IT TOOLS AND BUSINESS SYSTEMS

STRICTLY AS PER NEW DOEACC SYLLABUS

M1 - R4

Dr. R. K. Jain

KHANNA BOOK PUBLISHING CO. (P) LTD.

Publisher of Engineering and Computer Books

4C/4344, Ansari Road, Darya Ganj, New Delhi-110002

Phone : 011-23244447-48 **Mobile:** +91-9910909320

E-mail : contact@khannabooks.com

Website : www.khannabooks.com

Dear Readers,

To prevent the piracy, this book is secured with HIGH SECURITY HOLOGRAM on the front title cover. In case you don't find the hologram on the front cover title, please write us to at contact@khannabooks.com or whatsapp us at +91-99109 09320 and avail special gift voucher for yourself.

Specimen of Hologram on front Cover title:

Moreover, there is a SPECIAL DISCOUNT COUPON for you with EVERY HOLOGRAM.

How to avail this SPECIAL DISCOUNT:

Step 1: Scratch the hologram
Step 2: Under the scratch area, your "coupon code" is available
Step 3: Logon to www.khannabooks.com
Step 4: Use your "coupon code" in the shopping cart and get your copy at a special discount
Step 5: Enjoy your reading!

Thanks,
Khanna Publishing House

Price: ₹450.00

IT Tools and Business Systems
by **R.K. Jain**

ISBN: 978-93-80016-61-0

Edition: 2017
Reprint: 2023, 2024, 2025

To view complete list of books, please scan the QR Code:

Published by:
Khanna Book Publishing Co. (P) Ltd.
CIN: U22110DL1998PTC095547

Visit us at: www.khannabooks.com
Write us at: contact@khannabooks.com

Printed in India.

Preface

The new syllabus of DOE's various levels of courses, popularly called O-level, A-level, B-level and C-level is out. Keeping in mind the various developments taking place around the world in the field of computers, these syllabus include most of them. While keeping in mind the level of students studying the various levels, the degree of difficulties of the syllabus have been very well designed. I hope that after the new syllabus the courses would be as popular as they were before.

There had been a long struggle between Training Institutes and Government Organizations, since these organizations would not recognize the degree/diploma given by them. Students passing out from these institutions were not given jobs based upon the said diplomas/degrees. Ultimately, the Government formed a society under the Department of Electronics, called DOEACC, who conducts tests and gives grades to the students irrespective of the institutes where they have studied. It is also possible to give the test without having any proper institutional studies. This is more or less on the terms of SAT and GRE conducted by USA. The only difference is that this is not online. There are fixed dates for the exams.

The course for this has been designed for students to appear in the exams at various levels. These levels are O-level, A-level, B-level, C-level. The most popular among these is the O-level, since it is the entry level. Once you have cleared the O-level, you are eligible for a government job. Each course has been divided into various modules. Various books are available for various modules. This book is also made for you to prepare for the O-level course.

This book has been written totally in accordance with the syllabus provided. Each chapter has been embedded with the screen shots for you to know what to expect on the screen, while running the application. Each chapter contains examples which can be attempted to supplement the reading. At the end of the chapter, there is a thorough revision of the text read. Not to mention of the questions provided in the beginning, both in the form of objective and subjective. The book also contains Sample papers which are based on the samples provided by DOEACC society. These would help you in preparing for the exams.

R. K. Jain

SYLLABUS

M1-R4: IT TOOLS AND BUSINESS SYSTEMS

The goal of this course is to present overview of IT tools used in day to day use of computers and database operations. The Course has been designed to provide knowledge on various hardware and software components of computer, operating system, various packages used to different applications, database concepts & operations and various issues related to IT and application of IT.

At the end of the course the students will be able to:

- Acquire the foundation level knowledge required to understand computer and its operations.
- Understand the hardware and software components of the computer.
- Understand the basic concept of operating system and get knowledge about various different operating systems.
- Understand to use the packages of word processing, spreadsheet and presentation in detail.
- Understand varioud databse concepts and operations.
- Undestand the issues related to IT and IT applications.

Outline of Course

S.No.	*Topic*	*Minimum No. of Hours*
1.	Computer Appreciation	04
2.	Computer Organization	06
3.	Operating System	13
4.	Word Processing	06
5.	Spreadsheet Package	09
6.	Presentation Package	05
7.	Database Operations	13
8.	Information Technology and Society	04

Lectures = 60

Practicals /Tutorials = 60

Total = 120

Detailed Syllabus

1. Computer Appreciation — 04 Hrs.

Characteristics of Computers, Input, Output, Storage units, CPU, Computer System, Binary number system, Binary to Decimal Conversion, Decimal to Binary Conversion, ASCII Code, Unicode

2. Computer Organization — 06 Hrs.

Central Processing Unit: Processor Speed, Cache, Memory, RAM, ROM, Booting, Memory. Secondary Storage Devices: Floppy and Hard Disks, Optical Disks, CD-ROM, DVD, Mass Storage Devices: USB thumb drive. Managing disk partitions, File System. Input Devices: Keyboard, Mouse, joystick, Scanner, Web cam. Output Devices: Monitors, Printers – Dot matrix, inkjet, laser. Multimedia: What is Multimedia, Text, Graphics, Animation, Audio, Images, Video; Multimedia Application in Education, Entertainment, Marketing. Names of common multimedia file formats. Computer Software: Relationship between Hardware and Software; System Software, Application Software, Compiler, names of some high level languages, free domain software.

3. Operating Systems — 13 hrs.

Microsoft Windows: An overview of different versions of Windows, Basic Windows elements, File management through Windows. Using essential accessories: System tools – Disk cleanup, Disk defragmenter, Entertainment, Games, Calculator, Imaging – Fax, Notepad, Paint, WordPad. Command Prompt - Directory navigation, path setting, creating and using batch files. Drives, files, directories, directory structure. Application Management: Installing, uninstalling, Running Applications. Linux: An overview of Linux, Basic Linux elements: System Features, Software Features. File structure, File handling in Linux, H/W, S/W requirements, Preliminary steps before installation, specifies on Hard drive repartitioning and booting a Linux System.

4. Word Processing — 06 Hrs.

Word processing concepts: Saving, Closing, Opening an existing document, Selecting text, Editing text, Finding and replacing text, printing documents, Creating and Printing Merged Documents, Character and Paragraph Formatting, Page Design and Layout.

Editing and Proofing Tools: Checking and correcting spellings. Handling Graphics, Creating Tables and charts. Document Templates and Wizards.

5. Spreadsheet Package — 09 Hrs.

Spreadsheet Concepts. Creating, Saving and Editing a Workbook, Inserting, Deleting Work Sheets, entering data in a cell / formula Copying and Moving data from selected cells, handling operators in Formulae, Functions: Mathematical, Logical, Statistical, Text, Financial, Date and Time functions, Using Function Wizard.

Formatting a Worksheet: Formatting Cells – changing data alignment, changing date, number, character, or currency format, changing font, adding borders and colors, Printing worksheets, charts and Graphs – Creating, Previewing, Modifying Charts.

Integrating word processor, spread sheets, web pages.

6. Presentation Package **05 Hrs.**

Creating, Opening and Saving Presentations, Creating the Look of Your Presentation, Working in Different Views, Working with Slides, Adding and Formatting Text, Formatting Paragraphs, Checking Spelling and Correcting Typing Mistakes, Making Notes Pages and Handouts, Drawing and Working with Objects, Adding Clip Art and other Pictures, Designing Slide Shows, Running and Controlling a Slide Show, Printing Presentations.

7. Data Base Operations **13 Hrs.**

Data Manipulation - Concept: Database, Relational Database, Integrity. Operations: Creating, dropping, manipulating table structure, Manipulation of Data: Query, Data Entry Form, Reports.

8. Information Technology and Society **04 Hrs.**

Indian IT Act, Intellectual Property Rights - issues. Application of Information Technology in *Railways, Airlines, Banking, Insurance*, Inventory Control, *Financial systems*, Hotel management, Education, Video games, Telephone exchanges, Mobile phones, Information kiosks, special effects in Movies.

Contents

Computer Appreciation 1

1.1 Characteristics of Computers

The word computer has been derived from two words, mainly, Compute and Calculator. A computer is a dievice used for performing calculations automatically. Most of us use computers either at work or home. We can use computers for creating office documents or formating presentations and at home we can use it for checking our e-mails, playing games, or browse Internet for local news updates.

A computer is made of different parts which when looked at from any user angle will give a different definition. We should just remember that a computer:

1. Cannot think
2. It has vast capabilities of calculations like addition, substraction, etc. and
3. It is totally under the control of the user.

So, we can say that a computer is a machine, totally at the command of the user, which can perform operations at a much higher speed than a human being.

There is nothing magical about a computer. It is actually a friendly machine which is totally at your command. Do you remember the story Aladdin and the Magic Lamp? Just like the Genie of the magic lamp, a computer will obey your command. If you make a mistake in giving commands to the computer, it will carry out these commands giving wrong results.

1.1.1 Computer Age

Though the first fully operational electronic computer was introduced to the world in 1946, but the historian assumes the starting of a computer age from 1951, when first commercial computer UNIVAC was introduced. The remarkable thing about the computer age is that so much has happened in so much short time. We have leapfrogged four generations of technology in about 50 years - a span of time whose events are within the memories of many people today. The first three computer generations are pinned to three technological developments:

1. vacuum tube
2. transistor and
3. integrated circuit

Each has drastically changed the nature and size of computers. We define the timing of each generation according to the beginning of commercial delivery of the hardware technology. Defining subsequent generations has become more complicated because the entire industry has become more complicated.

If you see, the computer is physically divided into 3 main parts:

Monitor
Central Processing Unit
Keyboard

1.2 Input Unit

Input units are those units which provide inputs to the the computers. These include keyboard, floppy disks, CD ROM, etc. They provide the data to the computer which is then processed. In the next chapter, you would read about the various input units available.

1.3 Output Unit

The output unit consists of the output devices attached to the computer. These devices take machine-coded output results from the processor and convert them into a form that can be understood by the user.

1.4 Primary Storage Unit

This is main storage area, which is also called the main memory area. Its main functions are listed below:

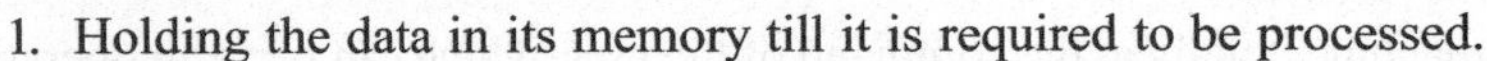

1. Holding the data in its memory till it is required to be processed.
2. Holding the result of the processed data.
3. Holding program instructions which are required for processing.

1.5 Central Processing Unit (CPU)

It is actually the main brain of the computer system. It is here that the whole processing takes place. It consists of 2 main units:

Arithmetic Logic Unit
Control Unit

Let us read about them one by one.

1.5.1 Arithmetic Logic Unit

This is used for the most of the logical processing, for example, for calculations or comparisons. The arithmetic operations like, +, –, *, and / are performed here. The logical operations like, <, >, =, <=, >=, and <> are also performed here. In most of the arithmetical operations the result is in numerical form while in the case of logical operations the result can be YES/NO or TRUE/FALSE.

1.5.2 Control Unit

This unit controls the flow and manipulation of data and information. It also controls the flow of data from input devices to memory and from memory to output devices.

1.6 Computer System

CMost of the things we learned so far has been pertaining to the items attached to the Central Processing Unit of the computer. Now we will go through the various components which are inside the CPU. Most of them are the various type of cards which are there and then there is microprocessor which controls the whole working of the system.

1.6.1 Microprocessor

As mentioned above it is the brain of the whole computer. This is where the whole processing takes place. All arithmetical, logical and other basic processing steps are done here. The thousands of instructions that the microprocessor executes one at a time to carry out the actions of each program is done here. In short a processor which is short for both microprocessor and central processor unit (CPU) is a piece of electronic circuitry that uses digital logic to perform the instructions of your software.

1.6.2 Semiconductors

A microprocessor is constructed of layer upon layer of electronic circuits that are liberally carved out of silicon. Silicon is a very commonly element in the world. In fact, after oxygen, there is more silicon available than any other element and you can find it easily on the beach in rocks and sand. However, the silicon used for manufacturing integrated circuits is found in white quartz. Silicon is the primary building material used in manufacturing the electronic integrated circuits (chips) that are used to conduct the processor and ultimately the computer. It is used in electronic circuits because it is an excellent semiconductor. A semiconductor is a material that is neither a conductor nor an insulator but can be chemically altered to be either one.

1.6.3 Conductors and Insulators

A material that is a conductor allows electrical current to pass through it. Without getting too technical, materials like copper, aluminum or gold are good conductors of electricity because they have free electrons through which the current can pass. While, a material that does not allow an electrical current to pass through it is called an insulator. Insulators like rubber, wood or glass do not have many free electrons through which the current can pass.

1.6.4 Integrated Circuit

An integrated circuit (IC) is a combination of electronic components, such as transistors, capacitors and resistors. An IC is designed to fulfill some logical function and can be built to be a timer, counter, a bank of computer memory, or even a microprocessor.

The basic building block of an IC is a logic gate. A logic gate performs the Boolean algebra AND operation by testing two input signals (each stored in a transistor). If both the positive (representing true or 1) it sets the signal of a result value to positive. Otherwise, the value is set to negative (representing false of 0).

1.7 Number System

Symbols could be combined to represent specific quantities, but the order of their combination followed no consistent rules. None of the early symbolic systems included all the concepts necessary for straight forward mathematical computation. Separate symbols were needed for each possible digit value (included zero) and other symbols were needed to separate the whole part of the number from the fractional part.

1.7.1 Arithmetic Systems

To a computer, everything is a number. Numbers are numbers, letters are numbers and punctuation marks, symbols and even the computer's own instructions are numbers. Computers do not use the same number system as the one we use. In fact, people who program computers use several different number systems, in addition to the familiar base 10 (or decimal) scheme that we use all the time. The most important of these are the binary or base 2 system and the hexadecimal or base 16 system.

1.7.2 Number System

Any system for representing numeric values or quantities, e.g., the decimal system utilizes ten digits 0 to 9. These digits can be arranged in groups, the contribution of each digit being made according to the value of the digit and the significance of its position in the group. The decimal number system is used almost universally by humans.

1.7.3 Decimal System

The decimal system is important because it is universally used to represent quantities outside a digital system. This means that there be will situations where decimal values have to be converted to binary values before they are entered into digital system, e.g., computer. Likewise, there will be situations where the binary values at the outputs of a digital circuit have to be converted to decimal values for presentation to the outside world.

In addition to decimal and binary number system, two other number systems find wide spread applications in digital systems. The octal (base 8) and hexadecimal (base 16) number systems are used to provide a convenient and efficient means for representing large binary numbers. In digital system, three or four of these number systems may be in use at the same time, so that an understanding of the system operation requires the ability to convert from one number system to another. You would learn about these conversions later in the chapter.

1.8 Binary System

The turning point in the history of number system occurred in 1666 A.D. when Leibniz generalized treatise on positional number system. Thirteen years later Leibniz defined the binary number system which today is so important that every beginner in computer science has to learn this number system.

Many of the electronic components of a computer are bistable in nature, i.e., they can be in either of two states ON or OFF. Reliable recording and reading on a magnetic surface is achieved when the surface is magnetized in either clockwise or anticlockwise directions.

Thus all data to be stored and processed in computers are transformed as strings of two symbols 0 and 1, which are also the symbols for digits of the binary number system. It is an example of positional numeration system.

Programmers usually use data and other information in the form of decimal digits, alphabets and special symbols. This information is converted to binary codes within the computer because a digital computer operates on binary bits only.

Binary number system has a base or radix of 2. Its two digits are denoted by 0 & 1 and are called **bits**. There is no digit in the binary number system to represent 2 or 3 etc. Therefore, using positional technique

2 is written as 10

3 is written as 11

4 is written as 100

and so on.

The weight of each binary bit of a binary number depends on its relative position within the number, i.e., the weight of a digit in any positional number system depends on its relative position within the number and the base of the number system in binary number system with base 2 the weight of nth bit of the number from R.H.S. = n^{th} bit x 2^{n-1}

1.9 Conversion from Binary to Decimal (to base 10 from base 2)

In this process we first mark the bit position and then we give the weight of each bit to the number depending on its position. The sum of the weight of all bits gives the equivalent decimal number. Also we know that the weight of nth bit of the number from R.H.S. in binary system = nth bit x 2^{n-1}. For example consider the following binary numbers.

Example: Convert $(10111011)_2$ to decimal.

Bit Position

	8	7	6	5	4	3	2	1
	1	0	1	1	1	0	1	1
Weight of each bit	2^7	2^6	2^5	2^4	2^3	2^2	2^1	2^0

Sum of weight of all bits

$= 1 \times 2^7 + 0 \times 2^6 + 1 \times 2^5 + 1 \times 2^4 + 1 \times 2^3 + 0 \times 2^2 + 1 \times 2^1 + 1 \times 2^0$

$= 128 + 0 + 32 + 16 + 8 + 0 + 2 + 1$

$= (187)_{10}$

Another Example: Convert $(101001010)_2$ to decimal

Bit Position

	9	8	7	6	5	4	3	2	1
	1	0	1	0	0	1	0	1	0
Weight of each bit	2^8	2^7	2^6	2^5	2^4	2^3	2^2	2^1	2^0

Therefore, decimal number = sum of weight of all bits

$= 1 \times 2^8 + 0 \times 2^7 + 1 \times 2^6 + 0 \times 2^5 + 0 \times 2^4 + 1 \times 2^3 + 0 \times 2^2 + 1 \times 2^1 + 0 \times 2^0$

$= 256 + 0 + 64 + 0 + 0 + 0 + 8 + 0 + 2 + 0$

$= (330)_{10}$

1.10 Conversion from Decimal to Binary

External to computer we use decimal numbers whereas internally we use binary representation, so we have to convert decimal numbers to binary. Also it is sometimes convenient to use a number in a base different from the base currently being used, i.e., to change the number from one base to another.

In a decimal number the value of the

1st digit from R.H.S. = $10^0 = 1$

2nd digit from R.H.S. = $10^1 = 10$

3rd digit from R.H.S. = $10^2 = 100$

Similarly in a binary number the value of the

1st digit from R.H.S. = $2^0 = 1$

2nd digit from R.H.S. = $2^1 = 2$

3rd digit from R.H.S. = $2^2 = 4$

.... and so on.

The process, often called the remainder method, is basically a series of repeated divisions by the number of the base to which you are converting (in our case base is 2). There are two points to remember:

Keep dividing until you reach a zero quotient

Use the remainder in reverse order.

Under the process of conversion we determine which multiples of 2 are present in a given decimal number. Consider the following examples.

Example

$(187)_{10} =$

2	187		
2	93	1	Least significant bit. (L.S.B.)

2	46	1	
2	23	0	
2	11	1	
2	5	1	
2	2	1	
2	1	0	
	0	1	Most significant bit. (M.S.B.)

$$(187)_{10} = (10111011)_2$$

Another Example

$(330)_{10}$

2	330		
2	165	0	Least significant bit. (L.S.B.)
2	82	1	
2	41	0	
2	20	1	
2	10	0	
2	5	0	
2	2	1	
2	1	0	
	0	1	Most significant bit. (M.S.B.)

$$(330)_{10} = (101001010)_2$$

The binary equivalent of the decimal number is given by the sequence of remainders obtained during division. L.S.B. of the binary number is the 1st remainder obtained and M.S.B. is the last remainder.

1.11 ASCII Code

It is the most commonly used code in the computer industry. By ASCII, we mean American Standard Code for Information Interchange (ASCII). It is a 7 bit code (usually the 8th bit is inserted for parity) and so it has $2^7 = 128$ possible code groups. It is used for the transfer of alphanumeric information between a computer and input/output devices such as video terminals or printers. Out of 128 ASCII codes 94 are printable and 34 non printing character used for various control functions. Following is the list of complete ASCII codes.

Character	*Hex code for ASCII*	*ANSI code*	*Description*
NUL	0000	0	Null
SOH	0001	1	Start of heading
STX	0002	2	Start of text
ETX	0003	3	End of text
EOT	0004	4	End of transmission
ENQ	0005	5	Enquiry
ACK	0006	6	Acknowledge
BEL	0007	7	Bell
BS	0008	8	Backspace
HT	0009	9	Horizontal tabulation
LF	000A	10	Line feed
VT	000B	11	Vertical tabulation
FF	000C	12	Form feed
CR	000D	13	Carriage return
SO	000E	14	Shift out
SI	000F	15	Shift in
DLE	0010	16	Data link escape
DC1	0011	17	Device control 1

Character	Hex code for ASCII	ANSI code	Description
DC2	0012	18	Device control 2
DC3	0013	19	Device control 3
DC4	0014	20	Device control 4
NAK	0015	21	Negative acknowledge
SYN	0016	22	Synchronous idle
ETB	0017	23	End of transmission block
CAN	0018	24	Cancel
EM	0019	25	End of medium
SUB	001A	26	Substitute
ESC	001B	27	Escape
FS	001C	28	File separator
GS	001D	29	Group separator
RS	001E	30	Record separator
US	001F	31	Unit separator
SP	0020	32	Space
!	0021	33	Exclamation point
“	0022	34	Quotation mark
#	0023	35	Number sign
$	0024	36	Dollar sign
%	0025	37	Percent
&	0026	38	Ampersand
‘	0027	39	Apostrophe
(	0028	40	Left parenthesis
)	0029	41	Right parenthesis
*	002A	42	Asterisk
+	002B	43	Plus sign
,	002C	44	Comma
-	002D	45	Hyphen
.	002E	46	Full stop
/	002F	47	Solidus
0	0030	48	Digit zero
1	0031	49	Digit one
2	0032	50	Digit two
3	0033	51	Digit three
4	0034	52	Digit four
5	0035	53	Digit five
6	0036	54	Digit six
7	0037	55	Digit seven
8	0038	56	Digit eight
9	0039	57	Digit nine

Character	Hex code for ASCII	ANSI code	Description
:	003A	58	Colon
;	003B	59	Semicolon
<	003C	60	Less-than sign
=	003D	61	Equals sign
>	003E	62	Greater-than sign
?	003F	63	Question mark
@	0040	64	Commercial at
A	0041	65	Latin capital letter A
B	0042	66	Latin capital letter B
C	0043	67	Latin capital letter C
D	0044	68	Latin capital letter D
E	0045	69	Latin capital letter E
F	0046	70	Latin capital letter F
G	0047	71	Latin capital letter G
H	0048	72	Latin capital letter H
I	0049	73	Latin capital letter I
J	004A	74	Latin capital letter J
K	004B	75	Latin capital letter K
L	004C	76	Latin capital letter L
M	004D	77	Latin capital letter M
N	004E	78	Latin capital letter N
O	004F	79	Latin capital letter O
P	0050	80	Latin capital letter P
Q	0051	81	Latin capital letter Q
R	0052	82	Latin capital letter R
S	0053	83	Latin capital letter S
T	0054	84	Latin capital letter T
U	0055	85	Latin capital letter U
V	0056	86	Latin capital letter V
W	0057	87	Latin capital letter W
X	0058	88	Latin capital letter X
Y	0059	89	Latin capital letter Y
Z	005A	90	Latin capital letter Z
[	005B	91	Left square bracket
\	005C	92	Reverse solidus
]	005D	93	Right square bracket
^	005E	94	Circumflex accent
_	005F	95	Low line
‘	0060	96	Grave accent
a	0061	97	Latin small letter a
b	0062	98	Latin small letter b

Character	Hex code for ASCII	ANSI code	Description
c	0063	99	Latin small letter c
d	0064	100	Latin small letter d
e	0065	101	Latin small letter e
f	0066	102	Latin small letter f
g	0067	103	Latin small letter g
h	0068	104	Latin small letter h
i	0069	105	Latin small letter i
j	006A	106	Latin small letter j
k	006B	107	Latin small letter k
l	006C	108	Latin small letter l
m	006D	109	Latin small letter m
n	006E	110	Latin small letter n
o	006F	111	Latin small letter o
p	0070	112	Latin small letter p
q	0071	113	Latin small letter q
r	0072	114	Latin small letter r
s	0073	115	Latin small letter s
t	0074	116	Latin small letter t
u	0075	117	Latin small letter u
v	0076	118	Latin small letter v
w	0077	119	Latin small letter w
x	0078	120	Latin small letter x
y	0079	121	Latin small letter y
z	007A	122	Latin small letter z
{	007B	123	Left curly bracket
|	007C	124	Vertical line
}	007D	125	Right curly bracket
~	007E	126	Tilde
DEL	007F	127	Delete
	0080	128	Reserved
	0081	129	Reserved
	0082	130	Reserved
	0083	131	Reserved
IND	0084	132	Index
NEL	0085	133	Next line
SSA	0086	134	Start of selected area
ESA	0087	135	End of selected area
	0088	136	Character tabulation set
	0089	137	Character tabulation with justification
	008A	138	Line tabulation set

Character	Hex code for ASCII	ANSI code	Description
PLD	008B	139	Partial line down
PLU	008C	140	Partial line up
	008D	141	Reverse line feed
SS2	008E	142	Single shift two
SS3	008F	143	Single shift three
DCS	0090	144	Device control string
PU1	0091	145	Private use one
PU2	0092	146	Private use two
STS	0093	147	Set transmit state
CCH	0094	148	Cancel character
MW	0095	149	Message waiting
	0096	150	Start of guarded area
	0097	151	End of guarded area
	0098	152	Start of string
	0099	153	Reserved
	009A	154	Single character introducer
CSI	009B	155	Control sequence introducer
ST	009C	156	String terminator
OSC	009D	157	Operating system command
PM	009E	158	Privacy message
APC	009F	159	Application program command
	00A0	160	No-break space
¡	00A1	161	Inverted exclamation mark
¢	00A2	162	Cent sign
£	00A3	163	Pound sign
¤	00A4	164	Currency sign
¥	00A5	165	Yen sign
¦	00A6	166	Broken bar
§	00A7	167	Section sign
¨	00A8	168	Diaeresis
©	00A9	169	Copyright sign
ª	00AA	170	Feminine ordinal indicator
«	00AB	171	Left-pointing double angle quotation mark
¬	00AC	172	Not sign
-	00AD	173	Soft hyphen

Character	Hex code for ASCII	ANSI code	Description
®	00AE	174	Registered sign
¯	00AF	175	Macron
°	00B0	176	Degree sign
±	00B1	177	Plus-minus sign
²	00B2	178	Superscript two
³	00B3	179	Superscript three
´	00B4	180	Acute accent
µ	00B5	181	Micro sign
¶	00B6	182	Pilcrow sign
·	00B7	183	Middle dot
¸	00B8	184	Cedilla
¹	00B9	185	Superscript one
º	00BA	186	Masculine ordinal indicator
»	00BB	187	Right-pointing double angle quotation mark
¼	00BC	188	Vulgar fraction one quarter
½	00BD	189	Vulgar fraction one half
¾	00BE	190	Vulgar fraction three quarter
¿	00BF	191	Inverted question mark
À	00C0	192	Latin capital letter A with grave
Á	00C1	193	Latin capital letter A with acute
Â	00C2	194	Latin capital letter A with circumflex
Ã	00C3	195	Latin capital letter A with tilde
Ä	00C4	196	Latin capital letter A with diaeresis
Å	00C5	197	Latin capital letter A with ring above
Æ	00C6	198	Latin capital ligature AE
Ç	00C7	199	Latin capital letter C with cedilla
È	00C8	200	Latin capital letter E with grave
É	00C9	201	Latin capital letter E with acute
Ê	00CA	202	Latin capital letter E with circumflex

Character	Hex code for ASCII	ANSI code	Description
Ë	00CB	203	Latin capital letter E with diaeresis
Ì	00CC	204	Latin capital letter I with grave
Í	00CD	205	Latin capital letter I with acute
Î	00CE	206	Latin capital letter I with circumflex
Ï	00CF	207	Latin capital letter I with giaeresis
Ð	00D0	208	Latin capital letter ETH
Ñ	00D1	209	Latin capital letter N with tilde
Ò	00D2	210	Latin capital letter O with grave
Ó	00D3	211	Latin capital letter O with acute
Ô	00D4	212	Latin capital letter O with circumflex
Õ	00D5	213	Latin capital letter O with tilde
Ö	00D6	214	Latin capital letter O with diaeresis
×	00D7	215	Multiplication sign
Ø	00D8	216	Latin capital letter O with stroke
Ù	00D9	217	Latin capital letter U with grave
Ú	00DA	218	Latin capital letter U with acute
Û	00DB	219	Latin capital letter U with circumflex
Ü	00DC	220	Latin capital letter U with diaeresis
Ý	00DD	221	Latin capital letter Y with acute
Þ	00DE	222	Latin capital letter thorn
ß	00DF	223	Latin small letter sharp s
à	00E0	224	Latin small letter a with grave
á	00E1	225	Latin small letter a with acute
â	00E2	226	Latin small letter a with circumflex

Character	Hex code for ASCII	ANSI code	Description
ã	00E3	227	Latin small letter a with tilde
ä	00E4	228	Latin small letter a with diaeresis
å	00E5	229	Latin small letter a with ring above
æ	00E6	230	Latin small ligature ae
ç	00E7	231	Latin small letter c with cedilla
è	00E8	232	Latin small letter e with grave
é	00E9	233	Latin small letter e with acute
ê	00EA	234	Latin small letter e with circumflex
ë	00EB	235	Latin small letter e with diaeresis
ì	00EC	236	Latin small letter i with grave
í	00ED	237	Latin small letter i with acute
î	00EE	238	Latin small letter i with circumflex
ï	00EF	239	Latin small letter i with giaeresis
ð	00F0	240	Latin small letter eth
ñ	00F1	241	Latin small letter n with tilde
ò	00F2	242	Latin small letter o with grave
ó	00F3	243	Latin small letter o with acute
ô	00F4	244	Latin small letter o with circumflex
õ	00F5	245	Latin small letter o with tilde
ö	00F6	246	Latin small letter o with diaeresis
÷	00F7	247	Division sign
ø	00F8	248	Latin small letter o with stroke
ù	00F9	249	Latin small letter u with grave
ú	00FA	250	Latin small letter u with acute
û	00FB	251	Latin small letter u with circumflex
ü	00FC	252	Latin small letter u with diaeresis
ý	00FD	253	Latin small letter y with acute
þ	00FE	254	Latin small letter thorn
ÿ	00FF	255	Latin small letter y with diaeresis

1.12 Unicodes

Decimal (Base 10)	Hexadecimal (Base 16)	Octal (Base 8)	Binary (Base 2)
1	01	01	00000001
2	02	02	00000010
3	03	03	00000011
4	04	04	00000100
5	05	05	00000101
6	06	06	00000110
7	07	07	00000111
8	08	10	00001000
9	09	11	00001001
10	0A	12	00001010
11	0B	13	00001011
12	0C	14	00001100
13	0D	15	00001101
13	0E	16	00001110
15	0F	17	00001111
16	10	20	00010000
17	11	21	00010001
18	12	22	00010010
19	13	23	00010011
20	14	24	00010100
21	15	25	00010101
22	16	26	00010110

Decimal (Base 10)	Hexadecimal (Base 16)	Octal (Base 8)	Binary (Base 2)
23	17	27	00010111
24	18	30	00011000
25	19	31	00011001
26	1A	32	00011010
27	1B	33	00011011
28	1C	34	00011100
29	1D	35	00011101
30	1E	36	00011110
31	1F	37	00011111
32	20	40	00100000
33	21	41	00100001
34	22	42	00100010
35	23	43	00100011
36	24	44	00100100
37	25	45	00100101
38	26	46	00100110
39	27	47	00100111
40	28	50	00101000
41	29	51	00101001
42	2A	52	00101010
43	2B	53	00101011
44	2C	54	00101100
45	2D	55	00101101
46	2E	56	00101110
47	2F	57	00101111
48	30	60	00110000
49	31	61	00110001
50	32	62	00110010
51	33	63	00110011
52	34	64	00110100
53	35	65	00110101
54	36	66	00110110
55	37	67	00110111
56	38	70	00111001
57	39	71	00111000
58	3A	72	00111010
59	3B	73	00111011
60	3C	74	00111100
61	3D	75	00111101
62	3E	76	00111110
63	3F	77	00111111
64	40	100	01000000
65	41	101	01000001
66	42	102	01000010
67	43	103	01000011
68	44	104	01000100
69	45	105	01000101
70	46	106	01000110
71	47	107	01000111
72	48	110	01001000
73	49	111	01001001
74	4A	112	01001010
75	4B	113	01001011
76	4C	114	01001100
77	4D	115	01001101
78	4E	116	01001110
79	4F	117	01001111
80	50	120	01010000
81	51	121	01010001
82	52	122	01010010
83	53	123	01010011
84	54	124	01010100
85	55	125	01010101
86	56	126	01010110
87	57	127	01010111
88	58	130	01011000
89	59	131	01011001
90	5A	132	01011010
91	5B	133	01011011
92	5C	134	01011100
93	5D	135	01011101
94	5E	136	01011110
95	5F	137	01011111
96	60	140	01100000
97	61	141	01100001
98	62	142	01100010
99	63	143	01100011
100	64	144	01100100
101	65	145	01100101
102	66	146	01100110
103	67	147	01100111
104	68	150	01101000

Decimal (Base 10)	*Hexadecimal (Base 16)*	*Octal (Base 8)*	*Binary (Base 2)*
105	69	151	01101001
106	6A	152	01101010
107	6B	153	01101011
108	6C	154	01101100
109	6D	155	01101101
110	6E	156	01101110
111	6F	157	01101111
112	70	160	01110000
113	71	161	01110001
114	72	162	01110010
115	73	163	01110011
116	74	164	01110100
117	75	165	01110101
118	76	166	01110110
119	77	167	01110111
120	78	170	01111000
121	79	171	01111001
122	7A	172	01111010
123	7B	173	01111011
124	7C	174	01111100
125	7D	175	01111101
126	7E	176	01111110
127	7F	177	01111111
128	80	200	10000000
129	81	201	10000001
130	82	202	10000010
131	83	203	10000011
132	84	204	10000100
133	85	205	10000101
134	86	206	10000110
135	87	207	10000111
136	88	210	10001000
137	89	211	10001001
138	8A	212	10001010
139	8B	213	10001011
140	8C	214	10001100
141	8D	215	10001101
142	8E	216	10001110
143	8F	217	10001111
144	90	220	10010000
145	91	221	10010001

Decimal (Base 10)	*Hexadecimal (Base 16)*	*Octal (Base 8)*	*Binary (Base 2)*
146	92	212	10010010
147	93	223	10010011
148	94	224	10010100
149	95	225	10010101
150	96	226	10010110
151	97	227	10010111
152	98	230	10011000
153	99	231	10011001
154	9A	232	10011010
155	9B	233	10011011
156	9C	234	10011100
157	9D	235	10011100
158	9E	236	10011110
159	9F	237	10011111
160	A0	240	10100000
161	A1	241	10100000
162	A2	242	10100001
163	A3	243	10100011
16 4	A4	244	10100100
165	A5	245	10100101
166	A6	246	10100110
167	A7	247	10100111
168	A8	250	10101000
169	A9	251	10101001
170	AA	252	10101010
171	AB	253	10101011
172	AC	254	10101100
173	AD	255	10101101
174	AE	256	10101110
175	AF	257	10101111
176	B0	260	10110000
177	B1	261	10110001
178	B2	262	10110010
179	B3	263	10110011
180	B4	264	10110100
181	B5	265	10110101
182	B6	266	10110110
183	B7	267	10110111
184	B8	270	10111000
185	B9	271	10111001
186	BA	272	10111010

Decimal (Base 10)	*Hexadecimal (Base 16)*	*Octal (Base 8)*	*Binary (Base 2)*
187	BB	273	10111011
188	BC	274	10111100
189	BD	275	10111101
190	BE	276	10111110
191	BF	277	10111111
192	C0	300	11000000
193	C1	301	11000001
194	C2	302	11000010
195	C3	303	11000011
196	C4	304	11000100
197	C5	305	11000101
198	C6	306	11000110
199	C7	307	11000111
200	C8	310	11001000
201	C9	311	11001001
202	CA	312	11001010
203	CB	313	11001011
204	CC	314	11001100
205	CD	315	11001101
206	CE	316	11001110
207	CF	317	11001111
208	D0	320	11010000
209	D1	321	11010001
210	D2	322	11010010
211	D3	323	11010011
212	D4	324	11010100
213	D5	325	11010101
214	D6	326	11010110
215	D7	327	11010111
216	D8	330	11011000
217	D9	331	11011001
218	DA	332	11011010
219	DATABASE	333	11011011
220	DC	334	11011100
221	DD	335	11011101
222	DE	336	11011110
223	DF	337	11011111
224	E0	340	11100000
225	E1	341	11100001
226	E2	342	11100010
227	E3	343	11100011
228	E4	344	11100100
229	E5	345	11100101
230	E6	346	11100110
231	E7	347	11100111
232	E8	350	11101000
233	E9	351	11101001
234	EA	352	11101010
235	EB	353	11101011
236	EC	354	11101100
237	ED	355	11101101
238	EE	356	11101110
239	EF	357	11101111
240	F0	360	11110000
241	F1	361	11110001
242	F2	362	11110010
243	F3	363	11110011
244	F4	364	11110100
245	F5	365	11110101
246	F6	366	11110110
247	F7	367	11110111
248	F8	370	11111000
249	F9	371	11111001
250	FA	372	11111010
251	FB	373	11111011
252	FC	374	11111100
253	FD	375	11111101
254	FE	376	11111110
255	FF	377	11111111

Let us Revise

1. A computer is made of different parts.
2. Computer is a machine, totally at the command of the user.
3. The computer is physically divided into 3 main parts: Monitor, Central Processing Unit and Keyboard.
4. CPU consists of 4 main units: Primay Storage, Arithmetic Logic Unit, Control Unit and Output Unit.
5. The main functions of the Primary storage are: Holding the data in its memory till it is required to be processed; Holding the result of the processed data and Holding program instructions which are required for processing.
6. Arithmetic Logic Unit is used to process Arithmetic and Logic problems.
7. To a computer, everything is a number.
8. Various number systems are used in computers.
9. Most common is the Binary (base 2) system.
10. Decimal numbers use digits from 0 to 9.
11. Binary system is based on 1s and 0s.
12. All numbers in binary are expressed as 0s and 1s.
13. Binary system's digits are denoted by 0 and 1 and are called bits.
14. You can convert numbers from one base to another.
15. For converting numbers from Decimal to Binary, we process a series of divisions.
16. For converting from Binary to Decimal, each bit position is marked and given the weight.
17. Most commonly used code for representing numbers in computers are ASCII codes.

Multiple Choice Questions

1. Computer uses which number system.
   (a) Decimal (b) Binary (c) Octal
2. Decimal system uses the numbers from 0 to:
   (a) 8 (b) 9 (c) 16
3. Decimal systems have the base :.
   (a) 8 (b) 10 (c) 16
4. A Binary system number can be represented as 0 and :
   (a) 1 (b) 8 (c) 16
5. Binary system numbers are usually :
   (a) short (b) long (c) zeros
6. RAM stands for:
   (a) Random Allowed Memory (b) Ready Access Memory (c) Random Access Memory
7. RAM consists of binary numbers 1s and :
   (a) 0s (b) 2s (c) 3s

True/False Questions

1. A computer is made of different parts.
2. Computer is a machine, which runs on its own.
3. The first three computer generations were based on : vacuum tube, transistor and integrated circuit.
4. The computer is physically divided into 3 main parts: Monitor, Central Processing Unit and Keyboard.

5. Primary storage is not a part of the CPU.
6. The main functions of the Primary storage are: Holding the data in its memory till it is required to be processed; Holding the result of the processed data and Holding program instructions which are required for processing.
7. Arithmetic Logic Unit is used to process Arithmetic and Logic problems.
8. Numbers represent everything in computers.
9. A single type of number system is used in computers.
10. Binary (base 2) system and Hexadecimal (base 16) systems are the commonly used number systems used in computers.
11. Decimal system is of the base 0.
12. Octal system is of the base 8.
13. Decimal numbers can use digits from 0 to 10.
14. All digits here are expressed in 10 to the power of the digits.
15. Binary system is based on 1s and 0s.
16. Binary system's digits denoted by 0 & 1 are called bits.
17. You cannot convert numbers from one base to another.
18. For converting numbers from Decimal to Binary, we process a series of divisions.
19. For converting from Binary to Decimal, each bit position is marked and given the weight.
20. In Octal number system the digits are used from 0 to 8.
21. In Hexadecimal system numbers used are 0 to 9, A, B, C, D, E and F.
22. Most commonly used code for representing numbers in computers are ASCII codes.

Match Columns

Match the matter in Column A with the matter in Column B.

Column A	Column B
A. Binary system	1. Central Processing Unit
B. Octal System	2. American Standard Code for Information Interchange
C. Hexadecimal System	3. Second generation computer base
D. Decimal System	4. Binary Coded Decimal
E. CPU	5. Base 2
F. ALU	6. First generation computers base
G ASCII	7. Third generation compuers base
H. BCD	8. Base 16
I. Vacuum Tubes	9. Arithmetic Logic Unit
J. Integrated Circuits	10. Base 10
K. Transistors	11. Base 8

a.	10	b.	short	c.	F	d.	1
e.	8	f.	16	g.	Binary	h.	Random
i.	0s	l.	9				

Fill in the Blanks with Appropriate Words

1. Computer uses _____________ number system.

2. Hexadecimal system has a base of _______.
3. Decimal system uses the numbers from 0 to _______.
4. Decimal systems have the base _______.
5. A Binary system number can be represented as 0 and ___.
6. Binary system numbers are usually _____.
7. Octal number system uses numbers from 0 to _______.
8. Hexadecimal number system uses numbers from 0 to _________.
9. RAM stands for _______ Access Memory.
10. RAM consists of binary numbers 1s and ____:

Descriptive Type Questions

1. Which are the various number systems in use?
2. What is the base of Decimal system?
3. What is the base of Binary system?
4. What is the drawback of Binary system?
5. How would you convert a Decimal number to its Binary counterpar?
6. How would you convert a Binary number to its Decimal counterpart?
7. What is an Octal system?
8. What is hexadecimal system?
9. What are BCD codes?
10. What are ASCII codes?
11. Convert the following numbers

$(479656)_{10}$ to Binary — $(11101001111)_2$ to Decimal

$(56.789)_{10}$ to Binary — $(1101.0101)_2$ to Decimal

Multiple Choice Questions

1. b	2. c	3. b	4. a
5. a	6. b	7. a	

True False Questions

1. T	2. F	3. T	4. T
5. F	6. T	7. T	8. F
9. F	10. T	11. T	12. T
13. F	14. T	15. T	16. T
17. F	18. T	19. T	20. T
21. T	22. T		

Matching Columns

A. 5	B. 11	C. 8	D. 10
E. 1	F. 9	G. 2	H. 4
I. 6	J. 7	K. 3	

Fill in the Blanks

1. g	2. f	3. l	4. a
5. d	6. b	7. e	8. c
9. h	10. i		

Computer Organization 2

2.1 The Processor (Central Processing Unit)

The processor, more formally known as the central processing unit (CPU), has the electronic circuitry that manipulates input data into the information people want, as well as it communicates with the input, output and storage devices. It coordinates and controls the activities of input, output and storage devices, and performs all the arithmetic and logical processes to be applied to data. All program instructions to be executed must be held within the central processor and all data to be processed must first be loaded into this unit. The complex procedure that transforms raw input data into useful information for output is called processing. To perform this transformation, the computer uses central processing unit which consists of

- Internal Memory (Primary Storage)
- Arithmetic-Logic Unit (ALU) and
- Control Unit

2.1.1 Internal Memory

Computer memory also known as primary storage, is closely associated with the central processing unit but is separate from it. It holds the data after it is fed in to the system and before it is processed; also it holds the data after it has been processed but before it has been released to the output device. In addition, it holds the programs (computer instructions) needed by the CPU. Internal memory consists of a series of magnetic storage devices organized to hold data or program instructions in a series of locations as either words or characters. In many computing systems the internal memory is stored within the cabinet housing the other sections of the CPU, but in large systems separate cabinets may be used to contain sections of internal memory. Nevertheless the memory can always be considered as part of the CPU.

2.1.2 Computer Registers

Registers are temporary storage areas for instructions or data. They are not a part of memory rather they are special additional storage locations that offers the advantage of speed. Registers work under the direction of the control unit to accept hold and transfer instructions or data and perform arithmetic or logical comparisons at high speed.

The number and type of registers in a CPU vary according to the CPU's design. Their size or capacity and number can dramatically affect the processing power of a computer system. In general, the larger the resister, the more bits it can carry at once, the greater the processing power. Some personal computers have general purpose registers that hold only 8 bits; others hold 16 bits; newer micromputer have 32-bit registers. The difference in processing power due to difference in register size. Most of the conventional modern computers are based upon the sored program computer concept.

A CPU usually consists of following:

Instruction Interpreter: The instruction interpreter is a group of electrical cicuits that performs the intent of instructions fetched from memory.

Location Counter: The location counter, also called Program Counter (PC) or Instruction Counter (IC), is a hardware memory device that denotes the location of the current instruction being executed.

Intruction Register: A copy of the current instruction is stored in the Instruction Register (IR).

Working Register: The working registers are memory devices that serve as scratch pads for the instruction interpreter, while the general registers are used by the programmer as locations and for special functions.

The main interface between the memory and the CPU is via the memory address register and the memory buffer register. The Memory Address Register (MAR) contains the address of the memory location that is to be read from or stored into. The Memory Buffer Register (MEB) contains a copy of the designated memory location specified by the MAR after a READ or the new contents of the memory location prior to a WRITE. The memory controller is hardware that transfers data between the MBR and the core memory location the address of which is in the MAR.

2.2 Processor Speed

The clock rate is the rate in cycles per second (measured in hertz) for the frequency of the clock in any synchronous circuit (such as a CPU). For example, a crystal oscillator frequency reference typically is synonymous with a fixed sinusoidal waveform, a clock rate is that frequency reference translated by electronic circuitry (AD Converter) into a corresponding square wave pulse [typically] for digital electronics applications. In this context the use of the word, speed (physical movement), should not be confused with frequency or its corresponding clock rate. Thus, the term "clock speed" is a misnomer.

A single clock cycle (typically shorter than a nanosecond in modern non-embedded microprocessors) toggles between a logical zero and a logical one state. Historically, the logical zero state of a clock cycle persists longer than a logical one state due to thermal and electrical specification constraints.

CPU manufacturers typically charge premium prices for CPUs that operate at higher clock rates. For a given CPU, the clock rates are determined at the end of the manufacturing process through actual testing of each CPU. CPUs that are tested as complying with a given set of standards may be labeled with a higher clock rate, e.g., 1.50 GHz, while those that fail the standards of the higher clock rate yet pass the standards of a lesser clock rate may be labeled with the lesser clock rate, e.g., 1.33 GHz, and sold at a relatively lower price. The clock rate of a CPU is normally determined by the frequency of an oscillator crystal. The first commercial PC, the Altair 8800 (by MITS), used an Intel 8080 CPU with a clock rate of 2 MHz (2 million cycles/second). The original IBM PC (c. 1981) had a clock rate of 4.77 MHz (4,772,727 cycles/second). In 1995, Intel's Pentium chip ran at 100 MHz (100 million cycles/second), and in 2002, an Intel Pentium 4 model was introduced as the first CPU with a clock rate of 3 GHz (three billion cycles/second corresponding to ~3.3 10-10seconds per cycle).

With any particular CPU, replacing the crystal with another crystal that oscillates half the frequency ("underclocking") will generally make the CPU run at half the performance. It will also make the CPU produce roughly half as much waste heat. Conversely, some people try to increase performance of a CPU by replacing the oscillator crystal with a higher frequency crystal ("overclocking"). However, the amount of overclocking is limited by the time for the CPU to settle after each pulse, and by the extra heat created.

After each clock pulse, the signal lines inside the CPU need time to settle to their new state. That is, every signal line must finish transitioning from 0 to 1, or from 1 to 0. If the next clock pulse comes before that, the results will be incorrect. Chip manufacturers publish a "maximum clock rate" specification, and they test chips before selling them to make sure they meet that specification, even when executing the most complicated instructions with the data patterns that take the longest to settle (testing at the temperature and voltage that runs the lowest performance).

Also, some energy is wasted as heat (mostly inside the driving transistors) whenever a signal line makes a transition from the 0 to the 1 state or vice versa. When executing complicated instructions that cause many transitions, higher clock rates produce more heat. If electricity is converted to heat faster than a particular computer cooling system can cool it, then the transistors may get hot enough to be destroyed.

Engineers continue to find new ways to design CPUs that settle a little quicker or use slightly less energy per transition, pushing back those limits, producing new CPUs that can run at slightly higher clock rates. The ultimate limits to energy per transition are explored in reversible computing, although no reversible computers have yet been implemented.

Engineers also continue to find new ways to design CPUs so that, although they may run at the same or a lower clock rate as older CPUs, they get more instructions completed per clock cycle.

2.3 Cache Memory

In computer science, a cache (pronounced "cash" /kæʃ]) is a collection of data duplicating original values stored elsewhere or computed earlier, where the original data is expensive to fetch (due to slow access time) or to compute, relative to the cost of reading the cache. In other words, a cache is a temporary storage area where frequently accessed data can be stored for rapid access. Once the data is stored in the cache, future use can be made by accessing the cached copy rather than re-fetching or recomputing the original data, so that the average access time is lower.

Caches have proven to be extremely effective in many areas of computing because access patterns in typical computer applications have locality of reference. There are several kinds of locality, but this article primarily deals with data that are accessed close together in time (temporal locality). The data might or might not be located physically close to each other (spatial locality).

Xeon model	Core 2 Duo model	Speed (GHz)	L2 Cache (MB)	FSB (MHz)
3040	E6300	1.86	2	1066
N/A	E6320	1.86	4	1066
3050	E6400	2.13	2	1066
N/A	E6420	2.13	4	1066
3060	E6600	2.4	4	1066
3070	E6700	2.66	4	1066
3080	X6800	2.93	4	1066
3065	E6550	2.33	4	1333
3075	E6750	2.66	4	1333
3085	E6850	3.00	4	1333

2.3.1 How cache works?

A cache is a block of memory for temporary storage of data likely to be used again. The CPU and hard drive frequently use a cache, as do web browsers and web servers.

A cache is made up of a pool of entries. Each entry has a datum (a nugget of data) which is a copy of the datum in some backing store. Each entry also has a tag, which specifies the identity of the datum in the backing store of which the entry is a copy.

When the cache client (a CPU, web browser, operating system) wishes to access a datum presumably in the backing store, it first checks the cache.

2.3.2 Disk cache

To speed up the transfer of data and programs from the hard disk drive to RAM, a section of primary memory or some additional memory placed on the disk controller card is used to hold large blocks of frequently accessed data. Cache memory is usually a small amount of static random access memory or SRAM. SRAM is made up of transistors that don't need to be frequently refreshed (unlike DRAM, which is made up of capacitors and must be constantly refreshed). SRAM has access speeds of 2ns (nanoseconds) or faster; this is much faster than DRAM, which has access speeds of around 50ns. Data and instructions stored in SRAM-based cache memory are transferred to the CPU many times faster than if the data were transferred from the PC's main memory. In case you're wondering why SRAM isn't also used for primary memory, which could eliminate the need for cache memory all together, there are some very good practical and economic reasons. SRAM costs as much as six times more than DRAM and to store the same amount of data as DRAM would require a lot more space on the motherboard. There are two types of cache memory:

2.3.2.1 Internal cache

Also called primary cache; placed inside the CPU chip.

2.3.2.2 External cache

Also called secondary cache; located on the motherboard

2.4 RAM

RAM or random access memory, is used in the PC for its primary memory. RAM is where all active programs and data are stored so that they are readily available and easily accessed by the CPU and other components of the CPU. When you execute a program on your PC, a copy of the program is copied into RAM from whatever secondary storage it is on, usually the hard disk. Once it is in RAM, the instructions that make up the program are passed one at a time to the CPU for execution. Any data the program accepts or reads from a disk is also stored in RAM. There are several reasons that RAM is used in a PC but perhaps the most important is that RAM can transfer data to and from the CPU much faster than all secondary storage devices. Without RAM, all programs instructions and data would be read from the disk drive, slowing the computer to a crawl. With RAM speeds as fast, if not faster, than the speed of the CPU, the entire PC operates much more efficiently.

RAM is a group of integrated circuits (ICs or chips) that contain small electronic components (called capacitors) that store binary 1s and 0s. A variety of memory chips can be used for RAM, but some are better suited to storing large amounts of data, fit better in the space available in the PC and are less expensive. However, not all memory applications in the PC need to store a large amount of data, so most PCs use three different layers of memory: primary memory, level 1 (l1) cache and level 2 (l2) cache. RAM in its common usage refers to the primary memory layer of the PC's memory.

2.4.1 Random Access

Random access refers to the ability to access a single storage location in RAM without touching the locations that neighbour it. A good illustration is the difference between a cassette tape and a music CD. If you wish to listen to the third song on a cassette tape, you must fast forward over the first two songs on the tape. This is called sequential or serial access. Everything is accessed in its physical sequence or in series. To listen to the third song on a music CD, however, you merely indicate that you wish to move to track 3 and bingo – there you are. This is called direct or random access. You pick where you'd like to go randomly and then go directly there. Accessing something, a program or data, in RAM is very much like music CD, except that your choice are millions of individual storage locations (byes) each of which can be addressed directly by your programs.

2.5 ROM

It's logical then that data stored on read-only memory (ROM) cannot be changed, as its name implies. ROM also has the added feature of being nonvolatile, which means that it can keep its contents even without a power source. This makes it ideal for storing the PC's startup instructions and system BIOS (Basic Input/Output System). While virtually all ROM chips are packed in a DIP (dual inline packaging) form, there are three types of ROM used in a PC:

2.5.1.1 PROM (programmable read-only memory)

This type of ROM chip is programmed using a special type of programming device called a RPOM burner (a.k.a. PROM programmer), which permanently stores machine language (binary instructions) code on the PROM chip. A PROM chips is also referred to as OTP (One Time Programmable) memory.

2.5.1.2 EPROM (erasable programmable read-only memory)

This type of ROM, pronlunced "e-prom," is erasable and can be reprogrammed. Unlike a PROM chip that cannot be reused and can only be thrown out when it becomes obsolete, an EPROM chip can be reprogrammed and reused. An EPROM has a quartz window on the face of the chip that exposes the chip's interior circuits. When ultraviolet (UV) light is shined through this window, it causes a chemical reaction that erases the EPROM. In order to reprogram an EPROM, it must be removed from the computer, erased with UV light and then reprogrammed on a PROM programmer.

2.5.1.3 EEPROM (electronically erasable programmable read-only memory)

Most newer PCs now include an EEPROM (pronounced"e-e-prom") that can be reprogrammed like an EPROM, but unlike the EPROM doesn't need to be removed from the CP to be reprogrammed. An EEPROM can be reprogrammed, a process called flashing, using specialized software that runs on your PC. An EEPROM is also referred to as flash ROM. Flashing lets you upgrade your computer's BIOS easily without removing and replacing the ROM chip. One thing that all DIP chips suffer from including removable and replaceable PROMs and EPROMs is a condition called chip creep. DIP chips are inserted into what are called through-hole sockets and can and do squirm out of their sockets. Should a ROM chip creep out of its socket, it can cause startup problems. If you have an older motherboard that includes removable DIP ROM or memory chips, you should check them occasionally for creep.

2.6 Booting Process

The BIOS runs off the PROM, EPROM or, most commonly, flash memory when the computer is powered on. It initializes several motherboard components and peripherals, including:

- the clock generator,
- the processors and caches,
- the chipset (memory controller and I/O controller),
- the system memory,
- all PCI devices (by assigning bus numbers and resources),
- the primary graphics controller,
- mass storage controllers (such as SATA and IDE controllers),
- various I/O controllers (such keyboard/mouse and USB).

Finally, it loads the boot loader for the operating system, and transfers control to it. The entire process is known as Power-on self-test (POST). On the original IBM PC, the hardware only needed minimal configuration and POST was indeed used for testing; on modern systems, most of POST actually consists of hardware configuration. Once system memory is initialized, the BIOS typically copies/decompresses itself into that memory and keeps executing from it. Nearly all BIOS implementations can optionally execute a setup program interfacing the nonvolatile BIOS memory (CMOS). This memory holds user-customizable configuration data (time, date, hard drive details, etc.) accessed by BIOS code. The 80x86 source code for early PC and AT BIOS was included with the IBM Technical Reference Manual.

In most modern BIOS implementations, users select which device boots first: CD, hard disk, floppy disk, flash keydrive and the like. This is particularly useful for installing operating systems or booting to Live CDs, and for selecting the order of testing for the presence of bootable media.

Some BIOS's allow the user to select the operating system to load (e.g. load another OS from the second hard disk), though this is more often handled by a second-stage boot loader.

2.7 Memory

So far at every stage we have said that computer cannot think on its own and cannot remember anything unless we store in hard disk with save. While working all the information is stored in what is called the memory of the computer till we press the button to save it. Till that point all the information and results are stored in memory. So usually a big memory means a faster and more useful computer.

A PC's memory is made up of electronic components in which the PC temporarily stores data and instructions. Technically, any device that stores data or instructions on the PC can be called memory, including the hard disk, floppy disks, ROM, CMOS, RAM and cache. However, what is commonly referred to as memory on the PC is its primary storage, which is also known as system memory, temporary storage or RAM. With the exception of ROM, the other forms of storage (hard disk, floppy disk, CD-ROM and the like) are known as secondary storage.

2.7.1 CMOS

Because of the initial cost of Complementary Metal Oxide Semiconductor (CMOS) technology, memory, transistors and large parts of most microprocessors were once reserved for storing the startup configuration of the PC. With technology advances and lower costs, however, CMOS technology is now used throughout the PC. CMOS memory requires only about one-millionth of an amp to hold any data stored on it. Using only a lithium battery, CMOS memory is able to store the startup configuration of a PC for many years. The term CMOS is still synonymous with the PC's startup configuration data.

2.7.2 Bits, Bytes and Words

Nearly everything the PC connects to is measured in bits these days, especially modems and Internet connections, but RAM is still measured in bytes – actually, Kilobytes, megabytes or gigabytes. The following table lists the various data units commonly associated with RAM.

Unit	*Size*	*Description*
Bit	One binary digit	Stores either a binary 0 or 1
Byte	Eight bits	One character
Word	16 to 64 bits	One character
Kilobyte (KB)	1 thousand bytes	About one page of double-spaced text
Megabyte (MB)	1 million bytes	About the size of a short book
Gigabyte (GB)	1 billion bytes	1,000 short books
Terabyte (TB)	1 trillion bytes	An entire library
Petabyte (PB)	1 quadrillion bytes	Just about all the libraries in the U.S.

2.7.3 Memory Speeds

RAM is much faster than a hard disk, floppy disk, CD-ROM or any other form of secondary storage. On the average, accessing data from a hard disk drive takes from 8 to 16 milliseconds (ms). Accessing the same data from RAM takes from 50 to 80 nanoseconds (ns.) There are 1,000ms and 1 billion nanoseconds in a second. What this works out to is that RAM at 50ns is over a million times faster than a hard disk. Other secondary storage devices, such as the CD-ROM or floppy disk, are even slower.

2.7.4 Video RAM

At the time of black and white monitors, it was easy to put aside 2K of memory to support the display. However, for a multicolour display significant memory is needed for display. Today's monitors need a memory source much closer and faster than standard RAM. To provide the video system with the RAM it needs, memory has been added to the video adapter card, which places it much closer to the video controller and the monitor itself. This memory is called video memory or video RAM. Some of the video memory technologies in use are:

2.7.4.1 Video RAM (VRAM)

The most commonly used form of VRAM is also called video RAM. VRAM is a dual-ported DRAM that acts as a buffer between the CPU and the video display.

2.7.4.2 Windows RAM (WRAM)

Although its name suggests otherwise, this type of video memory has nothing at all to do with the operating system with a similar name. Its name comes from the fact that this type of video memory is accessed in blocks or windows, which means it slightly faster than VRAM. Windows RAM is a high-performace video RAM that is better than standard VRAM for high-resolution images.

2.7.4.3 Synchronous Graphics RAM (SGRAM)

SGRAM is a single-ported DRAM technology imporved to run almost four times faster than normal DRAM. It is a single-ported clock-synchronized video RAM that users specialized instructions to perform in a few instructions what would be a series of instructions for other forms of VRAM.

2.7.5 Logical Memory Configuration

Prior to Windows NT and Windows 2000, operating systems such as MS-DOS, PC-DOS or Windows 3.x or 9x organized the physical primary memory into a logical organization that fit its processing needs. DOS and Windows operating systems define memory into four basic divisions.

2.7.5.1 Conventional Memory

Conventional memory is the first 640KB or system memory (RAM). Two things came together in the early days of PCs to fix its size to 640KB. The early processors could not address more than 1MB of RAM and IBM reserved the upper 348 KB of that space of its BIOS and utilities, which left the lower 640KB for the operating system and programs. In use, conventional memory usually contains the kernel of the operating system, user application programs, routines that terminate-and-stay-resident (TSR) and system-level device drivers.

2.7.5.2 The Upper Memory Area

The Upper memory area was originally designated by IBM for use by the system BIOS and video RAM, the 384KB that remains in the first 1MB of RAM after conventional memory. As the need for more than the 640KB available grew, this area was designated as expanded memory and special device drivers were developed, such as EMM386.EXE, to facilitate its general use. The use of this are frees up space in conventional memory by relocating device drivers and TSR programs into unused space in the upper memory area.

2.7.5.3 Extended Memory and the High Memory Area

All of a PC's memory beyond the first 1MB of RAM is called extended memory. Every PC has a limit of how much total memory it can support. The limit is induced by a combination of the processor, motherboard and operating system. The width of the data and address bus is usually the basis of the limit of how much memory the PC can address. The memory maximum usually ranges form 16MB to 4GB, with some newer PCs now able to accept and process even more RAM. Regardless of the amount of RAM a PC can support, anything above 1MB is extended memory. Extended memory is often confused with expanded memory. Expanded memory (the upper memory area) expands conventional memory to fill up the first 1MB of RAM. Extended memory extends RAM all the way to its limit. The first 64KB of extended memory is reserved for use during the startup processes of the PC. This area is called the high memory area.

2.8 Secondary Storage Units

Memory is not the only place where you store the data or program, since it is volatile. So you need to have storage devices which can store your data and programs permanently. For this we use so called storage units. These can be used for storing the data and then, maybe, transferring it to another computer or storage media.

2.8.1 Hard Disk Drives

Hard disks have been there since the time of mainframe systems of 3rd generation computers. The only difference is that the disks at that time were removable and were of very small capacity. However, the basic technology used in the earliest hard disks has not changed all that much over the years, although the size and capacity of the drives has.

2.8.2 Floppy Disk Drives

Although manufacturers have been trying for years to replace the floppy disk, with a device that holds more data, the 3.5 inch floppy disk drive is still very common on most PCs sold today.

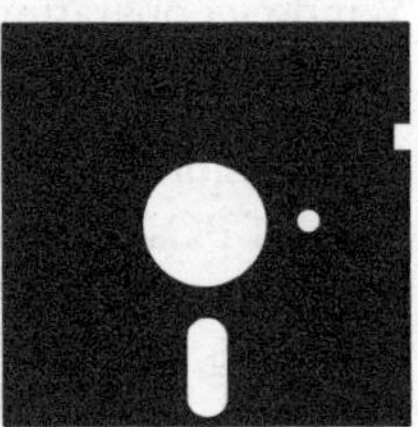

The floppy disk has survived well beyond what anyone expected. It has changed in size over the years and is available in drives that fit inside the system case as well as outside. The floppy disk has come in a variety of sizes over its lifetime, but for about the past ten years the most popular size has been the 3.5 inch diskette.

2.8.3 Optical Disks

Optical disks differ from magnetic disk storage by the way data is stored and read from the storage media. A laser beam is used to write and read data on these reflective disks, so they are also known as laser disks. In this technology a laser hits a layer of metallic material spread over the surface of a disk. When data is being entered heat from the laser produces tiny spots on the disk surface. To read the data, the laser scans the disk, and a lens picks up different light reflections from the various spots.

Optical disks are becoming a very inviting option for users. They are less sensitive to environmental fluctuations, and they provide more direct-access storage at a cost than is much less per megabyte of storage than the magnetic disk alternative.

Optical disk technology is still emerging and has yet to stabilize; however at present there are three different types of optical disks in common use:

- read-only
- recordable, and
- erasable

2.8.4 CD-ROMs and DVDs

The CD-ROM and its comparatively huge storage capacity (over 600 floppy disks) has been very attractive to software and multimedia producers and soon virtually all software, including databases, books encyclopedias and other materials not available to the PC in the past suddenly became very available and accessible for the PC.

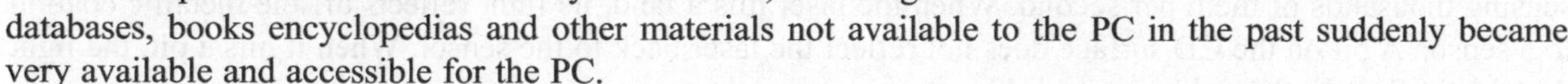

A CD-ROM drive is as common on PCs today as floppy drives were only a few years ago. In fact, some manufacturers now replace the floppy disk drive with a single CD-ROM on their latest PC models. The CD-ROM is by far the most common method of software distribution and data storage due to their combination of high capacity and easy, inexpensive manufacturing. A PC without a CD-ROM drive simply is not able to install the vast majority of PC software available on the market today. Some CD-ROM software even requires that your PC's drive meet a specific minimum requirement. For example, if you have an older CD-ROM drive, such as a 4X, in your system, it may need to be replaced before it can run some newer CD-ROM titles that require at least a 12X drive.

2.8.4.1 CD-ROM Technology

The CD-ROM uses compact disc (CD) technology, the same technology used to record the music on your favorite audio CDs. The physical media used for recording data, programs, music and multimedia on a CD-ROM is the same as that used to record music. In fact, the physical disc is the same for both.

2.8.4.2 Video CD (VCD)

The video CD (VCD) is used to store compressed video information using a standard also defined in the White Book. VCDs use MPEG (Motion Picture Experts Group) compression to store 74 minutes of full-motion video in the same space used by CD-DA audio. To play a video CD requires a CD-ROM drive or video CD player that is video CD-compatible. The compression algorithm used for VCD does not produce a high quality video; this format will likely give way to the DVD.

2.8.4.3 CD-Recordable

Each of the CD types covered to this point have been CD-ROMs or read-only discs, which means that except for during their manufacturing processes, data cannot be stored to them and they cannot be modified, other than to be destroyed. To take advantage of its large storage space, methods have been developed, along with special CD media that allow data to be written to a CD.

A CD Recordable (CD-R) disc is manufactured essentially the same as a CD-ROM disc, with some slight variations. In place of the substrate is a layer of organic dye, over which is placed a reflective gold-colored metallic coating. Over this is the protective lacquer layer, just like a CD-ROM.

Two general types of CDs that can be modified in a special CD-R are:

2.8.5 CD Media

Like other computer storage, such as discs and floppy disks, a CD stores data in digital form, which means that it actually stores only two values: 1s and 0s. However, where the hard disk and diskette stored data in magnetic form, data on a CD recorded in a physical recording technique. A CD starts out as a round piece of polycarbonate substrate about 4.75 inches in diameter and 1.2 millimeters (approximately) 1/20th of an inch) thick. A metal stamp, made from a master of a finished disc, is then used to stamp indentations into the substrate, a process called mastering. A CD-ROM produced this way is said to have been mastered.

The indentations are referred to as pits, and the flat, unpitted surfaces are referred to as lands. The substrate surface and its pits are then covered with a shiny, reflective silver or aluminum coating, which plays a very important part in reading and playing the contents of the CD. A clear plastic cover is then placed over the silver coating on which a paper or silk-screened label is applied. A disc manufactured in this way is called a single-session disc.

2.8.6 Reading the CD

When a CD is loaded into a player or CD-ROM drive, it spins and laser moves over the lands and pits, sensing thousands of them per second. When the laser hits a land, its light reflects off the metallic coating to a sensor. A pit on the CD surface does not reflect the laser back to the sensor. When it hits a pit, the light does not reflect back to the sensor.

Whether the sensor sees a reflection or not is how it knows if the bit on the CD is a 1 or a 0. Unlike a floppy or hard disk, a CD is recorded on a single long (about three miles long, in fact) spiral rather than in discrete tracks. The spiral is wound onto the disc in a pattern that is the equivalent of about 16,000 tracks per inch on a hard disk drive.

The first sector on the CD is located at two minutes, no seconds and no hundredths of seconds (00:02:00) or 600 blocks. On a CD-ROM using 512-byte blocks a minute of data contains 18,000 blocks, which means that there are 300 in a second and 600 in the first two seconds. This also means that Logical Block 0 is at 00:02:00 as well.

2.9 Mass Storage Devices

So far what we have read is what was relevent only a few years ago, The latest in this line are the various mass storage devices which have been deviced only recently. These are mentioned here.

2.9.1 USB Thumb Drive

USB flash drives are NAND-type flash memory data storage devices integrated with a USB (universal serial bus) interface. They are typically small, lightweight, removable and rewritable. As of November 2006, memory capacities for USB Flash Drives currently are sold from 32 megabytes up to 64 gigabytes. Capacity is limited only by current flash memory densities, although cost per megabyte may increase rapidly at higher capacities due to the expensive components. (USB Memory card readers are also available, whereby rather than being built-in, the memory is a removable Flash memory card housed in what is otherwise a regular USB flash drive, as described below.)

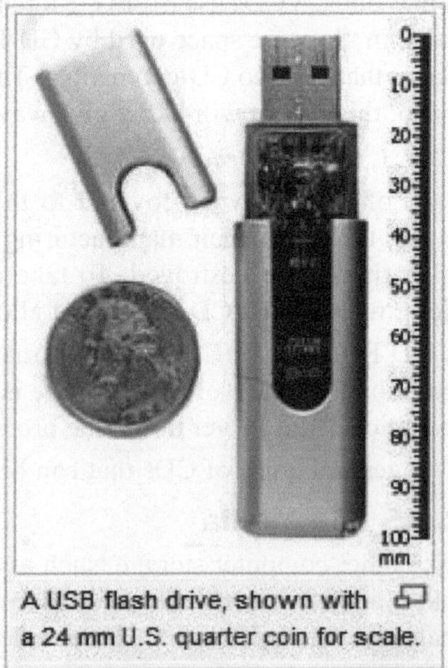

A USB flash drive, shown with a 24 mm U.S. quarter coin for scale.

USB flash drives offer potential advantages over other portable storage devices, particularly the floppy disk. They are more compact, generally faster, hold more data, and are more reliable (due to both their lack of moving parts, and their more durable design) than floppy disks. These types of drives use the USB mass storage standard, supported natively by modern operating systems such as Linux, Mac OS X, Unix, and Windows.

A flash drive consists of a small printed circuit board encased in a plastic or metal casing, making the drive sturdy enough to be carried about in a pocket, as a key fob, or on a lanyard. Only the USB connector protrudes from this protection, and is usually covered by a removable cap. Most flash drives use a standard type-A USB connection allowing them to be connected directly to a port on a personal computer.

To access the data stored in a flash drive, the drive must be connected to a computer, either by plugging it into a USB host controller built into the computer, or into a USB hub. Flash drives are active only when plugged into a USB connection and draw all necessary power from the supply provided by that connection.

However, some flash drives, especially high-speed drives utilizing the USB 2.0 standard, may require more power than the limited amount provided by a bus-powered USB hub, such as those built into some computer keyboards or monitors. These drives will not work unless plugged directly into a host controller (i.e., the ports found on the computer itself) or a self-powered hub.

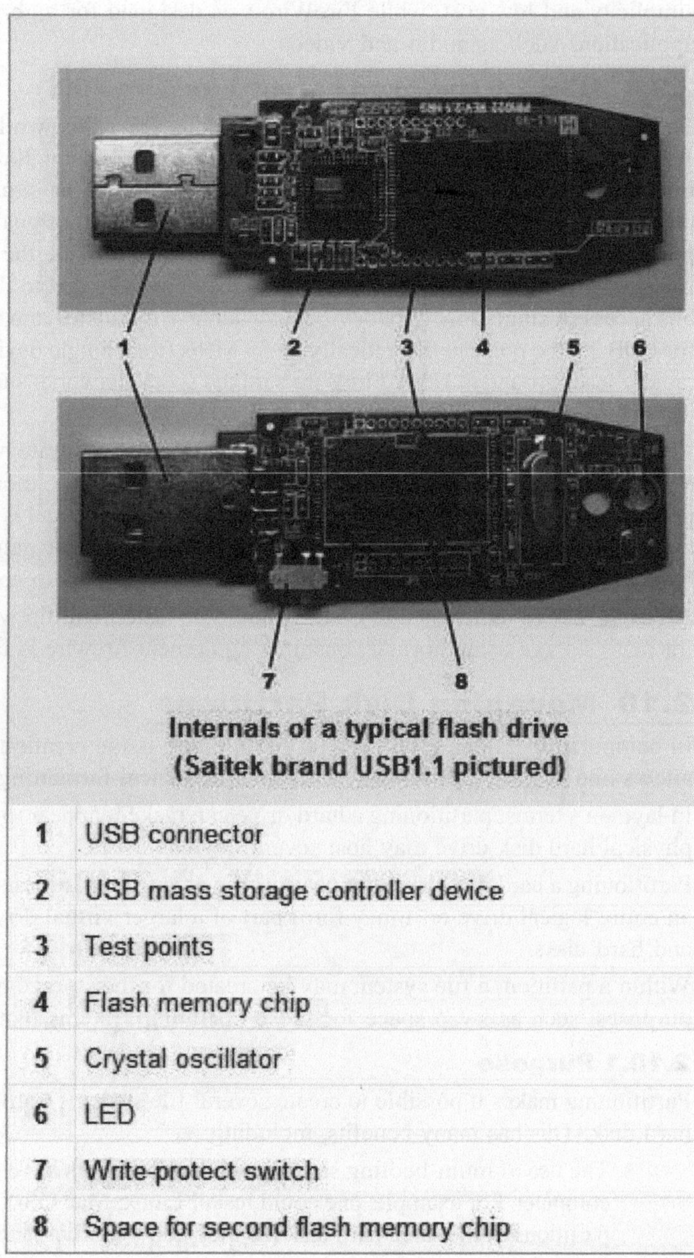

Internals of a typical flash drive (Saitek brand USB1.1 pictured)

1	USB connector
2	USB mass storage controller device
3	Test points
4	Flash memory chip
5	Crystal oscillator
6	LED
7	Write-protect switch
8	Space for second flash memory chip

2.9.2 USB 2.0

Its speed reached a performance level sufficient for consumer equipment while retaining compatibility with older devices. An example of how the popularity of USB displaced FireWire in a commercial device is the Apple iPod. It was originally released with a FireWire connector, which was eventually modified to allow for both USB and FireWire connections when the product was released for Windows. 3rd generation iPods used USB and Firewire for data transfer and only allows a FireWire connection to charge the battery from the main adapter. The iPod does charge via both cables when connected to the host computer. With the 4th generation and newer, iPods use USB for data transfer and both USB and Firewire for charging. The Firewire controller chip set has been removed in favour with reduced costs. The iPod Nano and shuffle don't even support Firewire, only supporting USB.

Today, USB Hi-Speed is used in many consumer products. FireWire, however, retains its popularity in areas such as video and audio production.

2.9.3 Technical differences

The most significant technical differences between FireWire and USB include the following:

- USB networks use a tiered-star topology, while FireWire networks use a repeater-based topology.
- USB uses a "speak-when-spoken-to" protocol; peripherals cannot communicate with the host unless the host specifically requests communication. A FireWire device can communicate with any other node at any time, subject to network conditions.
- A USB network relies on a single host at the top of the tree to control the network. In a FireWire network, any capable node can control the network.

These and other differences reflect the differing design goals of the two buses: USB was designed for simplicity and low cost, while FireWire was designed for high performance, particularly in time-sensitive applications such as audio and video.

2.9.4 USB 2.0 Hi-Speed versus FireWire 400

The signaling rate of USB 2.0 Hi-Speed mode is 480 Mb/s, while the signaling rate of FireWire 400 (IEEE 1394a, the slower, yet more common variant of firewire as of 2007) is 393.216 Mb/s, which would appear to indicate that USB should be slightly faster, but in reality the situation is far more complicated than that and other design factors can dwarf a relatively small difference in signaling rate. USB requires more host processing power than FireWire due to the need for the host to provide the arbitration and scheduling of transactions. USB transfer rates are theoretically higher than FireWire due to the need for FireWire devices to arbitrate for bus access. A single FireWire device may achieve a transfer rate for FireWire 400 as high as 41 MB/s, while for USB 2.0 the rate can theoretically be 55 MB/s (for a single device). In a multi-device environment FireWire rapidly loses ground to USB: FireWire's mixed speed networks and long connection chains dramatically affect its performance.

The peer-to-peer nature of FireWire requires devices to arbitrate, which means a FireWire bus must wait until a given signal has propagated to all devices on the bus. The more devices on the bus, the lower is its peak performance. Conversely, for USB the maximum timing model is fixed and is limited only by the host-device branch (not the entire network). Furthermore, the host-centric nature of USB allows the host to allocate more bandwidth to high priority devices instead of forcing them to compete for bandwidth as in FireWire.

All of the above indicates that USB 2 should be faster than firewire 400 but tests have generally shown that for mass storage using normal consumer equipment firewire is faster often by a significant margin.

2.10 Managing Disk Partitions

In computer operating systems, disk partitioning is the creation of logical divisions upon a hard disk that allows one to apply operating system-specific logical formatting.

In layman's terms, partitioning a hard drive can make it appear to be more than one hard drive. Thus, a single physical hard disk drive may host several logical drives.

Partitioning a hard disk drive defines specific areas (the partitions) within the disk. A partition may constitute an entire logical drive or it may form part of a larger virtual drive which could span over several partitions and hard disks.

Within a partition, a file system may be created for the storage of files, or a partition may be used for other purposes, such as swap space for those operating systems that support "swap partitions".

2.10.1 Purpose

Partitioning makes it possible to create several file systems (either of the same type or different) on a single hard disk. This has many benefits, including:

- The use of multi-booting setups, which allow users have more than one operating system on a single computer. For example, one could install Linux, Mac OS X, Microsoft Windows or others onto different partitions of the same hard disk (so they don't conflict) and have a choice of booting into any operating system (supported by the hardware) at power-up.

- Sharing swap partitions between multiple Linux distributions, so such partitions use less hard drive space.
- Protecting or isolating files, to make it easier to recover a corrupted file system or operating system installation.
- Raising overall computer performance. For instance, large hard drives with only one NTFS filesystem typically have a very large Master File Table (MFT), and it generally takes more time to read this MFT than the MFTs of hard drives with multiple partitions (because each partition has fewer files).
- Higher levels of data organization, raising the user efficiency of the system, for example separate partitions dedicated to digital movie processing, photos, email mailboxes or browser cache.

Partitions may be customized to different requirements, for example, allowing for read-only partitions to protect data: if one partition is damaged, none of the other file systems are affected, and the drive's data may still be salvageable.

2.10.2.2 PC BIOS Partition Types

This section describes partitions as used in MS-DOS, Microsoft Windows and Linux on PC compatible computer systems; for examples of partitioning schemes used in other operating systems, see Slice (disk) and BSD disklabel. Technically, a hard disk should contain either as many as four primary partitions, or one to three primaries along with a single extended partition. Each of these partitions are described by a 16-byte entry in the Partition Table which is located in the Master Boot Record.

The "type" of a partition is identified by a 1-byte code found in its partition table entry. Some of these codes (such as 0x05 and 0x0F) may be used to indicate the presence of an extended partition, but most are used by operating systems that examine partition tables to decide if a partition contains a file system they can mount/ access for reading or writing data.

Once a specific partition's type has been identified, additional information about its purpose and probable contents may be found (see: Andries Brouwer. List of partition identifiers for PCs. as one such resource). For example, some type codes are used to hide a partition's contents from various operating systems. However, if an OS or some partitioning tool has been programmed to also examine the boot sectors of any partition, then its file system may no longer remain hidden. There are no officially assigned partition types; thus, more than one kind of file system may lay claim to the same code value.

2.10.3 Primary (or Logical)

A primary (or logical) partition contains one file system. In MS-DOS and earlier versions of Microsoft Windows systems, the first partition (C:) must be a "primary partition". Other operating systems may not share this limitation; however, this can depend on other factors, such as a PC's BIOS.

The "partition type" code for a primary or logical partition can either correspond to a file system contained within (e.g. 0x07 means either an NTFS or an OS/2 HPFS file system) or indicate the partition has a special use (e.g. code 0xBC may mean an Acronis Secure Zone and code 0x82 usually indicates a Linux swap file partition). The FAT16 and FAT32 file systems have made use of quite a number of partition type codes over time due to the limits of various DOS and Windows OS versions. Though a Linux operating system may recognize a number of different file systems (ext2, ext3, reiserfs, etc.), they have all consistently used the same partition type code: 0x83 (Linux native).

2.10.4 Extended

An extended partition is secondary to the primary partition(s). A hard disk may contain only one extended partition; which can then be sub-divided into logical drives, each of which is (under DOS and Windows) assigned additional drive letters. For example, under either DOS or Windows, a hard disk with one primary partition and one extended partition, the latter containing two logical drives, would typically be assigned the three drive letters: C:, D: and E: (in that order).

Extended partitions are useful if you want more than four partitions on a single physical drive. Technically, the number of logical drives is no longer limited in later operating systems, but under Windows there is an effective limit if they are to be assigned drive letters (only 24 letters, C: through Z:, are generally available. Later operating systems may allow more drives to be mounted/accessed by using A-A:, A-B:, A-C:, etc.).

2.10.5 Compressed disks

Hard disks are sometimes compressed to create additional space. Under MS-DOS and early Windows, programs such as STACKER (DR-DOS except 6), SuperStor (DR-DOS 6), DoubleSpace, or DriveSpace (Windows 95) were used. This compression was done by creating a very large file on the partition, then storing the disk's data in this file. At startup, device drivers opened this file and assigned it a separate letter. Frequently, to avoid confusion, the original partition and the compressed drive had their letters swapped, so that the compressed disk is C:, and the uncompressed area (often containing system files) is given a higher name. (SuperStor required a separate device driver to be loaded, DEVSWAP.COM).

Versions of Windows using the NT kernel, including the most recent versions, XP and Vista, contain intrinsic disk compression capability. The use of separate compression utilities has declined sharply.

2.10.6 Partitioning schemes

2.10.6.1 Microsoft Windows

With Microsoft Windows, the standard partitioning scheme is to create a single active primary partition, the C: drive, where the operating system, user data, applications, and page file all reside. Some users, however, prefer to create multiple partitions so that the operating system can be stored separately from other kinds of data. While this scheme generally results in slightly lower performance due to additional work needing to be done by both the hard drive and the operating system, proponents of multiple partitions generally point to the benefit of being able to erase a single partition (typically the operating system itself) while retaining the other data.

When used in conjunction with 3rd-party partition management programs such as Acronis True Image, Norton PartitionMagic, Norton Ghost, or specialized recovery programs that come with computers manufactured by most major manufacturers, the use of multiple partitions allows computer users to quickly recover from viruses, rootkits, and trojan horses or an otherwise damaged, corrupt or compromised operating system.

2.10.6.2 Unix

For Unix-based and Unix-like operating systems such as Linux and Mac OS X, the creation of separate partitions for /boot, /home, /tmp, /usr, /var, /opt, swap and all remaining files under the "/" (root directory) is possible. (The same is true for Sun-based operating systems, except their partitions are called slices.) Such a scheme has a number of potential advantages: if one file system gets corrupted, the rest of the data (the other file systems) stay intact, minimizing data loss; partitions can be accessed read-only and the execution of setuid files disabled thus enhancing security; performance may be enhanced due to less disk head travel. However, this method has the disadvantage of subdividing the drive into fixed-size partitions, so, for instance, a user could run out of hard drive space in his or her /home partition, even though other partitions still have plenty of usable space. A good implementation requires the user to predict how much space each partition will need, which may be a difficult task; especially for new users. Logical Volume Management, often used in servers, introduces a degree of flexibility by allowing data in these volumes to expand into separate physical disks (which can be added when needed); another option is to resize existing partitions when necessary. Typical desktop systems, though, are often comprised of a single "/" (root directory) containing the entire filesystem plus a much smaller swap partition. A separate /home partition, however, can be very useful, since it allows for a clean reinstall of the OS (or a fresh install of another Linux distribution) while leaving the user's data intact.

2.10.6.3 Partition Recovery

When a partition is deleted, in general, only its partition table entry is removed from a table; and although the data is no longer accessible, it still remains on the disk until it's overwritten. Specialized recovery utilities, (such as TestDisk and gpart), can locate lost file systems and recreate a partition table which includes entries for these recovered file systems. However, some disk utilities may also overwrite a number of beginning sectors of a partition they delete. For example, if Windows Disk Management (Windows 2000/XP, etc.) is used to delete a partition, it will overwrite the first sector (relative sector 0) of the partition before removing it. Hopefully any FAT32 or NTFS partition you wish to recover will still have an available backup boot sector, so the boot sector can be restored.

2.11 File System

Before formatting a volume or partition, consider the file system with which to format it. Windows 2000 and Windows XP support the NTFS file system, File Allocation Table (FAT), and FAT32. NTFS is the recommended file system for Windows 2000 and Windows XP because it supports several features that the other file systems do not, such as file and folder permissions, encryption, large volume support, and sparse file management. However, you must format the volume or partition as FAT if you plan to access files on that volume or partition from other operating systems, including MS-DOS, Windows 95, Windows 98, Windows Millennium Edition, and Windows NT 4.0.

Choose NTFS only if you are running Windows 2000 or Windows XP and you want to take advantage of NTFS features.

The following features are unique to NTFS:

- Compression
- Disk quotas
- Encryption
- Mount points
- Remote storage

In addition, NTFS is required on all dynamic disks and GUID partition table (GPT) disks.

2.11.1 Choosing between NTFS, FAT, and FAT32

You can choose between three file systems for disk partitions on a computer running Windows XP: NTFS, FAT, and FAT32. Use the information below to compare the file systems.

NTFS is the recommended file system for the following reasons:

- NTFS is more powerful than FAT or FAT32, and includes features required for hosting · Active Directory as well as other important security features. You can use features such as Active Directory and domain-based security only by choosing NTFS as your file system.
- It is easy to convert partitions to NTFS. The Setup program makes conversion easy, whether your partitions used FAT, FAT32, or the older version of NTFS. This kind of conversion keeps your files intact (unlike formatting a partition). If you do not need to keep your files intact and you have a FAT or FAT32 partition, it is recommended that you *format* the partition with NTFS rather than *convert* from FAT or FAT32. Formatting a partition erases all data on the partition and allows you to start with a clean drive.

  Whether a partition is formatted with NTFS or converted using the convert command, NTFS is the better choice of file system. For more information about Convert.exe, after completing Setup, click **Start**, click **Run**, type **cmd**, and then press ENTER. In the command window, type **help convert** and then press ENTER.

- In order to maintain access control on files and folders and support limited accounts, you must use NTFS. If you use FAT32, all users will have access to all files on your hard drive, regardless of their account type (administrator, limited, or standard.)

·NTFS is the file system that works best with large disks. (The next best file system for large disks is FAT32.)

There is one situation in which you might want to choose FAT or FAT32 as your file system. If it is necessary to have a computer that will sometimes run an earlier version of Windows and other times run Windows XP, you will need to have a FAT or FAT32 partition as the primary (or startup) partition on the hard disk. Most earlier versions of Windows cannot access a partition if it uses the latest version of NTFS. The two exceptions are Windows 2000 and Windows NT 4.0 with Service Pack 4 or later. Windows NT 4.0 with Service Pack 4 or later has access to partitions with the latest version of NTFS, but with some limitations: It cannot access files that have been stored using NTFS features that did not exist when Windows NT 4.0 was released.

For anything other than a situation with multiple operating systems, however, the recommended file system is NTFS.

Let us Revise

1. The processor, more formally known as the central processing unit (CPU), has the electronic circuitry that manipulates input data into the information people want.
2. CPU coordinates and controls the activities of input, output and storage devices, and performs all the arithmetic and logical processes to be applied to data.
3. Computer memory also known as primary storage, is closely associated with the central processing unit.
4. Registers are temporary storage areas for instructions or data.
5. The number and type of registers in a CPU vary according to the CPU's design.
6. The instruction interpreter is a group of electrical cicuits that performs the intent of instructions fetched from memory.
7. The location counter, also called Program Counter (PC) or Instruction Counter (IC), is a hardware memory device that denotes the location of the current instruction being executed.
8. A copy of the current instruction is stored in the Instruction Register (IR).
9. The working registers are memory devices that serve as scratch pads for the instruction interpreter, while the general registers are used by the programmer as locations and for special functions.
10. SIC is a concept devised to explain the most commonly encountered hardware features and concepts.
11. Instruction sets in SIC are there to test all the conditions.
12. The ALU contains the electronic circuitry that executes all arithmetic and logical operations.
13. The control unit contains electronic circuit that uses electrical signals to direct the entire computer system to carry out, or execute, stored program instructions.
14. Computers provide the processing speed essential to our fast-paced society.
15. Computers are extremely reliable.
16. Computer systems can store tremendous amounts of data.
17. A PC's memory is made up of electronic components in which the PC temporarily stores data and instructions.
18. Data stored on read-only memory (ROM) cannot be changed.
19. RAM is a group of integrated circuits that contain small electronic components that store binary 1s and 0s.

20. Various storing units of memory are: Bit (One binary digit); Byte (Eight bits); Word (16 to 64 bits); Kilobyte (KB) (1 thousand bytes); Megabyte (MB) (1 million bytes); Gigabyte (GB) 1 billion bytes; Terabyte (TB) (1 trillion bytes); Petabyte (PB) (1 quadrillion bytes).
21. Accessing data from a hard disk drive takes from 8 to 16 milliseconds.
22. A storage device is used to store the data in the computer.
23. Floppy disks of 3½" are used these days.
24. CD-ROMs are now used as media for computers.
25. CDs can be used as recording media too.

Multiple Choice Questions

1. RAM stands for:
   (a) Random Allowed Memory (b) Ready Access Memory (c) Random Access Memory
2. RAM consists of binary numbers 1s and :
   (a) 0s (b) 2s (c) 3s
3. CPU contains Primary Storage, Arithmetic Logic Unit and
   (a) Control Unit (b) Data Unit (c) Alpha Unit
4. System software controls:
   (a) Hard disk (b) Internal computer system (c) Floppy disk
5. Data stored in ROM cannot be changed:
   (a) Yes (b) No
6. A copy of the current instruction is stored in:
   (a) Instruction Register (b) Working Register (c) General Register
7. Floppy disk popular these days is of size:
   (a) 3½" (b) 5¼" (c) 5½"
8. CDs are of which shape:
   (a) round (b) square (c) rectangular
9. Hard disks has
   (a) cubicles (b) platters (c) keys

True/False Questions

1. CPUs full form is Central Processing Unit.
2. CPU coordinates and controls all the activities of the computer.
3. Registers are permanent storage areas for instructions or data.
4. A copy of the current instruction is stored in the Instruction Register (IR).
5. The working registers are memory devices that serve as scratch pads for the instruction interpreter.
6. There are no instruction sets in SIC.
7. The ALU contains the electronic circuitry that executes all arithmetic and logical operations.
8. The control unit of computer contains electronic circuit .
9. Computers provide the processing speed essential to our fast-paced society.
10. Computers can store tremendous amounts of data.

11. A PC's memory temporarily stores data and instructions.
12. Data stored on read-only memory (ROM) can be changed.
13. RAM is a group of integrated circuits that contain small electronic components that store binary 1s and 0s.
14. Accessing data from a hard disk drive takes from 8 to 16 milliseconds.
15. A storage device is used to store the data in the computer.
16. Floppy disks of 5½" are used these days.
17. CD-ROMs are now used as media for computers.
18. CDs can be used as recording media too.

Matching Columns

Match the text of the column A with the action of Column B.

Column A	Column B
A. SIC	1. Read Only Memory
B. Registers	2. Compact Disk-Read Only Memory
C. RAM	3. CD Recordable
D. ROM	4. Simplified Instructional Computer
E. CPU	5. Arithmetic Logic Unit
F. CD-ROM	6. Programable Read Only Memory
G CD-R	7. Erasable Programable Read Only Memory
H. ALU	8. To store information temporarily
I. PROM	9. Central Processing Unit
J. EPROM	10. Random Acess Memory

a. Read b. System c. Memory d. Programmable
e. Windows f. Erasable g. Access h. Semiconductor
i. Processing j. Logic

Fill in the Blanks

1. Complementary Metal Oxide __________ (CMOS).
2. Arithmetic ________ Unit (ALU).
3. Random ________ Memory.
4. ________ RAM (WRAM).
5. Windows is a __________ software.
6. _______ Only Memory (ROM).
7. CD Read Only ________ (CD ROM).
8. _______ Read Only Memory (PROM).
9. Central __________ Unit.
10. ________ Erasable Programable Read Only Memory (EEPROM).

Descriptive Type Questions

1. Describe the various functions of CPU.
2. What does CPU consist of ?
3. What is Internal memory?
4. What are Registers? What function do they play?
5. What happens inside ALU?
6. Describe the various type of software.
7. Describe the various characteristics of computers?
8. What do you understand by SIC?
9. Describe the various features of SIC.
10. Describe the various types of memory in computers.
11. What do you understand by Logical Memory Configuration?
12. What is a hard disk?
13. Which type of Floppy Disks are in use?
14. Describe the various types of CDs available.
15. How a CD is read?
16. Describe the following terms:

Arithmetic Logic Unit
Central Processing Unit
Data Formats
Addressing Modes
Instruction Set
Application Software
System Software
Speed of computers
Storage capacity of computers
High Memory Area
Upper Memory Area
RAM
ROM
Extended Memory
Byte
Kilobyte
Gigabyte
Tetrabyte
Terabyte
Megabyte
PROM
EPROM
EEPROM
CMOS
VRAM
WRAM
SGRAM
Cache Memory
Disk Cache
Internal Cache
External Cache
VCD
CD-R
CD Media
DVDs
Floppy Disks

Answers to Objective Type Questions

Multiple Choice Questions

1. c	2. b	3. a	4. b
5. a	6. a	7. a	8. a
9. b			

True False Questions

1. T	2. T	3. F	4. T
5. T	6. F	7. T	8. T
9. T	10. T	11. T	12. F
13. T	14. T	15. T	16. F
17. T	18. F		

Matching Columns

A. 4	B. 8	C. 10	D. 1
E. 9	F. 2	G. 3	H. 5
I. 6	J. 7		

Fill in the Blanks

1. h	2. j	3. g	4. e
5. b	6. a	7. c	8. d
9. i	10. f		

Input and Output Devices 3

3.1 Introduction

As was mentioned in the last chapter, computer processes data which is fed into it and gives results in the form you like. You can feed in this data for processing using a number of input mediums available and take the resultant output on various other medias available. In this chapter we will read about all these input and output devices through which we can input the data and take the processed output.

Since output is dependent on the data which is inputted, it must be ensured that the data is correct else the result will be wrong too. If by mistake you type the bank account 9634 instead of 9631 then the amount would be credited to a different person. So one must ensure that the data is accurate. As you will read later in the chapter, there are devices which allow you to feed the directly to the computer whereas there are others which allow you to feed the data off line, record it in some media and then feed this media into the computer.

In this chapter I have divided the devices into 2 sections, namely; **Input Devices** and **Output Devices**. Let us start with Input Devices and most important of them all, the keyboard.

3.2 Input Devices

On the basis of input, computer gives an output. Clerical kind of mistakes occasionally occur during the inputting of data, e.g., if Student Identification Number 6346 is wrongly inputted as 6364 can lead to the wrong result. Input phase is an excellent place to detect and correct errors. A right input protects computer files, i.e., inputted data which is stored in file on disks can be used later in some task. Accurate input is therefore vital to protect these files from "contamination".

Data preparation is often labour intensive. This makes data preparation comparatively costly and therefore an important site for cost control.

There are 3 important characteristics for a good data input

1. Timeliness
2. Accuracy and
3. Potential Usefulness

3.2.1.1 Timeliness

Timely data is data that is collected and processed fast enough for action to be taken. For example, in on-line system in electricity department data of voltage and current is input continuously. Whenever the data of voltage or current is below or above the danger mark, i.e., data is also processed simultaneously, alarm gets on and whole system is shut down.

3.2.1.2 Accuracy

Data must be accurate to save the informational needs of the alarm to get on. For example, alarm should not run on any other which are not equivalent to the specified value.

3.2.1.3 Potential Usefulness

Data as such is raw and is of no use unless it is logical, i.e., related to the requirement. When this data is processed it becomes an information which helps in making decision. So the preparation of computerized input is the first step in the creation of useful information.

3.2.2 Keyboards

One look at it and you would be reminded of the old typewriter keypad. Well yes, the placing of alpha keys is exactly the same. This is called the QWERTY type of keyboard. This has been done specially keeping in mind the migration of people from typewriter to keyboard.

It is the most important part of the computer. I am yet to see a computer without it. It is there in each computer. There are some software available in the market which teach you how to master the keyboard, but the old asdf method of typing would be sufficient. If one does not have speed for typing, it is ok but, the placcment of keys is very important before you sit down on computer.

Let us sec how the various keys are placed on the keyboard.

3.2.2.1 Keyboard Keys

Most keyboard layouts are still a variation of the key layout of a typewriter, at least for the alphabetic, numerical and special character keys. Keyboards are available for various other languages than English too, but, for our purposes we would stick to the English one. There are mostly **101 keys** on the keyboard. The important keys are as follows:

Alpha Keys: Alphabet keys are marked from a to z. As in typewriter, you can use S to make them capital, i.e., ABCDE, etc. So if you press a b c d e .... etc., with S key already pressed, you will get A B C D E .... etc. Similar results can be obtained by putting CAPS LOCK key ON. For typing capital A, you press S key and then while keeping S key pressed, press the "a" key. Otherwise for typing a, you don't need to press the S key, just press the a key.

Numeric Keys: The numeric keys (with the characters 0 to 9) are located on the computer's keyboard at two places. You can see them in the top row above the alpha keys (as in typewriter). A second set of these keys is provided on the right-hand side of the keyboard. The numeric keys in the top row can be used straightaway to type in numeric characters. By simultaneously holding down the Shift key (as in the typewriter), you can also type in special upper characters like ! % $ *, etc. However, to type numeric characters by using the keys on the right side, you will need to press the Num Lock key ON.

Function Keys: These keys are marked ! to +. These keys are used for specific purposes as defined in the computer (a computer program is a set of instructions given to a computer to perform a specific task) which you may be using. For example, in BASIC programming (BASIC is a computer language used for writing programs) # will load the program, ! will list the program after loading and @ will run the program.

Arrow Keys: On 101 keys keyboard these are placed at two places. The first is called the cursor pad which works independently. The other is the numeric-cum-cursor pad. It is similar to the one on the 84 key keyboard. When the Num Lock key is not in the ON position, pressing the key of the numeric keypad moves the cursor in the direction shown on each key. Otherwise, this portion is used to enter numbers.

Special Keys including Spacebar: There are several other keys which serve some definite purposes. Some of these keys are available on the typewriter too. The special keys are:

S **Shift Key:** It is used for typing capital letters and special characters. In combination with both Control and Alternate keys, it is sometimes used to execute a particular command too.

C **Control Key:** On its own, this key does not have any purpose. However, combined with different keys, it performs some useful operations. For example, in WordStar software, Control if pressed alongwith B, will make the character Bold.

Q **Backspace:** It allows the cursor to go back by one character. Some types of computer programs allow the backspace to delete the last character. A cursor is usually a blinking line (_), on the screen, which shows where he character you type on your keyboard will appear.

Spacebar: As in the typewriter, the Spacebar is used to leave space between words.

E **Enter Key:** It informs the computer that the line of the matter, you are typing, has come to an end. After that you begin typing from a new line. It is also used, while programming, to tell the computer to execute certain commands which you give. Thus, while writing a computer program, you can also use this key to indicate the end of a given command.

= **Del Key:** If, by mistake, you have typed in something which you did not want to, you can erase the wrong character by pressing the DEL (short for Delete) key.

3.2.2.2 The Numeric Pad

As mentioned earlier the numeric pad is used for entering the numeric data, from 0 to 9. But, there are other keys too, which are shown here.

NUM LOCK: As mentioned you need to put this ON for typing the numeric data. When you put on the computer system, this key is put on.

Arithmetic operators: The number pad includes keys for the four standard arithmetic operators, / (divide), * (multiply), - (subtract) and + (add).

Numbers/cursor keys: When the Num Lock key is off, the various keys here act differently. They act as they are mentioned on the keys. For example, there is Home on the 7 key, there is Up Arrow at the 8 key. So while the Num Lock key is off, you can use the numeric pad for other purposes.

INSERT/DELETE: These two keys are the zero and period of the number pad when it is in number mode; in cursor control mode, they duplicate the actions of the INSERT key and the DELETE keys.

ENTER: This is a second ENTER key that remains an ENTER KEY regardless of the number pad's mode.

3.2.2.3 Special-Purpose Keys

These keys are used for some special purposes. Each key has a special purpose attached to it and can be used for it:

Esc: The Escape key is typically enabled as an exit key by most software applications. It is used to cancel out of a command or to exit an application. It is also used in combination with other keys to create special key values and to indicate other actions. For example, in Windows the ESC key can be used to close a context menu.

Print Screen/SysRq: The PRINT SCREEN mode of this key got its name back in the MS-DOS days, when pressing it sent the image of the display to the printer. On a Window system, the image of monitor's display is sent to the Windows Clipboard.

Pause/Break: In its default mode (PAUSE), this key will, it enabled by software, pause the display or the action of an application program. If used in combination with the CTRL key, the alternate mode of this key interrupts or halts some software programs, primarily MS-DOS commands and applications. Using the CTRL and BREAK keys together is the same using the CTRL and C keys to break an action.

3.2.3 Mouse

These days even the mouse has become very important part of computer. It has become integral part of computer since Windows has become the operating system for computers. It is in fact a pointing device. With this you can point at any place on the monitor and start the typing or clicking from that point. All Windows-based programs use mouse, making working with computers easier as you are not required to type commands.

3.2.3.1 Types of Mouse

There are three basic types of Mouse

1. Mechanical Mouse
2. Optomechanical Mouse
3. Optical Mouse

3.2.3.2 Mechanical Mouse

A mechanical mouse has a rubber or metal ball on its underside that can roll in all directions. Mechanical sensors within the mouse detect the direction of the rolling ball and make a movement of the screen pointer accordingly.

3.2.3.3 Optomechanical Mouse

Optomechanical mouse is also similar to a mechanical mouse except that it uses optical sensors to detect the movement of the ball on the Mouse Pad.

3.2.3.4 Optical Mouse

Optical mouse uses a laser beam to detect the movement of mouse on specially designed Mouse Pad. We must move the mouse along a special mat with a grid so that optical mechanism has a frame of reference. This type of mouse has no mechanical moving parts. Optical mouse respond more quickly and precisely than any other mouse. These are expensive than the other two.

3.2.4 Joysticks (or Paddle)

You must have seen a joystick with a video game at various video game parlours. Well the same joystick can be attached to the computer too. For playing game obviously. It consists of a small, vertical lever (called the stick) mounted on a base that is used to steer the screen cursor around. Some joysticks are mounted on a keyboard, others function as stand- alone units. The joystick can be moved left or right, forward or backward, springs are often used to return the joystick to its home center position.

3.2.5 Scanners

Whereas a keyboard, mouse or trackball requires manual input of data, scanners allow input of printed data. A scanner reads text, photographs and graphics from paper which are then converted into bit patterns for processing, storage or output. Scanner is a device that examines a spatial pattern one part after another and generate analog or digital signals corresponding to the pattern. Scanners are often used in mark sensing, pattern recognition or character recognition. Practically scanner uses light for examining the spatial patterns. In a scanner, as the image is scanned, it is converted into light and dark picture elements, or pixels, similar to newspaper photo. Colour scanners can assign a specific colour to a pixel. The pixel are then stored as bit patterns. This technique makes the images usable by word processing, desktop publishing, and graphic packages. There are two types of scanners, Hand-held scanner and Flat-bed scanner

3.2.5.1 Hand-Held Scanner

These devices read data on price tags, shipping labels, inventory part number, book ISBNs, and the like. Hand-held scanner, sometimes called wand scanners, use either contact or laser technology. It has a set of light emitting diodes. It is placed over the material to be scanned and slowly dragged from the top to the bottom. The light emitted by the diodes are not reflected by black lines and are reflected by whole areas. The material is converted and stored in a bitmap. Typical applications are to store images and reproduce them in publications.

3.2.5.2 Flat-bed Scanner

It consists of a box with glass plate on top, which is used for placing the document to be scanned. The light beam is situated below the glass plate and is moved from left to right horizontally. After scanning one line the beam moves up little and scans the next line. The scanner can also store colour images.

3.2.6 Web Cameras

It is fast becoming an integral part of the computer specially for those who use Internet quite often. With this you can take an instant picture of the object to whom you focus it. It is very useful specially for those who have to show their designs, products, etc., on the computer to the clients. The picture transfer is almost instant.

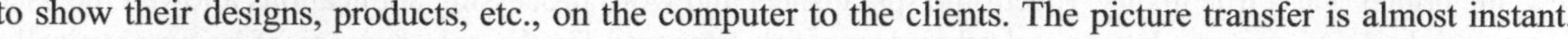

3.3 Output Devices

The success of business today can depend to a large extent on how meaningful and timely the information a computer can produce, i.e., the output. So the two most important requirements of computer output are that it is meaningful and convenient to use.

3.3.1 Monitors and Displays

There would be no What You See Is What You Get (WYSIWYG) on PCs, if there were no monitors or displays on which to see what you get. The PC must produce outputs that can be handled by the senses of humans and so far, technology is limited to sight and sound. Given a choice, most of us still prefer sight over sound. You can accomplish a lot on a PC without sound, but not much would get done without the ability to see what you are working on. The two general categories of PC visual presentation are the monitor and the display. A monitor has a CRT (cathode ray tube) and look something like a traditional television set (without the controls, of course). On the other hand, a display is a flat-panel device that can be attached to a portable PC or hung on the wall. A monitor is largely desk or table-bound, but a display can get up and move about. A flat-panel display is really an adaptation of the monitor, but because it uses different technology, they are treated as two different components.

The PC Monitor: With personal computer technology advancing as fast as it is, it is hard to believe that any part of a PC could be considered an investment. However, the PC monitor is the only part of the personal computer that actually hold its value and has some durability. A good quality monitor will last for years through several generations of the PC systems.

Video Cards: In general, the video card processes the graphics data produced by software running on the PC and prepares it for use by the monitor for converting it from digital data to an analog signal. The video card also sends out the data needed by the monitor to refresh the image or renew it as it changes.

Video cards, graphics cards and accelerator cards are all names for the adapter card inside the PC that is responsible for generating the signals that tell the monitor what to display. The relationship between the video card and the monitor should be carefully matched. These two device must be compatible in terms of the signal used to communicate to the monitor, the type of connector used to connect them together, the video display standards they support and their speed.

Dumb Terminal: It has been named as such since it is really dumb. It has no memory or processing unit, just a keyboard and the monitor. It takes everything else from the computer which it is attached.

Smart Terminal: If you add microprocessor to dumb terminal, then it becomes a smart terminal. But, it still depends upon the main computer for programming and other jobs.

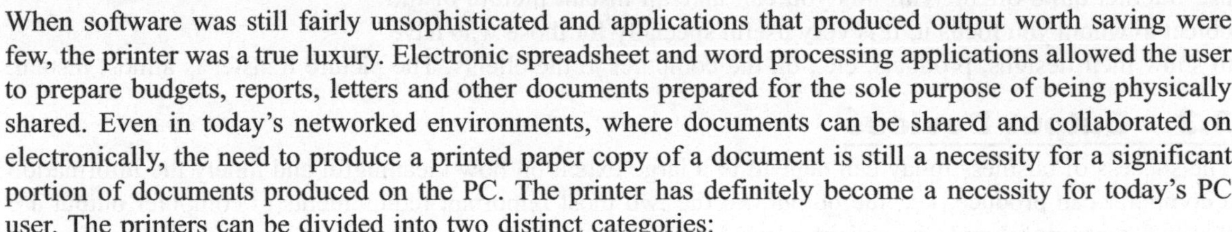

Intelligent Terminal: First we add microprocessor, now we add everything else. It is full-fledged computer in itself but connected to a large computer. It can be programmed and has processing power. Most of the work can be done at the terminal itself. Only for jobs that require large processing and storage facility, the main computer is used.

3.3.2 Printers

Once considered an expansive luxury for any PC, especially for home or small office systems, a printer is now virtually a necessity on any PC system. Technology has advanced to the point that good quality, color printers are available for less than Rs.8,000 and it is common for PC sale bundles to include one.

When software was still fairly unsophisticated and applications that produced output worth saving were few, the printer was a true luxury. Electronic spreadsheet and word processing applications allowed the user to prepare budgets, reports, letters and other documents prepared for the sole purpose of being physically shared. Even in today's networked environments, where documents can be shared and collaborated on electronically, the need to produce a printed paper copy of a document is still a necessity for a significant portion of documents produced on the PC. The printer has definitely become a necessity for today's PC user. The printers can be divided into two distinct categories:

1. Impact Printers
2. Non-impact Printers

3.3.2.1 Impact Printers

A printer in which printing is the result of mechanically striking the printing medium. An impact printer makes contact with the paper to produce an image. The impact may be produced by a print hammer character, like that of a typewriter key striking a ribbon against the paper or by a print hammer hitting paper and ribbon against a character. An impact printer must be used if printing a multiple copy report so that the duplicate copies will receive the imprint. Impact printers are of following types:

3.3.3 Dot-Matrix Printer

In it the individual characters are formed by a matrix of wires or styluses. Dot-matrix printers are also called serial printers. The images are formed by a print head that is composed of a series of little print hammers that look like the heads of pins. The print head usually has nine pins or 24 pines. The bottom 2 pins are used to form the descenders of lower case letters, viz., p, q, g and y. Many expensive dot-matrix printers do not provide descenders, but print quality is improved when they are used.

Features common to most dot-matrix printers include boldface, underline, subscript and superscript and compressed print (narrowed letters). Optional features include proportional spacing (using more or less space, depending on the width of the character) and italics. Dot matrix printers are very versatile since the character set can be changed by software or firmware such as a PROM for different styles, alphabets or graphic symbols. Dot-matrix printers are comparatively inexpensive and one of the fastest types of character-at-a-time printers available. The speed ranges from 50 cps to 400 cps (character per second).

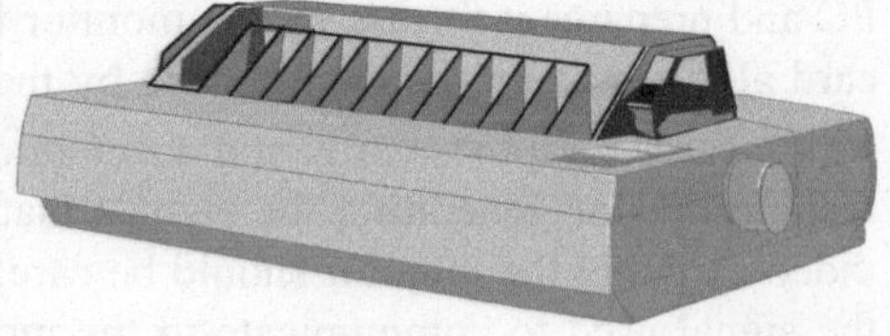

Their abilities to use different type fonts, different line densities and different types of paper are also important.

3.3.3.1 Non-Impact Printers

Printers that do not strike characters against ribbon or paper when they print, are non-impact printers. Example of non-impact printers include

1. Ink-jet printers
2. Laser printers

These printers makes much less noise than impact printers. If you are using a non-impact printer, do not try to print on multiple-part carbon forms: because no impact is being made on the paper you will end up with no copies.

3.3.4 Ink-jet Printers

It uses a technique of projecting droplets of ink at paper to form the required image. Ink-jet printer create an image directly on paper by spraying ink through as many as 64 tiny nozzles. It provides a print resolution of around 360 dots per inch.

3.3.5 Laser Printers

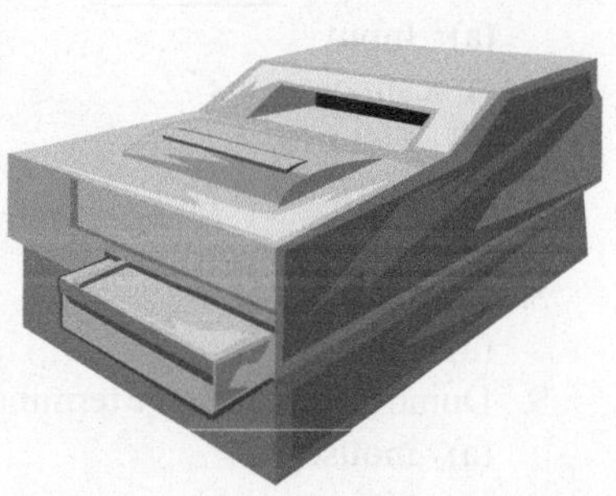

The physical properties of LASERs (Light Amplification by Stimulate Emission of Radiation) allows for the very precise positioning of narrow beam of light, transferring a high energy source to a very small area. This property is used to control printing, i.e., laser printers, to read information from bar codes and to read and write information in optical storage devices. Laser printer is a non-impact printer that creates, by means of a laser beam directed on a photosensitive surface, a latent image which is then made visible by a toner and transferred and fixed on paper. A separate computer is built into the printer to interpret the data that it receives from the computer and to control the laser. Just as electron gun in a graphic monitor can target any pixel, the laser in a laser printer can aim at any point on a drum creating an electrical charge. The resolution of laser printers is 600 DPI both horizontally and vertically; some high-end models have resolution of 1200 DPI.

Let us Revise

1. Input device is used to input data into computer.
2. Output device is used to get result from the computer.
3. Keyboard has 101 keys.
4. Alpha keys are there for typing alphabets A to Z.
5. Numeric keys are there for typing numerals 0 to 9.
6. Function keys are used in programming.
7. Arrow keys are used for moving the cursor on the screen.
8. Special keys are used for special purposes.
9. Numeric pad has other keys too besides the numeric ones.
10. Mouse is basically a pointing device.
11. There are three basic types of Mouse: Mechanical Mouse; Optomechanical Mouse and Optical Mouse.
12. Joystick is used for playing games.
13. A scanner reads text, photographs and graphics from paper which are then converted into bit patterns for processing, storage or output.
14. Monitor is like a TV and is used to display output.
15. The printers can be divided into two distinct categories: Impact Printers and Non-impact Printers.
16. Dot matrix printers use hammers to print characters.
17. Laser printer is a non-impact printer that creates a laser beam transfers the same on the paper for printing.

18. Web cameras are used for sending and receiving pictures on the Internet.
19. Dumb terminals have only keyboard and monitors.
20. Smart terminals have microprocessors too.
21. Intellignet terminals have everything except big storage capacity.

Multiple Choice Questions

1. For seeing the output, you use:
   (a) Monitor (b) Keyboard (c) Mouse
2. In programming, you use the following keys:
   (a) Arrow keys (b) Function keys (c) Alpha keys
3. Keyboard has ________ number of keys.
   (a) 100 (b) 88 (c) 101
4. Printer is an ________ device.
   (a) Input (b) Output (c) Both
5. Mouse is a ________ device.
   (a) Input (b) Output (c) Both
6. A scanner scans
   (a) Pictures (b) Text (c) Both
7. Laser printer is an ________ device.
   (a) Input (b) Output (c) Both
8. Trackball has a
   (a) ball (b) track (c) football
9. Dumb terminals have terminals and
   (a) mouse (b) speakers (c) keyboard
10. Dot matrix printers uses ______ for printing
    (a) hammers (b) slugs (c) mouse

True/False Questions

1. Keyboard has 100 keys.
2. Function keys are used in programming.
3. Numeric pad has other keys too besides the numeric ones.
4. Mouse is basically a pointing device.
5. There are three basic types of Mouse: Mechanical Mouse; Optomechanical Mouse and Optical Mouse.
6. Joystick cannot be used with computers.
7. A scanner reads text, photographs and graphics from paper which are then converted into bit patterns for processing, storage or output.
8. Trackball is not a pointing device.
9. Monitor is like a TV and is used to display output.
10. There are two type of printers: Impact Printers and Non-impact Printers.
11. Dot matrix printers use hammers to print characters.
12. Laser printer does not use laser beam for printing.
13. Web cameras are used for sending and receiving pictures on the Internet.
14. Dumb terminals have only keyboard and monitors.
15. Smart terminals have microprocessors too.

Matching Columns

Match the text of the column A with the action of Column B.

Column A	Column B
A. Keyboard	1. Camera used for sending pictures on Internet

B. Mouse	2. Upside down mouse with ball on top
C. Joystick	3. A pad on which whatever you write goes to the computer
D. OCR	4. Machine to read punched cards
E. Hand held scanner	5. A device to convert computer output to speech
F. Flat bed scanner	6. Pen with light sensors
G Bar codes	7. Printer which uses a wheel of characters to print
H. Digial camera	8. A pointing device
I. MICR	9. Printer which uses jets of ink to print
J. Card reader	10. Entering data by speaking
K. Web cameras	11. Printer using laser beam for printing
L. Light pens	12. Camera which can store pictures
M. Trackball	13. Plotter which plots on ream of paper
N. Touch screen	14. Computer Output on Microfilm
O. Touch pad	15. It has 101 keys
P. Voice input	16. Plotter which plots full page
Q. Multimedia projector	17. Scanner which can scan a full page
R. Speech synthesizer	18. Scans text or graphics by sliding on it
S. Dot matrix printers	19. Printer which prints one line at a time
T. Daisywheel printers	20. Used for playing games
U. Line printers	21. Printer which prints characters in the shape of dots
V. Inkjet printers	22. Vertical bars used to represent numbers
W. Laser printers	23. Projecters used for multimedia presentations
X. Flatbed plotters	24. Optical Character Reader
Y. Drum Plotters	25. It allows you to enter data by touching screen
Z. COM	26. Magnetic Ink Character Reader

Fill in the Blanks with appropriate words

a. Text	b. Mechanical	c. Trackball	d. Speech synthesizer
e. Impact	f. Line	g. Optical	h. Joystick
i. Light pen	j. Character	k. Non impact	l. Optomechanical
m. Flatbed	n. Computer Output Microfilm	o. Pictures	p. Graphics
q. Touch screen	r. Voice Input	s. hammers	t. Presentations
u. Bar codes	v. Numeric	w. paper	x. Function

1. Printers are of two types ___________ and ___________.
2. Mouse are of 3 types ___________, ___________ and ___________.
3. ________ is used for playing games.
4. OCR is Optical ________ Reader.
5. Scanner is used to scan ________ and ________.
6. Digital camera stores ________.
7. ________ uses light sensors.
8. ________ has ball on the top.
9. Multimedia projector is used for multimedia ___________.
10. ___________ converts computer data to speech.
11. Dot Matrix Printer uses ________ to print characters.
12. ________ printers print one line at a time.
13. ________ plotters plot a full page

14. Full form of COM is ___________, ___________, on ___________
15. ___________ is used for writing by touching the screen.
16. ________ allows you to speak data to the computer
17. Card readers used cards made up of ________ for reading the data.
18. _________ consits of various codes in the form of vertical bars.
19. ________ keys are at two places on the keyboard.
20. ________ keys are used in programming.

Descriptive Type Questions

1. Describe the various type of keys on the keyboard.
2. Describe the various types of mouse available.
3. What is a trackball?
4. What is the difference between Impact and Non-impact printers?
5. Describe the working of joystick.
6. What is the difference between hand held and flat bed scanners?
7. What is a trackball?
8. Describe the various types of terminals available.
9. Decscribe the working of Dot Matrix Printer.
10. How do the daisywheel printers print?
11. What is an inkjet printer?
12. Describe the working of laser printer.

Answers to Objective Type Questions

Multiple Choice Questions

1. a	2. b	3. c	4. b
5. a	6. c	7. b	8. a
9. c	10. a		

True False Questions

1. F	2. T	3. T	4. T
5. T	6. F	7. T	8. F
9. T	10. T	11. T	12. F
13. T	14. T	15. T	

Matching Columns

A. 15	B. 8	C. 20	D. 24
E. 18	F. 17	G. 22	H. 12
I. 26	J. 4	K. 1	L. 6
M. 2	N. 25	O. 3	P. 10
Q. 23	R. 5	S. 21	T. 7
U. 19	V. 9	W. 11	X. 16
Y. 13	Z. 14		

Fill in the Blanks

1. e, k	2. b, g, l	3. h	4. j
5. a, p	6. o	7. i	8. c
9. t	10. d	11. s	12. f
13. m	14. n	15. q	16. r
17. w	18. u	19. v	20. x

Multimedia and Other Software 4

4.1 What is Multimedia

First thing first, let us understand what Multimedia means. Multi- means many, i.e., not one, more than one. Media means medium to communicate or talk. Now how would a computer talk to you. It would either create a sound, show a picture or some text on the screen. All this would be communicated to you by computer using medium like Monitor to show the text and picture, speaker to broadcast sound. All these mediums of the computer, like monitor and speaker are collectively called Computer Media.

Now what we make of Multimedia. It is a process by which computer communicates with you using more than one computer medium like sound, text, graphics, animation or video. Any two or more combinations from the above can be used and the net result can be displayed on the monitor screen or transferred to your web or the web site which you may create.

Among the various applications of multimedia are the dazzling effects you can see in most of the advertisements on the TV. How about Pepsi advertisement of Oh Bubbly. It makes good use of sound, graphics, and animation. Most of the advertisements which you see on the TV are the results of computer created animation (using software called Flash, about which you would be reading in a later chapter) and combinations of pictures shot by either still or video camera. These pictures are then changed to suit according to needs using a software called Photoshop, about which too you will read in a later chapter.

A perfect example of Multimedia is the creation of a motion picture called Toy, which was totally made in the studio using the various animations and live actors. It used live pictures and merged them with animations and fit in the sound to create an effect which had been highly appreciated by many. Some time back Japanese made a complete film on Ramayan, totally animated with Hindi sound.

4.2 Text

How do you read a book, for example, this one. Chapter by chapter, page by page. While you are on page 43, do you have any idea what is there on page 28. No. The solution to this lies in linkage which is provided by Hypertext. Thus, Hypertext is a process which puts links or anchors, as they are called, for easy accessing to another page while reading one page.

It may not be very clear here, since these things do not happen in the printed book like this one, which you are reading. But, it is very common in web pages. There while on a page, you can refer to any other page by just a click, using so called Anchors.

Let us see how it is done. While publishing material on the web site page, the information is divided into various small "chunks". These are called nodes. Then links are put into these nodes. These links in the language of the web are called Hyperlinks. The process of finding a node among other nodes is called Browsing, which is sometimes referred for searching on the net. What are you doing? Browsing the Internet. That is you are searching something on the Internet. The World Wide Web (WWW) is a hypertext system accepted throughout the World.

Hypertext applications are particularly useful while working with massive amounts of text such as encyclopaedias and multi volume case law reports .

4.3 Graphics

Image a teacher at his home and you as a student at your home. He has got his computer and you have got yours. He is sending out the lecture and you are receiving it. No more going to College and sitting in the class. He can send the lecture whenever he wants, may be in the night. You can catch (download) the lecture when you are free, may be after dinner. Does it sound impossible? No, it is true. It is quite common in USA. It is fast catching up here too. I know of some MBA courses being conducted like this.

This whole process is called e-schooling or Hypergraphics. So what we gather is that Hypergraphics is the process where the education is not done on one-to-one basis but teacher puts the lecture into the computer and students catch the same. This self-learning approach has been used for most of the practical research in, and applications of, computer-based training. This approach, which has been favoured even for interactive video, ensures a one-on-one interaction between student and computer. The only drawback of this is that the student must have the computer. Alternatively, he can go to the Cyber Cafe.

4.4 Animation

Animation literaly means moving objects. You can have more than one object moving. Like in a Cartoon film you can have one or more animals or characters moving. All cartoon films are examples of animation. Have you got any idea of what animation is all about. Take the following small experiment to learn more about animation.

Take 12 blank papers each of the size of a playing card. It would not be a bad idea if you have some waste playing cards lying around. Stick papers on them. Mark them 1 to 12 on the top right hand side with a pencil. Now you have cards 1 to 12. On card 1 draw a line of 2 inches. On card 12 draw a line of 4 inches. On card 2 draw the line of 2.2 inches, on card 3 draw the line of 2.4 inches and so on. Remember that the line should start at the same spot on each card increasing the width on outer side.

Now you have 12 cards each with line drawn in it but with a different dimension. Stack the cards from serial number 1 to 12 with 1 on top. Firmly hold the inside of the stack of the cards and run them as you would do in a fan. What do you see. You would see the line growing from 2 inches to 4 inches. Faster you run it, more effective it will be. This is the fundamental base of animation.

In computer animation, these cards are replaced by frames. Each frame has a text, picture, sound, etc., on it. The next frame has the same but with a slight change as was in card ranging from 2 inches to 2.2 inches. These frames are placed in an order and run one by one by computer at a speed to give the effect of animation. This is how most of the cartoon movies are made. Do you know something? India is now the leading country in creating these animations. Most of the Hollywood cartoon movies are made making use of the facilities available in South India.

4.5 Audio

When you create multimedia, it is likely that you will deal with file formats and translators for text, sounds, images, animations or digital video clips. A sound file's format is simply a recognized methodology for organizing the digitized sound's data bits and bytes into a data file. The structure of the file must be known, of course, before the data can be saved or later loaded into a computer to be edited and/or played as sound. The following table shows some of the common sound formats used for multimedia. In Windows, digitized sounds are most commonly stored as WAV files. For the Internet, new formats are emerging as companies develop solutions for streaming and playing sound on the Web. There are many ways to store the bits and bytes that describe a sampled waveform sound. The method used for Red Book Audio data files on consumer-grade music CDs is Linear Pulse Code Modulation.

The wave format (WAV) was introduced by Microsoft and IBM with the introduction of Windows. Windows make use of MIDI files. A MIDI interface is built into many sound boards on the PC.

4.5.1 Sound for the World Wide Web

In the early days of the Internet, when connected machines typically ran in a Unix environment, the common file format for sounds (.au) was the international telephone format of µLaws (also known as Mu-law or µ-law, nicknamed the "TalkRadio" or "Greek of the Week" format and pronounced "mew-law"). It provided meager 8kHz sampling rates at 8-kHz at 16 bits in 2:1 compression. aLaw is the European equivalent of µLaw. Many more sound file types are now commonly found on the Web as shown in the last table. There are two methods for playing either digital or MIDI sound on the Web.

- First, you can wait for the entire sound file to download to your computer, then play it back with a helper application.
- Second, you can begin to play a downloading sound file as soon as enough of the sound is cached in your computer's buffer and the downloading continues to fill the butter faster than you empty it by playing the sound file streams into your computer in the background, keeping ahead of what has already been played so the playback doesn't pause or break up.

Streaming files are dependent upon connection speed: you must wait longer (streaming latency) before the streamed sound begins to play when using a 28.8 kbps modem (low bandwidth) than using a high-speed T1 connection (high bandwidth). Macromedia's Flash allows you to integrate the sound tracks that you have made using a sound editor into a Web-based multimedia presentation, including both event sound like button clicks and streaming sound like background music. Able to read and save .mp3 files, Flash offers Web designer serious and powerful options for solving the quality conundrum of high-quality (big) files and slow downloads versus low-quality (small) files and speedy delivery – with nice results.

4.5.2 Adding Sound to Your Multimedia Project

Apple was the first company to have sound and video interleaved into the computer. It outpaced Microsoft's Audio/Video Interleaved technology, with the release of QuickTime. QuickTime has become a standard file format for displaying digitized motion video from hard disk or CD-ROM without special hardware.

Digital audio data is interleaved with video information in the file and when it is played back the audio stays synchronized to the motion picture. You can use QuickTime just to play stereo sounds and MIDI; the video part of QuickTime is not required. QuickTime will display many graphic image formats as well.

Whether you're working on a Macintosh or in Windows, you will need to follow certain steps to bring an audio recording into your multimedia project. Here is a brief overview of the process:

1. Decide what kind of sound is needed (such as background music, special sound effects and spoken dialog). Decide where these audio events will occur in the flow of your project. Fit the sound cues into your storyboard or make up a cue sheet.
2. Decide where and when you want to use either digital audio or MIDI data.
3. Acquire source material by creating it from scratch or purchasing it.
4. Edit the sounds to fit your project.
5. Test the sounds to be sure they are timed properly with the project's images. This may involve repeating steps 1 through 4 until everything is in sync.

When it's time to import your compiled and edited sounds into your project, you'll need to know how your particular multimedia software environment handles sound data. Each program handles it a bit differently, but the process is usually fairly straightforward: just tell your software which file you want to play and when to play it. This is usually handled by an importing or "linking" process during which you identify the files. Scripting languages such as OpenScript (ToolBook), Lingo (Director) and ActionScript (Flash) provide a greater level of control over audio playback, but you'll need to know about the programming language and environment. In authoring environments, it is usually a simple matter to play a sound when the user clicks a button, but this may not be enough.

If the user changes screens while a long file is playing, for example, you may be needed to program the sound to stop before leaving the current screen. If the file to be played cannot be found on the hard disk, you may need to code an entire section for error handling and file location. Sample code is generally provided in both printed and online documentation for software that includes sound playback.

4.6 Images

It is not that you would be typing the text in all the cases. You may enter the text in computer by scanning it from the matter already available. In fact, while using scanner you cannot only scan the text, but can scan the images too, which can be stored in the computer.

For all this you need to have what is called as OCR software, meaning Optical Character Reader software, which reads all the characters on the image character by character. OCR software turns bitmapped characters into electronically recognizable ASCII text.

Most OCR applications claim about 99% accuracy when reading 8- to 30- point characters at 300 dpi and can reach processing speeds of about 150 characters per second. These programs, however, have difficulty in reading poor copies of originals where the edges of characters have bled; these and poorly received faxes in small print may yield more recognition errors than it is worthwhile to correct after the attempted recognition.

4.6.1 Image Editing Tools

Image editing applications are specialized and powerful tools for enhancing and retouching existing bitmapped images. These applications also provide many of the features and tools of painting and drawing programs and can be used to create images from scratch as well as images digitized from scanners, video frame-grabbers, digital cameras, clip art files, or original artwork files created with painting or drawing package.

Here are some features typical of image-editing applications and of interest to multimedia developers:

- Multiple windows that provide views of more than one image at a time.
- Conversion of major image-data types and industry-standard file formats.
- Direct inputs of images from scanner and video sources.
- Employment of a virtual memory scheme that uses hard disk space as RAM for images that require large amounts of memory.
- Capable selection tools, such as rectangles, lassos, and magic wands, to select portions of a bitmap.
- Image and balance controls for brightness, contrast, and colour balance.
- Good masking features.
- Multiple undo and restore features.
- Anti-aliasing capability, and sharpening and smoothing controls.
- Colour mapping controls for precise adjustment of colour balance.
- Tools for retouching, blurring, sharpening, lightening, darkening, smudging, and tinting.
- Geometric transformations such as flip, skew, rotate, distort, and perspective changes.
- Ability to resample and resize an image.
- 24-bit colour, 8-or 4-bit indexed colour, 8-bit gray-scale, black-and-white, and customizable colour palettes.
- Ability to create images from scratch, using line, rectangle, square, circle, ellipse, polygon, airbrush, paintbrush, pencil, and eraser tools, with customizable brush shapes and user-definable bucket and gradient fills.

- Multiple typefaces, styles, and sizes, and type manipulation and masking routines.
- Filters for special effects, such as crystallize, dry brush, emboss, facet, fresco, graphic pen, mosaic, pixelize, poster, ripple, smooth, splatter, stucco, twirl, watercolour, wave, and wind.
- Support for third-party special effect plug-ins.
- Ability to design in layers that can be combined, hidden, and recorded.

4.7 Video

Various video formats are mentioned here.

4.7.1.1 S-VHS Video

In S-VHS video, colour and luminance information are kept on two separate tracks. The result is a definite improvement in picture quality. This standard is also used in Hi-8. Although basically consumer oriented, this format is gaining rapid acceptance among lower-end broadcasters. Still, if your ultimate goal is to have your project accepted by broadcast stations, this would not be the best choice.

4.7.1.2 Component (YUV)

In the early 1980s, Sony began to experiment with a new portable professional video format based on Betamax. Called Betacam, it required speeding the tape up considerably (a 2-hour tape was used up in 20 minutes) and laying the signal on the tape in three channels, one for red, one for blue and one for luminance information. The resulting format (called "component") produced images that had none of the problems of traditional composite video such as colour shift and bleed and crawling edges on graphics.

This has evolved into Betacam SP, which features four channels of audio and is superior to 1-inch and even the D-2 digital format in some cases. Though Panasonic has developed their own standard based on a similar technology, called "MII," Betacam SP has become the industry standard for professional video field recording. This format may soon be eclipsed by a new digital version called "Digital Betacam." Featuring four channels of CD-quality audio, its video quality is almost equal to D-1 digital.

Betacam SP is without doubt the choice for the broadcast industry. No format is so widely used and praised. When you should start thinking of full screen/full motion picture then this becomes a little small.

4.7.1.3 Component Digital

Around the same time when Sony was developing Betacam, they also began research into digital video, where the signal was converted to digital information before it was recorded, as bits and bytes. The advantages were many, including better colour and image resolution and an ability to make almost unlimited copies without loss of quality.

The result of this research was D-1 or "Component Digital." Using a 19 mm (3/4-inch) tape and recording the signal in a digital version of the component technology developed for Betacam, it quickly proved itself as the format of choice for graphics. Although it is the oldest of digital video formats, D-1 is the standard by which all others are compared. It has most recently spawned DCT (from Ampex), D-5 (from Panasonic) and Digital Betacam (from Sony).

4.7.1.4 Composite Digital

Although D-1 was a vastly superior recording format, its steep price scared away broadcasters: recording decks, for example, cost $110,000 or more. To reduce hardware costs, other less expensive formats were developed to record an NTSC composite signal in digital form: D-2 and D-3 (from Panasonic). Though surpassed in quality by D-1, composite digital may be the most common digital standard for broadcast and editing facilities. Again, this format is more expensive to work with than is justified for multimedia.

4.7.1 Microsoft Video for Windows

Audio video Interleaved (AVI) is a Microsoft-developed format for playing full-motion interleaved video and audio sequence in Windows, without specialized hardware. Video data is interleaved with audio data within the file that contains the motion sequence, so the audio portion of the movie remains synchronized to the video portion. The AVI file format is not an extensible, "open" environment and lacks features needed for serious video editing environments. To improve this situation, a group of interested companies recently created the OpenDML file format to make AVI more useful for the professional market. But because QuickTime works with OpenDML files and delivers on Windows platform and across the Web, look for a growing number of neat multimedia projects housed in a QuickTime container. AVI provides the following features:

- Playback from hard disk or CD-ROM.
- Playback on computers with limited memory; data is streamed from the hard disk of CD-ROM player without using great amounts of memory.
- Quick loading and playing, because only a few frames of video and a portion of audio are accessed at a time.
- Video compression to boost the quality of your video sequences and reduce their size.

4.7.2 Movie Editors

With the invention of QuickTime and Video for Windows, desktop video publishing (DVP) on PCs had become a digital process. Improved compression and decompression techniques allow quarter – half and full-screen/ full-motion movies instead of the small, 160x120-pixelized movies characteristic of earlier digital video experiments. With desktop editing software and an appropriate video digitizing board, you can digitize video clips, edit the clip offline, add special effects and titles, mix sound tracks and save the finished products as a digital file on magnetic or optical media. The Targa board from TrueVision, VideoBlaster from Create Labs, Super VideoWindows SL from New Media Graphics and other boards are available for making AVI movies for Windows. Specialized video editors have been designed around this technology for PC environments – for example, AVID's VideoShop, Media100, Fast's VideoMachine, Adobe's Premiere and Ulead's Media-Studio Pro.

These applications let you mix video clips, audio recordings, animation, still images and graphics to create QuickTime or AVI movies. You arrange your clips linearly, cutting and pasting and layering them into transitions with special effects such as dissolves, page turns, spins, tinting, distorting and replicating. A familiar push-button control panel is used for stop, rewind, play, fast-forward, record and single-stop and these applications display time references, frame counts and audio and transparency levels.

4.8 Multimedia Application in Education

It is another form of training. Though the concept is quite new in India, but, is catching up fast in other countries. The teaching method is more and more interactive using the multimedia concepts and instead of teacher asking the questions the questions are asked by the computer and students have to reply on the computer itself by pressing various keys. Thus, the result is compiled on the spot.

From homework helpers to literature guides to school registries at home pages and information servers, education is finding a place on the World Wide Web

Lots of Indian companies, I know, are planning to introduce interactive CDs in the market to make students learn on their own. The CDs for primary classes are already available in the market. Very soon we will see students working on the computers for their homework.

4.9 Entertainment

With built-in filters in Movie Player, you can adjust colours, contrast and brightness and you can apply special effects to your composition, such as film noise and edge detection. The Picture Viewer application is used for viewing and converting still images among many standard image-file formats, including Photoshop's native format. QuickTime includes built-in support for ten different media types (video, audio, text, timecode, music/MIDI, sprite/animation, tween, MPEG, VR, 3-D) and offers a comprehensive set of "services" such as:

- Timing and synchronization
- Audio and image data compression and decompression
- Image blitting, format conversion, scaling, composition and transcoding.
- Audio mixing, sample rate conversion and format conversion
- Audio and video effects and transitions
- Synchronized storage and read and write
- Media import and export
- Standard user interface elements, such as movie controller, media previewers and media capture dialogs.

4.10 Marketing

I am quite sure that you must have seen a sales conference of a company. If not atleast must have heard about it. There the speaker while talking about the sales has the various charts and graphs displayed on the board using the overhead projector. This becomes the part of the sales display and supports the figures given by the speaker. The same can now be done using the various facilities of the multimedia with graphs and sounds. The most common software used here is the presentation software from Microsoft named as Microsoft PowerPoint.

Multimedia is enjoying widespread use in training programs. The teacher replaces speaker in the above example. Flight attendants learn to manage international terrorism and security through simulation. Mechanics learn to repair engines. Salespeople learn about product lines and leave behind software to train their customers. Fighter pilots practice full-terrain sorties before spooling up for the real thing.

4.11 Names of Commom Multimedia File Formats

Different types of movie file formats which contain all the sound and videos are:

DAT Digital Audio Tape System

They provide a tape based 44.1 Khz, 16 bit record and playback capacity. DAT is high fidelity file which can give 2 accurate recordings, background noises, microphone pops and coughs from the next room.

AVI Audio Video Interleaved

This system depends upon special algorithms that control the amount of information per video frame that is sent to the screen, as well as the rate at which new frames are displayed. It also provides a methodology for interleaving audio data with video data so that they remain synchronized. It allows data to stream from disk into memory in a buffered and organized manner.

MPEG Moving Picture Experts Group

It is a standard used to encode motion images. It allows compression of audio, its compression speeds are fast, and decompression occurs in real time. It shows observable degradation of the image.

MOV This is the Apple Quick Time format for digital media/video files. This file format can be imported into Flash only if Quick Time is installed.

SWF This file extension is used for a Flash document that can be played with a Flash player. Before it is published, a Flash document, while it is being developed, has the extension .fla.

4.12 Computer Software

So far we have talked about one side of the computer system, i.e., the hardware, the machine itself. Now, we will talk about its usage. How this machine can be used with the help of various programs. This is called Software. There are various types of software. Some are needed for some particular type of operations and others for running the computer. The basic difference between Hardware and Software can be explained by simple term that Hardware is something which can be seen and touched whereas Software cannot be seen or touched. Software is essential for running the computer.

As mentioned it is needed to run the computer, but, what is it? It is nothing but a set of instructions that directs the computer to process information. These instructions are called programs. A set of programs is called Software. There are mainly two types of software—System software and Application software.

4.13 Relationship between Hardware and Software

There are two ways of looking at it. First is this that Hardware is something which we can see with our eyes and touch whereas Software is something which we don't see and works in the background and definitely we can't touch it. A very practical example of this can be given in the form of a VCR. In this case the VCR where the video cassette is put is the hardware whereas the video cassette which has the film in it can be called as Software. Without each other they have no value. You cannot run video cassette without a VCR and VCR is nothing but a machine in itself has no movie to run.

Similarly in computers Hardware and Software go neck-in-neck. They are totally dependent upon each other. This is why when you buy a software, it has the hardware requirements mentioned on it since without that much of hardware, it will not work. But, software is a very vast field. Lots and lots of software are available, which one would suit your requirements, you have to use according to your needs.

4.14 System Software

As the name implies it is needed to run the system. It also coordinates the operations of the various hardware components of the computer. It is needed to run the computer system. It also acts as an coordinator between the computer and its user.

Most of the system software are machine based so usually the manufacturer of the machine provides the software. There are two types of system software and they are:

(a) The Operating System; and

(b) The Language Translators

4.14.1 Operating System (OS)

It is a collection of programs that controls the overall operations of a computer. It helps the computer to supervise and manage its resources. Operating system calls the application program whenever needed, translates the programs and manages data needed to produce the output.

4.14.2 Language Translators

There are different type of translators available.

Assembler It is used to convert the program written in assembly language into machine language.

Compiler It translates a source program that is usually written in a high level language by a programmer into machine language, which the computer understands. It is capable of replacing source program with a series of machine-language instructions or with a subroutine. It is different for different languages. A compiler creates a unique object program, i.e., if a source program is compiled there is no need of that source program because output can be obtained by executing that object program.

Interpreter It translates each source program statement into a sequence of machine instructions and than executes these machine instructions before translating the next source language statement. Interpreters are also unique for each high level language. Basically, the function of the compiler and interpreter are the same; the only difference is that compiler provides a separate object program but the interpreter does not. At the time of using interpreter each and every time the source program is needed. Another difference is that interpreter translates the source program line wise, i.e., it would not execute the next line unless the first one has not error.

4.15 Application Software

It is a set of programs designed for specific uses or applications such as word processing, graphics or spreadsheet analysis. In fact, most of the commercial software fall under this category. Application software can be custom-made but is usually purchased off the shelf.

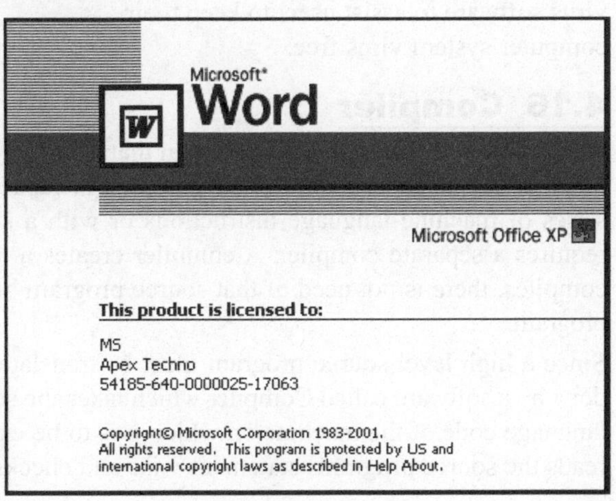

4.15.1 Popular Software Packages

4.15.1.1 Word Processors

This is the software where you play with the text. You enter the text by typing and manipulate it to create a good looking letter, brochure, thesis, etc., and print them according to your needs.

4.15.1.2 Spreadsheets

A spreadsheet is a matrix of rows and columns. These columns and rows are used for entering text and numbers, which can then be used for calculations. An ideal software for accounting purposes and is very widely used for creating balance sheet, etc.

4.15.1.3 Database System

These software are used to create and extract data from a database in the form needed by you. Most of the information needed by you can be totalled too. It also helps you in arranging the data in a particular format too.

4.15.1.4 Accounting Packages

Various accounting packages are available in the market which would take care of all your accounting needs from ledgers to reports. There are provisions for creating exclusive reports too.

4.15.1.5 DTP Packages

Without these packages, this book would not have been possible. It sort of acts as via media between computer and printing press. All the pre-press work can be done using these software. From designing a page with text and graphics to creating complicated art works, everything can be done using them.

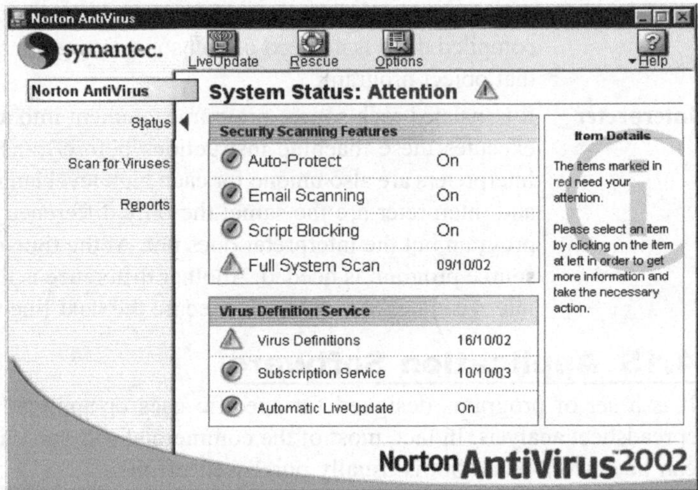

4.15.1.6 Graphic Packages

These are used for working with pictures and graphics instead of numbers and text. Computer-accessible data can readily be converted to graphic form on the screen as well as on paper using dot-matrix printers, ink-jet printers or plotters.

4.15.1.7 Anti Virus Software

Though viruses are mushrooming at a faster rate than virus vaccines, still there are few very good and reasonable anti-virus software to assist users to keep their computer system virus free.

4.16 Compiler

A compiler translates a source program that is usually written in a high level language by a programmer into machine language as a whole. The compiler is capable of replacing single source program statement with a series of machine-language instructions or with a subroutine. For each high level language, the machine requires a separate compiler. A compiler creates a unique object program, i.e., when a source program is compiles, there is not need of that source program because output can be obtained by executing that object program.

Since a high level source program must be translate first into the form of machine can understand, this is done by a software called Compiler which takes the source code as input and produces as output that machine language code of the machine on which it is to be executed. During the process of translation, the compiler reads the source programs statement-wise and checks the syntax (grammatical) errors. Of there is any error, the computer generates a printout of the errors it has detected. This action is known as Diagnostics. The compiler and interpreter have different approaches to translation.

4.17 Names of Some High Level Languages

A language is a system of communication. In order to communicate with each other, humans need languages like English, Hindi, etc. In the same manner, for communicating with the computer, we use computer language called programming language. A programming language consists of all the symbols, characters and usage rules that permit people to communicate with computers. Learning to program requires learning all these symbols and rules.

There are many programming languages available and each one has its symbols, character set and syntax but each language has an instruction set that permits those familiar operations to be performed. We know that the computer can neither think nor can make any decision on its own. It needs instructions to understand what to do. A program is a set of logically related instructions that are arranged in a sequence that guides the computer to solve a problem. The process of writing a program is called programming. If a system is not correctly programmed; it delivers incorrect information.

4.17.1 Machine Language

This is a sequence of instructions written in the form of binary numbers consisting of 1s and 0s to which the computer responds directly. A machine language would have two parts. The first part is the command or an operation that tells the computer what functions are to be performed. The second part of the instruction is the operand that tells the computer where to find or store the data on which the desired operation is to be performed.

The machine language is the only one that computer can understand directly. In the earlier computers programmers had to translate instructions directly into machine language from the computers understood. This task was very difficult and very few programmers could do this job. So, this language was very difficult to understand. But the main advantage of this language is that it is faster in execution as the computer directly starts executing it.

4.17.2 Assembly Language

To ease the burden of the programmer, mnemonic operation codes and symbolic addresses were developed during the early 1950s. The mnemonic refers to a memory aid. One of the first steps for improving the program preparation process was to substitute letter, symbols and mnemonics for the mnemonic machine-language operation codes. Today every computer has a mnemonic code, though the actual symbols vary among makes and models. Machine language is still used by the computer as it process data but assembly language software first translates the specified operation code symbol into its machine language equivalent.

A program written by a programmer in an assembly language is called a Source Program. After this source program has been converted into machine code by an assembler, it is referred to as an Object Program. The main advantage of assembly language is that the programs written in it are easy to understand as compared to the programs of machine language. And a big drawback is that they are machine-oriented, depending upon the model of processor being used.

Also, the programs written assembly language are slower to execute as compared to those in the machine language.

4.17.3 High Level Language

The development of mnemonic technique and macro-instruction led, to the development of high level languages that are often oriented towards a particular class of problem. Unlike assembly programs, high-level language programs may be used with different makes of computes with the little modifications.

Thus re-programming expense may be greatly reduced when new equipment is acquired. The time and cost of creating machine and assembly languages was quite high. And this was the prime motivation for the development of high level languages.

Some of the programming languages with their main characteristics have been described as follows:

LOGO It allows you to draw pictures on the computer screen using a friendly little cursor called TURTLE. Most of the school going children are taught computers using this software.

FORTRAN In early 90s, it was the most popular software used for carrying out scientific and mathematical computations. Since it is suitable for large amount of data, it is not used for business programming applications.

COBOL If FORTRAN was for scientific purposes then this was for business purposes. It was capable of handling any type of data. COBOL programs are characterised by their easy readability due to their verbose syntax and good data organization and file handling.

BASIC Probably the first computer language you would learn while learning programming. Its ease of use made it more popular with the users. But the main problem in BASIC is that most versions of this language do not support indexed files.

PROLOG It lays stress on the usage of logic to solve problems. PROLOG is basically known as a theorem-providing system, using a formal logic technique known as predicate calculus to prove the truth of propositions from a set of axioms.

PASCAL It is a general-purpose language that can be used for a wide range of numeric and non numeric applications. It is a well-structured and well organized programming language.

C It is a general-purpose structured programming language characterised by the ability to write very concise source programs. The compiler of C is commonly available for the computers of all sizes. The compilers are usually compact and they generate object programs that are small and highly efficient as compared to the programs written in any other language.

C++ It is an object-oriented programming language. It is based on the concept of Object-oriented programming. Most of the new software are developed using this language.

JAVA The language for the Internet. JAVA is an object-oriented programming language that was developed after C++. Java was designed to be small, simple and portable across platforms.

4GL Language The fourth generation of language has not been defined as that of the other generations. Fourth generations of languages are commonly referred to as 4GL. These are high level languages that requires significantly fewer instructions to accomplish a particular task than a third generation language does. Thus a programmer should be able to write a program faster in a 4GL than in a third generation language.

4.18 Free Domain Software

As the name suggests, it is available free. Whatever maybe the reason behind it, the fact of the matter remains that it is free. Sometimes a researcher who has developed a new software, would like it to be distributed just for the heck of it. So there are agencies who would do it for you and would charge the minimum fee for handling and media. Now-a-days with the advent of Internet, the things have become more easier. You just download from the sites and start using the software without bothering about the copyright and even paying for it. Usually what happens is that when you have got used to using the software and want to know more about it, then they would charge for updation. So if are of the type who does not want to grow, then it is ok to use free software else be prepared to pay more.

Let us Revise

1. Multimedia means working with more than one media.
2. You can combine text, graphics, sound, animation and video to form a multimedia project.
3. A multimedia project can be both interactive and non-interactive.
4. CD-ROMs are the most popular media of packaging multimedia.
5. Multimedia is widely used in Business specially when you have to make a audio-visual presentations.
6. Lots of interactive school CDs are available to help students in their studies.
7. Multimdia kiosks are also available at various public places.
8. Most popular hardware for multimedia is PC.
9. Operating system in most of the PCs is Windows.
10. There are various software available for creating multimedia.
11. Hardware is something which can be seen and touched whereas Software cannot be seen or touched.
12. A set of programs is called Software.
13. There are two types of system software and they are: Operating System; and Language Translators.
14. There are 3 types of translators: Assembler, Interpreter and Compiler.
15. Word processors are used for manipulating text.
16. Spreadsheets are used for calculations.
17. DTP packages are used for text and graphics.
18. Anti virus software are used for virus detection and removal.
19. For communicating with the computer, we use computer language called programming language.
20. The machine language is the only one that computer can understand directly.
21. A program written by a programmer in an assembly language is called a Source Program.
22. LOGO programming allows you to draw pictures on the screen.
23. COBOL is basically used for business applications.
24. PASCAL is a general purpose language.
25. JAVA programming is used on Internet.

Multiple Choice Questions

1. You can work with how many media in multimedia?
   (a) 1 (b) 2 (c) Many
2. A multimedia project can be active?
   (a) Yes (b) No
3. Which software is usually used for making overhead presentations?
   (a) Microsoft Frontpage (b) Microsoft Powerpoint (c) Microsoft Word
4. What is usually used for displaying information at public places?
   (a) Monitors (b) Overhead projections (c) Touch screen kiosks
5. Which is the most popular media for multimedia packaging?
   (a) Floppy disk (b) CD-ROM (c) Hard disk
6. Which is the most popular hardware for the multimedia creations?
   (a) PCs (b) Mini Computers (c) Mainframe Computers
7. What is MP3?
   (a) A mouse (b) A printer (c) A sound format
8. Can you create a multimedia project alone?
   (a) Yes (b) No

9. A computer language which is used for drawing pictures on the screen is:
   (a) LOGO (b) COBOL (c) BASIC
10. Computer program which controls the operations of computer is called:
   (a) Assembler (b) Operating System (c) Interpreter
11. A computer program used for Business applications is:
   (a) LOGO (b) COBOL (c) BASIC
12. A software package for creating printing artworks is called:
   (a) Word Processing (b) DTP (b) Spreadsheet
13. Computer understands the ________ language.
   (a) Machine (b) Assembly (c) High level language
14. Computer language used on Internet is
   (a) PASCAL (b) JAVA (c) BASIC

True/False Questions

1. Multimedia means working with more than one media.
2. You can combine text, graphics, sound, animation and video in a multimedia project.
3. CD-ROMs are the most popular media of packaging multimedia.
4. Multimedia is not used in Business by making presentations.
5. Lots of interactive school CDs are available to help students in their studies.
6. PC cannot be used for multimedia.
7. There are various software available for creating multimedia.
8. Software is something which can be seen and touched whereas Hardware cannot be seen or touched.
9. A set of programs is called Software.
10. Assembler is a type of translator.
11. Word processors are used for manipulating text.
12. DTP packages cannot work with graphics.
13. Anti virus software are used for virus detection and removal.
14. The machine language is the only one that computer can understand directly.
15. LOGO programming allows you to draw pictures on the screen.
16. COBOL cannot be used for business.
17. JAVA programming cannot be used on Internet.

Matching Columns

Match the text of the column A with the action of Column B.

Column A	Column B
A. Hardware	1. A program to draw on screen
B. Software	2. An internet language
C. COBOL	3. Mainly used for accounts
D. LOGO	4. Software to work with text
E. BASIC	5. A transaltor of computer language
F. JAVA	6. Something which can be seen
G Word Processing	7. Working with more than one media
H. Spreadsheet program	8. Something which works in the background
I. Assember	9. First commercial computer language

J. Multimedia	10. A computer language for business

Fill in the Blanks with appropriate words

a. JAVA	b. Compiler	c. DTP	d. Word Processing
e. COBOL	f. Multimedia	g. BASIC	h. Spreadsheet
i. CDs	j. LOGO		

1. _______ allows you to work on two media.
2. The first computer language was _________.
3. The language used for drawing by children is called ____________.
4. The language used for Internet is called _____.
5. The software used for mixing graphics with text is called ________.
6. _________ is used for converting source program to machine language program.
7. A programming language for business _____.
8. A process for working with words _______.
9. Accountant's favourite program ________.
10. Multimedia is usually packed in ______.

Descriptive Type Questions

1. What is multimedia?
2. How would you assemble a multimedia project?
3. Write short notes on use of:
   Multimedia in Schools
   Multimedia in Business
   Multimedia in Public Places
   Multimedia at Home
4. Describe the process of planning a multimedia project.
5. Describe what all you need for a multimedia project in terms of Hardware, Software?
6. How is a CD-ROM used in multimedia?
7. What is the difference between Hardware and Software?
8. What are the different type of system software?
9. Describe the various language translators.
10. Which are the various popular software packages?
11. What are assembly and machine languages?
12. Describe briefly the following languages:
    LOGO
    FORTRAN
    COBOL
    BASIC
    PROLOG
    PASCAL
    C
    C++
    JAVA
13. What is Internet?
14. Describe the process of connecting to Internet.

Answers to Objective Type Questions

Multiple Choice Questions

1. c	2. a	3. b	4. c
5. b	6. a	7. c	8. b
9. a	10 b	11. b	12. b
13. a	14. b		

True False Questions

1. T	2. T	3. T	4. C
5. T	6. F	7. T	8. F
9. T	10. T	11. T	12. F
13. T	14. T	15. T	16. F
17. F			

Matching Columns

A. 6	B. 8	C. 10	D. 1
E. 9	F. 2	G. 4	H. 3
I. 5	J. 7		

Fill in the Blanks

1. f	2. g	3. j	4. a
5. c	6. b	7. e	8. d
9. h	10. i		

Operating System Microsoft Windows

5

5.1 An overview of different version of Windows

Windows is nothing but graphics-based operating environment from Microsoft. It provides a desktop environment similar to the Macintosh, in which each active application is displayed in a resizable, moveable window on the screen. Initially Windows ran on DOS platform, but now-a-days it runs on its own platform.

Windows 1.x, Windows 286 (2.x) and Windows 386 were first attempts. Windows 3.0 had its own enhanced user interface and ability to manage extended memory, upto 16MB with built-in DOS extender.

Windows 3.1 (1992) was faster and supported multimedia, true type fonts, drag and drop, among other features. It was the last of the Windows versions based to work on DOS platform. From this point onward Microsoft introduced Windows 95 which was independent of DOS and had its booting capabilities.

Windows for Workgroups for introduced in 1993. It was the first version of Windows which truly supported networking. This was later enhanced to Windows NT, which was introduced in 1993. Next came Windows 95, Windows 98, Windows 2000 and then Windows XP. Recently we had Windows Vista and Window 7 too. But, still Windows XP remais the favourite and we would stick to this version in this chapter.

5.2 Basic Windows elements

Windows XP is a new Windows that represents a major shift in personal computing. Windows XP gives users the freedom to experience the digital world by building on the momentum of the internet and digital media with improvements that increase dependability and productivity for home users (Windows XP Home Edition) and businesses of all sizes (Windows XP Professional). Windows XP puts the exciting experiences of the digital age at user's fingertips by uniting PCs, devices and services with enhanced reliability, security and performance.

5.2.1 What does Windows XP stand for?

The XP stands for experience. The name Windows XP represents Microsoft's focus on enabling end-to-end experience, unlocking the power of the PC and empowering users to make the most of their computer experience in the simplest way possible. With Windows XP Microsoft is extending the power of the PC to devices, web services and applications that enable the broadest set of experiences.

5.2.2 Difference between Home Edition & Professional Edition

Windows XP Home Edition is designed to deliver the power and reliability of Windows 2000 to the home user, while improving on the best of Windows Me and providing application compatibility for users moving from either Windows 2000 or Windows Me/98/98 SE. Windows XP Professional is a superset of Windows XP Home Edition and offers numerous additional technologies and features including roaming profiles, remote desktop, domain account support and dual processor support. Windows XP Professional meets the requirements for C2 security certification and includes Encrypting File Systems (EFS).

5.2.3 System Requirements for Windows XP

Following is the recommended configuration for loading Windows XP in your computer.

Hardware: PC with 300 MHz or higher processor clock speed recommended; 233 MHz is minimum required.

Memory: 128 MB of RAM or higher recommended (64 MB minimum supported; may limit performance and some features).

Hard Disk: 1.5 GB of available hard disk space.

CD-ROM: CD-ROM drive.

Input Device: Keyboard and Mouse or compatible pointing device

Multimedia: **For sound**: Sound card and speakers or headphones. **For DVD video playback**: DVD drive and DVD decoder card or DVD decoder software & 8 MB of video RAM. For Windows Movie Maker: Video capture feature requires appropriate digital or analog video capture device & 400 MHz or higher processor for digital video camera capture.

5.2.4 Exploring Windows XP Desktop

On the desktop, there are few icons which are a must for all the desktops being used by Windows XP and there are few which are optional and are created by the users according to their likings.

Among the permanent ones are: **My Computer**, **Recycle Bin**, **My Documents**, etc.

Before we go into details of all these and see how they help us in working, we explore the other parts of the desktop. At the bottom most left corner of the desktop is the **Start** button. By pressing it you can launch the following options: (A typical set of options as available on pressing Start button are shown next). For those of you who have used earlier versions of Windows, this would look very different from the earlier ones. The main difference being that it is in 2 cols.

Various options on the Start button, as shown on the next page, are:

Internet: It opens up Internet Explorer version 6.0 for you to access Internet.

e-mail: If opens up Outlook Express for you to send and receive e-mail.

Shortcut to Cricket: A program loaded by me.

Recently used programs: Windows XP shows here the recently used programs so that you can access them easily. The ones shown here are: Windows Media Player, Winamp, WinZip 8.0, Microsoft Office Word 2003, Microsoft Office Excel 2003 and Adobe PageMaker 7.0.

All Programs: It gives you access to all programs loaded in your computer. You *can start these programs* by *just* clicking at them.

My Recent Documents: It gives you access to the last 15 documents opened.

My Pictures: It gives you the list of pictures stored by you in your computer.

My Music: It gives you the list of music files stored in the computer.

Control Panel: You can access to Control Panel from here.

Connect To: It provides access to connecting you to your own connection or show all the connections available in the computer.

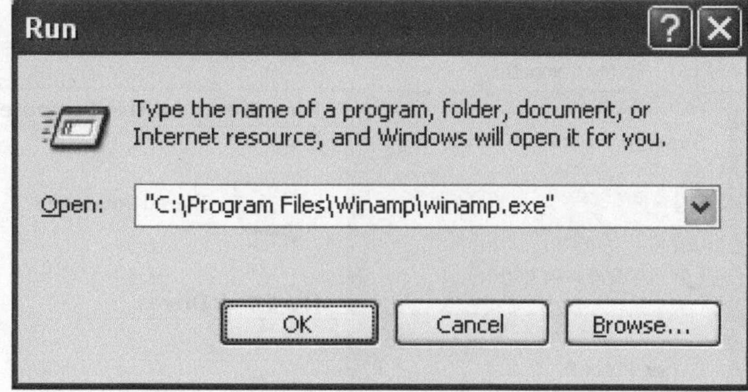

Printers and Faxes: It shows you the various printers and faxes connected to your computer.

Help & Support: It opens the extensive Windows XP Help system and gives you access to the Troubleshooting.

Search: This allows you to search for a file or folder.

Run: Allows you to run a particular program using a dialog box.

Log Off..: It logs off the system quickly so that you can log back with a different user profile or so that another user can log on.

Turn Off Computer: This gives rise to a dialog box, which asks you what you want to do. The options are: **Hibernate**: Alternate to Standby. **Turn off**: To turn off the computer. **Restart**: To restart the computer

5.2.5 Exploring the Taskbar

It the bottom key line on the desktop. Please refer to the earlier figure of desktop for the details. Starting with the right most corner, we see the following:

Date and Time : It shows you the date and time of the system.

Quick Launch Toolbar: Various icons here are the ones used for launching different programs. You have an option to put these icons here for the programs which you often use.

Running Tasks: When you have a program running in your system, its name will be reflected here on this taskbar to show that this program is open.

Now we come to the various options of the desktop.

5.2.6 My Computer

It helps you browse the contents of your computer, open folders, open documents and run your favourite applications. As shown here, it is divided into 3 sections, System Tasks, Other Places, Details. You click at any icon on the right hand side of the dialog box and then choose the option on the left hand side. Details will give you the detail of the item selected. System tasks will allow you to perform a task. You can access other places by clicking at any one of them. On the right hand side, you have the users first. Then the hard drives and then removable ones like Floppy and CD drive. By clicking at any one of them, you can see the details of the files in it.

The buttons on the top are useful for going and coming back to the various folders. Seeing the various views of the files, etc.

5.3 File Management through Windows

When you open Windows Explorer, it shows the hierarchy of folders in the All Folders pane (left pane) and the contents of the selected folder in the Contents pane (right pane).

You can run Explorer multiple times and drag items between each Explorer window.

5.3.1 From Desktop

Using Start Button

1. Click **Start Button**.
2. Point to **Programs ➢ Accessories**.
3. Click **Windows Explorer**.

By Right Clicking

1. Right click the desired **drive or folder icon**.
2. Click **Explore**.

By Shift, Double-Clicking

1. Click the desired **drive or folder icon**.
2. Press shift and double click the **drive or folder icon**.

Size Explorer All Folders and Contents Panes

1. Point to Pointer till it becomes a **split bar**.
2. Drag **split bar outline** to left or right.

5.3.2 Use Explorer to Browse Folders and Open Files

Explorer shows the hierarchy of folders in the All Folders pane (left pane) and the contents of the selected folder in the contents pane (right pane). The current folder name appears in the **Go to a different folder** list box on the toolbar.

Open Any Folder

1. Click **Folder icon** in All Folders pane.

   Or

2. Click **Folder icon** in contents pane.

Go to a Different Folder

1. Show toolbar.
2. Select desired folder in the list.

Open Parent Folder

1. Show Toolbar.
2. Click Up One Level button.

Expand Folder Levels

From All Folders Pane

1. Click **[+]** to the left of folder to show folder it contains.

Collapse Folder Levels

1. Click **[–]** to the left of folder to hide folders it contains.

Open a File

1. Click **File icon** in the Contents pane.

5.3.3 Arrange Files and Folders in Sort Order

Arrange files on the desktop, in a folder window, the Explorer Contents pane, the Find result list, and a common dialog box. Sort options will depend on the type of folder or workspace.

By Right Clicking

1. Right click empty area on **desktop**.

   Or on **Folder workspace**

   Or on **Explorer contents pane**

   Or on **Find result list**

2. Point to **Arrange Icons**.
3. Select desired options:

   Folder or desktop: by *Name*, by *Type*, by *Size*, by *Date*.

   My Computer folder: by *Drive Letter*, by *Type*, by *Size*, by *Free Space*

   Network Neighborhood folder: by *Name*, by *Size*, by *Date*

   Common dialog box: by *Name*, by *Type*, by *Size*, by *Date*

Using Menu

Not available from the desktop or a common dialog box.

1. Click **View**.
2. Point to **Arrange icons**.
3. Select desired options:

   Folder: by Name, by *Type*, by *Size*, by *Date*.

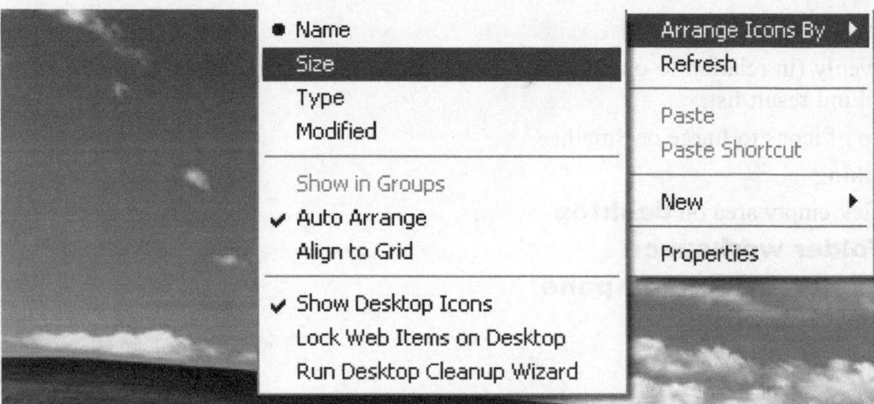

My Computer folder: by *Drive Letter*, by *Type*, by *Size*, by *Free Space*

Network Neighborhood folder: by *Name*, by *Size*, by *Date*

Find result list: by *Name,* by *Folder*, by *Type*, by *Size*, by *Date*

Using Column Headings

1. Set appearance of files and folders to Details.
2. Click to sort by **column heading**.

5.3.4 Set Appearance of Files and Folders

Set appearance of files or folders in a folder window, the Explorer contents pane, a common browse dialog box.

Using Menu

Not available from a common browse dialog box.

1. Click **View**.

Select one the following :

Large Icons;

Small Icons;

List;

Details

Using Toolbar

Not available from Find window

1. Show toolbar.
2. Click desired button on the toolbar.

5.3.5 Arrange Icons

Position icons on the desktop, in a folder window, and the Explorer Contents pane.

From Desktop, Folder or Explorer Window

1. If necessary, set appearance of files and folders to Large or Small Icons.
2. Select items to arrange.
3. Drag **selected outline** to the desired position.
4. Deselect the Auto Arrange option if icons do not remain where placed.

5.3.6 Line Up Icons

Align icons evenly (in relation to one another) on the desktop, in a folder window, the Explorer Contents pane, and the Find result list.

Set appearance of icons to Large or Small.

By Right Clicking

1. Right click empty area on **desktop**.
   Or on **Folder workspace**
   Or on **Explorer contents pane**
   Or on **Find result list**
2. Click **Line Up icons**.

Using Menu

1. Set appearance of files and folders to Large or Small icons.
2. Click **View, Line up icons**.

5.3.7 Set Auto Arrangement of Icons

Select to arrange icons automatically when appearance of icons is set to Large or Small.

By Right Clicking

1. Right click empty area on **desktop**.
   Or on **Folder workspace**
   Or on **Explorer contents pane**
   Or on **Find result list**
2. Point to **Arrange icons**.
3. Click **Auto Arrange**.

Using Menu

No available from the desktop or a common dialog box.

1. Click **View**
2. Point to **Arrange icons**.
3. Click **Auto Arrange** to select or deselect.

5.3.8 Use Common Dialog Boxes

Common dialog boxes help locate, select, save and open files. In a common dialog box, the list of items shows the contents of the current folder—the folder name in the Look in list box.

From any Common Dialog Box

The common dialog box is used to browse while creating a shortcut or when selecting browse from the run dialog box.

Open Any Folder

1. Select desired folder in the **Look in...**

Open a Folder Appearing in List of Items

1. Click the desired **folder icon** in list of items.

Open Parent Folder

1. Click **Up One Level** button.

Limit File Names Displayed in the List of Items

1. Type filespec in **File name**.

2. Press **Enter**.

View Specific File types in List of Items

1. Click **file icon**.

   Or

2. Click **file icon** in the list of files.
3. Click **open**.

Create New Folder in Current Folder

1. Click **Create New Folder** button.

Set Appearance of Icons

1. Click **List button**

   Or

2. Click **Details button**.

Common Dialog Box—Right Click Options

1. Right click **File or Folder icon**. A shortcut menu appears.
2. Click appropriate shortcut menu item.

Common Dialog Box—Right Drag Options

1. Right drag **File or Folder icon** on destination item.
2. Click appropriate **menu item**.

5.3.9 Set File and Folder Attributes

From the desktop, a folder window, the Explorer Contents pane, a common browse dialog box, and the Find result list.

Change the attributes of a file or folder only if you understand the effect of the change.

1. Right click desired **File or Folder icon**.
2. Click **Properties**.
3. Select or deselect attribute options:
4. Click

   Read Only

   Archive

   Hidden

5. Click **Ok**.

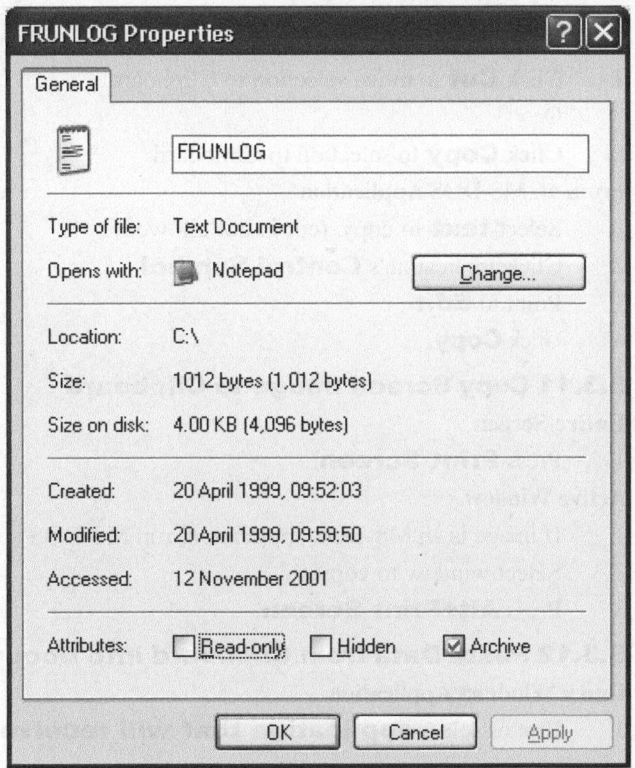

5.3.10 Cut or Copy Data in Document to Clipboard

Existing Clipboard data is replaced.

From a Windows Application

1. Select data to cut or copy.
2. Click **Edit**

   Or

3. Right click **Selection**.

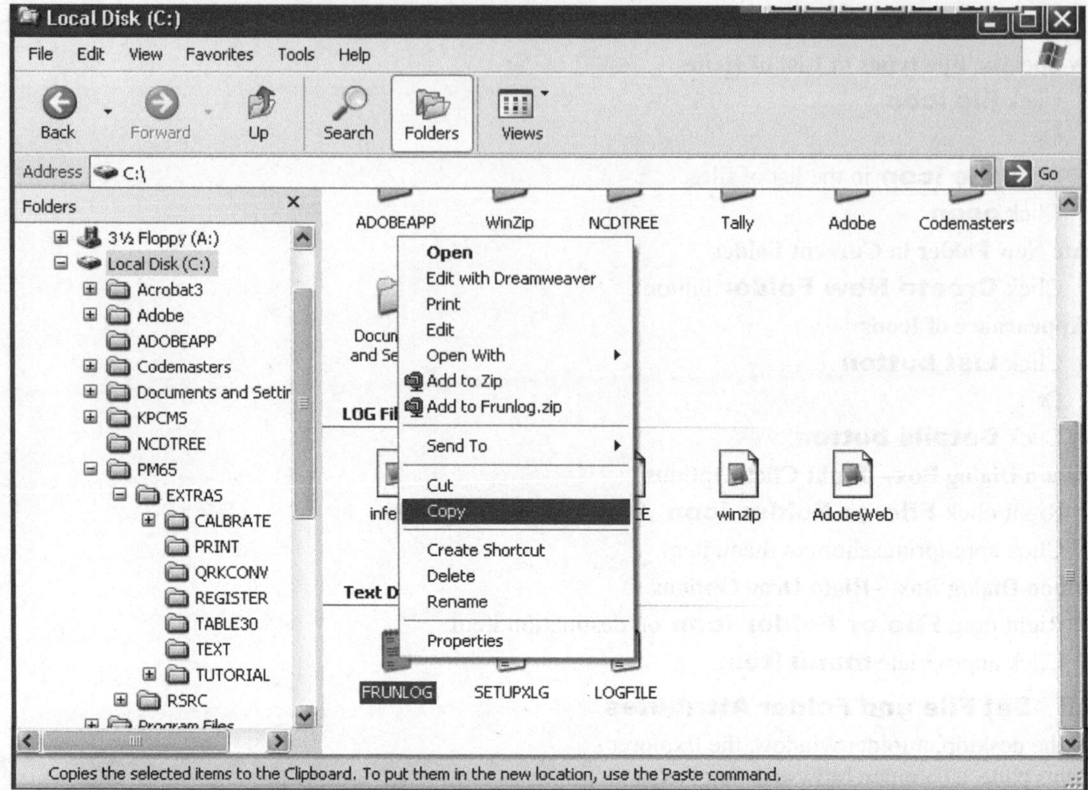

4. Click **Cut** to move selection to Clipboard.

   Or

5. Click **Copy** to selection to Clipboard.

From an MS-DOS Application

1. Select **text** to copy. (cut is not allowed)
2. Click application's **Control Symbol**.
3. Point to **Edit**.
4. Click **Copy**.

5.3.11 Copy Screen Image to Clipboard

Entire Screen

1. Press **Print Screen**.

Active Window

1. If image is an MS-DOS application, run MS-DOS application in a window.
2. Select window to copy.
3. Press **Alt+Print Screen**.

5.3.12 Paste Data from Clipboard into Document

Into a Windows Application

1. Run or select **application that will receive data**.

By Right Clicking

1. Right click on **workspace** where to place data.
2. Click **Paste**.

Using Menu

1. Click **workspace** where data is to be pasted.
2. Click **Edit**, **Paste**.

Into an MS-DOS Application

1. Run MS-DOS application in Window.
2. Position cursor in **workspace** where text will be pasted.
3. Click application's **control symbol**.
4. Point to **Edit**.
5. Click **Paste**.

5.3.13 Paste Data into Document as an OLE Object

Make sure that data has been copied to clipboard from an OLE object application such as Paint.

From Application to receive Object

1. Click on **workspace** where to place data.
2. *Click* ***Edit***, ***Paste Special***.
3. Select **Paste** to paste data as an embedded object
   Or
4. Select **Paste Link** to paste as linked object.
5. If Paste Link options are grayed, the application did not recognize the object; in such a case use Insert Existing File as Linked OLE Object in document.
6. Select format of object in **As: in list box**.

Display object as an icon

1. Select **Display as Icon**.
2. Click **Ok**.

5.4 Using essential Accessories

As in earlier versions of Windows, Windows XP too has its own set of accessories for making the working under Windows XP easier. Most of the earlier one have been retained but some new ones have also been added. As in the case of **Control Panel**, we will go through all of them, one by one so that you can use them whenever required.

5.4.1 Accessing Accessories

Accessories can be accessed from **Start Menu** and **Programs**.

As we can see there are various heads in Accessories, each giving rise to different options. Then there are options which are independent of categories.

These can be listed as:

Accessibility — Accessibility Wizard — Magnifier
— Narrator — On Screen Keyboard
— Utility Manager

Communications — Hyper Terminal — Internet Connection Wizard

	— NetMeeting	— Network Connections
	— Network Setup Wizard	— New Connection Wizard
	— Phone Dialer	— Remote Desktop Connection
Entertainment	— CD Player	— Sound Recorder
	— Volume Control	— Windows Media Player
System Tools	— Backup	— Character Map
	— Disk Cleanup	— Disk Deframenter
	— Files and Settings Transfer Wizard	— Scheduled Tasks
	— System Information	— System Restore

Address Book
Calculator
Command Prompt
NotePad
Paint
Program Compatibility Wizard
Synchronize
Tour Windows XP
Windows Explorer
Windows Movie Maker
Word Pad

5.5 System Tools

This category of accessories are there to enhance the working of the computer with different tools which not only speed up the computer but also keeps the system clean of any unwanted elements.

5.5.1 Backup

This option allows you to backup your files from hard disk to a removable media.

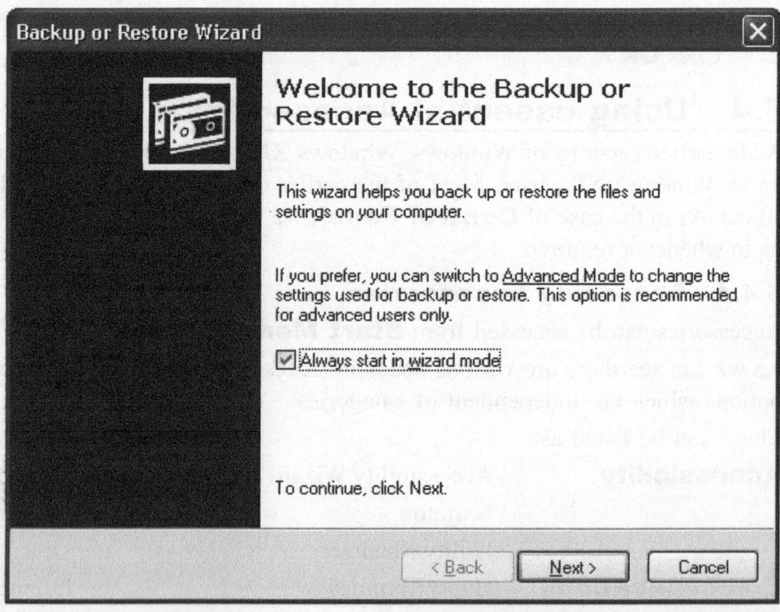

5.5.2 Character Map

This option helps you view the various characters of the fonts available in your Windows. After seeing the format of the character, you can decide whether to use it or not.

5.5.3 Disk Cleanup

The Windows operating system creates a mass of temporary files and cached files—all designed to speed up the performance of the graphical interface. These files do a pretty good job but, often do not

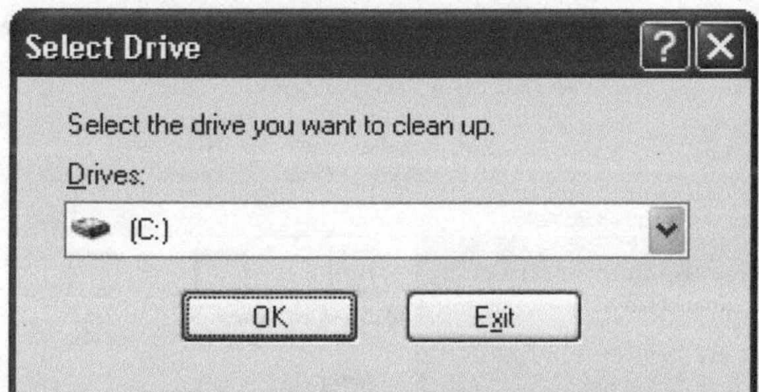

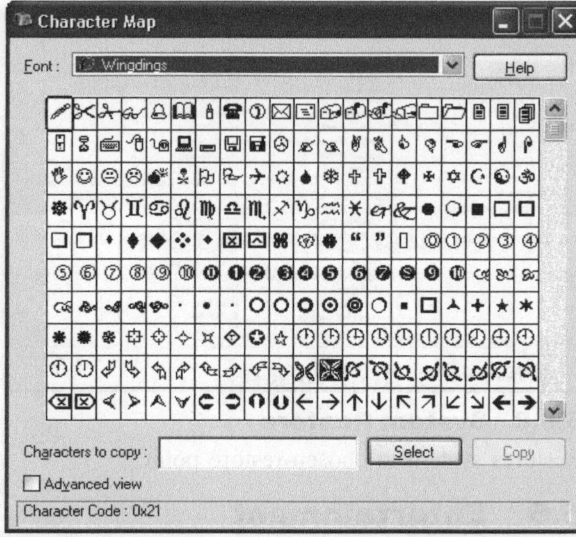

get deleted when they should be. This results in a lot of files cluttered up on your hard drive. When you run Disk Cleanup, it checks for files that can be safely deleted and then presents a list of such files.

5.5.4 Disk Deframenter

While writing files on hard disk, Windows keeps the files at random and keeps track of its position using FAT. This results in having the files placed in hard disk, quite staggered. This command, which was there even in DOS, does the job of housekeeping and puts the files on one side and the blank space in the hard disk on the other side. This results in speeding up the activity of the hard disk. It is advised that once you run Disk Deframenter, you must run Disk Cleanup after it.

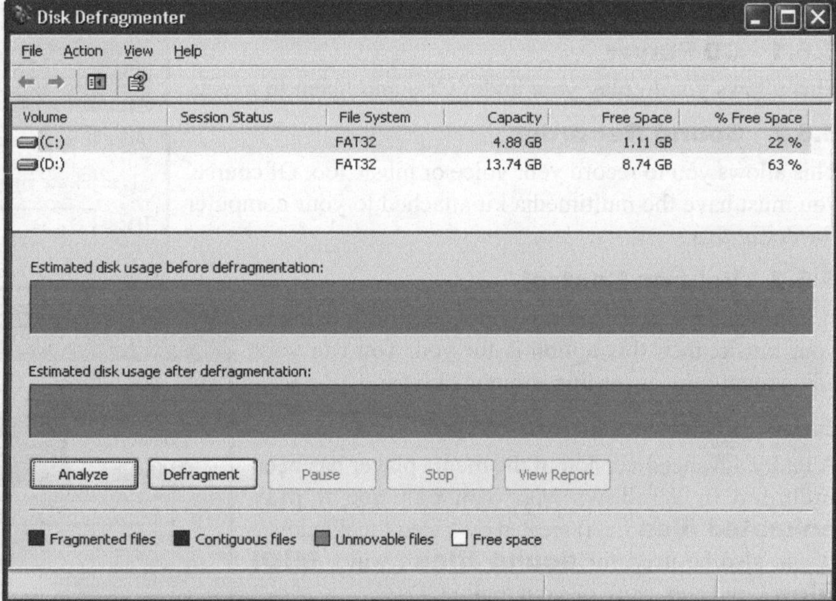

5.5.5 Files and Settings Transfer Wizard

Migrates files and settings from one computer to another.

5.5.6 Scheduled Tasks

As mentioned earlier in the case of Control Panel, you can run some tasks at regular intervals. This command will let you line up the programs for running.

5.5.7 System Information

This command is mainly used by the people who are supposed to correct your computer. It gives the specific information about your computer when he is troubleshooting your configuration. It quickly finds the data that is needed to resolve your system problem.

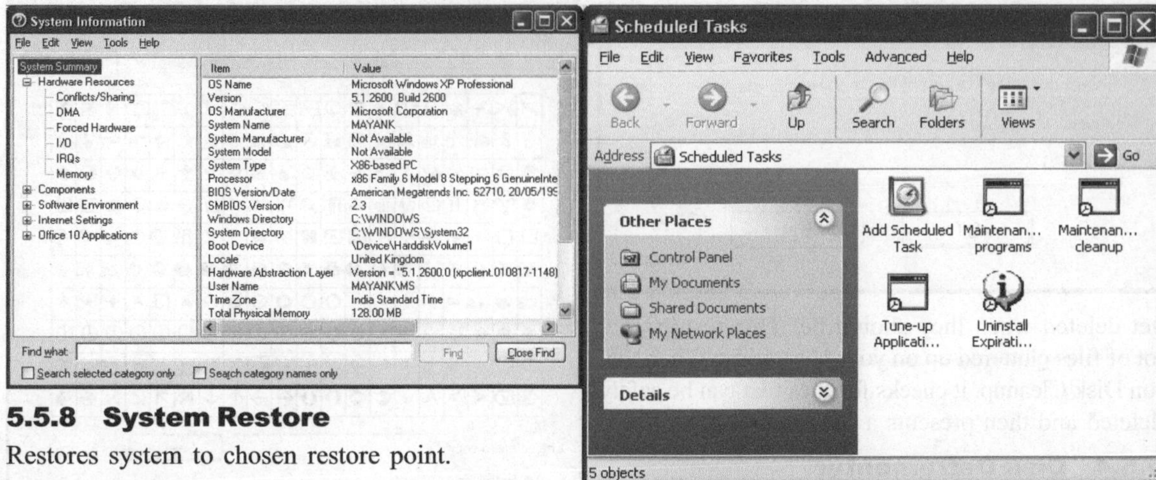

5.5.8 System Restore

Restores system to chosen restore point.

5.6 Entertainment

This category has the following accessories.

5.6.1 CD Player

This allows you to play your audio CDs and listen to music.

5.6.2 Sound Recorder

This allows you to record your voice or music too. Of course, you must have the multimedia kit attached to your computer for doing that.

5.6.3 Volume Control

If you want a sophisticated volume control to listen to your music, then this option is for you. You can your adjustment here according to your likings.

5.6.4 Windows Media Player

A really advanced version of the media player has been included in Windows Me. You can use it play **animated files** (.avi) created by Video for Windows. It can also be used for **sound files** (.wav), **MIDI files** (.mid and .rmi), or your audio CDs.

5.7 Games

As mentioned above a separate folder has been created in Windows XP for games. Various games are:

- Classic Hearts
- Classic Solitaire
- Freecell
- Internet Backgammon
- Internet Checkers
- Internet Hearts
- Internet Reversi
- Internet Spades
- Minesweeper
- Pinball
- Spider Solitaire

For playing the internet games like Backgammon, Spades, etc., you need to connect to Internet before playing the game.

5.8 Calculator

Windows XP gives you the choice of both Standard and Scientific calculator for doing the calculations while working on the computer.

A Scientific calculator is shown here.

5.9 Imaging

With the help of this option you can rotate, edit or change the colours of a picture.

5.10 Fax

It gives you the option of attaching and working with Fax.

5.11 Notepad

It is a simple text editor with quite a number of features of a good word processor. It can be used as a stop-gap word processor for viewing text files.

5.12 Paint

It is a full fledged program known by the name of Paintbrush. You can create, edit graphic files in **bit-map**

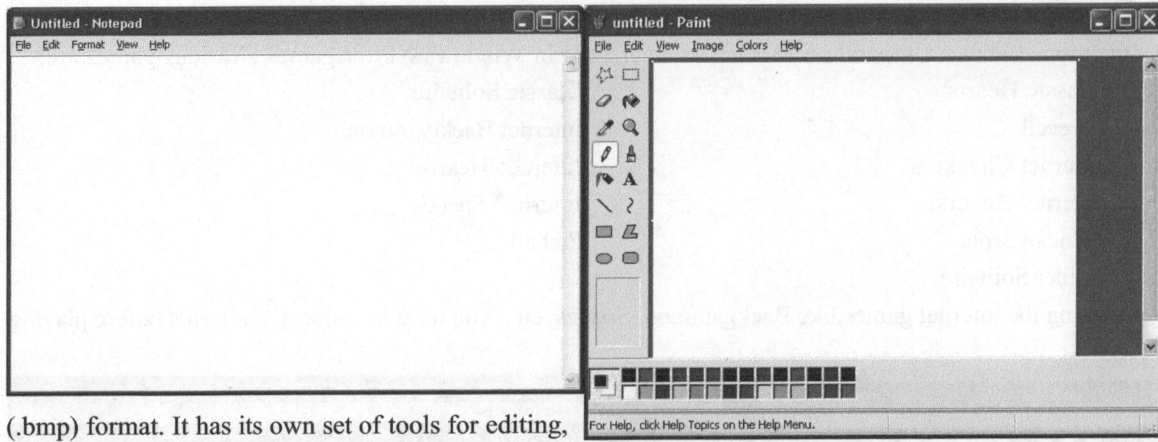

(.bmp) format. It has its own set of tools for editing, cropping of pictures. You can even draw your drawing using the freehand tools available.

5.13 WordPad

It is another simple word processing program. Though better than the Note Pad, it is still falls short of a full fledged word processing software.

5.14 Command Prompt

Something which would make the users of MS DOS happy. Using this you can run your DOS programs. DOS translates the commands that we enter through the keyboard into signals that can be interpreted by the computer. The CPU (Central Processing Unit) processes the raw data as per the commands we feed (Input) into the computer and returns the results (gives the Output).

The results are displayed on the Monitor in our language. The results can also be printed on a printer. Directed by the instruction that we type, the DOS operates and controls the operating system. With DOS we can do the following:

- Create new files
- Delete old files
- Rename existing files
- List all the files in the hard disk or floppy
- Enhance the storage capacity of the disk
- Format new floppy or hard disk for usuage
- Reorganize the storage files on the disk
- Make back up files on the hard disk or to the floppy diks

- Scan for viruses

5.14.1 Type of DOS Commands

There are 2 types of DOS commands, mainly, Internal and External commands.

5.14.1.1 Internel Commands

These commands can be given from the DOS prompt, irrespective of the fact the command is there in the DOS directory or not. These can be said to be the in-built commands of DOS. For example, the following commands are internal commands:

Chdir It changes the current directory, shortname is CD.

Cls It clears the screen.

Copy It is used for copying files, read more about it later in the chapter.

Copy cont It is used to create a quick batch file.

Ctty This command is used to redirect the keyboard and screen to the serial port.

5.14.1.2 External Commands

These commands are such they have to be present in the hard disk to be used. Some of external commands are given below:

Append It lets programs open data files as if they were in the current directory.

Assign It is used to reassign drives when programs work only with specific drives.

Attrib It changes file attributes, which are settings in every DOS file.

Backup/Restore It lets you backup your hard disk onto as many floppies as required. Restore command can be used to use backedup files.

Chkdsk It checks disk status, memory status, files and flags unidentifiable files.

Comp It compares two files for identical content and reports up to 10 mismatches.

5.15 Directory Navigation

To create a new directory, you have to assign a name to it. This should, as far as possible, signify the type of data or programs you are going to store into it. The command is given as following:

```
MD LAXMI
```

This will create a new directory by the name of LAXMI. In the beginning, it is blank. Your cursor will remain at the position of its start.

Supposing you want to enter this or any other directory, then the command will be:

5.15.1.1 Change Directory

This command can be given as following:

```
C:\>CD LAXMI
C:\>LAXMI>
```

This means that you have entered the directory called LAXMI. However, if you are in any other directory and want to enter the LAXMI directory from there, the command becomes:

```
C:>CD\
```

The backslash (\) means that you are entering a different directory. Actually (\) means more than that. If you type CD\ at the DOS prompt of any subdirectory, your cursor reaches the root directory. This is a quick way to go to the root directory, skipping several levels of subdirectories. If you write only CD then it will show the current directory.

5.15.1.2 Remove Directory

Sometimes, it is possible that you have finished using a software and do not want to keep it or have finished with a project and taken the backup too and don't want to burden your hard disk by keeping it. In this case you would like to remove the directory all together. This would help in having more space for working. This command has to be given from outside the directory which you want to remove. So, if you are in the directory, go out from it and then give the remove directory command. You can use either RD or RMDIR. The command is given as:

```
RD LAXMI
```

Before, you do this, however, you must make sure that you have removed all the files in the directory by using the DEL command. If you have not done so, this command will give you the message that the directory is not empty and cannot be deleted.

5.16 Path Setting

The PATH command creates a list of directories that DOS searches for executable files whenever you type a command that is not an internal DOS command. Running PATH with no command line parameters display the current PATH running it with nothing but a semicolon cancels the current PATH, PATH strings are stored as environment variables so you can also create and modify them with the SET command.

5.17 Creating and Using Batch files

Batch processing requires that a program, its related data and relevant control commands should be submitted together, in the form of a Job. Batch operating system allows no interaction between the users and the executing programs. Thus the programs that have long execution times (like payrolls, forecasting, statistical analysis and large scientific number-crunching programs) and require little operator interaction during execution, were well served by Batch Processing. However, due to long turn-around delays and infeasibility of online debugging, the Batch Processing was not at all suitable for software development.

5.18 Drives, files, directories

Files are stored in the hard disk just as we store packets in godown. A hard disk is divided into various subdirectories like rooms in a house. When you start your PC, the first directory that you see is the root directory. The root directory can be compared to a house. Within a subdirectory, you can have another subdirectory and files. You can create and delete these directories yourself. Related files are kept in the same directory.

5.19 Directory Structure

TREE graphically depicts the structure of the specified drive from the specified directory down listing all the subdirectories it encounters. If you use /F switch, it also displays the names of the files inside those subdirectories. Use /A when you direct the output from TREE to a printer that does not support the upper half of the IBM character set.

5.20 Application Management

An application can be run under Windows by various methods. They are:

5.20.0.1 By Icon

Clicking at the icon of the application at the desktop.

5.20.0.2 From Windows Explorer

Click at the file/icon of the application in Windows Explorer.

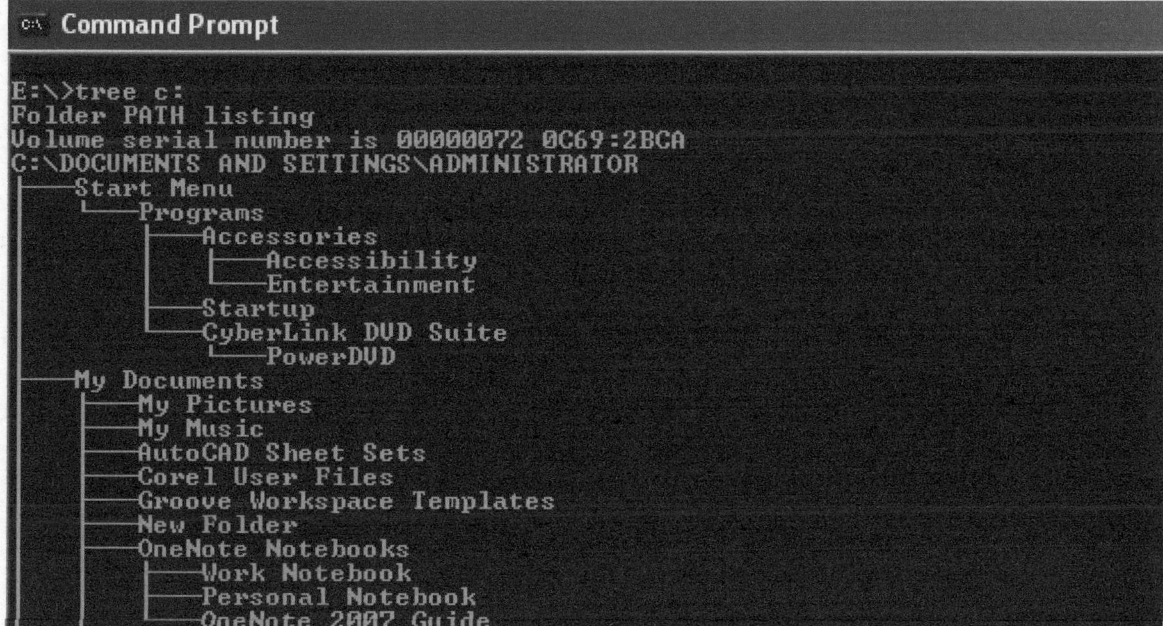

5.20.0.3 From Start Menu

Click at Program and then the program name from its sub-menu. For example, for running Paintbrush, you will have to go to Programs, Accessories and then Paint.

5.20.1 Working on Windows

So far you have seen how the various sections of Windows work. Now we see how you can control the working of the Windows or for that any of the Windows dialog box.

5.20.1.1 Minimizing the Windows

You can work on more than one application at the same time under windows. For this you have to minimize one application, which is done by using Minimize button, as shown here. Once you are though with the other application you can minimize that and come back to this application.

5.20.1.2 Restoring the Windows

If you have minimized an application, then there must be some button to restore it. Using this button you can restore the application back to its position on the screen. The restore button is in the centre here.

5.20.1.3 Maximizing the Windows

Using this button, you can make the full use of Windows screen.

5.20.1.4 Closing of Windows

Using this button you can close the running application. However, if the running application is not saved, then it will be pointed out to you.

5.21 Installing and Uninstalling

Using Add/Remove Programs option you can Add or Remove programs from the hard disk. The program files should never be deleted from the directory itself using delete command. This leaves the program infomation in Windows Registery and does not remove all the files.

This lists out all the programs loaded into the hard disk, their size and the date of last used.

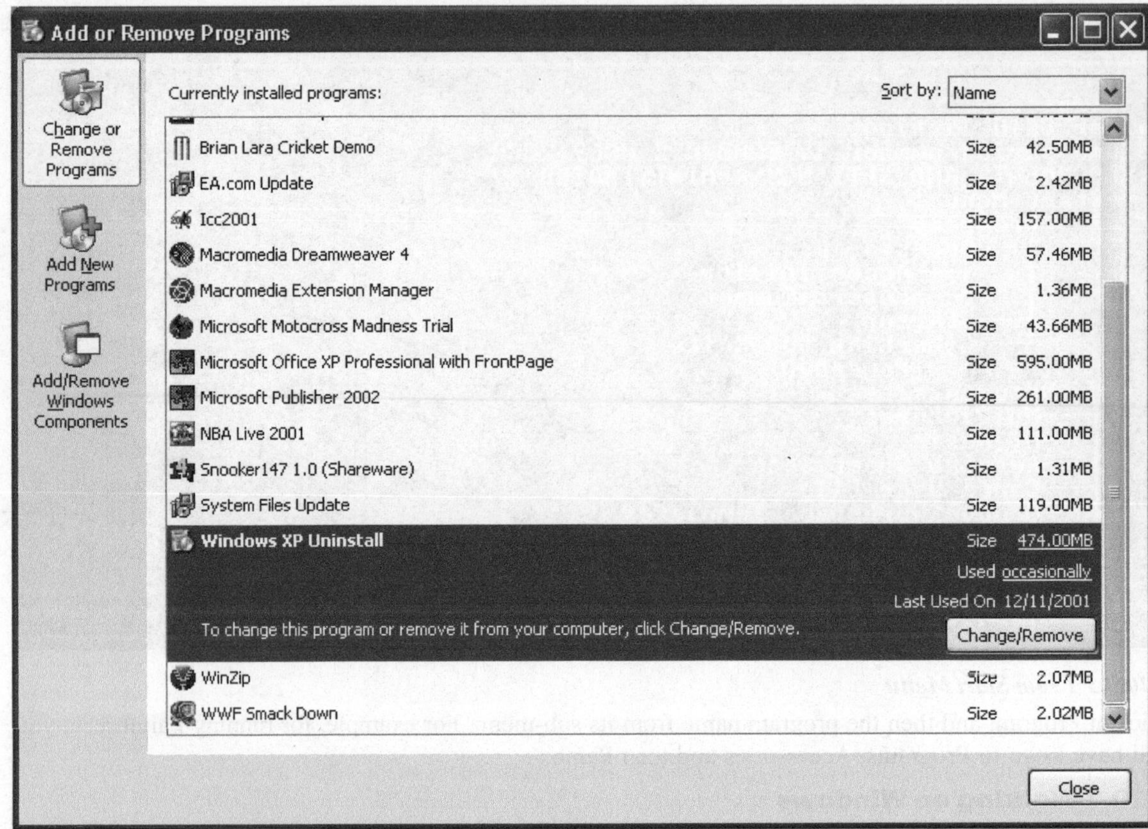

If you want to update it click at Program and then on Change/Remove button.

5.22 Running Applications

See application management.

Let us Revise

1. By using Windows Explorer you can: Create a folder, Copy a file/folder; Rename a file/folder or delete the file/folder.
2. A Windows dialog box has the following units: Title bar, Menu bar, Scroll bar and Status bar.
3. Accessories are additional programs which are there alongwith the main program called Windows.
4. Accessories can be accessed from Start Menu and Programs.
5. When you run Disk Cleanup, it checks for files that can be safely deleted and then presents a list of such files.
6. Disk defragmenter does the job of housekeeping and puts the files on one side and the blank space in the hard disk on the other side.
7. Drive Space allows you to see how of the space has been utilized in the hard disk.
8. Maintainance wizard allows you to set the time and dates for running various utility programs.

9. Scan disk scans the various partitions of the hard disk.
10. Scheduled tasks allow you to see what jobs have been scheduled.
11. System information gives the complete information about the system.
12. Character map allows you to see and use the various fonts available in the system.
13. Imaging allows you to see various graphics.
14. Paint is a useful graphics program which allows you to create graphics too.
15. Word pad is a small word processing program.
16. Calculator has 2 varities, standard and scientific.
17. DOS has internal and external commands.
18. Internal commands can be given from anywhere.
19. In DOS the filename is of 8 + 3 format.
20. Root directory is the main directory of the hard disk.
21. DIR command gives the listing of files in directory.
22. DIR/P allows you to view the files on screen page by page.
23. DIR/W gives the listing widthwise.
24. MD command allows you to create directory.
25. CD command is used for changing directory.
26. RD command is used for removing directory.

Multiple Choice Questions

1. Among the 2 types of calculators, one is standard and the other one is?
   (a) Ordinary (b) Scientific (c) Physical
2. Which accessory would you use to schedule your tasks?
   (a) Disk Cleanup (b) Disk Defragmenter (c) Task Scheduler
3. For fragmenting you hard disk which accessory you would use:
   (a) Disk Fragmenter (b) Tools (c) Fragmenter
4. For creating drawings, you would use:
   (a) Drawing (b) Paint (c) Painter
5. For viewing Video CDs you would use:
   (a) CD Player (b) Windows Media Player (c) Video
6. For sound recorder, what is necessary?
   (a) Speaker (b) Microphone (c) Mouse
7. For Phone dialer, what extra equipment you need to have in your computer?
   (a) Mouse (b) Printer (c) Modem
8. For seeing how the various fonts look, you would use:
   (a) Font (b) See (c) Character Map
9. A small word processing program available in Accessories is called:
   (a) Word (b) Processing (c) Word Pad
10. Solatire is a :
    (a) System tool (b) Game (c) Internet tool

11. Which command is used to shift the command from one directory to another?
    (a) CD (b) MD (c) RD
12. Which command would you use to create a new directory?
    (a) CD (b) MD (c) RD
13. The main directory of the hard disk is:
    (a) Main directory (b) Root directory (c) Final directory
14. Which command will always transfer to the root directory?
    (a) CD\ (b) CD/ (c) CD
15. For listing the files widthwise, we give the command as?
    (a) DIR/P (b) DIR/W (c) DIR

True/False Questions

1. Task Scheduler is used for defragmenting disk.
2. Scientific calculator is a part of Windows Accessories.
3. You can put computer on Stand by mode from the Shut Down button.
4. Small graphical items on desktop are known as icons.
5. *For drawings in Windows*, Paint can be used.
6. MD command is used to change the directory.
7. RD command is used to create a directory.

Matching Columns

In the following case, commands are given in the left hand columns and their actions in the right hand column. Match them.

Column A	Column B
A. Paint	1. For scheduling the maintaince jobs
B. Recycle Bin	2. Standard and Scientific
C. Solatire	3. Controlling the volume of speakers
D. CD Player	4. To see the various font formats
E. Volume control	5. For seeing items in bigger size
F. Phone dialer	6. For running an application
G Character Map	7. For finding file and folders
H. Maintainance Wizard	8. For creating small drawings
I. Magnifier	9. For dialing from the PC
J. Find	10. For playing an audio CD
K. Run	11. Game
L. Calculator	12. For collecting the deleted files

Fill in the Blanks with appropriate words

a. Recycle Bin b. Restore c. Icon d. Find
e. Accesories f. Direct Cable Connector g. Entertainment h. Run
i. Minimize j. Title bar k. Disk Defragmenter l. Desktop

1. An application can be started by using ________ in the Start button.
2. Calculator is part of ____________.
3. By clicking the ________ button you can restore the application window to its original format.
4. The deleted files and folders go to _________.
5. The accessory which allows you to defragment the hard disk is called _________.
6. The initial windows screen is called ________.
7. Graphical representation of applications is called _________.
8. The accessory which allows you to connect various computers is called _______________.
9. The button which is used to reduce the application window is called __________.
10. Games are there is accessories _________ subgroup.
11. For locating files and folders, you would use ______ utility.
12. The bar which displays the name of the document or application at the topmost in any application is called _________.

Descriptive Type Questions

1. How can you run an application in Windows?
2. What do you understand by:
   Minimizing the Windows Maximizing the Windows
   Restoring the Windows Closing the Windows
3. What is the function of Windows Explorer?
4. How would you do the following using Windows Explorer?
   Rename a file Copy a file
   Create a folder Delete a file
   Move a file
5. Describe the various components of a Windows dialog box.
6. What is the purpose of Disk clean up?
7. For what purpose do you use Disk Defragmenter?
8. How would you control the volume of the CDPlayer?
9. If you have a Video CD, how would you run it on your computer?
10. How would you see the shape of various fonts under Windows?
11. If you have to dial from your computer, what would you use?
12. If you have to create a drawing, which program would you use?
13. To clean up your hard disk, which program would you use?
14. What is the command to remove all files in a directory?
15. Is it possible to remove the root directory of your hard disk by using the RD command? If yes, how?
16. Type the command to remove a directory. Where must the cursor be to remove a directory or subdirectory?

Answers to Objective Type Questions

Multiple Choice Questions

1. b	2. c	3. a	4. b
5. b	6. b	7. c	8. c
9. c	10. b	11. a	12. b
13. b	14. a	15. b	

True False Questions

1. T	2. T	3. T	4. T
5. T	6. F	7. F	

Matching Columns

A. 8	B. 12	C. 11	D. 10
E. 3	F. 9	G. 4	H. 1
I. 5	J. 7	K. 6	L. 2

Fill in the Blanks

1. h	2. e	3. b	4. a
5. k	6. l	7. c	8. f
9. i	10. g	11. d	12. j

Linux Operating System 6

6.1 An Overview of Linux

Bill Gates is no doubt the richest man in the World. He made his money by selling commercial software, specially operating software like MS-DOS and Windows. Compare this with the Linux which is nothing short of a phenomenon. It is an operating software which has no financial strings attached to it. It can be just downloaded freely from the net. Imagine if the producers of this software too would have insisted on selling it commercially they would have been in league with Bill Gates. But, they choose not to do so.

It is not that since Linux is available cheaply it would be cheap in performance too. In fact, it lacks no punch as far as its competitors in operating system from Microsoft, Apple, Novell and IBM. It is also handling more demanding applications, it is also a serious contender against rival Unix-derivative operating systems such as Solaris, HP-UX and SCO-Unix for larger businesses.

6.1.1 History of Linux

Linux was created as an offshoot of Unix. It has more similarities to UNIX than to any other operating systems. As an operating system, Unix continues to be widely used in commercial environment, as well as in the educational world, although it is also often found running on today's client-server intranet networks too. While versions of Unix have long been available for PCs, they never had the grace or power of the operating systems available for minicomputers, mainframes and today's servers.

In addition, the early commercial versions of Unix were costly, sometimes costing more than the PC hardware they were destined to run on. This lack of accessibility ultimately gave birth to Linux as a means to make a Unix-like operating system available on a widespread basis. Richard Stallmand and the Free Software Foundation (FSF) began work on this alternative operative system in the mid-1980s. By the end of that decade, they had developed functional alternatives to every major Unix component except the kernel. Linux Torvalds at the University of Helsinki in Finland developed the original Linux kernel in 1991.

The combined work became the Linux as you know today. Torvalds originally intended to develop Linux as a hobby. Early versions of Linux didn't have consumers in mind; instead, they provided the barest bones of functionality to allow Unix programmers the apparent joy or programming the kernel. As the core of the operating system, the kernel keeps everything running smoothly – without a stale, powerful kernel, you don't have an operating system. But as programmers integrated the work of the FSF with the Torvalds kernel, the base software for a complete operating system emerged. It became clear to those involved that Linux was evolving the state where it could respectably be called an operating system.

In March 1992, version 1.0 of the kernel came into being, marking the first official release of Linux. At this point, Linux ran most of the common Unix tools from compilers to networking software to X Windows. Linux continues to evolve as the pre-eminent Unix-clone operating system for PCs. Hardware support is now broad, including the most popular and common peripherals; performance is strong, giving many PCs power comparable to that of mind range workstations such as Sun Microsystems' SPARC systems.

Linux is even now ported to the PowerPC and Compaq Alpha platforms, among others. Although technically today's Linux is not Unix because it fails it fails to quality for the brand name, Linux is functionally equivalent to Unix in almost every important way.

6.2 Basic Linux Elements

These can be listed out as following:

6.2.1 Linux As an Operating System

Linux is used in two ways: specifically to refer to the kernel itself-the heart of any version of Linux-and more generally to refer to any collection that run on the kernel, usually referred to as a distribution. The kernel's job is to provide the basic environment in which applications can run, including the basic interfaces with hardware and the systems for managing tasks and currently running programs. In the specific sense, there is only one current version of Linux at any one time the current revision of the kernel. Torvalds keeps the kernel as the domain in the world of Linux development, leaving all the applications and services that sit on top of the kernel to any of the thousands of other Linux developers in the world.

In the general meaning of the term Linux, referring to cohesive collections of applications that run on top of the Linux kernel, there are numerous versions of Linux. Each distribution has its own unique characteristics, including different installation methods, different collections of features and different upgrade paths. But since all distributions are fundamentally Linux, in almost every case an application that works with a current version of one distribution will work with a current version of another distribution. The interesting thing about this dichotomous use of the term "Linux" is that it exactly parallels the same confused usage of the term "operating system".

For consumers, an operating system has come to mean a large collection of applications centered around a kernel. This is what Windows 95, 98, Me, NT and 2000 are. This is what the Macintosh OS is. In a purist, technical sense, an operating system is a much smaller core kernel that provides those basic system functions needed to develop any application. In both ways, Linux is an operating system. One of the features of the Linux kernel that sets it apart from other consumer operating systems designed to run on desktop PCs is that it is both multitasking and multiuser.

6.2.2 A Multitasking Operating System

You are probably familiar with the term multitasking, even if you are not really sure what it means. When desktop computing graduated from Windows 3.1 to Windows 95, the multitasking capabilities of the then-new Windows 95 were among its biggest claims to fame. To say that a system can multitask is to say that it can appear to be running more than one application, or process, at a time. For example, the system can print a document, copy a file and dial into the Internet while the user is comfortably typing in a word processing program.

Even with these background tasks happening, the foreground word processor should not freeze up or be unusable. This is the wonder of multitasking: It allows a computer with a single processor to appear to be performing multiple tasks simultaneously. Of course, a single CPU an execute only a single instruction at a time – that is, only one action can be taking place at any one time. Multitasking creates the appearances of simultaneous activity by switching rapidly between tasks as the demands of those processes dictate. When multitasking words well, a user running a word processor while several other things happen will not be aware of the extra work the computer is doing.

All processes will seem to be running smoothly and the computer will be responsive. Historically, Unix systems have been much better than Windows at multitasking; Unix is able to run large numbers of simultaneous applications in a way that made it an ideal fit for large corporate servers and high-powered work stations. Today, only Windows 2000 and its predecessor Widows NT 4.0 can really claim to offer a similar robust multitasking implementation. Even Windows 95/98/Me, despite all of this fanfare, has trouble effectively handling large numbers of simultaneous processes. To take thing further, Linux, like Windows NT and Windows 2000, offers support for computer with multiple processors, such as dual-Pentium III systems.

These systems can in fact perform two actions at exactly the same time. Combining multitasking with multiple processors greatly increase the number of simultaneous applications a computer can run smoothly.

6.2.3 A Multiuser Operating System

Even more important than being a multitasking operating system, Linux-like all versions of Unix and Unix clones – is a multiuser operating system. All consumer versions of Windows and the Mac OS are single-user systems. In other words, only one user can be logged in and running applications at any one time in these operating systems. By comparison, Linux allows multiple simultaneous users, fully leveraging the multitasking capabilities of the operating system. The great advantage of this is that Linux can be developed as an applications server. From their desktop computers or terminals, users can log into a Linux server across a LAN and actually run applications on the server instead of on their desktop PCs.

6.2.4 Linux Applications

As an operating system, Linux can be used to develop almost any type of application. Among the applications available for Linux are the following:

6.2.4.1 Text and Word Processing Applications

In addition to commercial word processing software such as WordPerfect, StarOffice and Applixware, Linux offers powerful tools for editing text files and processing text in an automated fashion.

6.2.4.2 Programming Languages

A wide variety of programming and scripting languages and tools are available for Linux and all Unix operating systems. This abundance of programming tools makes it easy to develop new applications that can run not only on Linux but also on most Unix and Unix-like operating systems.

6.2.4.3 X Windows

X Windows is Unix's answer to the graphical user interface (GUI). X Windows is a highly flexible and configurable GUI environment that runs on Linux as well as on most Unix systems. Numerous applications that run in X Windows help to make Linux an easy-to-use operating system.

6.2.4.4 Internal tools

In addition to supporting well-known software such as Netscape and Mosaic, Linux provides a wide range of Internet software, including character-based and graphical mail-reading applications, the full range of software needed to create Internet serves (Web servers, mail servers and news servers), plus complete network support to connect to the Internet via a local network or modem.

6.2.4.5 Databases

Like all Unix platforms, Linux provides a robust platform for running client-server database applications. From its earliest days, powerful, free databases such as mSQL and PostgreSQL have been available for Linux. As Linux has grown in popularity, especially in corporate information systems, the number of commercial relational database servers for Linux has grown. Today, Oracle, Sybase and Informix all offer relational database products for Linux.

6.2.4.6 DOS and Windows compatibility software

Linux can be made to run DOS software with a high degree of stability and compatibility and offers several approaches to running Windows software. In fact, the entire text of this book was written using Microsoft Word for Windows on a computer running Linux. This provides strong evidence of Linux's ability to work well in a Windows environment. In addition, emulators are available for other popular computer systems, including the Macintosh and Atari ST computer lines.

6.3 Linux System and Software Features

Version 7.1 of Red Hat Linux offers several new features not found in earlier versions and still not found in all distributions of Linux. These features include the following:

6.3.1 The 2.4 Linux kernel

The evolution of the Linux kernel over the past year is impressive. While every revision to the Linux kernel is small, the development of the kernel over the past year has resulted in new features for the desktop, for servers and for smaller devices such as handlheld computers.

These new features include the following:

6.3.2 Integrated PC hardware support

While USB support is growing version 2.4 also promises improved performance for PCMCIA (PC Card) and Plug-and-Play ISA devices, by integrating their drivers directly into the kernel.

6.3.3 A diversity of platforms

With the new kernel, you can now run Linux on a wide variety of non-Intel platforms, including Alpha, Sparc, MIPS, PowerPC and ARM-based computers. The new kernel even supports the IBM s/390 mainframe computer.

6.3.4 Support for Smaller Devices

The new kernel is designed for use in compact devices such as handheld computers and other portable network devices.

6.3.5 Few Limits

The new kernel now supports a large amount of RAM (64GB), virtually unlimited multitasking and the ability to create a single volume over multiple disks for very large files.

6.3.6 New Configuration Tools

Linux has always had a strong of both command-line and graphical tools for configuring and administering a Red Hat Linux-based system. Starting with version 5, these were expanded to include a user information tool to set user information such as name and phone number, a user password tool that makes it easy to change users' passwords and a file system tool that allows the mounting and unmounting of file systems from a graphical interface.

Red Hat Linux also offers a tool for configuring the free version of X Windows, XFree86 called Xconfigurator. Xconfigurator has always been easier to use than the configuration program included with XFree86. In Red Hat Linux, Xconfigurator offers additional improvements such as automatic ditection of video cards and their features.

Red Hat Linux now includes new tools for configuring printers and firewalls, known as printconf and gnome-lokkit. Printconf allows you to set up printers locally or remotely through a standard graphical user interface. Gnome-lokkit allows you to configure a firewall to protect your computer and network from intruders, configuring firewall rules based on simple questions that determine your communication needs.

Altogether, these improvements make Red Hat Linux easy to manage for most usrs and help bring to the Linux word the types of graphical management tools found in rival systems such as Windows 2000.

6.3.7 Improved X window systems

Red Hat Linux 7.1 includes XFree86 version .0.3 the latest version of the Linux X Window System. This creates a more stable platform and improved 3-D graphics for the two major desktop environments, GNOME and KDE both of which are also included in Red Hat Linux 7.11. GNOME and KDE are desktop environments for X Windows designed to make application development easier and to provide a more consistent, professional quality desktop environment for Linux users.

6.3.8 Improved Performance Features

Red Hat Linux 7.1 offers several new or improved features that can be used to leverage high-end hardware to improve the performance and stability of Red Hat Linux systems. These features include better implementation of symmetric multiprocessing (SMP), which allows Red Hat Linux to leverage the performance gain offered by multiprocessor systems. In addition, Red Hat Linux 7.1 includes an improved version of Disk Druid, which detects errors as you set up partitions during installation.

6.4 File Structure and File Handling

Different from DOS and Windows, which use backslash (/) as separator for directories, LINUX uses forward slash (/). A subdirectory booksdir of the directory user, will be shown as /user/booksdir. The slash (/) before the user represents the root directory. Some of the prominent directories are mentioned below:

/bin It contains executable program files (binary files). Here, you can find the files for the LINUX commands.

/dev It contains the special device files. Printer may be a file known as prn in this directory, the hard disk may be hda file and its first partition would be hda().

/etc It contains all the system-wide configuration information as text files.

/kernel It contains all the kernel specific code. Kernel is the heart of the LINUX system. It is responsible for resource allocation, security and low-level hardware interfaces.

/lib It contains the library files. Library files contain the reusable functions and routines for the programmer to use.

/mnt It is the directory where the storage devices other than hard disks are mounted. This directory contains the subdirectories "floppy" and "cdrom" which when these devices are mounted show the contents of the floppy disk or CD-ROM respectively.

/tmp It contains all the temporary files, which will eventually be deleted from the system. Similar to the C:\windows\temp directory in Windows 98.

/usr It contains the home directories of the users, source text for the online manual (man) pages, games and other directories. There is one home directory for each user.

6.4.1 File Handling in LINUX

Through DOS we are familiar with pathname. In LINUX too, each directory or file has a pathname. Here it is referred to from the beginning of the root directory. For example, the directory user is referred to as /user; book is referred to as /user/book, where user is the parent directory of book directory.

A pathname can be of two types

- Absolute Pathname
- Relative Pathname

6.4.1.1 Absolute Pathname

It tells you the complete path of a directory starting from the root, as explained above. For example, absolute pathname of "ittools" directory is /usr/books/laxmi/doe/ittools.

6.4.1.2 Relative Pathname

It gives location of a directory, relative to the current working directory. For example, suppose your current working directory is /usr/books/laxmi/doe/ittools. Then the relative pathname to the "ittools" directory is ittools. Relative pathnames do not start with a "/".

If you do not start a pathname with "/", LINUX assumes that you are using relative pathname.

6.5 Hardware and Software Requirements

Since Linux runs on many different computers and supports a wide range of hardware, and because everyone has different needs, I won't make too many recommendations as to which specific hardware to buy. (Systems change too fast for such a list to ever be useful, anyway.) Before you make a hardware purchase, though, make sure that it's compatible with Linux -- that bargain video-capture board will be worthless if it has a proprietary interface that only works with a certain non-free operating system.

6.5.1 Hardware Requirements

For an ideal Linux based PC your computer must have the following:

- An IBM Compatible PC with minimum 80386. 80486 is better.
- Any processor from Intel, Sparc, Alpha or AMD
- Minimum 128 MB RAM
- Minimum 2 GB free hard disk space
- Input devices such as keyboard, mouse, etc.
- Controller cards such as SCSI, IDE, etc.
- A Network card such as ISA, PCI or USB etc.
- Sound card compatible to LINUX

6.5.2 Software Requirements

- A partitioning program such as fdisk or disk druid supplied by Red Hat.
- Linux Software package.

To find out whether your hardware will work under Linux, try the following:

1. Read the Linux Hardware Compatibility HOWTO, an up-to-date list of hardware that is compatible with Linux.
2. Search for it on the two sites that provide reviews and information about hardware that works with Linux, http://www.linuxhardware.net/ and http://www.linuxhardware.org/.
3. Search the Internet -- particularly Usenet news and the linux.com site -- for information on the hardware you intend to buy. Read any trouble reports people may have written about getting it to work with Linux, so that you won't be writing the next one about it.

It takes more than individual software programs to make something that we can use on our computers-someone has to put it all together. It takes time to assemble the pieces into a cohesive usable collection, test it all, and then keep up to date with the new developments of each piece of software (a small change in any one of which may introduce a new software dependency problem or conflict with the rest). A Linux distribution is such an assemblage. You can do it yourself, of course, and "roll your own" distribution -- since it's all free software, anyone can add to it or remove from it and call the resulting concoction his own. Most people, however, choose to leave the distribution business to the experts.

There are scads of distributions, although not more than a half-dozen make up the bulk of all Linux systems: Debian GNU/Linux, Fedora Linux, Mandrakelinux, Red Hat Enterprise Linux, Slackware Linux, and SuSE. So when people speak of Debian, Fedora, Mandrake, Red Hat, Slackware, SuSE and the like in terms of Linux, they're talking about the specific distribution of Linux and related software, as assembled and repackaged by these companies or organizations. The core of the distributions are the same -- they're all the Linux kernel, the GNU Project software, and many other free software packages -- but each distribution has its own packaging schemes, defaults, and configuration methods. Unless otherwise noted, recipes in this book are general to Linux and are not dependent on a specific distribution.

All of the major distributions today are reputable, and you should have no serious problems with any of them. Each has its loyalists and adherents, while some Linux users like to drift from distro to distro, trying them all. Among the distributions Debian has special qualities worth noting. It is the only one designed and assembled by volunteers in the same open manner that the Linux kernel and most other free software is written; it is also robust (the standard Debian CD-ROM set comes with more software than any other, with 2,500 different software packages), and is entirely committed to free software by design (yes, there are distributions that are not). In Debian's early days it was referred to as the "hacker's distro" because it could be very difficult for a Linux newbie to install and manage. However, that has changed.

6.5.3 The Penguin

You've surely seen the "Linux penguin" in advertisements arid all over Web. Larry Ewing's penguin drawing (made in the free-software GIMP image editor) has become a guaranteed sighting anywhere that Linux comes up, ami is the "official" Linux mascot. Yes, it has a name: Tux.

Many variations on the standard drawing now exist. Linus Torvalds' favorite is actually distributed right along with the Linux kernel sources now, so if your system has the Linux source code installed (it's kept in /usr/src/linux), you can see a copy of his favorite for yourself at /usr/src/linux/Documentation/logo.gif.

While it seems like he was always a part of Linux, Tux actually didn't conic to be until about 1994. In the earliest days of Linux, the storm petrel was a popular mascot, drawn by Peter Williams. His illustration shows the storm petrel in flight, from a perspective where its left wing appears raised and right wing sharply parallel to the view, so that its body forms an L shape.

6.5.4 Open Source, Free Content, and the Future

The term open source was first introduced by some free software advocates in 1998 as a marketing term for free software. They felt that some people unfamiliar with the free software movement -- specially the executives at certain large corporations who'd suddenly taken an interest in the more than ten years' worth of work that had been put into this software -- might be scared off by the word "free." They were concerned that said industry decision-makers might confuse free software with unrelated concepts such as freeware, which is software provided free of charge, but in executable form only.

The Open Source Initiative (osi) was founded to promote software that conforms with its public "Open Source Definition," which in turn was derived from the "Debian Free Software Guidelines" (DFSG), originally written by Bruce Perens as a set of software inclusion guidelines for Debian. All free software -- including software released under the terms of the GNU General Public License -- conforms with this definition.

But some free-software advocates and organizations, including the Free Software Foundation, loudly criticized the term "open source," believing that it obscured the importance of "freedom" in this movement.

However, even "free software" is now much too limited, because the very scope of the "movement" itself is a source of contention and debate. As long ago as 1994, I pointed out that it took more than computer program source code to make a complete and working operating system (non-software elements such as documentation, graphic icons, audio samples, and databases would be necessary).

In time, groups were formed to advance the free copying and modification of specific types of non-software works, such as audio recordings of pop music. New terms including "open content" and "free content" then became popular to differentiate these new works from free software. Eventually, even software organizations began to recognize the role of non-software works in achieving their stated goals, and some endorsed other kinds of works, like software documentation, as deserving of free licensing.

Today, the surfeit of so many amateur "free" or "open" works, sell published on the Web, shows that many people clearly want to share-but the outcome may not be what they expected. With so many specialized licenses and conflicting methods for "free" publishing, these works all remain incompatible with each other, enclosed in their own separate commons.

Other questions and concerns quickly arise: The goals of license makers are not always identical to those of publishers who use such licenses; the promise of "free" invites careless violation of license terms and conditions by casual users and amateur publishers alike; enforcement is difficult if not impossible; assistance is nonexistent, since the practice occurs outside of traditional publishing; what constitutes the open "source" for different works is heavily debated; and, while the availability of works on the Internet is generally transnational, it is unclear whether international law or the laws of sovereign nations apply to these licensed works and their copies and derivatives.

The situation is this. Computers have made it possible for machine-readable works to be published in such a way so that anyone can instantly access copies of these works from anywhere, and then sample from, modify, or distribute these copies free of charge and without harm to the originals (and theoretically preserving all access and authorship credit in some appropriate manner), but this has only been demonstrated by individual self-publishers who have released their works under unique licenses-there is no acknowledged universal standard or commons for such works, and no clear economic model to replace the old publication methods. The future of this practice, and of all the works already so published, is unclear.

6.6 Preliminary Steps before Installation

Every Linux system has an administrator -- someone who installs the hardware and software, maintains the system, and generally keeps things running smoothly. A single-user home Linux system, once installed and running, needs little adniinistration -- but the occasional upgrade or maintenance task is neccessary. This appendix exists as a reference for those users who will also forming the administrative duties on their systems. While a complete administrative guide is out of the scope of this book, the goal of this chapter is to point the new Linux administrator in the right direction, giving tips on how to choose the computer you'll use for Linux, install Linux on it, and get it ready for use. Unlike the rest of this book, this chapter contains recipes describes commands to be run by root, the superuser account. Many of these commands, cannot be run by an ordinary user. Instead of the normal "$" shell prompt used for examples throughout the rest of the book, the examples in these recipes use a pound sign (#), which is the default prompt for the root account.

6.6.1 Setting Up Hardware

In days gone by, Linux enthusiasts had to piece together computer systems from individual components, since the salesmen at computer stores had never even heard of Linux or the free software movement. But no more. Today, many dealers sell complete systems with Linux pre-installed, including corporation like Dell Computers and IBM.

6.6.2 Setting the System Date and Time

There are a few methods for setting the system date and time. The first is simple and works on all systems, but it relies on the operator to input an accurate, correct time; if you need or want a greater degree of accuracy, use one of the tools described in the second method.

6.6.2.1 METHOD #1

Use date with the -s option to set the system date. Give as an argument the time and date to use -- the system date is set to this date the moment the command is run. Quote long-format dates. Here are two ways to use this.

To set the system date to noon on March 4,1994, type:

```
# date -s "Mar 4 12:00 1994"
```

To set the system date to 4:15 p.m., type:

```
# date -s 16:15
```

In the second example above, the day, month, and year are not set,. and remain at the value they had before this command was run.

6.6.2.2 METHOD #2

Use one of the following tools to set the system date and time to that given by remote hosts on the Internet. This is good for keeping your time adjusted with various public time servers, such as the ones run by the United States Navy.

Chrony — Sets the date according to time servers availaible on the Internet, and adjusts for "drift" by periodicallv readjusting the system time from these servers.

```
DEB: chrony
RPM: chrony
WWW: http://chrony.sunsite.dk/index.php
```

Rdate — Sets the system date to the time and date givci a remote host.

```
DEB: rdate
RPM: rdate
```

6.6.2.3 Specifying Mount Points for Certain Devices

It is sometimes nice to set up a special mount point for a device, such as a CD or floppy drive you use all the time, so that when you specify that mount point as an argument to mount, that device is automatically mounted. To do this, edit /etc/fstab so that the particular mount point has an entry, and so the name of the device is given in the first column. For example, you might want to have a variation on the two lines given in following figure somewhere in your /etc/inittab.

```
/dev/fdo       /floppy  auto        defaults,user,noauto 0 0
/dev/cdrom    /cdrom iso9660 defaults,ro,user,noauto 0   0
```

This would mean that whenever any user (since both of these mount points have user access) typed mount/ f loppy, the disk corresponding to the /dev/fdo device (the first floppy drive) would be mounted on /f loppy, and its filesystem type would be detected automatically. If a user were to type mount /cdrom, the data CD in the drive corresponding to the /dev/cdrom device would be mounted on /cdrom as an ISO 9660 filesystem. If you do specify a particular mount point for a device adready in your /etc/fstab, that device will be mounted at the point you specify—this method doesn't limit your mount point to only the device specified in the hlc

6.6.3 Making a Boot Floppy

A boot floppy is a floppy disk with a bootable Linux kernel on it. It is useful to have a boot floppy in case your root partition—that is, the partition of your hard drive containing the bootable Linux kernel-should ever become corrupted. In an emergency, you can boot your system from the floppy, and then mount your other partitions.

If you didn't have a boot floppy, you would be stuck. This is why a boot floppy is sometimes called a "rescue disk". To make a boot floppy, you first need to find the file on your system containing the Linux kernel image that you want the floppy to have. Often there is a vmlinuz compressed kernel boot image file kept in /boot. You can also obtain a boot image from your distribution. Here are two ways to use this.

- For Debian systems, you can always get a rescue image for latest X86 release from the following URL (given all on one line):
  `ftp://debian.crosslink.net/debian/dists/stable/main/disks-i386/current/images-1.44/rescue.bin`
- For Red Hat systems, x86 boot images are available via FTP, from the host ftp.redhat.com. It's kept in a directorv named /pub/redhat/linux/version/en/os/i386/images, where version is your Red Hat version number, and the file is called either boot.img (on older versions) or bootdisk. img.

To make a boot floppy from a Linux kernel image, use dd, giving the name of the kernel image as the input file and the name of the floppy device as the output file. To make the floppy in the first floppy drive a boot disk, containing the boot image file bootdisk. img, type:

```
#    dd if=bootdisk.img of=/dev/fd0
```

To remove the master boot record (MBR) of a disk, use dd to write the contents of /dev/zero over the first 512 bytes of the disk. To remove the master boot record of /dev/hda, type:

```
#    dd if=/dev/zero of=/dev/hda bs=512 count=1
```

Use caution with this command. If you erase the MBR on a disk that you rely on for booting, you won't be able to boot with it until you write a new, bootable image on that MBR.

6.6.4 Setting Up a Printer

Magicfilter

```
DEB: rnagicfilter
RPM: magicfilter
WWW: http://www.pell.portland.or.us/~orc/Code/magicfilter/
```

When a printer is properly configured on Linux, it is a pleasure to use, but a misconfigured printer can lead to all kinds of trouble -- including the dreaded "staircase effect," where a text file prints with each subsequent line of output offset to the right by the length of the previous line. If print services haven't been configured yet on your system, I strongly recommend that the rnagic filter package be installed; it includes filters for the automatic detection of file types -- when you print a file, it automatically converts it to the proper format for your printer.

6.6.5 Shutting Down the System

The most proper way to shut down a system is to use shutdown, which only root can do. This command notifies all users and processes of the impending shutdown, blocks new logins, and brings the system down cleanly. Options allow you to halt the system upon shutdown, or reboot it and begin again.

To halt the system once the shutdown is complete, use the -h option; to reboot the system after shutdown, use -r instead. The following recipes describe ways of using shutdown to do useful things. You can also bring the system down and then reboot it by typing Ctrl + Alt + Del from the console terminal; the shutdown process starts immediately when you press this key combination.

6.6.6 Shutting Down Immediately

Normally, you order the system shutdown by giving the time to do it as an argument; use the special now argument to begin the process immediately. Here are two ways to use this.

- To immediately shut down and halt the system, type:

```
#    shutdown -h now
```

- To immediately shut down the system, and then reboot, type:

```
#    shutdown -r now
```

You can follow the now argument with a quoted message that will be displayed on all terminals of all users currently logged in. To immediately shut down and halt the system, and send a warning message to all users, type:

```
#    shutdown -h now "The system is being shut down now!"
```

6.6.7 Shutting Down at a Certain Time

To shut down the system at a certain time, give that time (in 24-hour format) as an argument. Here are two ways to use this.

- To shut down and then reboot the system at 4:23 a.m., type:

```
#   shutdown -r 4:23
```

- To shut down and halt the system at 8:00 p.m., type:

```
#   shutdown -h 20:00
```

To shut down the system in a certain number of minutes, give that number of minutes prefaced by a plus sign (+). To shut down and halt the system in five minutes, type:

```
#   shutdown -h +5
```

Follow the time with a quoted message to be displayed on the terminals all logged-in users. To shut down and halt the system at midnight, and give a warning message to all logged-in users, type (all on one line):

```
#   shutdown -h 00:00 "The system is going down for maintenance at midnight"
```

6.6.8 Canceling a Shutdown

If you have given shutdown orders and decide that you don't actually want to shut the system down after all, run shutdown again with the -c optton. T~i~ command stops any shutdowns in progress. To cancel any pending shutdown, type:

```
#   shutdown -c
```

As with a normal system shutdown, you can send out an explanatory message with the cancel to be shown to all users. To cancel any pending shutdown and send an explanatory message to all logged-in users, type:

```
#   shutdown -c "Sorry, I hit the wrong key!"
```

This command cancels any pending system shutdown and displays the message, "Sorry, I hit the wrong key!" on all the terminals of anyone logged in. If the shutdown process has advanced to the point where all ter1iHI1~ii~ are stopped, you won't be able to run this command.

6.6.9 Going into Maintenance Mode

Sometimes it is useful to go into single-user maintenance mode -- maybe for running e2fsck on a hard drive partition or for performing some other system diagnostic. Do this by shutting the system down, and then give the root password to enter maintenance mode. To go into maintenance mode, type:

```
#   shutdown now
    shutdown messages

    Give root password for maintenance: abracadabra

#
```

This command will put you in a root shell on the console, where you can run e2f sck or do whatever it is you intended to do. In the example, the root user has the simple password of "abracadabra." To exit the shell, type Ctrl + D; depending on what you did, you may wish to reboot again with Ctrl – Alt – Del.

6.6.10 Managing Software

All Linux distributions come with a multitude of software programs (also called binaries, because programs are usually contained in a binary file that is executable). People are constantly contributing to the free software movement pubishing, their work online. This means that new software programs are constantly being added to Linux distributions, and current software programs are continually being improved -- new features to match new hardware, faster program execution, security updates, and so forth. A Linux system, therefore, needs to be kept up to date in order to reap the benefits of the latest free software. And sooner or later, you will want to install more programs, or you will want to upgrade your existing software when newer versions are available with some feature you desire.

The following recipes are for installing software on your system.

6.6.11 Getting and Installing a Linux Distribution

You can get a copy of Linux on CD-ROM from local or online vendors, or from a friend. Some distributions also allow for download off the Internet (recommended only if you have a fast Internet connection, of course). Wherever you get your copy of Linux, be sure you get the most recent version of a reputable distribution. If you are offered only an older version, you might pass on it: The software might not work with your brand-new hardware! If you'd rather buy a copy online, a recommended source is Cheap*Bytes ([http://www.cheapbytes.com]. There you can find various Linux distributions on CD-ROM for sale at affordable prices. Installation procedures vary from distribution to distribution, and specifics for installing any one distribution and version is outside this book's scope. However, the process usually involves making a Linux "boot disk" from a tool provided on CD-ROM, or starting Linux on your system. The hard drives are partitioned and formatted, and the Linux software is loaded onto them. Many users then recompile a Linux kernel that is customized for their needs and hardware. If you find this difficult, or need assistance, you should find your local Linux User Group and bring your computer there -- there are ways some LUG members who are especially happy to help install Linux oh a first-timer's computer, and many LUGs have regular "InstallFests" for this purpose, where participation is always free of charge.

6.6.12 Installing Packages for Your Linux Distribution

Linux distributions place software programs in packages, which are single files, usually compressed, that contain an archive of all of the files necessary for that particular program. Distributions have a software management system for installing and maintaining packages; upon installation, a package is first checked for other packages it might depend on to function correctly (its dependencies) In this way, you can be assured that the software you have installed on your system will function correctly. There are two primary package formats in the Linux world: the Debian DEB format, and Red Hat's Package Manager format, RPM. The former is used by the Debian and KNOPPIX distributions; the latter, by Red Hat, Mandrakc-linux, SuSE, and others. Still other distributions may not use packages at all, or may use source packages.Most of the software that you need for your system will be in the package format of your distribution, but you are not limited to even that. You can always install source packages, and even software that is packaged in another distribution's format: Debian has long been able to read and install RPM packages through special software, and the distributions that default to RPM (including Fedora and Red Hat Enterprise) equally have tools to use DEB. I am a bit old-fashioned in that I don't like to mix packaging systems with distributions, but some people may need to do so.

6.6.13 Installing a Source Package

Usually a source package is distributed in a compressed tar archive as a single file with a .tar .gz or .tgz file name extension. This collection of file is often called the sources of a computer program.

These files are usually placed in /usr/local/src and are uncompressed into their own directories. If they are source distributions, the software will have to be compiled. Usually a file named INSTALL or README in the package directory will instruct you how to do that. Many source packages come with a script named configure that is run to configure the compilation routine for your system, and then make is run with either install or all as an argument depending on what the package's particular documentation instructs. To compile and install a software package from its source directory, you generally type..

```
#    ./configure
     configuration messages
#    make install
     compilation messages
     installation messages

#
```

When you install source packages on your system, you are said to be installing local software-the files are kept in the /usr/local directory tree. Binaries are placed in /usr/local/bin, libraries in /usr/local/lib, man pages in /usr/local/man, and documentation in either /usr/local/doc or /usr/local/share/doc.

6.6.14 Installing a Shell Script

When you have a shell script that you want to install on the system, you first make sure that the script file is executable. Generally, the administrator installs new shell scripts in the /usr/local/bin directory. If you are on a multi-user system and you are the only user liable to run a particular script, you can put it in a special directory in your home directory tree -- the ~/bin directory is the standard recommendation here -- and then add that directory to your path. Not all executable script files are shell scripts. The first line of a script contains the full path name of the shell or other program that is to interpret and execute the script; sometimes the path may differ on your system from the one the script was written on, so you may have to change this line. For example, a script may start with the following line:

```
#    !/usr/local/bin/perl
```

This line means that the script is written in the perl language; the text after the "#!" is the full path name of the perl program, which in this case is /usr/local/bin/perl. If the location for a tool here in the first line of the script is different from the location on your system, it will not work. For example, if perl is located on your system at /usr/bin/perl, you will have to edit the first line in this script so that it matches that actual location. If you try to execute this script, and the system reports an error finding the file, you will have to change that first line to correspond to the location of the perl binary on your system. The which tool will output this location. To find out where perl is installed on your system, type

```
#    which perl
```

If the command returns /usr/bin/perl or some path name other than /usr/local/bin/perl, you will have to change the location in the first line of the script to the path name given below:

```
#    !/usr/bin/perl
```

If the output of the which command returns nothing, that means that the perl program is not installed on your system at all; in that case, you should install the perl software in order to run the script.

6.7 Hard Drive Partitioning

I have mentioned about hard disk partitioning above in step 2. Here I give you an optimum partition of a hard disk.

/swap directory	About double the main directory size. For example, a system having 128 MB memory should get 256 MB swap space.
/directory (root)	About 60% of the available space. That is about 1200 MB in a 2 GB hard disk.
/bin directory	About 20% of the available space. This is about 400 MB in a 2 GB hard disk.
/user directory	Remaining space

The size of /user should be the largest one. This is because all the users' directories and files, installed application softwares, web pages, log files etc. will be stored here only. You can have a perfectly running LINUX system on a single partitioned hard disk also. Partitioning the hard disk however, has the following advantages:

(a) Reduces the time required to perform file system checks.

(b) Mounting of one or more of your partitions as read only.

(c) Protects filesystem. If a filesystem gets destroyed due to some reason, you will probably lose only the files on a single partition. All other partitions will remain unaffected.

(d) Allows you to have multiple operating systems.

6.8 Booting a LINUX System

The booting process may differ from system to system and depending upon the type of hardware platforms being used. Generally, it involves checking of the basic subsystems of your computer, such as amount and validity of RAM, CPU time and speed, presence of floppy, CD-ROM or hard drive, keyboard and other attributes and peripherals. The booting process will fail, if there is hardware failure or if there is mismatch in the configuration. Next, comes the software part which is there in the BIOS of the bootable disk or CD, whichever may be mentioned in the bootable process of the BIOS. Then it will look for the boot code in the Master Boot Record (MBR) of the first hard disk. This area of the disk (MBR) contains the boot sector which loads the boot loader (viz. LILO, GRUB or BootMagic).

Once the operating system of Linux is loaded, Kernel takes over and performs the following operations:

- Initializes the RAM disk image.
- Performs timing tests
- Parse for any boot time kernel arguments.
- Recognise, set-up and initialise the CPU.
- Set up kernel memory and process handling.
- Open a console for displaying kernel boot messages.
- Initialize configured system devices.
- *Start memory handling*
- Set up and mount the file system
- Start the init command

The entire sequence of events that take place when the LINUX kernel is loaded can be found in the file usr/src/linux/init/main.c. If all goes well, you will see a "login" prompt. You can now login using your username and password.

6.9 Other Applications of Linux

6.9.1 Linux As a File Server

Perhaps the most fundamental need on a small network is a file server. File servers supply common places to store data, thus allowing shared files to be accessed by all users who need them and providing centeralized locations for backing up files (thereby eliminating and need for daily backups on each workstations on a network).

On a Windows or Novel network, this is generally done in one or two ways:

Using dedicated file servers

Using peer-to-peer networks

6.9.1.1 Dedicated File Servers

A dedicated file server is a system that is not used as a workstation but is set up as a central file server for the network. Users at different workstations or computers on the network can access directories on the file servers as if these were directories or disk drives on their own computes. Dedicated file serves offer the advantage or centralising the management of shared data and the backup process, but they cost more than peer-to-peer networks. They also offer the benefit of being able to set up network access control policies for confidential, core or shared data to ensure that unauthorised users don't have easy access to the information.

Linux is ideally suited to run as a low-cost file server for a small network. Linux can act as a file server to Unix/Linux, Windows and Novel networks making it an easily developed universal file server for a network containing different types of computers and workstations. In addition, the stability and the true multitasking capabilities of Linux make it a better choice than some other well-known options (such as Windows 95/98/Me) when a robust file-server solution is needed.

6.9.2 Peer-to-Peer File Sharing

In a peer-to-peer network, there is no central file server. Instead, each user decides which directories and drives on their PC should be shared on the network and what level of access control to impose. In this way, each workstation or computer on the network becomes a small file server.

While there is flexibility in this approach, allowing users to decide what data to share and with whom, there are also drawbacks. These include no centralized management of file sharing and access control policies, no centralized location for the backing up of critical data and a performance impact on a user's desktop when several other individuals on the network are accessing shared files on that user's PC. Linux can act as a reasonable peer-to-peer file server because of its ability to share with multiple types of networks. In addition, the true multitasking abilities of Linux mitigate much of the impact on performance when multiple users access files on a PC being used for other work.

Ultimately, though the low cost of setting up a Linux-based dedicated file server for a small network makes the dedicated file server approach more attractive because of the management and centralized backup benefits it provides.

6.9.3 Linux As a Print Server

In addition to file servers, print servers are another component of the network. Generally, dedicated file server also plays the role of offering print services to the network, serving double duty. It is not uncommon to find print services provided in both a centralised, dedicated fashion and the peer-to-peer method on the same network. Some users who use a printer heavily may warrant their own printers at their desks, while others who use the printers less frequently may share a printer located n a common area.

Often, a user with a dedicated printer shares it on the network so that other users can print documents for that user's attention directly to the dedicated printer rather than to the common shared printer. Linux, of course, can work in both environments. Linux supports a healthy range of printers, including most PostScript and HP-compatible PCL printers. In addition, its printer-sharing option include the ability to share printers on Unix/Linux, Windows and Novel networks.

6.9.4 Linux As a Database Server

Like most Unit platforms, Linux has long had a wide selection of free database packages available for it, including PostgreSQL and mSQL.

- Starting in 1998, though, major commercial database vendors gave Linux a boost in the database market by announcing and releasing Linux vesions of their products. For example:
- Red Hat has just released as of this writing the Red Hat Database, which integrated PostgreSQL7.1.2, optimized for Red Hat Linux 7.1. This database is targeted at mid-size businesses and independent corporate business units as an alternative to the large corporate database systems that seem to dominate the market.
- Oracle released in early 2001 its 9i suite of database/application server tools, optimized for the Linux 2.4 kernel. This promises to move a number of heavier business databases from higher-end Unix system to Linux.
- Sysbase Builder supports the SQL. Anywhere database Studio application on Linux. They have documented examples where the total cost of this package is about half the cost of the equivalent Window sNT/2000-style solution.
- IBM has released its flagship DB2 Universal Database for Linux, which encourages users to move their databases from higher-end Unix as well as Windows NT/2000 systems.

- Where Linux once provided only an alternative for file servers and Web servers in an organization, Linux can now be deployed as a robust, scalable database platform for an organizing using standard, widely-used relational database system.

As we mention late, combining a Linux-powered database with a Linux-powered Web server allows Linux to serve as a complete intranet server solution.

6.9.5 Linux As an Intranet server

If you follow the computing trends today, you have probably heard a lot about intranets: internal corporate network that use Internet technology such as TCP/IP, Web browsers and Internet-standard e-mail to share information and applications within an organisation. Many articles that discuss intranets and the hardware and software used to deploy them depict intranets as expensive endeavours suited only to large corporations and organizations. This couldn't be further form the truth.

Even in small offices, an intranet can provide a convenient way to publish information to be read by all employees through a Web browser. With a little forethought, you can eliminate some of the paperwork in your office by introducing electronic, online, Web-based forms for everything from leave requests to expense report submissions. In addition, if you have small database scattered across your organisation, each used on a daily basis by different users, an intranet can provide a common means by which occasional users of the data can access the information in a database without needing full accesses to the database tools used to create, maintain and update the data. By integrating the database with an intranet Web server, simple Web-based forms can be used to query the database.

Linux, which offers a wealth of powerful and flexible Web server as well as fully functional relational databasc systems, can allow the creation of an intranet server without the cost involved in deploying Windows Nt/ 2000, a commercial database such as Oracle and an expensive Web database integration tool. There are even some free tools for Linux that make it relatively easy to produce intranet programs and applications that make use f your corporate databases.

6.9.6 Linux As an Applications Server

Linux is by nature designed to act as both a file/print/intranet server and a full fledged applications servers. With an applications server, applications actually run on the server and are only displayed on a terminal or workstation, using the X Windows protocol or a terminal connection such as Telnet.

In contrast, on many typical Windows networks the applications run on the desktop and the data is stored on the server and accessed there. For some types of applications and in some situations, centralizing the running of applications can bring both performance and management benefits. If you are running a Windows or Novell network, a Linux system can act as an application server for several purposes:

Running character-based programs such as powerful Unix/Linux mail software.

Running a custom-designed, character-based database interface to centralised Linux database.

Accessing custom in-house applications, such as a corporate telephone book, designed to run in a Unix/Linux shell.

If you install an X server on a Windows desktop, you can even deliver centrally managed X Windows applications to the desktop while running the applications on a Linux applications server. Where budgets are low, Linux can create full-fledged GUI networks without the hardware or software expense of running Windows 95/98/Me or NT/2000. For instance, I have deployed a 10-desktop network running Linux exclusively. The desktops are all 486-class machines with 8MB of RAM. It would be exceptionally difficult to run Windows plus Microsoft Office on them and the cost for the necessary software licenses would run over US$300 per desktop. But with Linux on their older hardware, these systems can act as simple X terminals, displaying applications that run on a single applications server. In this case, the applications server is a Pentium 2000MHz system with just 98 MB or RAM. With the development and free release of several Linux office suites, software licensing costs are essentially down to zero.

A network like this can provide performance to the user that feels like a low end Pentium system with 32MB of RAM running Windows 95/98/Me. All of the management of software, user accounts, backups and system maintenance can be done centrally on one or two servers. Of course, this type of solution takes a fundamental strategic decision: not to use popular Windows-based productivity applications. But where cost is of the essence of the availability of modern hardware is limited, Linux makes a strong candidate for an organisation-wide computing platform.

6.9.7 Linux As a Router

The concept of a router is simple: Where two or more networks need to be connected, a router is the device that makes it possible to communicate between the networks. Routers come in all shapes and sizes from software-based routers running on Windows NT/2000 servers to hardware routers form well-known vendors such as Cisco. Routers can connect to networks in different ways, using technology ranging from regular modems to Ethernet cards to ISDN connections. Let's consider an example: an office with a small network that is connected the Internet by a high-speed connection such as DSL or a cable modem. That is, a small company has a single high-speed connection to the Internet but has a network of two or more computers that would like to share the connection.

A router for this situation offers a single Ethernet connection to the local network and corresponding high-speed connection to the Internet. All computers on the network send all packets to the router. The router decides if the packet is destined for another location on the local network or for an outside address (in other words, somewhere on the Internet). All local packets are sent by the router back out in on the Ethernet connection to the local network. If a packet is destined for the outside world, it is sent through the high-speed connection. Since it is always connected, network packets do not have to wait for a modem connection to get to the Internet. Similar routing situation include connecting two separate Ethernet networks through a router that has two or more Ethernet connections. The basic configuration of other high-speed networks such as Fast Ethernet (100Mbps), Gigabit Ethernet (1000Mbps), or Asynchronous Transfer Mode (155Mbps and up) 9s similar.

Linux has all the features needed to act as a router:

- Support for multiple Ethernet cards
- Support for regular modems and high-speed connections such as DSL and cable modems.
- Support for IP forwarding (the means by which packets can be received, analyzed and routed by the Linux-based router)

In fact, for small Ethernet to-Ethernet interconnectivity or Ethernet-to-high-speed-connection Internet routing, a Linux-based solution can be far less expensive than dedicated hardware routers and once it is properly configured can be very secure and reliable.

6.9.8 Linux As a Workstation

A final use of Linux in a small office environment is as the actual desktop operating system. If the application base available in Linux is suitable to the work of the office, then Linux-based desktops provide the following advantages:

- Stability and performance
- Full remote management by the network administrator
- Full network backup capabilities
- Lower cost of ownership in comparison with Windows-based desktops.

Where money is available, high-powered Linux workstations can offer speed rivalling that of the more expensive Windows-speed Systems. Linux also offers peer-to-peer networking that is more robust and offers better performance than is seen on many systems, especially those running Windows 95/98/Me. Also, as mentioned in the previous section, Linux can enable low-end or old hardware that can't run the latest Windows software to become full-fledged X terminals, providing performance on obsolete desktop hardware that feels like that of a low-end Pentium system.

6.9.9 What is X Windows?

Put in its simplest terms, X Windows is a complete graphics interface for Unix and by extension, for Linux. But this doesn't say it all. X Windows is a highly configurable environment that provides a broad range of flexible options for both the user and the application developers producing software to run under X Windows.The core X Windows concept is the client-server framework. What this means in practical terms is that X Windows provides an environment that is not bound to a single processor.

Applications can run on different servers and machines on a network and applications can display to X Windows terminals and workstation elsewhere on the network.This separation between where an application runs and where it is displayed is a concept missing in the Windows and Macintosh environments, which tie the application to the display. The benefit of this separation is that in a networking environment, it is possible to have sophisticated graphics desktops displaying applications that are running on well-maintained, powerful and easy-to-manage central application servers. In fact, this very capability is what gives Unix/Linux and X Windows such a good reputation among professional system administrators of large networks.

Another concept introduced in the X Windows environment is the separation of windowing form the interface. On an X windows system, two applications must run to provide a complete GUI. The first is the X server, which sets up the graphics displays (i.e, resolution, refresh rate and color depth), displays the windows and tracks mouse movements, keystrokes and multiple windows. But an X server does not provide menus, windows borders, or mechanism for moving, switching, minimizing or maximizing windows. There is no fancy color background no sophisticated window borders or menu controls, and no other features that make a complete GUI. All these features are provided by a second application called a window manager. The features of the window frames the control buttons and the control menus as well as a Taskbar and a virtual desktop system. The window manager provides all of these. The window manager talks to the X server in a standard predefined way as does the X server to the X applications. This means that different window manages with different interface features can all talk in this standard way to the X server. Likewise, the variety of X server that are available, which offer support for different graphics cards, monitors, and other performance features, can also talk in a standardised way to application.

610 Microsoft Windows vs. X Windows

Given some of the descriptions of X Windows you have seen, it would be natural to assume that Microsoft Windows and X Windows are pretty much the same thing. The reality though, is that they are fundamentally different beasts. For example, Microsoft Windows is a complete operating system, with everything from a kernel to a shell to a windowing environment and more. X Windows is just one piece of that operating system puzzle the windowing environment. Another contrast is in the interface: The Microsoft Windows interface is fairly rigid while the X Windows interface has an amazingly flexible and customizable design.

6.10.1 Similarities

So, what is similar about X Windows and Microsoft's current operating system? The main similarities are that they both provide graphical interfaces and make it possible to work with multiple windows. On top of this, they allow the user to interact with information using more than a keyboard and plain characters. Users can utilize a mouse as well as a keyboard, and can create interfaces that combine menus, forms, windows, and dialog boxes.

6.10.2 Differences

There are numerous differences between the two windowing systems. The main differences are in the following areas:

- Flexibility of the interface
- Fine tuned control over the interface configuration
- Client server technology

6.10.2.1 Flexible Interface

The flexiblity of the X Windows interface is one of the joys of this environment for many users. As discussed already, the separation of the user interface layer from the basic windowing layer makes it possible to create multiple interfaces for X Windows through the creation of different window managers. Multiple interfaces do not simply provide subtle differences in appearance, as some customization tools for the Microsoft Windows interface offer, rather, they allow complete redesigns of the user interface from a window manager to window manager.

6.10.2.2 Fine Tuned Control

Another advantage of the X Windows environment is that if offers fine tuned control over all aspects of the windowing environment and the interface. By setting any of dozens of settings, it is possible to control all aspects of the environment, from the background and foreground window colours to cursor colour, default font, and default window size. Users can also define modes of interaction. For instance, it is possible to use the mouse pointer to make a window automatically jump to the foreground or to change cursor focus to a background window. In additon, these and other features can be defined on a per-applicaiton basis, creating different settings for each application so that each application lauches in the most convenient way possible. It is also possible to define which windows and applications open each time the X environment starts, as well as have the sytgem make logical choices about which window manager to use when starting X Windows.

6.10.2.3 Client Server Environment

As mentioned previously, the X Windows world works on a client server model in which applications are clients to an X server that drives the physical display. This has made X Windows well adapted to network environments, allowing applications to urn on one machine on the network while displaying their output on another. Microsoft Windows lacked this ability until recently and now has it only in a limited and expensive fashion through its Terminal Server services on high-end mulitiuser Windows NT and 2000 system. In the Linux, Unix, and X worlds, even the lowliest system is capable of playing either the client role or the server role in this X windows client server model.

6.11 Linux for PowerPc Processors

The LinuxPPC project is managed and developed by PowerPC Linux. It offers a stable and complete distribution that runs a wide range of Power Macintosh computers. Supported applications and features include the following:

- PCI bus systems
- SCSI and IDE hard disk drives
- Multimedia support
- Web browsers such as Netscape
- X Windows and a wide range of window managers
- Java JDK 1.2.2

A project is also under way to develop an emulator of the Mac OS to run inside Linux on the PowerPC just as Wine is an attempt to develop a Windows emulator for Linux on the Intel x86 CPU.

Let us Revise

1. Linux can be downloaded free from Internet.
2. Linux has roots in Unix.
3. There are various versions of Linux available depending upon distributor.
4. Linux is a multitasking operating system.
5. Linux offers support for computer with multiple processors, such as dual-Pentium III systems.
6. Linux can be developed as an applications server.
7. A wide variety of programming and scripting languages and tools are available for Linux and all Unix operating systems.
8. X Windows is a highly flexible and configurable GUI environment that runs on Linux as well as on most Unix systems.
9. Linux provides a wide range of Internet software.
10. Free databases such as mSQL and PostgreSQL have been available for Linux.
11. Linux kernel and most of the applications written for Linux are available for free on the Internet.
12. Kernel is the core of the Linux system.
13. Shell is the program which accepts commands from the users.
14. In Linux everything is a file.
15. Linux uses a forward slash instead of backward slash.
16. You can give either a Relative pathname or an Absolute pathname to the Linux files.
17. Linux can be installed using an installation disk which can be created from the Linux CD.
18. Hard disk has to be partitioned if you have to have more than one operating system.
19. Linux kernel takes over when the booting process of Linux finishes.
20. There are commercial applications for Linux as well as commercial distributions of Linux.
21. Red Hat Linux also offers a tool for configuring the free version of X Windows, XFree86 called Xconfigurator.
22. Distributors can be built on different versions of the kernel, can include different sets of applications, utilities, tools, and driver modules, and can offer different installation and upgrade programs to ease management of the system.
23. Red Hat Software (www.redhat.com) has emerged as the favourite Linux distribution for most users.
24. Debian offers more than 3950 software packages using its own package management system, which is designed to offer similar functionality to that offered by the Red Hat distribution.
25. It is possible to get Linux up and running on a 386-based computer with only 4MB of RAM.
26. Linux actually requires far fewer resources to perform far more functions than the average Windows 98 or Windows NT/2000 system.
27. A sound card will enhance your working under Linux.
28. In a peer-to-peer network, there is no central file server.
29. Linux, which offers a wealth of powerful and flexible Web server as well as fully functional relational database systems.
30. If you install an X server on a Windows desktop, you can even deliver centrally managed X Windows applications to the desktop while running the applications on a Linux applications server.

31. Linux in a small office environment is as the actual desktop operating system.
32. X Windows is a complete graphics interface for Unix and by extension, for Linux.

Multiple Choice Questions

1. Cost of Linux operating system is:
   (a) $100 (b) $480 (c) Its FREE
2. Windows version of Linux is:
   (a) L Windows (b) X Windows (c) M Windows
3. Linux can be loaded on PC:
   (a) Yes (b) No
4. There is no software based on Linux:
   (a) True (b) False
5. Database available on Linux is known as:
   (a) mSQL (b) lSQL (c) Not available
6. Popular distributor of Linux is:
   (a) Red Hat (b) Blue Hat (c) Green Hat
7. Linux can be installed from :
   (a) floppy disk (b) CD ROM (c) both
8. Linux components have :
   (a) kernel (b) shell (c) both
9. Hard disk is partitioned to have :
   (a) another operating system (b) more hard disk space (c) less hard disk space
10. There are two types of pathnames, Absolute and :
    (a) Relational (b) Relative (c) Reasonable
11. In Linux directory is also a :
    (a) shell (b) hard disk (c) file
12. Linux file system uses :
    (a) backslash (b) forward slash (c) both

True/False Questions

1. Linux can be downloaded free from Internet.
2. Linux is similar to Unix.
3. Linux has no versions.
4. Linux does not support multitasking operating system.
5. Linux can be developed as an applications server.
6. A wide variety of programming and scripting languages and tools are available for Linux .
7. X Windows is a highly flexible and configurable GUI environment that runs on Linux as well as on most Unix systems.

8. There are no software available for Linux operating systems.
9. Kernel is the core of the Linux system.
10. Shell is not there in Linux.
11. In Linux everything is a file.
12. Linux uses a backward slash in its file system.
13. You can give either a Relative pathname or an Absolute pathname to the Linux files.
14. Hard disk has to be partitioned if you have to have more than one operating system.
15. Red Hat Software is the most popular version of Linux.
16. It is not possible to get Linux up and running on a 386-based computer with only 4MB of RAM.
17. A sound card will enhance your working under Linux.
19. Linux, which offers a wealth of powerful and flexible Web server as well as fully functional relational database systems.
20. Linux in a small office environment is as the actual desktop operating system.
21. X Windows is a complete graphics interface for Unix and by extension, for Linux.

Matching Columns

Match the matter in Column A with the matter in Column B.

Column A	Column B
A. Red hat Linux	1. Operating system
B. Pathnames: Relative and	2. X Windows
C. Partition hard disk to have	3. Forward slash
D. Kernel	4. file
E. Cost of linux software	5. 128 MB
F. Linux is an	6. mSQL
G Everything in Linux is a	7. It is free
H. Linux uses	8. Absolute
I. Windows version of Linux	9. A version of Linux
J. RAM requirement for Linux installation	10. CD ROM
K. Linux database	11. Another operating system
L. Linux can be installed from	12. A Linux component

Fill in the Blanks with appropriate words

a. mSQL	b. Forward	c. X Windows	d. Networking
e. Relative	f. floppy disk	g. Shell	h. Partitioned
i. Absolute	j. Red	k. CD-ROM	l. 128
m. files	n. Operating	o. Kernel	

1. Linux can be installed from _______ and ________.
2. _______ is a Linux database.
3. Popular linux version is _______ hat linux.
4. Windows version of Linux is known as ______ .
5. A hard disk has to be __________ to have second operating system.
6. RAM requirement for Linux installation is _____ MB.
7. Linux files can have _______ and ________ pathnames.
8. Linux uses ______ slash.
9. Linux is an ________ system.
10. In Linux even directories are ______.
11. _____ and _____ are part of Linux components.
12. Linux supports __________.

Descriptive Type Questions

1. What is Linux?
2. How was Linux developed?
3. How can you use Linux as an operating system?
4. Is Linux a multiuser operating system?
5. Describe the various applications of Linux system.
6. How can Linux be obtained?
7. What are the feautes of Linux?
8. What is meant by Linux distribution?
9. Write a short note on Red Hat Linux distributor.
10. What are the minimum requirements for Linux working on PC?
11. How does Linux support the file system?
12. Write a short note on Linux as database server.
13. What is X Windows?
14. How does it differ from Microsoft Windows?
15. Describe the various components of Linux.
16. Which are the main directories of Linux?
17. How would you install Linux?
18. What are the hardware requirements for installing Linux?
19. What are the software requirements for installing Linux?
20. What steps you have to follow before installing Linux?

Answers to Objective Type Questions

Multiple Choice Questions

1. c	2. b	3. a	4. b	5. a
6. a	7. c	8. c	9. a	10. b
11. c	12. b			

True False Questions

1. T	2. T	3. F	4. F	5. T
6. T	7. T	8. F	9. T	10. F
11. T	12. F	13. T	14. T	15. T
16. F	17. T			

Matching Columns

A. 9	B. 8	C. 11	D. 12	E. 7
F. 1	G. 4	H. 3	I. 2	J. 5
K. 6	L. 10			

Fill in the Blanks

1. f, k	2. a	3. j	4. c	5. h
6. l	7. e, i	8. b	9. n	10. m
11. g, o	12. d			

Word Processing 7

7.1 Word Processing Concepts

Word processor is a computer program for processing of words, very similar to a food processor (*mixie*) which processes food. Most of the word processors would start from a blank screen assumed to be a blank page with a blinking starting point known as **Cursor**. For all practical purposes it is like a typewriter, but it is much more than that.

You can type the text (even enter graphics) in the word processor, save it under a name to recall it again and again. Spell check it for errors, format it to look good, and then if needed print it too.

This makes it much easier for writing the text since you can make as many mistakes as you like since you can correct them by just pressing a key. This way you save a lot of paper and make the document look more neat and clean.

7.1.1 Some Important Terms of Word Processing

Before we go any further and study word processing, let us understand few basic terms of word processing:

Text	It is the matter which you type.
Document	It is whole text matter which you create, like a letter, or a chapter, etc.
Fonts	In typewriting you have just one type of handwriting. In word processing you can have your text written in many writings, these are called Fonts. Each font has its own way to writing the alphabets (A to Z) and even numerals (0 to 9).
Cursor	It is as said before, the blinking point which tells you where to start typing or what your current position is.
Arrow keys	These keys are on the arrow pads of your keyboard and are shown as: Up-arrow (↑), Down-arrow (↓), Left-arrow (←) and Right-arrow (→).
Space bar	It plays a very important role in word processing. The space between the words is given by this.
Tabs	These are used to set the text into tabular form.
Backspace	This is another important keyboard key which is used to delete the wrongly typed character in your text. You can even use the Del key for this.

7.1.2 Things which can be done by Word Processing

Let us now see what are the things which can be done by Word Processing and cannot be done on the typewriter.

Alignment	You can set your text in any alignment, e.g., Left, Right or Centre. You can even do box setting, i.e., aligned from both sides.
Deleting Mistakes	You can delete word, line, paragraph in a stroke and the rest of the matter will get adjusted automatically.

Line Spacing You can set line spacing according to your liking from one to nine.

MailMerging A very important feature of any word processing. This helps you in sending the same text to the different people, all in original format.

Moving the Cursor You can move your cursor from word to word or from paragraph to paragraph, if needed.

Naming a Document As mentioned earlier, you can name a document and recall it anytime from hard disk for editing, updating, correcting and even printing.

Overwriting Mistakes You can overwrite your mistakes on the screen itself. No more messing of eraser and spoiling of paper.

Page Breaks You can set a page break at any place within the text so that while printing it will jump to next page.

Page Numbers You can set page numbers according to your liking.

Search and Replace You can search for a particular word in the whole document and replace it with another one. You can even replace all the occurrence of the same word.

Spell Checking Probably the most important part of any word processing. Each word processor comes with a dictionary built inside it. You can check your text with it see whether any word has been wrongly typed.

7.2 Saving a Document File

It is the process by which you give the name to the file and save under that name. For saving, just select the **Save** option under **File** menu. You will get the dialog box, as shown here. Just type the name in the space provided for typing the filename and click **Save**. Your file will be saved under this name and automatically the title bar will show the name of the file on the top of the Word screen.

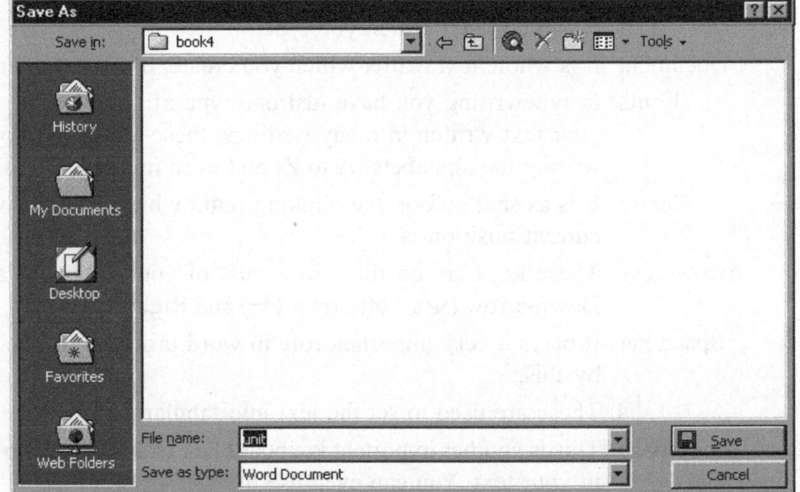

Let us understand the difference between **Save** and **Save As**. You save your document file as you save any other file. **Save As** option allows you to save with another name, maybe another format at another drive/directory.

It is not that the system will not allow you to save the file with the same name under **Save As** option. It will ask you whether you want to overwrite the file which exists. This is just a precautionary option so that you do not overwrite a file with the same name accidentally.

7.3 Closing a Document File

You can choose **Close** command from **File** menu to close the document file. Or you can do so by clicking at ☒ button on the extreme right top of the word document. But don't forget to save the file before closing else the software will ask you to do so.

7.4 Opening an Existing Document

Opening of the file can be done by 2 methods if you are already working under Word.

7.4.1 From File menu

There is an **Open** command under the **File** menu. Click at it to open the Open dialog box as shown next.

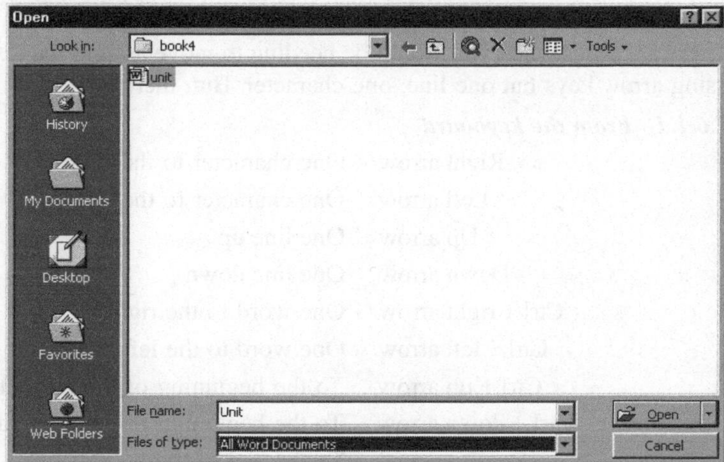

7.4.2 From Open Icon

You can get the same Open dialog box by clicking at Open icon on the **Standard** toolbar.

In both cases you will get the dialog box shown here. From here you can click the file you want to open. If it is not there on the screen, try to locate it in different directories with the help of icons on the left or from the drop-down list of directories.

7.5 Selecting Text

For any text to be formatted, it has to be selected. There are various ways of selecting the text.

7.5.1 Selecting from keyboard

For selecting, place the cursor at the left of the word to be selected and then do the following:

Press shift + right arrow	To select one character to the right
Press shift + right arrow	To select one character to the left
Press shift + up arrow	To select one line up
Press shift + down arrow	To select one line down
Press shift + end	To select to the end of the line
Press shift + home	To select to the beginning of the line
Press shift + ctrl + end	To select till end of the document
Press shift + ctrl + home	To select from the beginning of the document
Press ctrl + a	To the complete text

7.5.2 Selecting the text with the mouse

For this do the following:

1. Position the cursor to the left of the first character to select.
2. Hold down the left mouse button and drag it to where you want to stop.
3. Release the mouse.

7.5.3 Selecting with mouse clicks

1. Double click to select a word.
2. Triple click to select the full paragraph.
3. Ctrl + click in a sentence to select the full sentence.

7.6 Editing Text

For editing you can do various things with your text. Few of them are given here.

7.6.1 Moving the Text

There are times when you would be needing to move around the text in the document. This can be done by using arrow keys but one line, one character. But, there are other methods too.

7.6.1.1 From the keyboard

Right arrow	One character to the right
Left arrow	One character to the left
Up arrow	One line up
Down arrow	One line down
Ctrl + right arrow	One word to the right
Ctrl + lcft arrow	One word to the left
Ctrl + up arrow	To the beginning of the current paragraph
Ctrl + down arrow	To the beginning of the next paragraph
End	To the end of the current line
Ctrl + end	To the end of the document
Home	To the start of the current line
Ctrl + home	To thc start of the document
Page up	Up one screen
Page down	Down one screen
Ctrl + page up	To the first character on the current screen
Ctrl + page down	To the last character on the current screen

7.6.1.2 Moving with Mouse

To position the cursor using the mouse, move the mouse pointer to where you want it and click.

7.6.2 Changing Style of the Text

By style in Word, we mean the appearance of the text. The various formats supported by Word are:

Bold
Italics
Underline

These are the main styles and we had earlier used them in our letter. But, if you go deep into the working of the software, you would see that it allow you to convert the character to:

Strikethrough
Double strikethrough
Superscript
Subscript
Shadow
Outline
Emboss
Engrave

Small Caps
All Caps
Hidden

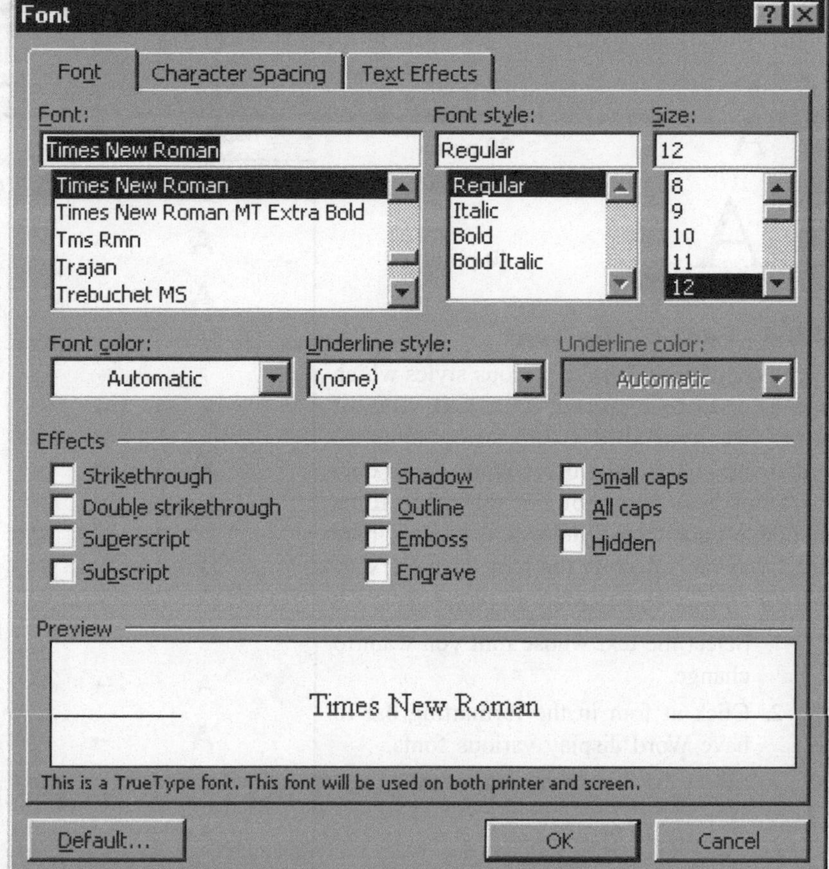

The first 3 are there on the Standard toolbar only. They can be used by just clicking at them. For example, if you have to make a word, Bold, then select the word and click at B in the Standard toolbar, it will be made Bold. Similarly, you can make the characters italics and underlined.

Bold
Italics
Undeline

The above example shows how they appear after changing the styles. For the other styles you have to do the following:

1. Select the text whose style you have to change.
2. Click at Format menu and select Font from it.
3. In the dialog box, select the option you want to use.
4. You text would be changed accordingly.
5. Various options of the text are shown above.

7.6.3 Size of Text

The size of the text, pertains to the thickness of the text. As the size increases, the width of the character also increases. In fact, the proportionate height of the character also increases. You can change the size of the text from 2 places in Word.

7.6.3.1 From the Formatting Bar

1. Select the text whose size you want to change.
2. Click at font size in the formatting bar to have Word display various sizes.
3. Select the size which you want.

7.6.3.2 From the Font Dialog Box

1. Select the text whose size you want to change.
2. Click at Format and select Font.
3. From the Font dialog box, select the size you want to have.
4. Click Ok to have your text changed to the required size.

The following examples would show how the font size make the difference:

A 12 point

A 20 point

A 40 point

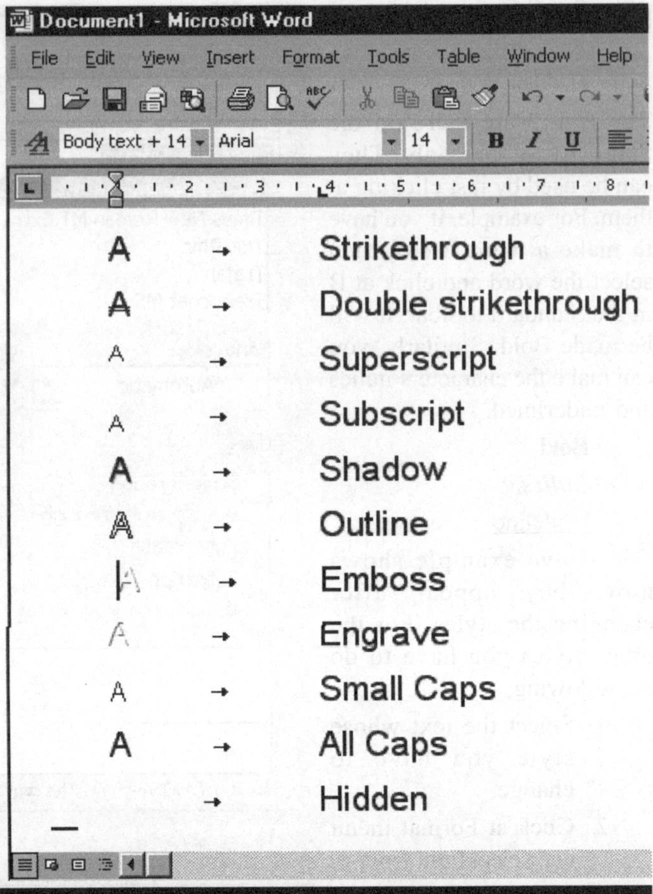

7.6.4 Font of the Text

Fonts are nothing but the various styles which can be used to represent your text. Lots of fonts are available from fancy ones to ornamental types. Microsoft Word on its own does not have fonts, but, it takes the fonts available under the Windows. As usual there are 2 ways of selecting the font for the text.

7.6.4.1 From Formatting Toolbar

1. Select the text whose font you want to change.
2. Click at font in the formatting bar to have Word display various fonts.
3. Select the font which you want.

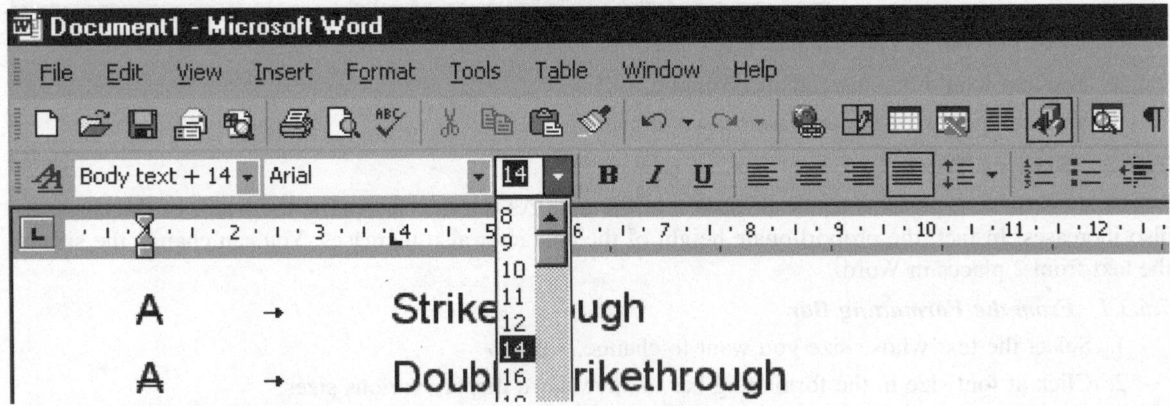

7.6.4.2 From the Font Dialog Box

1. Select the text whose font you want to change.
2. Click at Format and select Font.
3. From the Font dialog box, select the font you want to have.
4. Click Ok to have your text changed to the required font.

The figure next shows some of the fonts available.

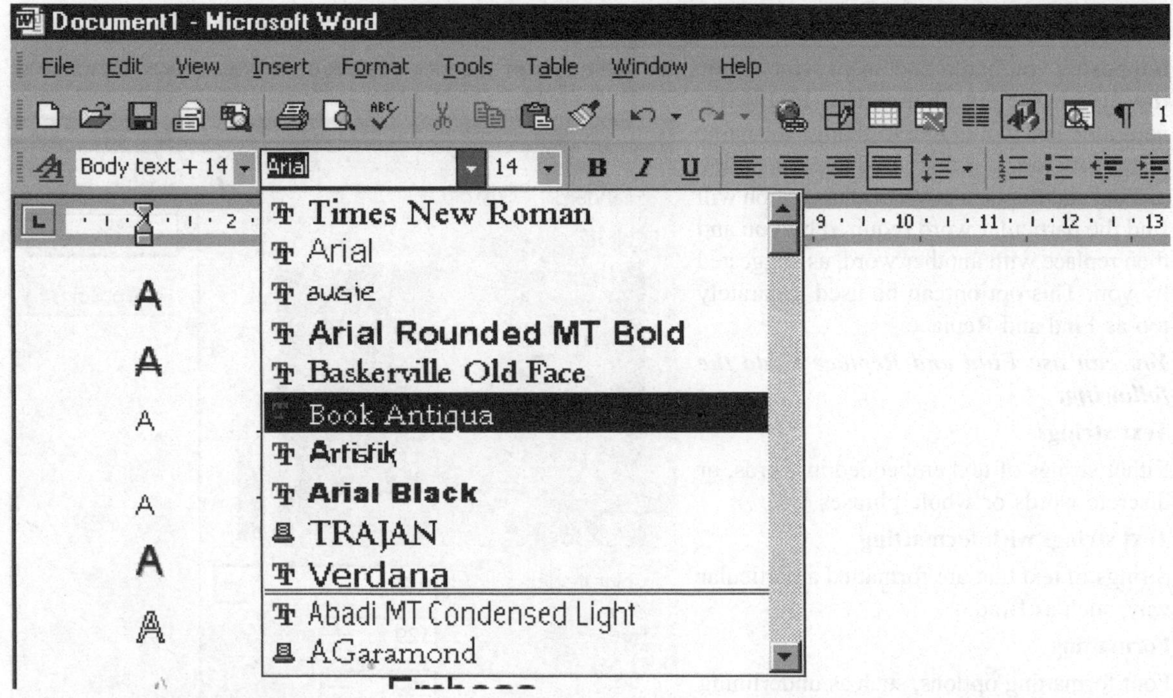

7.6.5 Colour of the Text

You can if you want can change the colour of the text too. Since of the printers now-a-days have the colour capabilities, you can print your letters in colours too. Microsoft Word supports the full colour features. You can have various colours for various portions of the text in your document.

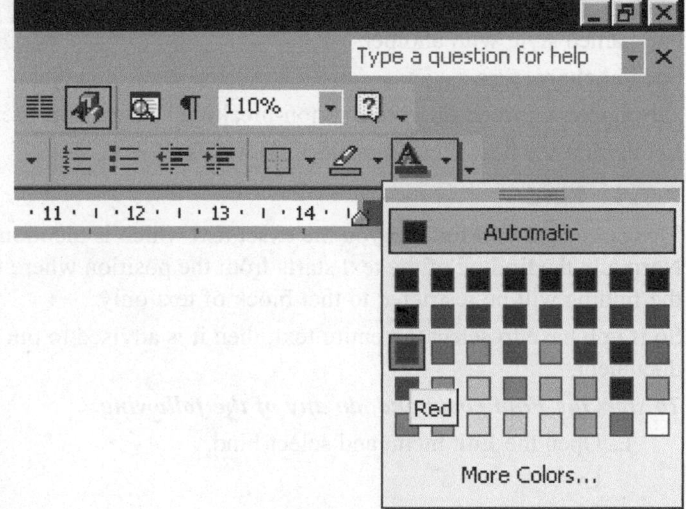

For changing the colour of the text, do the following:

1. Select the text whose colour you want to change.
2. Click at A on the formatting toolbar.
3. A colour template would be shown to you.
4. Select the colour which you want.
5. Your text would be changed to that colour.
6. If you click at More Colors, another dialog box would give you more options of colours to choose from.
7. Both the dialog boxes are shown .

7.7 Finding and Replacing Text

Supposing you had a document which contained the name of the city as **Calcutta**. Now since the name of the city has been changed to **Kolkatta**, naturally, you would like to change the name of the city too. For this you have the option of Find and Replace in Word. This option will find the particular word required by you and then replace with another word, as suggested by you. This option can be used separately too as Find and Replace.

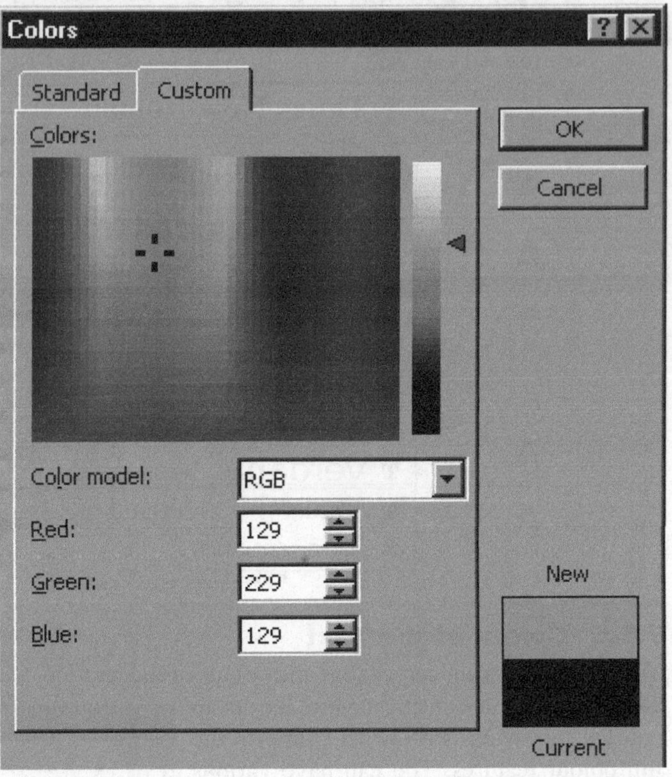

You can use Find and Replace to do the following:

Text strings

Either strings of text embedded in words, or discrete words or whole phrases.

Text strings with formatting

Strings of text that are formatted a particular way, such as Bold.

Formatting

Font formatting options, such as underlining and bold, that are not necessarily associated with words or text.

Styles

Find all instances of a named style or replace one named style with another.

Special characters

Tab markers, forced line breaks, non-breaking spaces, non-breaking hyphens, whitespace, and so on.

Let us first see how the command Find works.

7.7.1 Find

This command will find for you the exact text which is mentioned in its box and will stop for further action. Normally the finding of the text starts from the position where the cursor is. If you have selected some text, the finding will be restricted to that block of text only.

So if you have to select the entire text, then it is advised to put the cursor at the beginning of the text in the document.

To start the Find command, do any of the following:

1. Open the Edit menu and select Find.

   Or

2. Press Ctrl + F.

   Or

3. Click the Find icon, which is part of Standard toolbar. If it is not there you can add it on your toolbar from the Add and Remove buttons.

Find and Replace dialog box, as shown next will appear in each of the above cases.

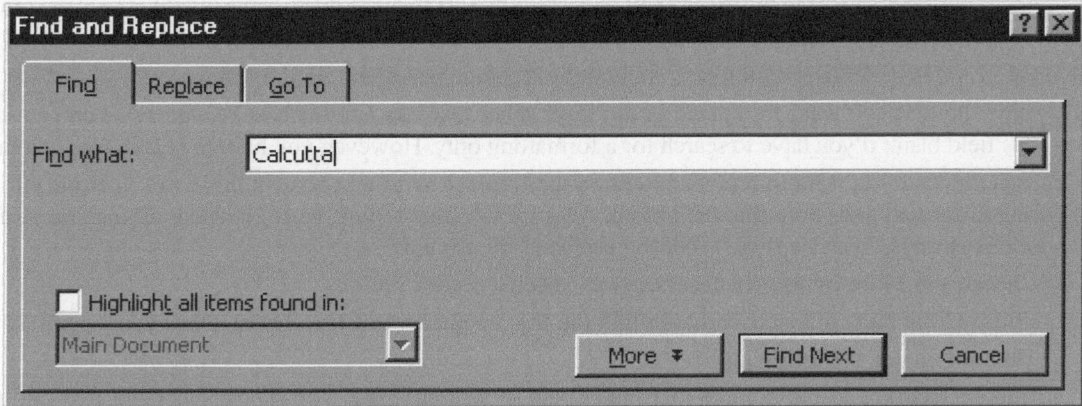

This is how you will use the Find command.

1. Type the text that you are seeking in the Find What? text box. This word or phrase is also referred to as the search string.
2. Choose the More button (if necessary) to specify search options.
3. Choose Find Next. Find looks through the document for text that matches your search strings. When it finds matching text, Word highlights the text in the document and stops. The Find and Replace dialog box remains on screen.
4. Choose Find Next if you want to continue the search for another instance of the search string. Click Cancel or press Esc to close the dialog box and return to the document. The text in the document is still highlighted.

When Word finishes the entire document, or if it could not find the search string in the document, a dialog box displays a message to that effect. Choose Ok to continue working in the document.

7.7.2 Replace Text

Next step after finding the required text is to replace it with some other text. For this we would call the command called Replace. To get the replace command do the following.

1. Open the Edit menu and select Replace.

   Or

2. Press Ctrl + H.

   Or

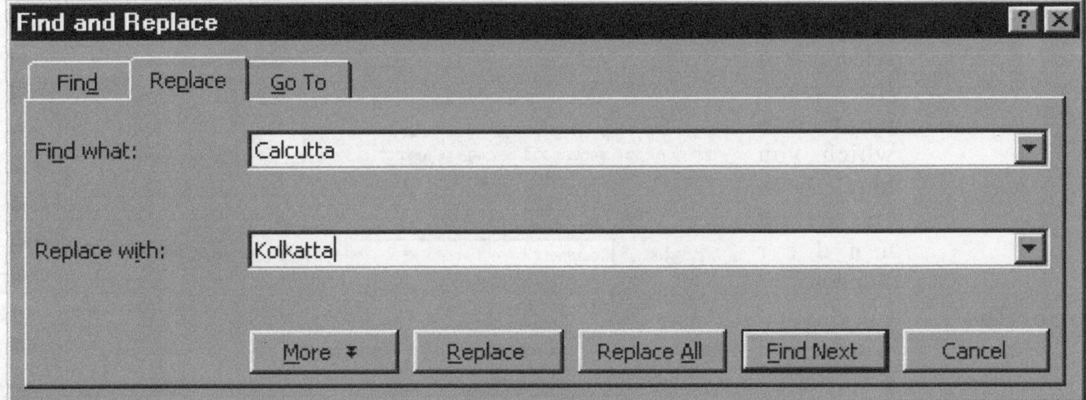

3. Click the Find icon, which is part of Standard toolbar. If it is not there you can add it on your toolbar from the Add and Remove buttons.

Now on the Find and Replace dialog box click at the Replace panel and do the following:

1. Type the text you want to replace in the Find What text box (in this case, *Calcutta*). You can leave this field blank if you have to search for a formatting only. However, you have to search for something.
2. Type the text you want to replace it with in the Replace With text box (in this case, *Kolkatta*). If you search for text and leave this field blank, you are in effect telling Word to delete all instances of the search strings, because they would be replaced by a blank.
3. Choose the More button (if necessary) to specify search options.
4. Choose Find Next to locate and highlight the first occurrence of text that matches your search string.
5. Then do one of the following:
   - Choose **Replace** to replace the text matching the search string with the replacement text and then locate the next occurrence of the search string in your document.
   - Choose **Find Next** to leave the text matching the search string unchanged and to locate the next occurrence of the search string.
   - Choose **Replace All** to replace text in the entire document that matches the search string with the replacement text.
6. Choose Cancel. Alternatively, press Esc to close the Find and Replace dialog box and return to the your document.

When Word has finished searching through the document and has replaced all occurrences of the search text or can't find any further occurrences, a message box appears. Click Ok to return to your document.

7.8 Printing Documents

No document preparation process is complete without printing it. For this we have the **Print** option under the **File** menu. Once clicked it gives rise to a dialog box as shown below. The various options on the dialog box are as follows:

Printer Select the printer to which you want to send the printing. From the drop-down list, you can select one of the many printers which you may have installed under Windows.

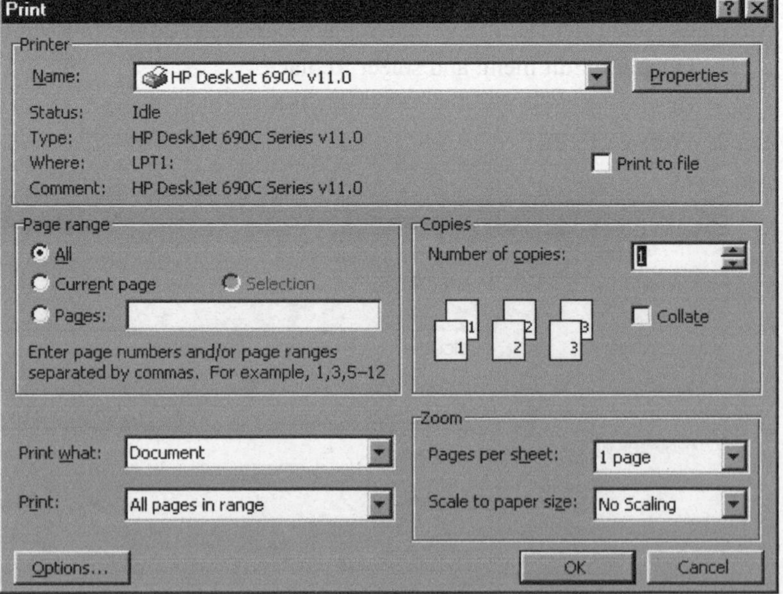

Properties Clicking at it would lead to a dialog

box having the properties of the selected printer. If some adjustments are to be made in the properties of the selected printer, they can be done here.

Print to file Sometimes it is possible that you may like to print the document to the printer which is not installed in your computer. In this case you will select this option and create a print file for that particular printer and copy the file and then print on that printer where it is installed.

Print range You may like to print few selective pages instead of printing the whole document. So either click **All**, for printing all pages of the document or **Pages**, for defining the pages you want to print. You can even print the current page, i.e., page on the screen.

Copies Word allows you to print multiple copies of the pages in the document. You can mention here the number of copies you want. What's more you can have the copies collated for you, if you select the **collate** option.

Print what Various options available here are Document, Document properties, Comments, Styles, AutoText entries, Key assignments. But, most of the time you would be printing with Document option.

Print You have the option of printing all pages or all **odd pages** or all **even pages**.

Zoom Pages per sheet allows you to print 1 to 16 pages of the document on one sheet. Scaling allows you to scale your document to the various sizes of the paper.

Options This will lead to the print options, already described under **Options** and select the option of your choice.

Once you are sure that you have selected all the options required by you, just click Ok to for document to start printing. However, do not forget to have the Printer ON before giving the final print command.

7.9 Creating and Printing Merged Documents

MailMerge is one of the very important application of any word processing software. Word has indeed made it very easy to operate. In MailMerge you have the variable data coming from a data source which can be either a database file, spreadsheet, or even a text file with fields marked in it. Then you have the document file whose text remains the same for all the subsequent merged files changing only the data which has been received from the source. So in fact you create multiple documents having the same text but having different fields depending upon the source. Well, one can think of various usages of the MailMerge. The most important being sending the same letter to various parties. Sending the same invitation to various guests. Sending payment reminders to various creditors. Calling all the directors to the same board meeting. In all these cases, the text would remain more or less the same but the name and address of the receiver would change. You can even change the salutation too, for example, Dear Mr. so and so, picking the name from the data source.

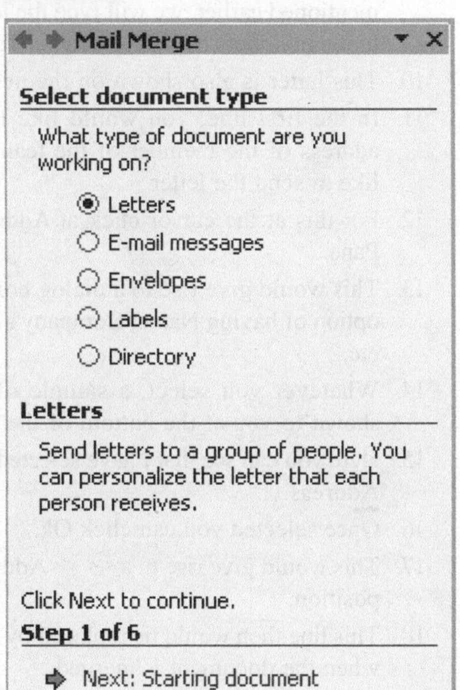

MailMerge in Word is done in steps. Creating document (text), data source and then merging them before printing. Let us see how it is done. For your information, here I am creating a appreciation letter for the various members of the victories Indian Cricket Team. So, lets start.

1. Start Word.
2. On the Tools menu, point to Letters and Mailing and then click Mail Merge Wizard to open the Mail Merge task pane showing Step 1 to 6 in the wizard.
3. In the task pane, click the Letters option, and then click Next: Starting document at the bottom of the pane, to reach the step 2, as shown on next page.
4. In the task pane, click the Use the current document option, then click Next: Select recipients at the bottom of the pane. Step 3 to 6 in the wizard appears, as shown on next pages.
5. In the task pane, click the Type a new list to type a new list of the recipients and click at Create to get a New Address dialog box, shown on next to next page.
6. Here type your first entry with all the details known to you. You can leave the fields blank too, if not required. After entering the first entry, you can click at New Entry to get the next blank form for filling. Once done click at Close to get Save dialog box, to name your data source.

Select starting document

How do you want to set up your letters?

- (•) Use the current document
- ( ) Start from a template
- ( ) Start from existing document

Use the current document

Start from the document shown here and use the Mail Merge wizard to add recipient information.

Step 2 of 6

➡ Next: Select recipients

7. Here you are shown the data that you have entered into the Mail Merge Recipients which you can edit, if you want to by clicking at the required field.
8. When pressed Ok, you are returned to Mail Merge with Step no. 4 displayed by Word, as shown on the next page.
9. In this step you have to type your document. Here as mentioned earlier, we will type the letter of congratulations to the members of Indian Cricket Team.
10. This letter is also shown on the next page.
11. In the first line, you would like to print the name and address of the member of the team to whom you would like to send the letter.
12. For this at the cursor click at Address Block in the Task Pane.
13. This would give rise to a dialog box, which gives you the option of having Name, Company's Name, Postal Address, etc.
14. Whatever you select, a sample of the same, would be shown to you at the bottom of the dialog box.
15. Here you can see that I have selected only Name and Postal Address.
16. Once selected you can click Ok.
17. This would give rise to a << <<Address Block>> >> at the position.
18. This line then would be replaced by the Name and Address when the document is merged.

Select recipients

- ( ) Use an existing list
- ( ) Select from Outlook contacts
- (•) Type a new list

Type a new list

Type the names and addresses of recipients.

 Create...

Step 3 of 6

➡ Next: Write your letter

⬅ Previous: Starting document

19. In the next line, I have typed Dear and after this I want the name of the member.
20. So I would again click at Address Block in the Task Pane to get the above dialog box, once again.
21. This time I will select the name only and not the address.
22. Once this is done, we would type the complete letter.
23. So now that the matter of Step 4 is complete, we will click at Next in Task Pane to go to the next step.

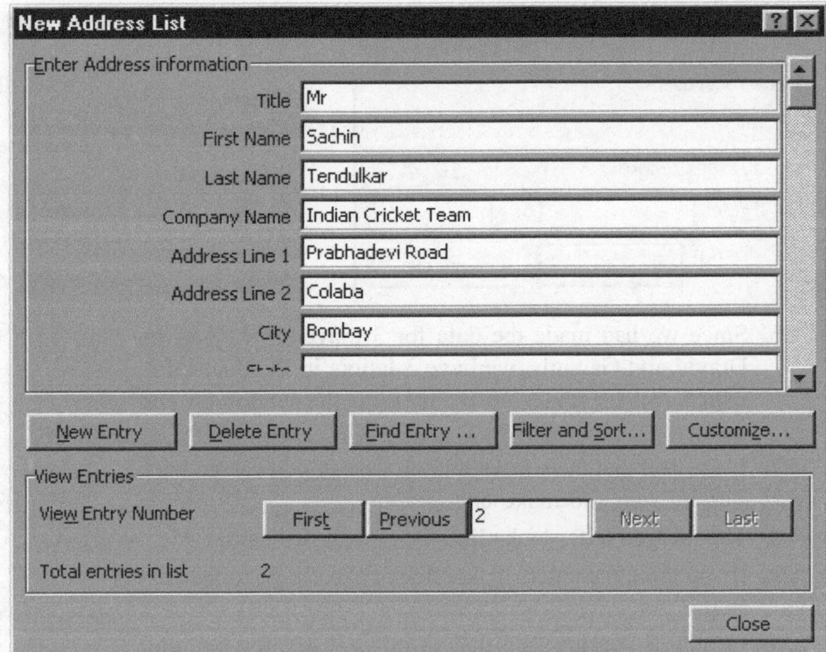

24. The Step 5 would ask you to preview the letter, which Word has already merged with your source data.
25. So now your document has number of letters, each belonging to one data source.

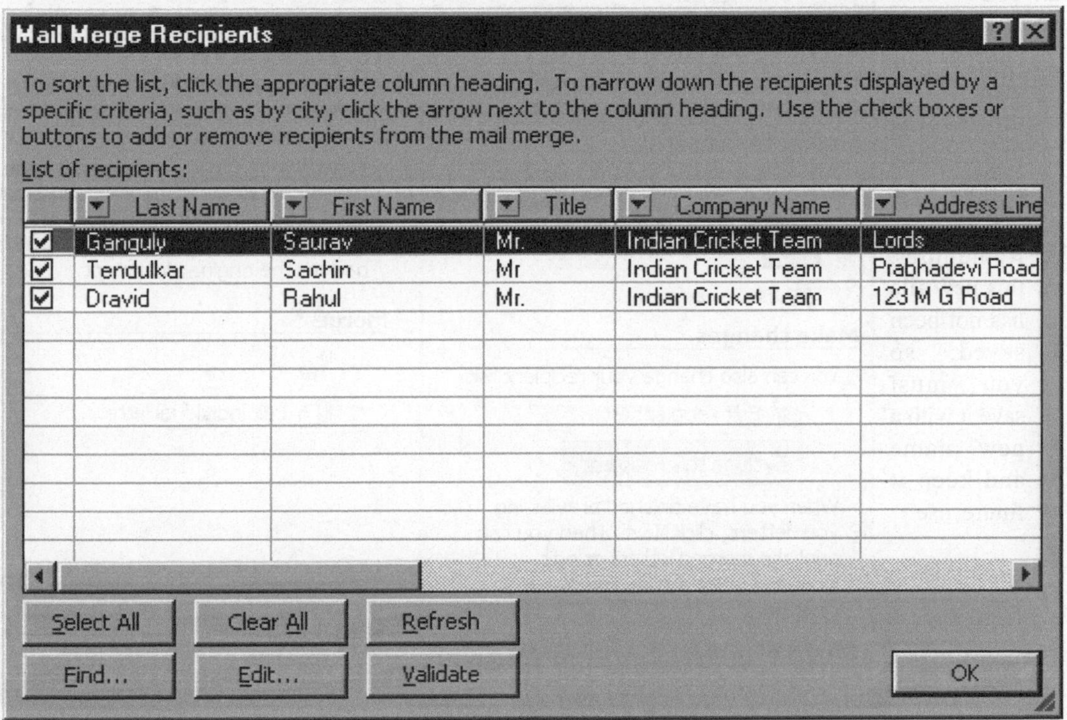

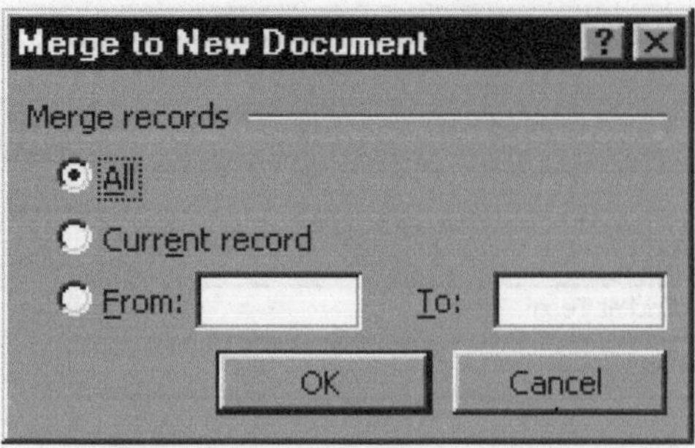

26. Since we had made the data for 3 players, i.e., Sachin, Dravid and Ganguly, we have 3 letters in the document, which can be reviewed by moving the cursor up and down.
27. If you feel that there is something wrong, you can go back step by step and make changes.
28. The merged letter looks like the one shown next.
29. If you think the letter is Ok, click at Next to go to the next step.
30. In Step 6 you are told that Word is ready for the mail merge, if you are.
31. You have the choice of either printing or editing the letters individually.
32. You also have the choice of merging all the records or some selected ones.
33. Remember, this new file has not been saved, so you must save it with a new name and keep it future use.

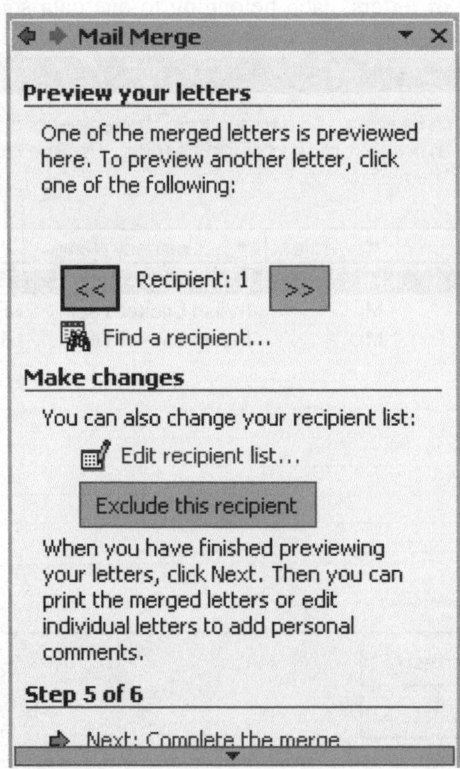

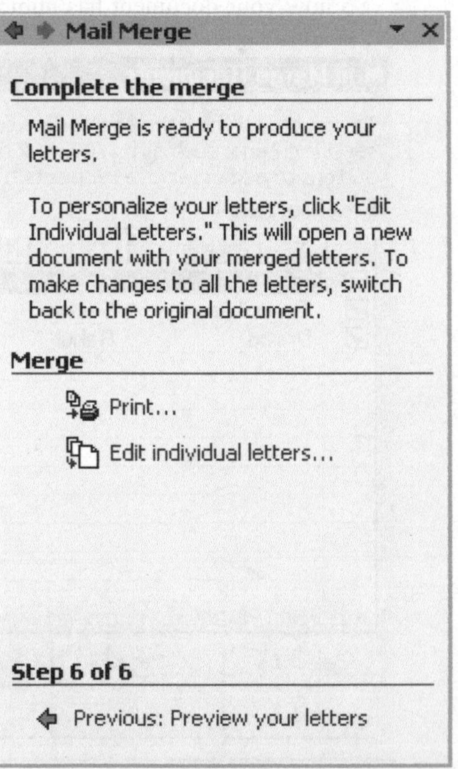

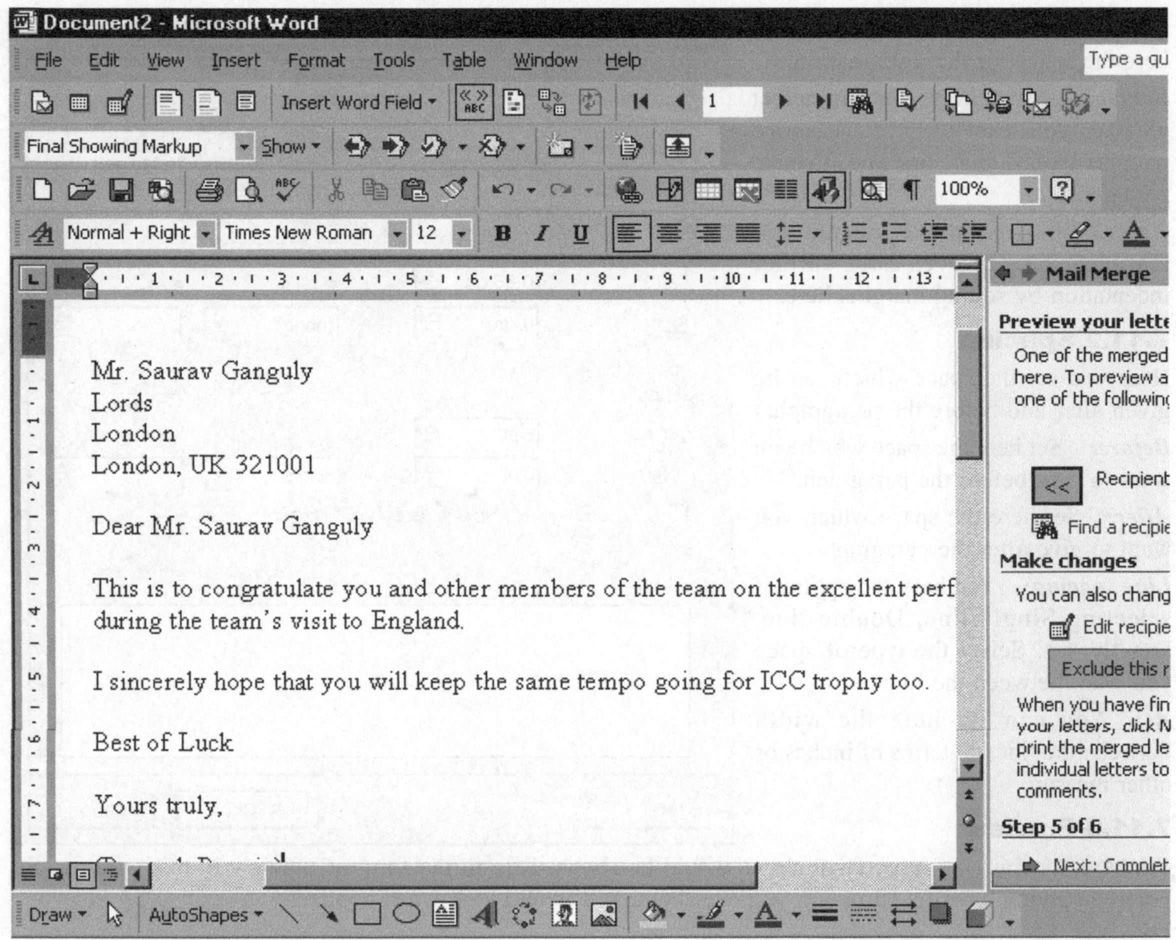

7.10 Character Formatting

See Editing Text.

7.11 Paragraph Formatting

Text in the document is typed in terms of paragraphs. A paragraph can have a number of lines. What we would learn now is how to leave some space between the paragraphs, lines of the paragraphs and their alignments.

For most of these we would be using the dialog box called Paragraph, which is available under Format menu and is shown on the next page. Various options which you can choose or change are given below:

7.11.1 General

This has the following options:

Alignment: As discussed above the various paragraph alignments are available here too for changing.

Outline Level: You can set here the various levels of text alignments.

Indentation: From here you can set the various options of paragraph spacing.

Left: Set here the margin from where the paragraph would be starting. If you set here 1", then the paragraph would start, leaving 1" space on the left.

Right: Similar to above, you can set here the space for the right margin.

Special: From here you can select whether you want to have the above margins applied to the first line or whole paragraph.

By: Within the above indentation/ margins you can even have further indentation by setting margins here.

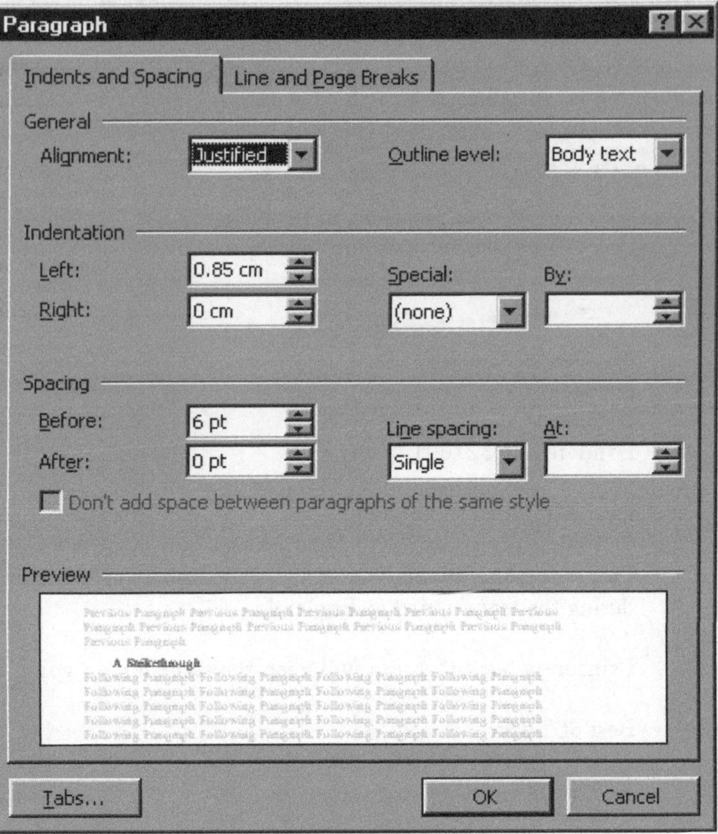

7.11.2 Spacing

Here you set the space which can be given after and before the paragraph.

Before: Set here the space which you want to give before the paragraph.

After: Set here the space which you want to give after the paragraph.

Line spacing: You have the option of selecting Single line, Double line, Exactly, etc. Select the type of space you want between the lines.

At: You can set here the width between the lines in terms of inches or other measure.

7.11.3 Preview

Whatever operation you perform above would be shown here in the form of preview in this window. So before applying a particular option you can see how it would look when applied.

7.12 Page Design and Layout

You can change the page layout of the document. Set the margins according to your likings. For all this you have the command called Pageset in File menu.

7.12.1 Change Page Margins

1. On the File menu, click Page Setup, and then click the Margins tab.
2. Under Margins, select the options you want.
3. To change the default margins, click Default after you select new margin settings. The new default settings are saved in the template on which the document is based.
4. Each new document based on that template automatically uses the new margin settings.

7.12.2 Set mirror margins for facing pages

Margins of the left page are a mirror image of those on the right page. That is, the inside margins are the same width, and the outside margins are the same width.

1. On the File menu, click Page Setup, and then click the Margins tab.
2. In the Multiple pages list, select Mirror margins.
3. In the Inside and Outside boxes, enter values for the mirror margins.

7.12.3 Set gutter Margins for Bound Documents

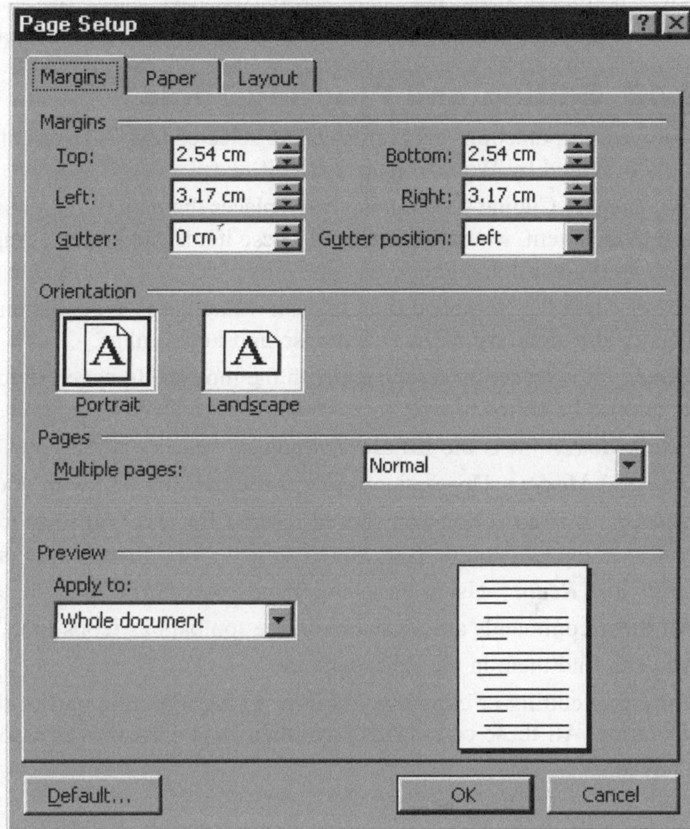

A gutter margin setting adds extra space to the side or top margin of a document you plan to bind. A gutter margin ensures that text isn't obscured by the binding.

1. On the File menu, click Page Setup, and then click the Margins tab.
2. In the Gutter box, enter a value for the gutter margin.
3. In the Gutter position box, click Left or Top.
4. To change the margins for part of a document, select the text, and then set the margins you want. In the Apply to box, click Selected text.
5. Microsoft Word automatically inserts section breaks before and after the text with the new margin settings. If your document is already divided into sections, you can click in a section or select multiple sections, and then change the margins.

7.12.4 Change the Orientation of Text

You can change the text orientation in drawing objects, such as text boxes (text box: A movable, resizable container for text or graphics. Use text boxes to position several blocks of text on a page or to give text a different orientation from other text in the document.), shapes, and callouts, or in table cells so that the text is displayed vertically or horizontally.

1. Click the drawing object or table cell that contains the text you want to change.
2. On the Format menu, click Text Direction.
3. Click the orientation you want.

7.12.5 Select a paper source

1. On the File menu, click Print.
2. Click Properties.
3. Click the Paper tab.
4. In the Paper source box, click the paper source you want.

7.12.6 Select paper size

1. On the File menu, click Page Setup, and then click the Paper tab.
2. Click a paper size.
3. To change the paper size for part of a document, select the pages and then change the paper size as usual. In the Apply to box, click Selected text. Microsoft Word automatically inserts section breaks

before and after the pages with the new paper size. If your document is already divided into sections, you can click in a section or select multiple sections, and then change the paper size.

7.13 Editing and Proofing Tools

Many editing functions are performed on selected text, such as cut, copy, move, and delete. There are various tools provided by Word to help you edit text:

Cut, Copy: Cutting and copying items places them on the Clipboard and you can paste these items anywhere in the document, wherever required. These items can be text, graphics, tables and any other object which is there in the word document. Cut and Copy can be performed using mouse and key strokes.

Paste: It is the command used to paste whatever is available on the Clipboard to paste it in the document. This is also done by the use of mouse and key strokes.

Move: It is an action associated with the mouse. However, if you cut and paste from one place to another, it can also be called move.

Insert Mode: It is the feature that adjusts spacing when you add new text to the document.

Overtype Mode: This option replaces the existing text with your new text.

Delete: It is an action you should reserve for text you want to permanently remove. Deleted text is not placed in the Clipboard. You can delete text with either mouse or key strokes.

Undo and Redo: Using these commands you can reverse the tasks performed earlier.

All these commands are available on the toolbars as icons too.

You can find them in the Edit menu too.

For either cutting or copying, you have to highlight the part of the text on which you want to perform this operation. All these commands have their keyboard strokes associated with them too.

They are:

Cut	Ctrl + X
Copy	Ctrl + C
Paste	Ctrl + V
Move	Ctrl + X and then Ctrl + V
Delete	Backspace or Delete
Undo	Ctrl + Z
Redo	Ctrl + Y

7.14 Checking and Correcting Spellings

As was mentioned earlier, Word points out the spelling errors by underling the word/words with red wavy line. Since our document is just one page long. It is not difficult to pin point the errors. I am quite sure you must have noticed them by now.

There are two methods of correcting these errors. One method is to correct these errors one by one, picking them up. Secondly, you spell check the whole document. Let us do both on our document. Looking from top to bottom of the text in the document file **Unit**, you will see few of the words underlined by **wavy red line**. Few of them are the proper words and thus cannot be corrected.

Words like Gulab is basically a *Hindi* word, so it cannot be in the dictionary of Word and that is why it has been shown as an error. Similar is the case with Bhawan which is again an *Indian* word and is not there in the dictionary and need not to be corrected. For this follow the following procedure:

1. Click with the mouse at any place within the word to be corrected, in this case againt. An alphabet s is missing in this.

2. Now right click the mouse button.
3. A pop-menu will pop-up as shown below.

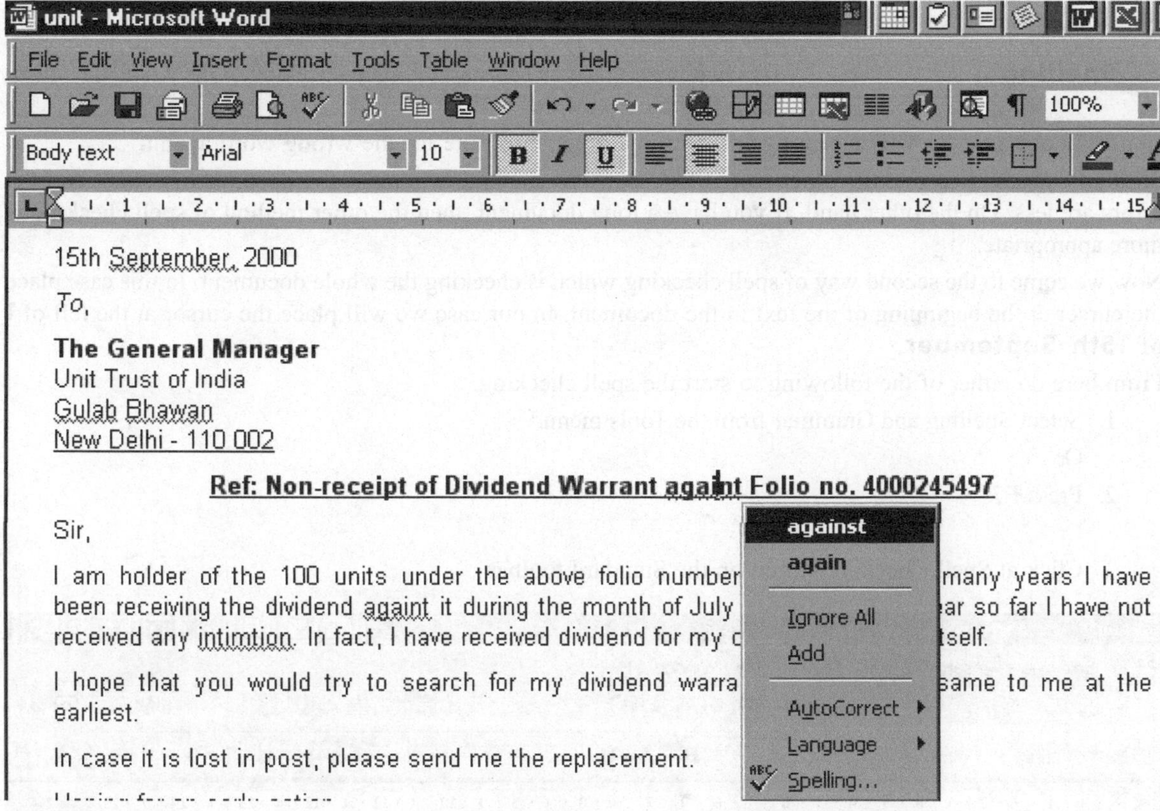

4. Among the various options are:

Alternative words Word displays few words which are similar to the word in question with a hope that these may had been word in your mind while typing this word wrongly. You can choose any one of them, which you feel is the right word by just clicking and selecting that and leaving the mouse. The word will stand corrected with the new word and will replace the wrong word.

Ignore All It is like over ruling the dictionary and saying that whatever you have typed is right and would like the dictionary to ignore this not only at this place but also at all other places within the document.

Add You feel that this word is right and would like this word to be added to the dictionary so that it is not shown as an error in the future.

AutoCorrect You will learn about AutoCorrect in the later chapter. But, only thing to understand here is that it is a list of mostly misplaced word which can be corrected without referring to the dictionary. For example, you may have the bad habit of typing *the* as *teh*. You can add this to AutoCorrect to correct *teh* to *the* always without even telling you.

Language You feel that this particular word which has been pointed as wrong by the current dictionary would be available in other language dictionary. So mention here the name of the other dictionary where this word could be found. If you do not have a second dictionary loaded, just ignore this.

Spelling By clicking at this, you can start the spell checking of the whole document from this point onward.

5. In our case we will accept against as the correct substitute for the wrong word againt.

Similarly you can correct the other words too. But, this method is good if the document is small and the errors are less. On the other hand, if you have a long document, then the other method of spell checking is more appropriate.

Now we come to the second way of spell checking which is checking the whole document. In this case place the cursor at the beginning of the text in the document. In our case we will place the cursor at the left of **1** of **15th September**.

From here do either of the following to start the spell checking.

1. Select Spelling and Grammar from the Tools menu.

   Or

2. Press F7

   Or

3. Click at Spell Checking button on the Standard toolbar.

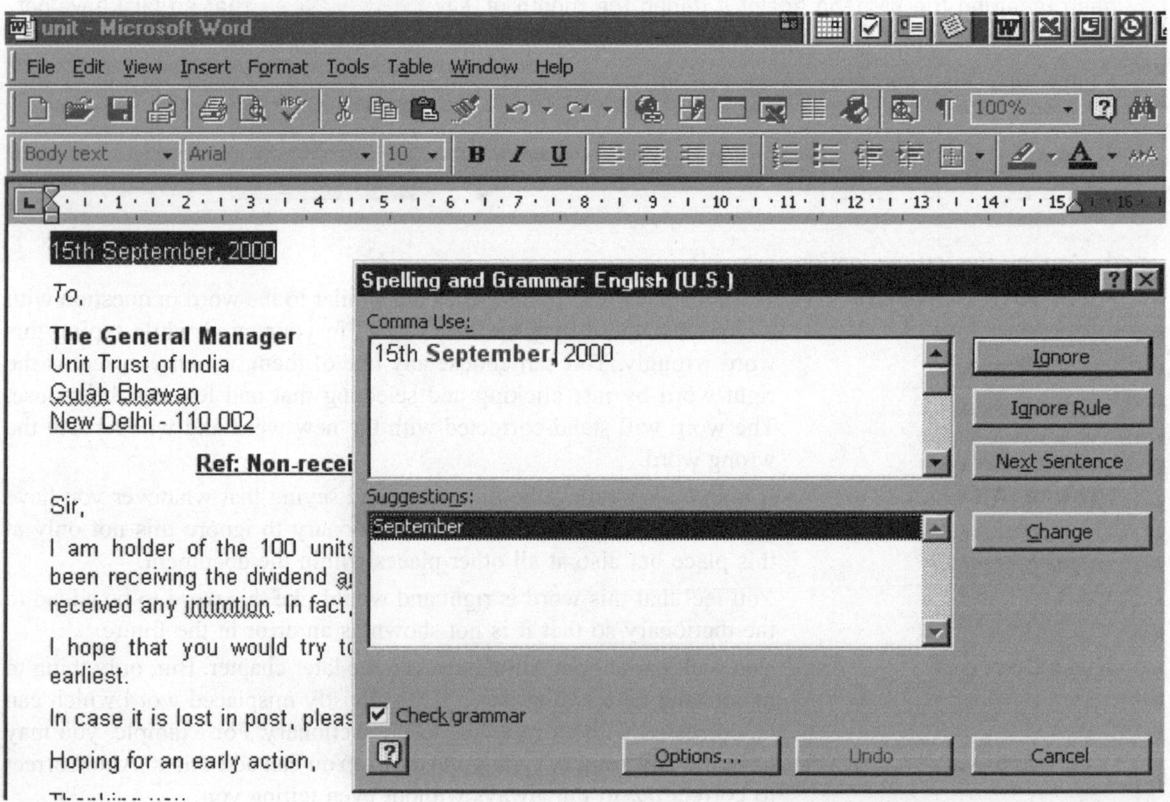

This will initiate the spell checking process and will start the spell checking of the document with each word of the document being searched with the similar word with the words available in the dictionary. If not found it will point out as shown below.

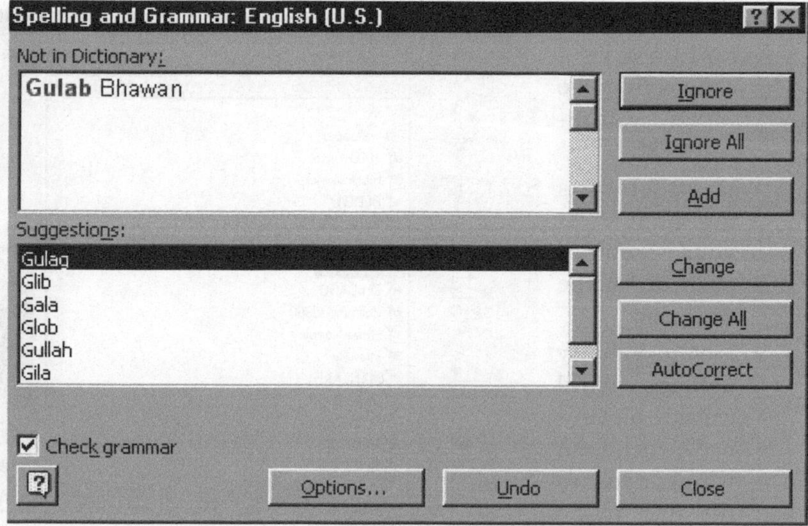

Consider the case shown on the next page, the error has been pointed out in the word September, which is not a spelling error, this is a grammatical error. The suggestion given here is that you put only **September** and not **September,** i.e., comma (,) after September is not required. Now the choice is yours to **Ignore** this or just accept the suggestion as it is and make it September. I suggest we let it remain as it is. For this click at **Ignore** and see what happens.

Now it selects *Gulab* of **Gulab Bhawan**. As was mentioned before it is a proper *Hindi* word, so it cannot be corrected. **Ignore** to proceed further. Other words in the document are also corrected till you reach the end of the document and it stops checking the spelling of the document. In between it will correct the words **againt** by **against** and **intimtion** by **intimation**.

After this there is no other word to correct and the spell checking ends with a dialog box, saying that the spelling checking is complete.

7.15 Handling Graphics

It is not that Word is only for text. You can have graphics into it. You can in fact enter graphics into it. This graphics could have been created in other software which is capable of creating graphics. However, Word has its own set of Clip Arts too, which can be used to enhance your word document.

7.15.1 Inserting Graphics

1. Place the cursor where you want to insert the graphic.
2. Click at Picture in the Insert menu. From the sub-menu select From File to open the Insert Picture dialog box.
3. If necessary, select the folder where the graphic is stored from the Look In drop-down list.
4. The Files of Type drop-down list is automatically set to display All Pictures, but you can select the specific type of graphic file you want to appear in the list.
5. Select the name of the file you want to use from the listed files, enter the name in the File Name text box, or highlight the file. Click the down arrow next to Views on the toolbar and then select Preview to see a preview of the selected file.

6. Click any of the following options from the Insert drop-down list:
   - Insert. Inserts the picture at your cursor position in the document.
   - Link to File. By default, Word embeds pictures in the document, which adds to the size of the file. Choose this option to reduce the size of the file by linking to it. One benefit of linking is that the graphic in the document updates immediately if any changes are made to the original file.
   - Insert and Link. Inserts the picture into the document and links to the source file so the picture is immediately updated if the original graphic is changed.

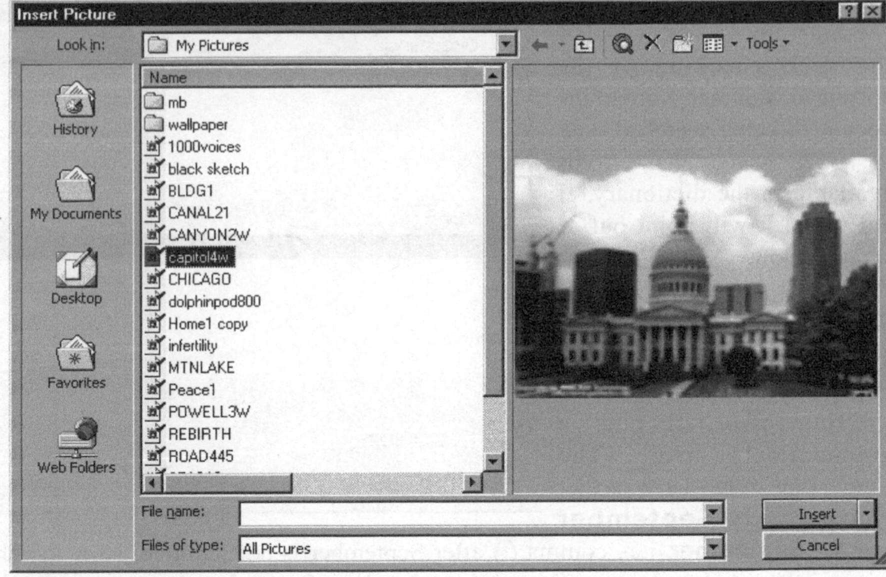

7. Choose Insert to add the graphics image to your document.

7.15.2 Insert Clip Art

Word comes with a library of Clip Art, which is comprised of drawings and pictures you use to add visual appeal and interest to your documents. Adding clip art to the documents is easy and it can be the added element that draws attention to your document versus someone else's in a competitive market.

7.15.2.1 Add Clip Art to a Document

1. Place your cursor where you want to put the clip art picture or drawing in your document.
2. Open the Insert menu and choose Picture, then choose Clip Art from the submenu to open the Insert Clip Art dialog box.

3. The Pictures tab is displayed, showing a set of clip art categories.
4. Click a category picture to display the clips in that category. When you point to one of the clips, the graphic format and categories of that clip appear as a pop-up.
5. Click once on the clip to see a menu.
6. Choose Insert Clip to insert the clip in your document.

7.15.3 Wrap Text around Graphics

A graphic causes a break in your text. The text immediately after the graphic does not start until the next line after the picture, leaving whitespace to the left or right of the graphic. It also leaves space on the top and bottom of the graphic. This is called text wrap and is Word's default setting for wrapping text around a picture.

7.15.3.1 Set Text Wrap Options

1. Select the image.
2. Open the Format menu and select Picture, choose Format Picture on the Picture toolbar, or right-click the graphic and select Format Picture from the pop-up menu.

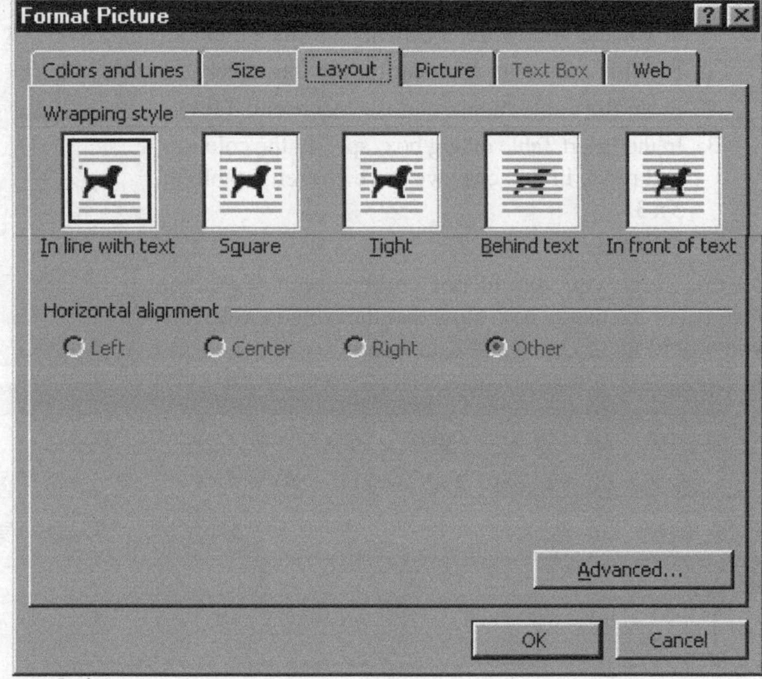

3. When the Format Picture dialog box appears, select the Layout tab.
4. Under Wrapping Style, select a style of text wrap—In Line with Text, Square, Tight, Behind Text, or In Front of Text—depending on how close you want the text to wrap around the picture.
5. Choose Advanced to set text wrapping specifics in the Advanced Layout dialog box.
6. Select the Text Wrapping tab. Under Wrap Text, select the sides on which you want the text to wrap—Both Sides, Left Only, Right Only, or Largest Only.
7. To set the distance between the edge of the picture and the beginning of the text wrapping around it, enter the distance in the **Top**, **Bottom**, **Left**, and **Right** boxes under Distance from Text.
8. Choose Ok to close the Advanced Layout dialog box.
9. Choose Ok to close the Format Picture dialog box.

The picture would be adjusted in the text as your needs.

7.16 Creating Tables

When you put the data in tabular form, it looks good. You can also show data in tabular form to highlight that particular data. Tabs were used in the earlier word processing software for this, but, now you have a full fledged table menu in the new Microsoft Word. Though you will still use Tabs to reach the next cell of the table but the working of the whole tables is much easier.

7.16.1 Creating a Table

A table can be created by two methods. You can create the table structure before you enter any text, or you can convert text you have already created to a table. There is an easy way to create the structure for a simple table and a way to create a more complex table.

To create the structure for a simple table

1. Position the insertion point at the location for the table.
2. Click the Insert Table button on the Standard toolbar.
3. Drag across, the number of columns and down, the number of rows you want

   An unformatted table appears

   or you can follow the following alternate method.

1. Position cursor at the location for the table.
2. From the Table menu, choose Insert and Table.
3. In the Insert Table dialog box, specify the columns and rows, in this case we have chosen a table of 3 x 3.
4. Click Ok.

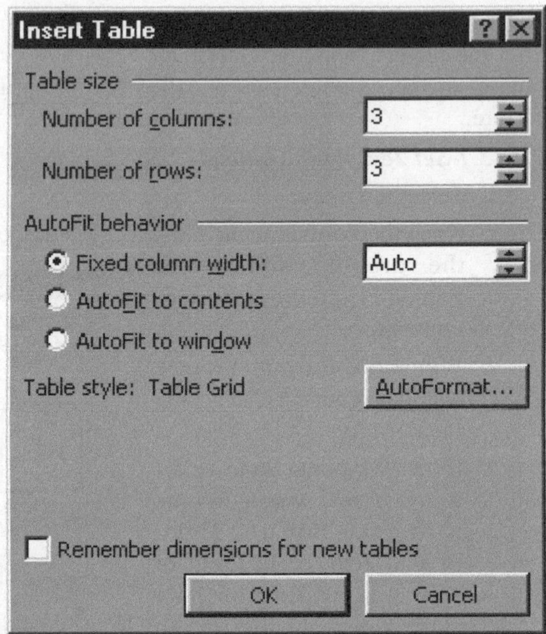

At this stage you should not bother about the other features of the dialog box. Now that the table in available you would like to enter the data into it.

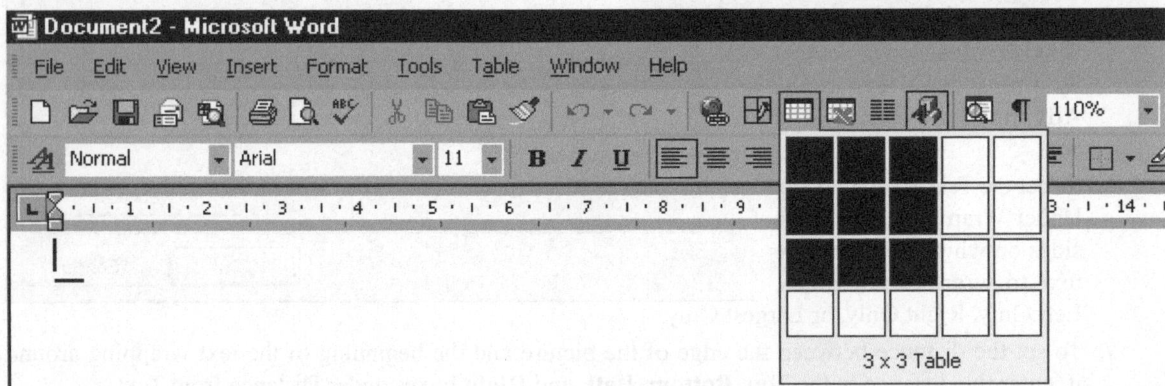

7.16.2 Entering Data in a Table

Data can be typed directly into the cells or it can be moved or copied from other cells.

7.16.2.1 To Enter Data in a Table

1. Click in a cell with the mouse and type the data required to be typed. As you type, the cursor wraps within the cell and the entire row will become taller if it needs to accommodate multiple lines of text.
2. Press Tab to move to the cell to the right, and type text in the next cell.

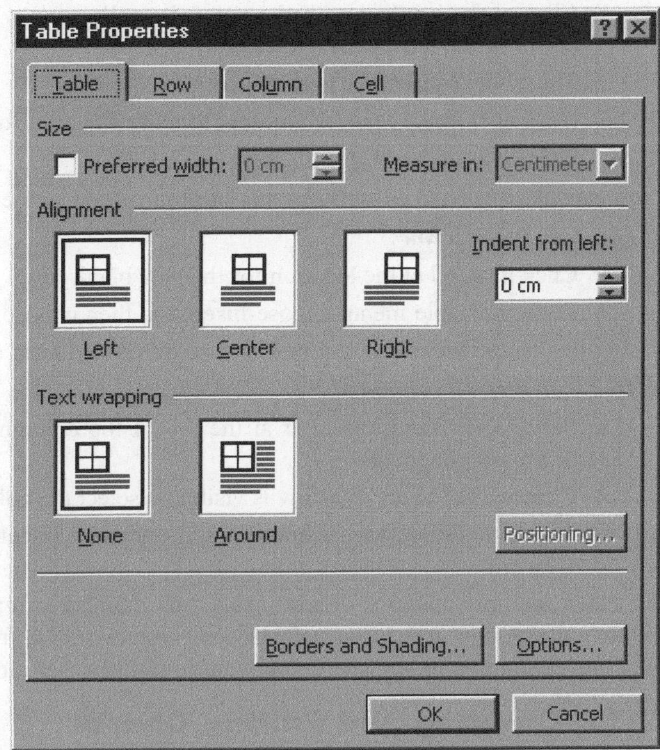

3. Continue pressing tab after you finish each cell.
4. When you finish entering text in the last cell of the table, press Tab to create a new row, if required.

7.16.2.2 Aligning Data in a Table

For aligning of the data, you can use either of the following:

7.16.2.3 To Align Data Vertically or Horizontally Within Cells

1. Select the cells you want to align.
2. Click the Table Properties in the Table menu.
3. A dialog box will appear.
4. From here select the Table panel and the alignment wanted by you.

7.16.2.4 Changing Direction of Text

1. Select the cells you want to change.
2. Click the Change Text Direction tool on the Tables and Border toolbar.
3. The text would change the direction as required by you.

Another thing which we can do to our table is to decorate a bit by turning the headings as **bold**. For this do the following:

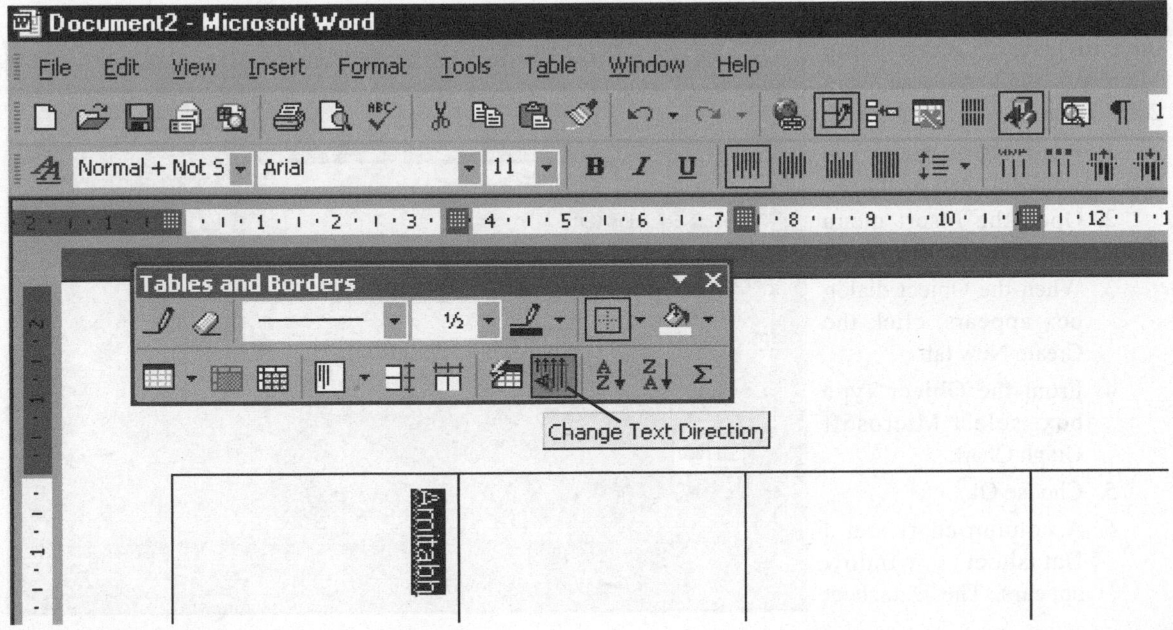

1. Click at the heading with the pointed small arrow which comes to the screen when you move the cursor to the left of the text within the cell.
2. The whole cell will be highlighted.
3. Click at B in the Standard toolbar to make the text Bold.

7.16.2.5 Inserting Rows and Columns

You can add rows and columns to any portion of your table on all the sides using the following options.

7.16.2.6 To insert a row

1. Click in a cell at the location for the new blank row.
2. From the Table menu, choose Insert and then choose Rows Below from the Insert submenu.

Using this option we will add a new row to our table in the document.

7.16.2.7 To insert a column

1. Position the mouse pointer at the top of the column at the location for the new column. A large down-arrow appears.
2. Click while the down-arrow is visible to select the column.
3. From the Table menu, choose Insert and then select one of the Columns options from the Insert submenu.

To insert multiple columns or rows, select the number of existing columns or rows corresponding to the number that you want to insert before you choose an option from the insert submenu. If there are not enough existing columns or rows where you want to do the insertion, do multiple Insert operations.

7.17 Creating and Editing Charts

Charts and graphs are another options of presenting your data in the form of pie charts and column graphs. Often, reports such as a annual report contain charts illustrating data such as sales and profits. Word does not create charts but uses a program called **Microsoft Graph**, which is installed by default.

7.17.1 Create a Graph

The following steps show you how to insert a chart using Microsoft Graph into your Word 2000 document.

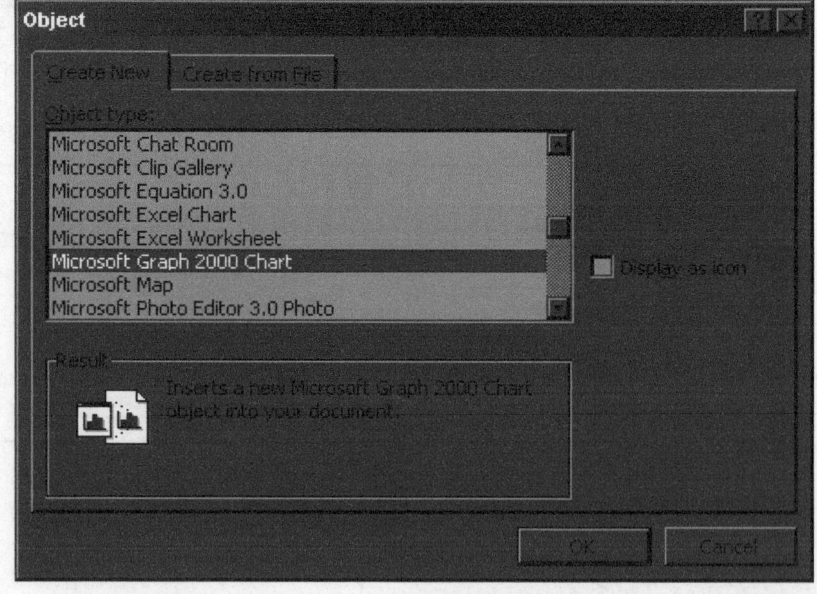

1. Place cursor where you want the chart to appear.
2. Open the Insert menu and select Object.
3. When the Object dialog box appears, click the Create New tab.
4. From the Object Type box, select Microsoft Graph Chart.
5. Choose Ok.
6. A column chart and a Datasheet window appears. The Datasheet

Bill.doc - Datasheet

		A	B	C	D	E
		1st Qtr	2nd Qtr	3rd Qtr	4th Qtr	
1	East	20.4	27.4	90	20.4	
2	West	30.6	38.6	34.6	31.6	
3	North	45.9	46.9	45	43.9	
4						
5						

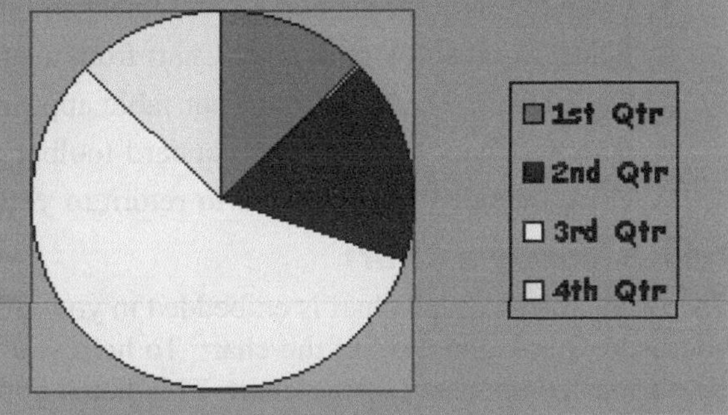

contains sample data that you replace to create your own graph. The chart is transformed automatically as you add your data and select formatting options, until it becomes the chart you want.

7. To replace the sample data, click in the cell in the Datasheet where you want to put new data and then type your own data there. Press Enter to accept the data and move down one row; press Tab to move one cell to the right and Shift+Tab to move one cell to the left (the arrow keys also help you navigate in the Datasheet). Choose View Datasheet on the Standard toolbar to close the Datasheet.
8. Click the down arrow next to the Chart Type button on the Standard toolbar to select a chart from the types shown. Then click the picture of the type of chart you want to create.
9. Click outside the border around the graph to return to the Word document (double-click on the chart to return to the Microsoft Graph program).

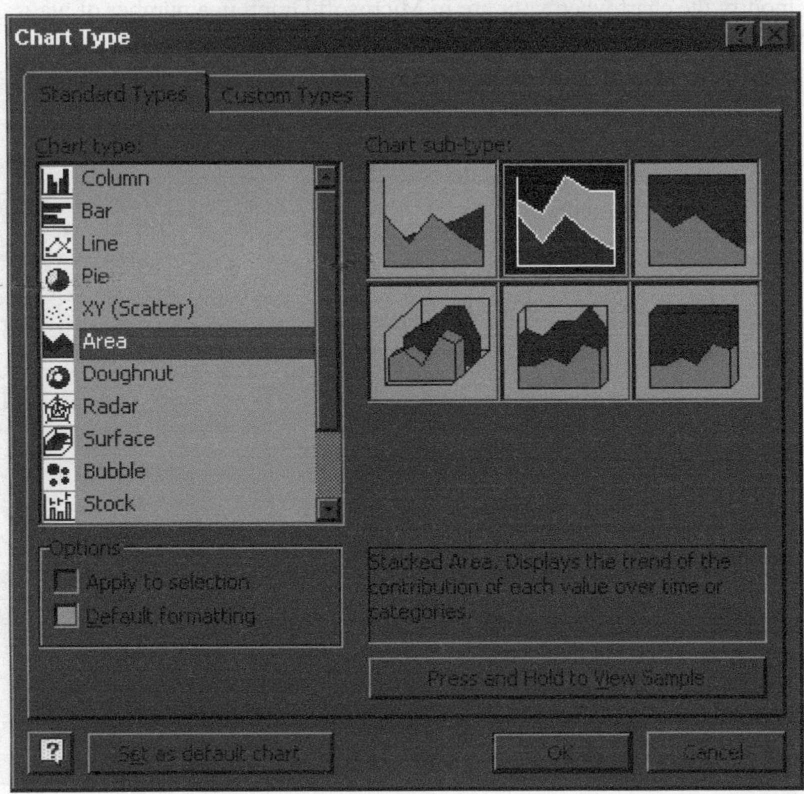

The sample data that appears in the Datasheet when you start a new chart is always the same. It serves as an aid that helps you enter the data in the right places. Be sure to delete any of the sample data that remains after you have entered you own information.

7.17.2 Create a Chart from a Table

Data that exists in a table (such as sales and profit data) can act as the data for your chart. If you have the data you need for a chart in a Word table, there is no need to enter the data again in the Datasheet. Instead, start the chart with the following steps.

1. Create the table in Word. Put text labels in the cells in the top row and in the left column. Put numbers in the other cells.
2. Select all the cells in the table (click in the table to put your insertion point there and then open the Table menu, choose Select, and then select Table from the submenu), unless your table includes a row and a column of totals. In that case, select all the cells except those total rows or columns.
3. Open the Insert menu and select Object and then select the Create New tab in the Object dialog box.
4. Select Microsoft Graph 2000 Chart from the Object Type box.
5. Choose Ok. The data from your table appears in the Datasheet.
6. Choose Chart Type on the Standard toolbar and then select a chart type.
7. Click outside the graph area to return to your Word document.

7.17.3 Modify a Chart

Once a Microsoft Graph chart is embedded in your document, double-click the middle of the chart to activate Microsoft Graph and modify the chart. To help you in modifying the chart, tips pop up when you point to the various components of the chart. This helps you in identifying the item you want to change. You can modify the chart when your are in Microsoft Graph in a number of ways, from changing the data to altering its appearance.

The following list gives you some suggestions on how you can modify your chart.

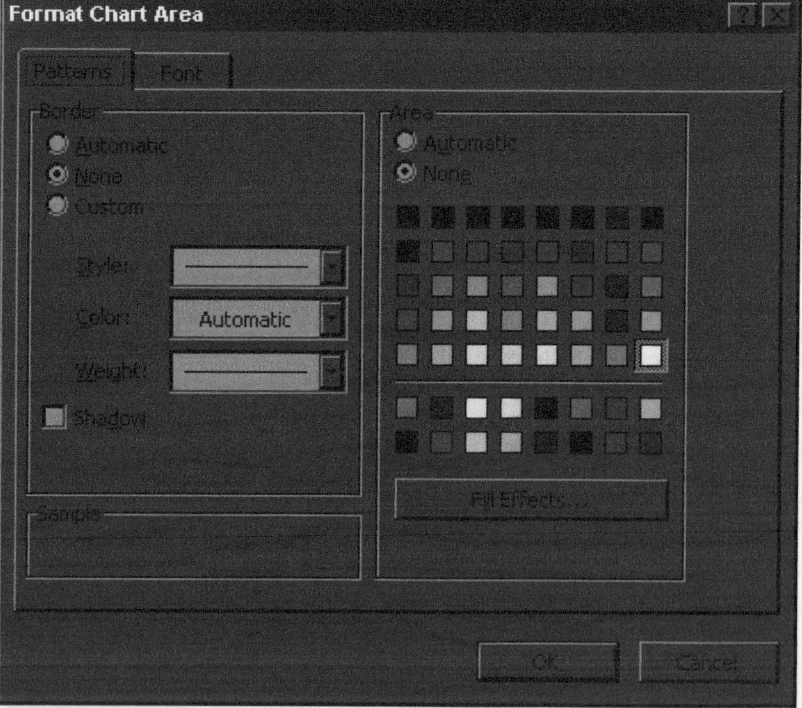

- To edit the data, open the Datasheet by choosing View Datasheet on the Standard toolbar. Replace data by clicking in the cell and typing the new value or label. Press Enter or move the insertion point to the next cell to accept the change.
- To change the chart type, open the Chart menu and select Chart Type to open the Chart Type dialog box. From the Chart Type list, select the type of chart

you want. Then make a selection from the Chart Sub-Type options and choose Ok.

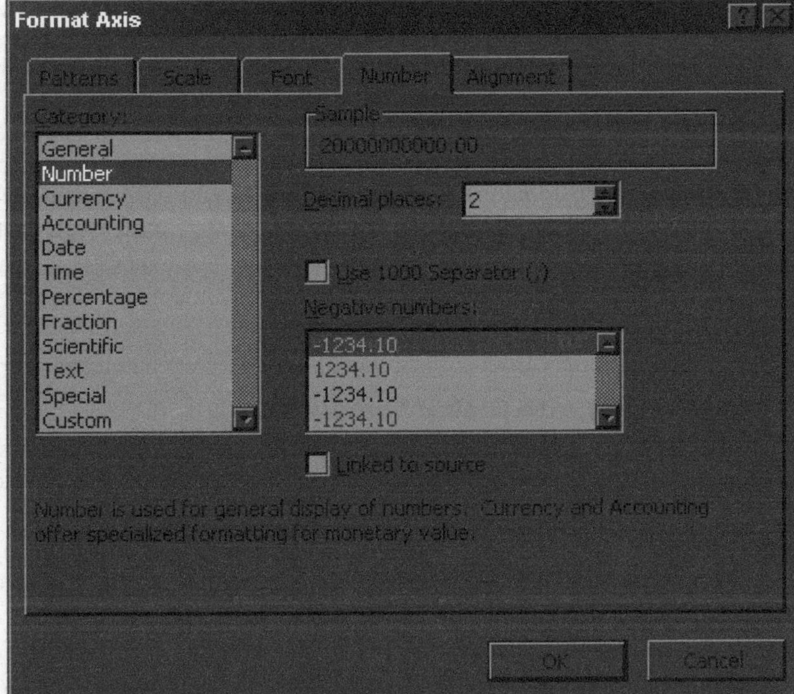

- To change the colour of bars, lines or areas, double-click on the item to open the Format Data Series dialog box. For pie chart slices, click once on the pie and then double-click the slice you want to change to open the Format Data Point dialog box. Set the line style and colour on the appropriate options. Then choose Ok to apply them to the chart.
- To change the number format (how the numbers appear) of the chart values, double-click the numbers on the value axis (Y-axis) to open the Format Axis dialog box and then select the Number tab. Choose a number format (such as currency or percentage) from the Category box. The options vary with each category, so you may have to specify number of decimal places, symbols, appearance of negative numbers, use of a thousand separator, data and time formats, and so on. Choose Ok.
- To set the interval between the numbers or specify the minimum or maximum values, double-click the numbers on the value axis (Y-axis) to open the Format Axis dialog box and then select the Scale tab. Change the Major Unit number to specify the interval between numbers, which also sets the spacing between the gridlines (lines that act as a reference to help you evaluate data in relation to the axes). Enter values in the Minimum and Maximum boxes to change those values. Choose Ok.
- To add titles to the value and category axes, click open the Chart menu and select Chart Options on the menu to open the Chart Options dialog box. Select the Titles tab and enter the title text in the Category (X) Axis or Value (Y) Axis box. Click in the Chart Title box and enter a title for the entire chart. Click Ok.

When you complete your modifications, click outside the graph border to return to your Word document. Move the graph by pointing in the middle of it and dragging it to a new position on the page. Change the size of the chart by selecting it and then dragging one of the handles (small hollow boxes surrounding the chart) toward or away from the center of the graph. After you click outside the graph, it acts like any graphic inserted into a word document.

Now that you have seen how Word 2000 handles all the graphics, Tables, Charts and other graphics, we will revert back to the text in the next chapter and see how Word 2000 handles the text of larger volumes, such as Books, Project Reports, etc., where you have more than one document file and the whole thing is divided into various sections.

7.18 Document Templates

Every Microsoft Word document is based on a template. A template determines the basic structure for a document and contains document settings such as AutoText entries, fonts, key assignments, macros, menus, page layout, special formatting, and styles. The two basic types of templates are global templates and document templates.

Global templates, including the Normal template, contain settings that are available to all documents.

Document templates, such as the memo or fax templates in the **New** dialog box, contain settings that are available only to documents based on that template. For example, if you create a memo using the memo template, the memo can use the settings from both the memo template as well as the settings in any global template.

Word provides a variety of document templates, and you can create your own document templates.

7.18.1 Working with Global Templates

When you work on a document, you can typically use only the settings stored in the template attached to the document or in the Normal template. To use any such items that are stored in another template, you can load the other template as a global template.

After you load a template, items stored in that template are available to any document during the remainder of the Word session. When you're finished with the items, be sure to unload the template to conserve system resources.

Add-ins and templates that you load are unloaded when you close Word. To load an add-in or template each time you start Word, copy the add-in or template to the Startup folder, whose location is specified on the **File Locations** tab (**Tools** menu, **Options** command).

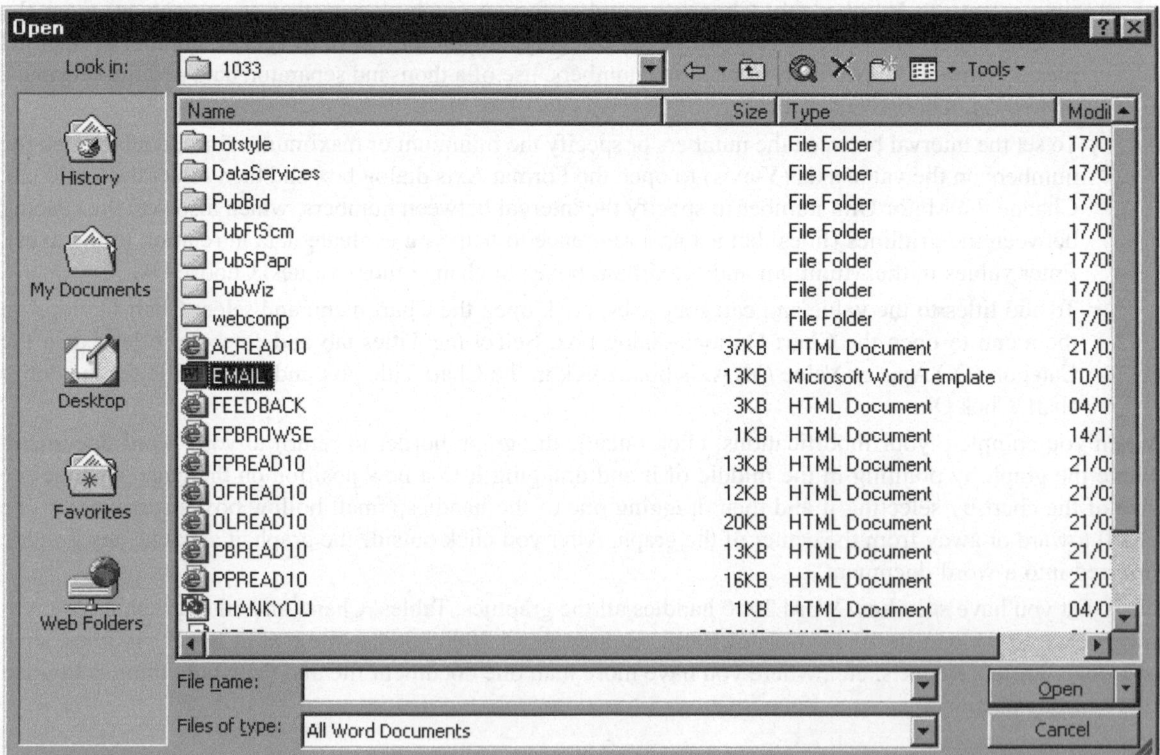

7.18.2 Locating templates

When you or someone in your workgroup clicks **New** on the **File** menu, two factors determine which document templates are available and which tab each template appears on: the location of the template and your file location settings for **User templates** and **Workgroup templates**.

To check your template file location settings, click **Options** on the **Tools** menu, and then click the **File Locations** tab.

7.18.3 Workgroup templates

It is recommended that your system administrator store templates that you share on a network in the **Workgroup templates** file location specified on the **File Locations** tab.

To keep custom templates from being inadvertently altered by others, the administrator should mark them as read-only or store them on a server with limited permissions.

7.18.4 User templates

Save your custom templates in the **Templates** folder. (In Microsoft Windows 95 or 98, the **Templates** folder is located by default in either the C:*Windows_folder*\Application Data\Microsoft folder or the C:*Windows_folder*\Profiles*User_name*\Application Data\Microsoft folder. In Microsoft Windows the **Templates** folder is located by default in the C:*Windows_folder*\Profiles*User_name* folder.)

Template files that you save in the **Templates** folder appear in the **New** dialog box (**File** menu). Any document (.doc) file that you save in the **Templates** folder also acts as a template.

Templates you save in the **Templates** folder appear on the **General** tab. If you want to create custom tabs for your templates in the **New** dialog box, create a new subfolder in the **Templates** folder and save your templates in that subfolder.

The name you give that subfolder will appear on the new tab. When you're saving a template, Word switches to the **User templates** location (**Tools** menu, **Options** command, **File Locations** tab), which by default is the **Templates** folder and its subfolders. If you save a template in a different location, the template will not appear in the **New** dialog box.

7.19 Wizards

Wizards are there in any software to guide and create for you in a flash the document/output which you are trying to create using the software. These are there for like having fast food instead of having a good sit down dinner. Here everything is ready made and you have to just fill in the data and the document is ready for you. I will start with Resume Wizard, which I am sure that at some stage of your life you must be needing it.

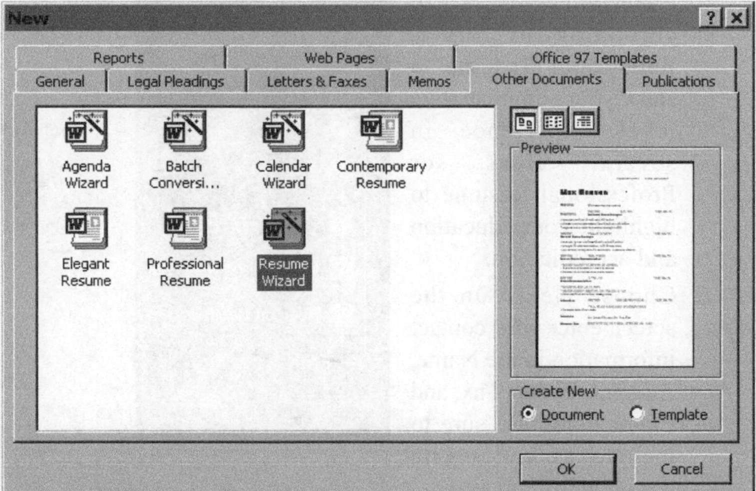

7.19.1 Resume Wizard

When you are looking for a job, the first thing you need a resume of yours or better known as Bio-data in this part of the World. Word helps you in preparing a professional looking, neat and organized resume in no time. The following steps you have to take to create a resume using the Wizard.

1. Click the File menu and select New.
2. When the New dialog box appears, select the "Other Documents" tab.
3. Click the Resume Wizard icon to select it and then choose Ok. The Resume Wizard dialog box appears.
4. Choose Next. The wizard offers you 3 styles of resumes—Professional, Contemporary, or Elegant. A preview of each style appears beneath the option. Click the style you want to use.
5. Choose Next. The Resume Wizard lets you select the type of resume you are preparing. Use Entry-Level Resume if you are entering the job market or have limited experience, Chronological Resume to list your experiences in chronological order, Functional Resume to show your administrative level experience in several areas, or Professional Resume to highlight your education and accreditation.
6. Choose Next. On the screen enter your contact information in the Name, Address, Phone, Fax, and Email fields. Be sure to include are codes with the phone numbers.

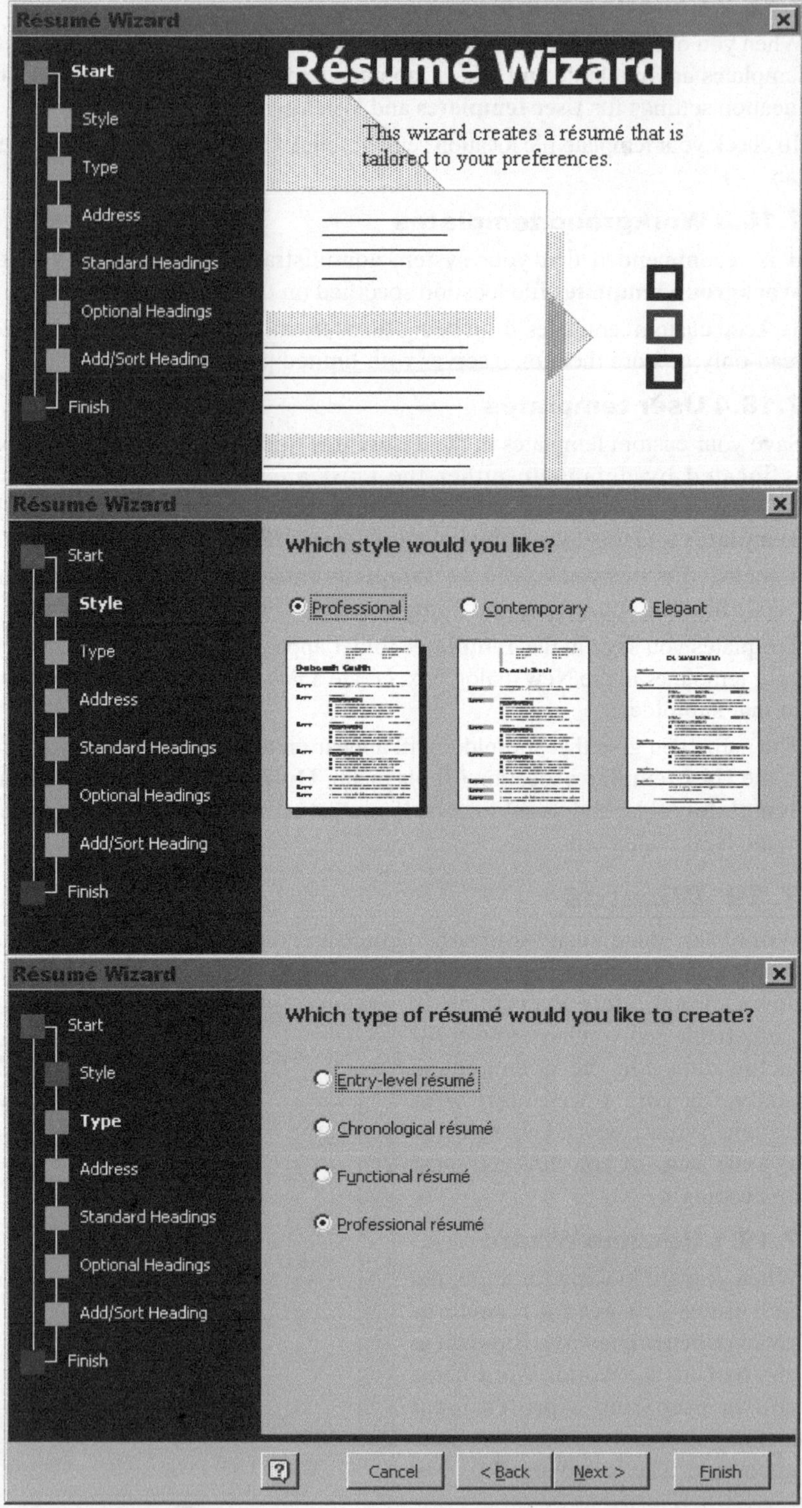

7. Choose Next. The Resume Wizard list a series of headings that can appear on the resume style you choose. Click the ones you want included on your resume to check those boxes and remove the check marks from the headings you don't want to use.
8. Choose Next. Another set of heading choices appears. These can be included, but you probably won't use them unless they are relevant to the objective of the resume. Click to check the headings you want to use.
9. Choose Next. The resume headings you selected are listed on this screen. If you want to add another heading, type the heading in the text box and then choose Add. To set the order of appearance in your resume, select a heading by clicking on it and then choose Move Up or Move Down to move the heading up or down in the list. To remove a heading from the list, select it and then choose Remove.
10. Choose Next. You have filled in all the information needed for the resume, so choose Finish.

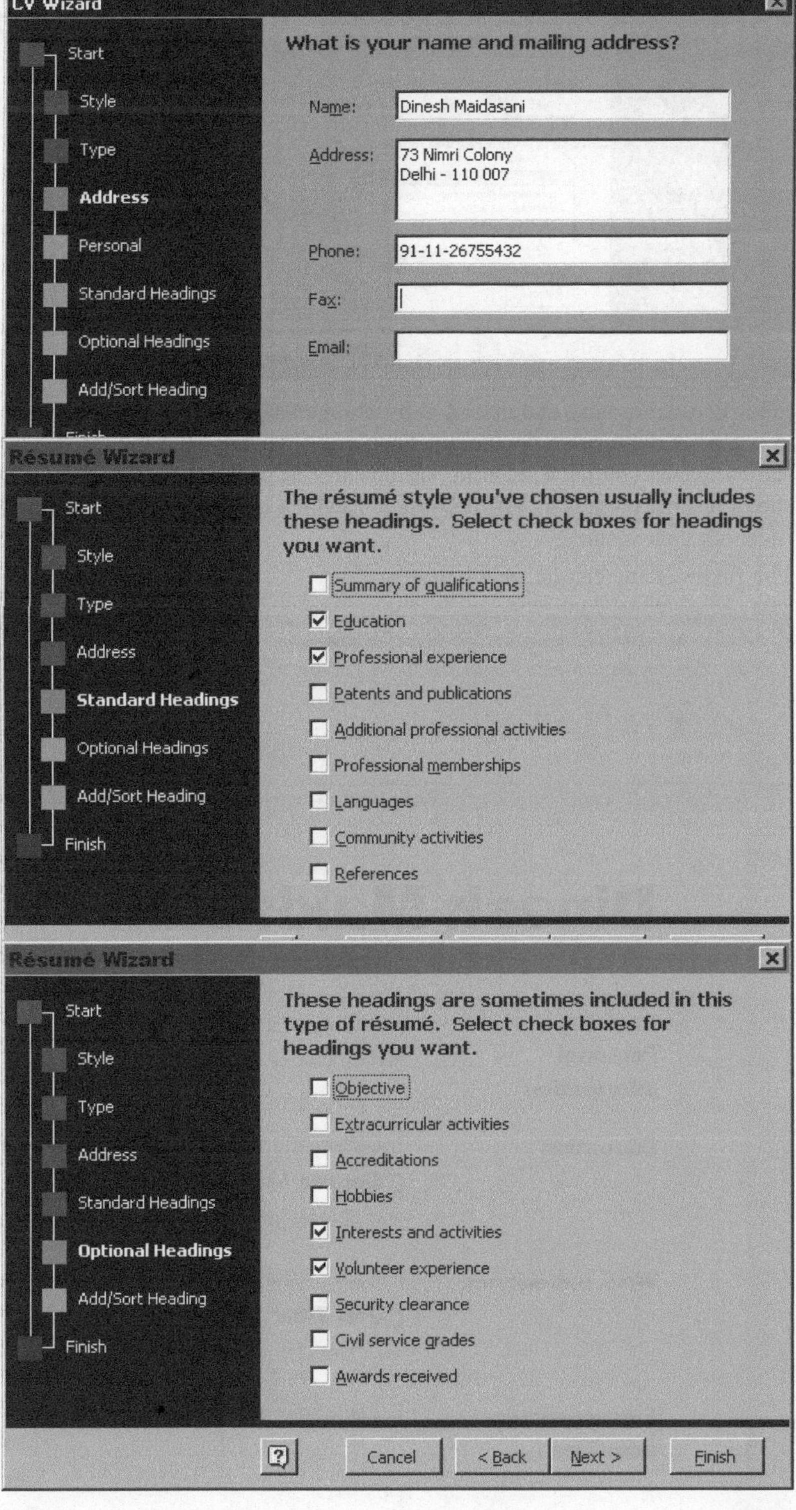

When the resume document opens, it displays a series of

Résumé Wizard
Start
Style
Type
Address
Standard Headings
Optional Headings
Add/Sort Heading
Finish
Are there any additional headings you would like to add to your résumé?
Add
These are your résumé headings.
Education
Professional experience
Interests and activities
Volunteer experience
Move Up
Move Down
Remove
Cancel
< Back
Next >
Finish

Résumé Wizard
Start
Style
Type
Address
Standard Headings
Optional Headings
Add/Sort Heading
Finish
Résumé Wizard
Those are all the answers the Wizard needs to create your résumé! Click Finish to view the document.
Cancel
< Back
Next >
Finish

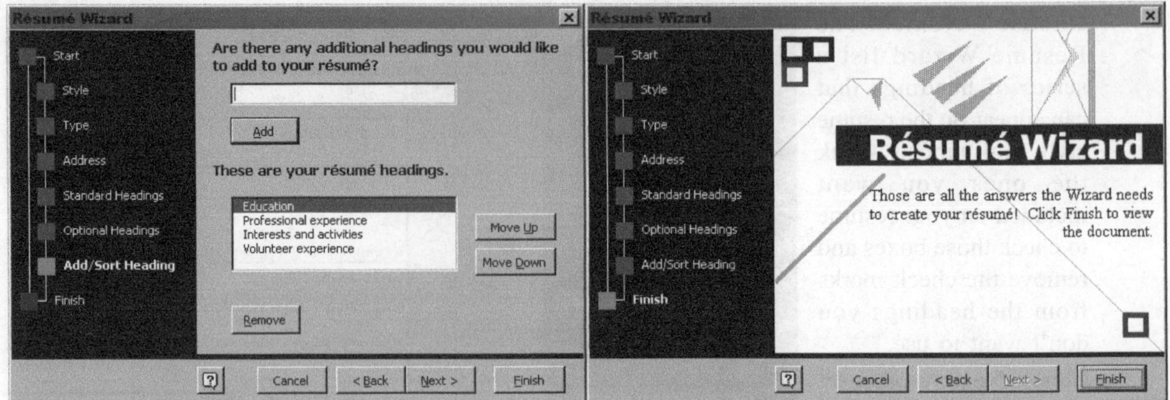

fields marked in gray and enclosed by brackets ([ ]). Close these fields and enter the necessary information to complete the resume document. Then you save and print the resume as you would any document. On the las few pages you have seen the various screen of the wizard and the finally the resume. As seen from the above resume there is an Office Assistant which offers help in the following options that you might need in finishing your resume.

The final resume can be seen below.

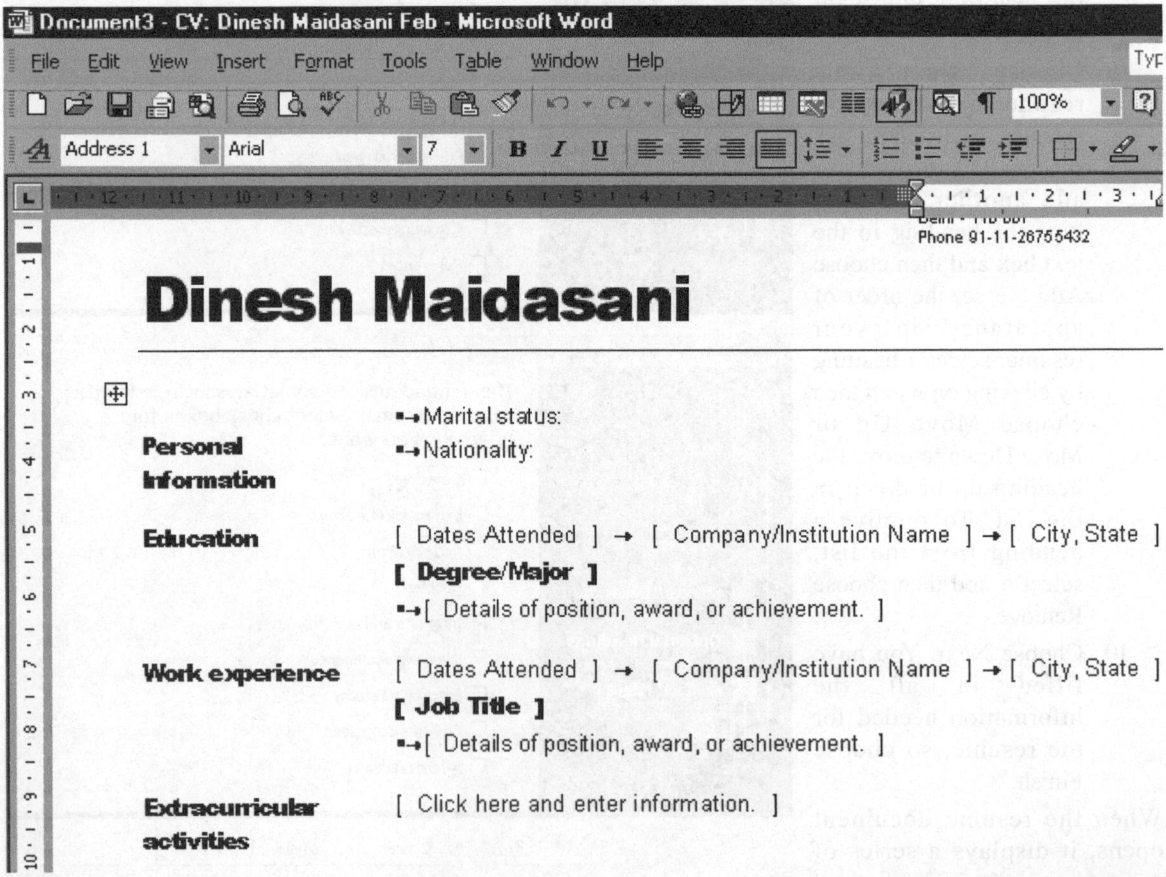

Document3 - CV: Dinesh Maidasani Feb - Microsoft Word
File Edit View Insert Format Tools Table Window Help
100%
Address 1
Arial
7
Phone 91-11-26755432
Dinesh Maidasani
Personal Information
Marital status:
Nationality:
Education
[Dates Attended] [Company/Institution Name] [City, State]
[Degree/Major]
[Details of position, award, or achievement.]
Work experience
[Dates Attended] [Company/Institution Name] [City, State]
[Job Title]
[Details of position, award, or achievement.]
Extracurricular activities
[Click here and enter information.]

7.20 Page Numbering

Printed documents longer than one page should have page numbers. You can set up page numbering in two ways. Either insert a page number code while editing headers and footers, or insert page numbers from the **Insert** menu. Both methods insert a page number code in you documents' header or footer, but there are two differences.

Putting the page numbers through header and footer, we will learn that when we learn Header and Footer, later in the chapter. Otherwise you do the following:

1. Click the Insert menu and select Page Numbers to open the Page Numbers dialog box, as shown here.

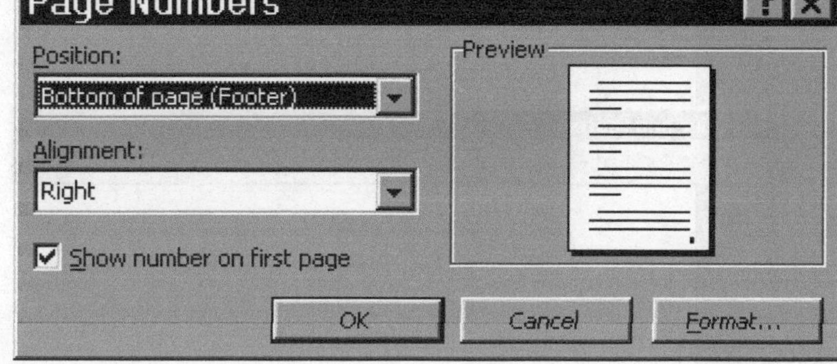

2. From the Position drop-down list, select the position on the page where you want your page numbers to appear. The options are:
   Top of the Page (Header)
   Bottom of the Page (Footer)
3. From the alignment drop-down list, select Left, Center, or Right to specify the horizontal position of the page number in relation to the right or left margins.
4. If you want the page number to appear on the first page, Show number on first page to place check mark there. Deselecting this option creates a separate header or footer for the first page.
5. Click Ok.

When you insert a page number, Word automatically switches you to Print Layout view so you can scroll to the portion of the page where the page number appears to check its appearance.

7.21 Header and Footer

As you must be knowing that **Header** appears on the top of the page and **Footer** appears on the bottom of the page. Word allows you to put both of them on the document pages.

Headers and footers can vary within a document. Choices include:

1. The same header and footer on every page.
2. A different header and footer for the first page only
3. Different headers and footers for odd numbered pages than those on even numbered pages.
4. Different headers and footers for each section of the document.

7.21.1 Adding a Header or Footer in Your Document

1. Click the View menu and select Header and Footer. The document appears in the Print Layout view with the header area indicated by a nonprinting dashed line box, as shown here. Regular document text is gray, and the header and footer toolbar is displayed.
2. Type the header or footer text. Edit and format the text as you would anywhere else in the document. Both the header and the footer have two tabs set to help you align your text a centre tab at the center of the page and a right tab at the right margin.
3. Use the toolbar buttons, as shown on next page, to add page numbers, total page numbers, date, time, etc.

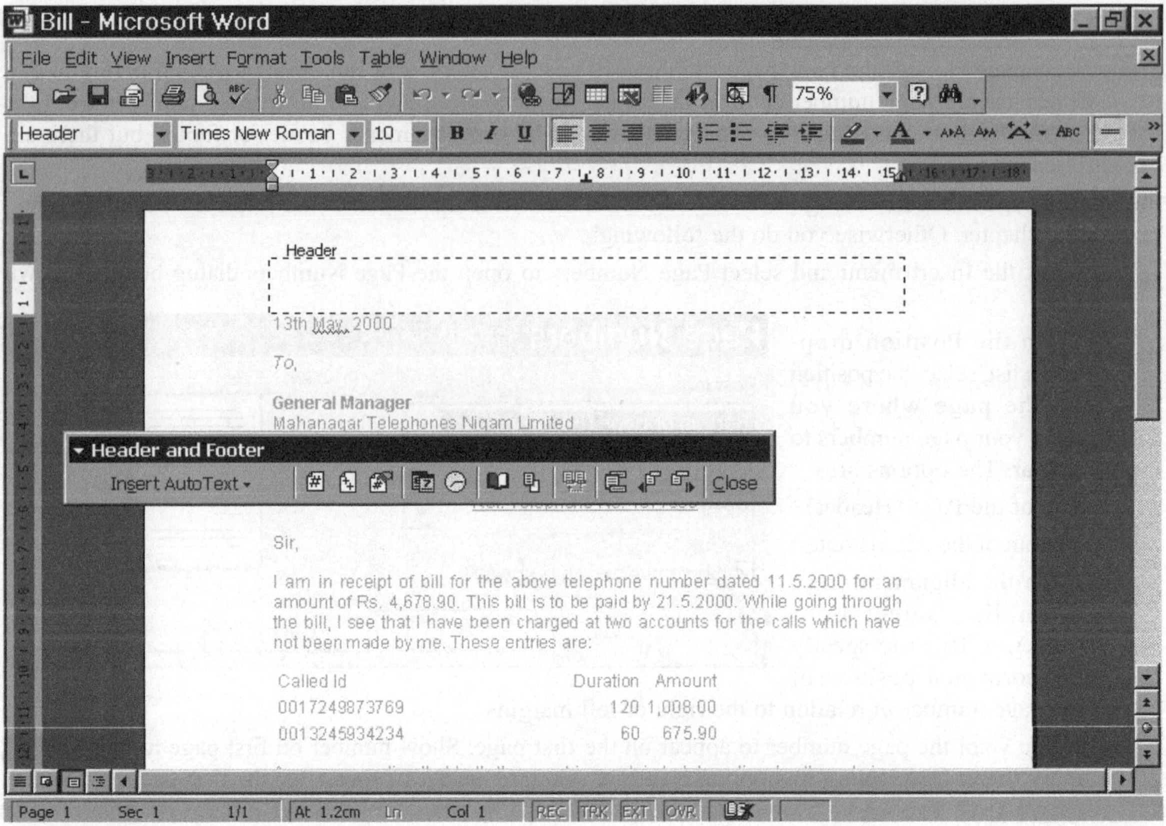

4. Choose Close on the Header and Footer toolbar to return to the document.

7.22 Insert a Symbol

The symbols will depend upon the fonts that you are using in your computer. Some of the popular fonts with symbols are: *Symbol*, *Wingdings*, *Zaph Dingbats*, *Monotype Sorts*, etc. You can insert symbols from these fonts into your document.

1. Place cursor where you want the symbol to appear.
2. Open the **Insert** menu and choose **Symbol** to open the **Symbol** dialog box. Click the **Symbols** tab if it is not already on top.

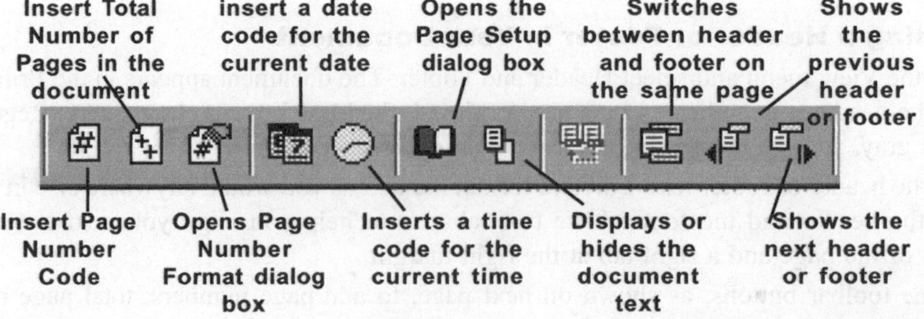

3. From the **Font** drop-down list, select the symbol set you want to use. Choose (normal text) to see the list for the current font, which includes letters with *diacritical marks*, *currency symbols*, *the paragraph symbol*, *the registered mark*, *the trademark symbol*, *the copyright symbol*, and so on. Using various fonts you can even get *mathematical symbols*, *arrows*, *pointing hands*, *snowflakes*, *bullets*, and more.

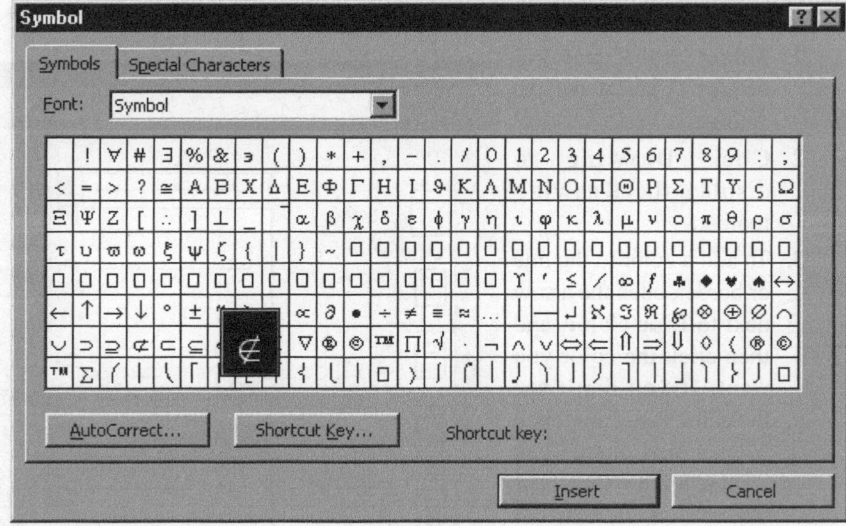

4. Look through the grid of symbols for the one you want. Click a symbol square to see an enlarged view of the symbol.
5. To insert the selected symbol in your document, choose **Insert** or double-click the symbol.
6. Choose **Close** to close the dialog box after you inset one or more symbols. Choose **Cancel** to close the dialog box without inserting a symbol.

7.23 Borders and Shading

You can add a border to any or all sides of each page in a document, to pages in a section, to the first page only, or to all pages except the first. You can add page borders in many line styles and colors, as well as a variety of graphical borders.

You can set apart paragraphs or selected text from the rest of a document by adding borders. You can also highlight text by applying shading. You can add borders to a table or individual table cell, and you can use shading to fill in the background of a table. You can also use the Table AutoFormat command to quickly give a table a polished look with a variety of borders, fonts, and shading.

You can add borders to drawing objects (including text boxes and AutoShapes) or to pictures, and you can enhance your drawing objects by adding a gradient (shaded), patterned, textured, or picture fill.

7.23.1 Add a Border to Text

Do one of the following:

1. To add a border to a paragraph, click anywhere in the paragraph.
2. To add a border only to specific text, select the text.
3. On the **Format** menu, click **Borders and Shading**, and then click the **Borders** tab.
4. Select the options you want, and make sure the correct option — **Paragraph** or **Text** — is selected under **Apply to**. For Help on an option, click the question mark and then click the option.
5. To specify that only particular sides get borders, click **Custom** under **Setting**. Under **Preview**, click the diagram's sides, or use the buttons to apply and remove borders.
6. To specify the exact position of the border relative to the text, click **Paragraph** under **Apply to**, click **Options**, and then select the options you want.

7.23.2 Add a Border or a Line to a Drawing Object

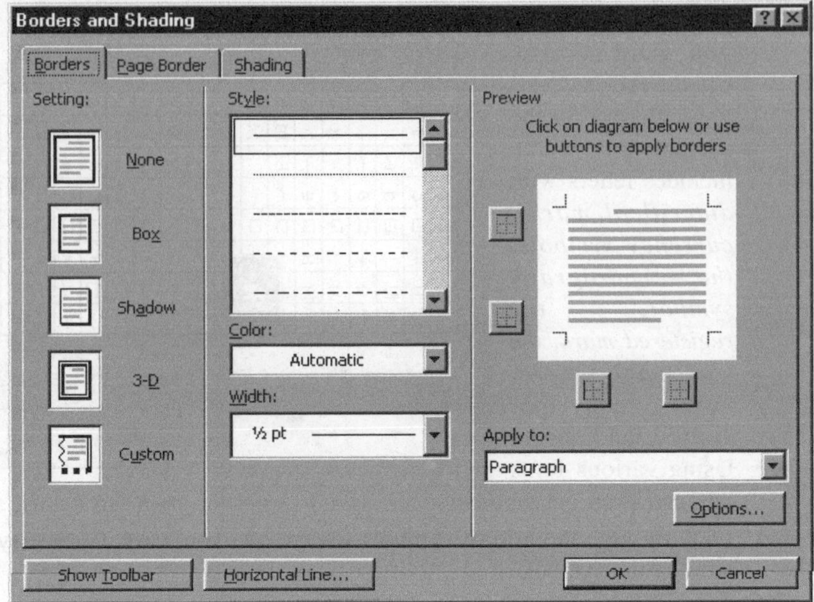

1. Select the drawing object you want to change.
2. Click **Drawing** to display the **Drawing** toolbar.
3. To add a color to the line or border, click the arrow next to **Line Color**, and then click the color you want. If you don't see the color you want, click **More Line Colors**. Click a color on the **Standard** tab, or click the **Custom** tab to mix your own color, and then click **OK**.
4. To give a line or border a different style, such as a heavier weight, click **Line Style**, and then click the style you want — or, click **More Lines**, and then click a style.
5. To make a dashed line or border, click **Dash Style** , and then click the style you want.

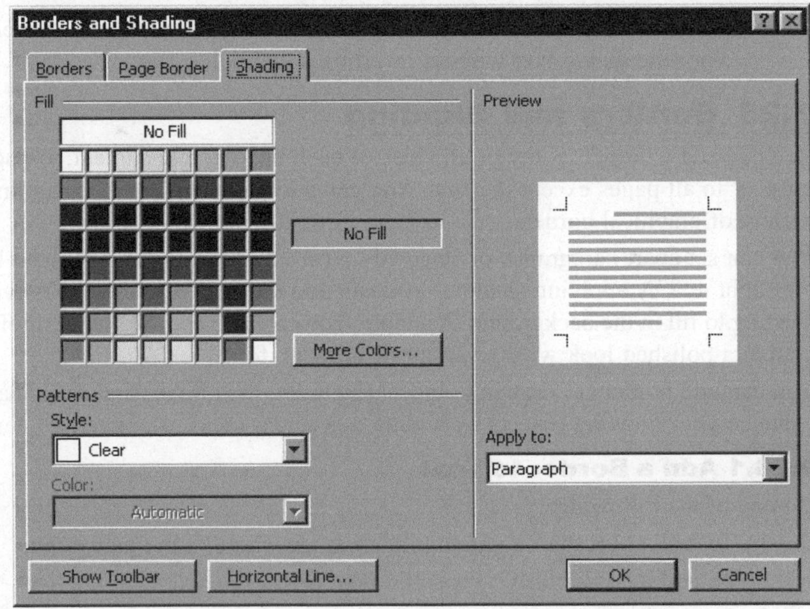

7.24 Columns

This command is used to make your text run into different columns. You can choose the number of columns you want to have in your text. You can make your text look like a newspaper having 5 coloumns.

1. Select the text which you want to divide into columns.
2. Select Columns from Format menu to get Columns dialog box as shown here.
3. Choose the option and click Ok.

7.25 Working with Longer Documents

Working with long documents is cumbersome, particularly when several files created by several users need to be combined into one seamless report. For example, documents and reports such as Books, Annual Reports,

Company Policies, are often the combined efforts of a team of people representing several departments. Each of these people create a separate file for their contribution to the report from which a final product is generated. When the files are bound into one large report, the need for page numbers, headers and footers, a table of contents, an index, and consistent formatting becomes apparent to the individual responsible for the final, printed version. Some of the features are covered here.

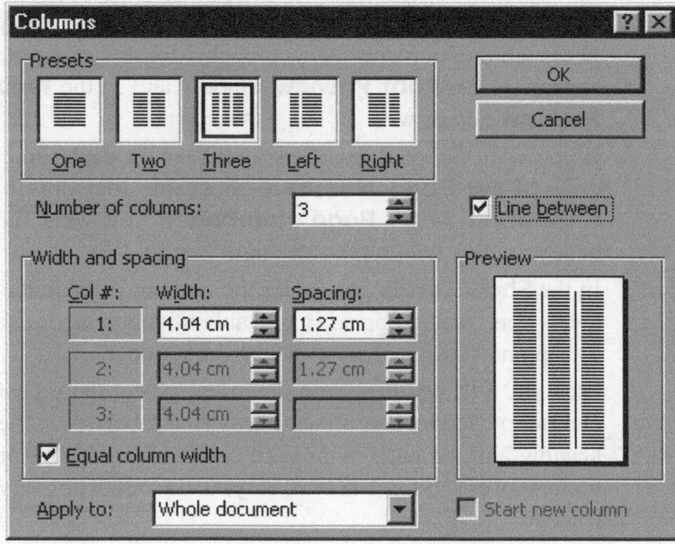

7.25.1 Create a Table of Contents

In all the books, in the beginning of the book, you will find a table of contents. It lists all the main topics in your document and notes on which page number each topic starts. Word helps you generate a table of contents for your document automatically. The easiest method for doing this is to assign one of Word's built-in heading styles (Heading 1 to Heading 9) to the headings you want to include in the table of contents. If you are not using Word's heading styles, you must assign a table of contents level to the styles you are using or mark text for inclusion in the table of contents.

7.25.1.1 Create a Table

1. Apply the built-in heading styles Heading 1 to Heading 9 to the headings in your document that you want to include in the table of contents.
2. Place the cursor in the document where you want the table of contents to appear. You may want to add a section or page break before your document text so the table of contents is on a separate page. You may also want to add a title for your page, such as "Table of Contents".
3. Click the **Insert** menu and select **Index and Tables**. The Index and Tables dialog box appears.
4. Select the **Table of Contents** tab if it is not already displayed.
5. From the **Formats**

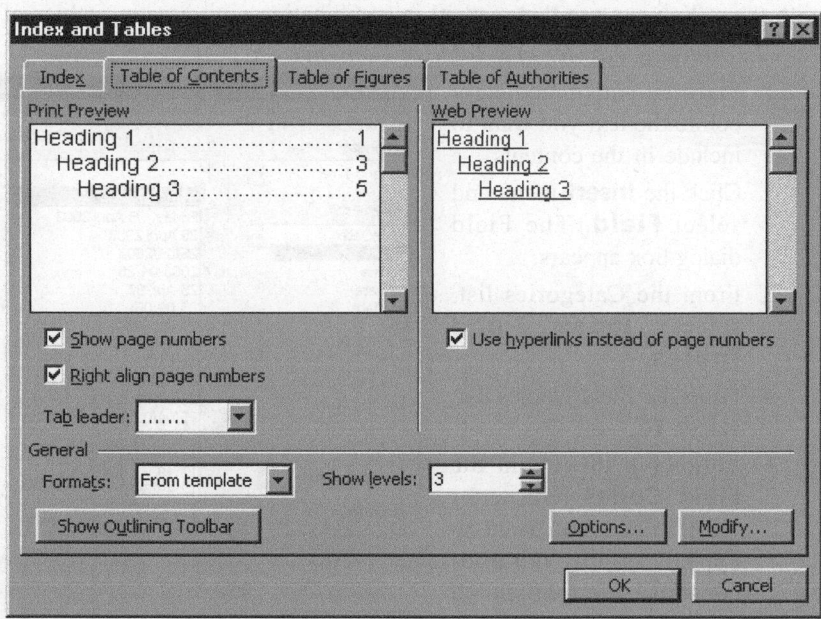

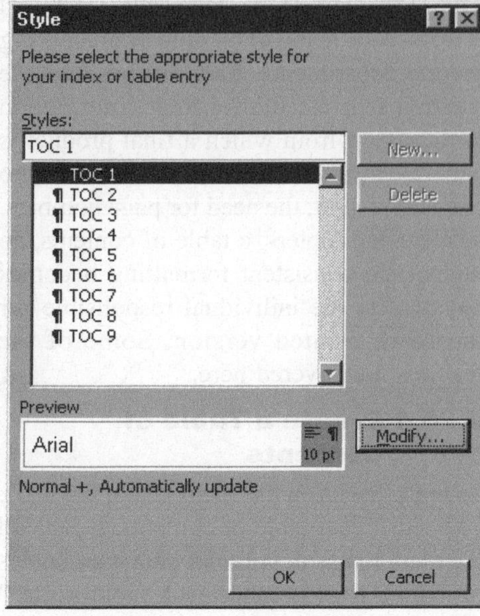

drop-down list, select the format that you want to apply to the table of contents. As you click a format, a sample appears in the **Print Preview** window and in the **Web Preview** window.

6. If you want the page numbers to appear for each topic, click **Show Page Numbers** to enable that option. Click **Right Align Page Numbers** if you want the page numbers lined up on the right margin.
7. In the **Show Levels** box, enter the number of headings levels you want to appear in the table of contents, or use the up and down arrows to select the number.
8. From the **Tab Leader** drop-down list, select the repeat character (leader) you want to appear between the heading and the page number (it can be dots, dashes or underscores). Select **None** if you do not want any leaders.
9. If you want to change the format, choose **Modify** to open the Style dialog box. From the Styles box, select the heading level you want to change in the table of contents and then choose Modify to open the **Modify Style** dialog box. Choose **Format** to select the type of format you want to specify and then select the formatting options you desire. Choose Ok to return to the Style dialog box, and then choose **Apply**.
10. Choose Ok. Word generates the table of contents for your document.

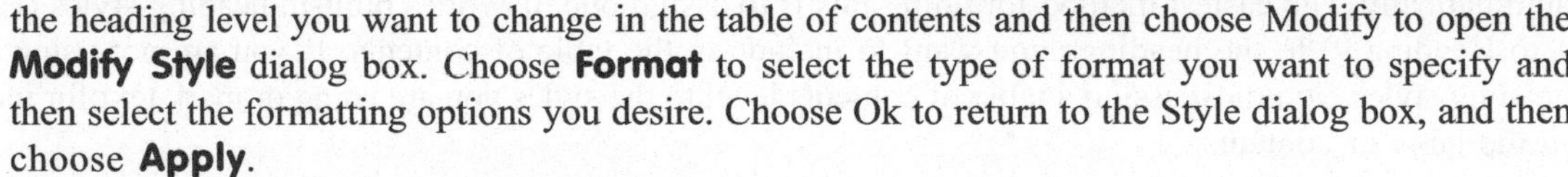

7.25.2 Marking Text for Table of Contents

Table of contents entries can be marked by field codes, marking each entry as you type. Use this method if you have items you want to include in the table of contents, but those items do not have styles associated with them. You can use this method in combination with creating tables of contents using styles.

7.25.2.1 Marking Entries of a Table of Contents

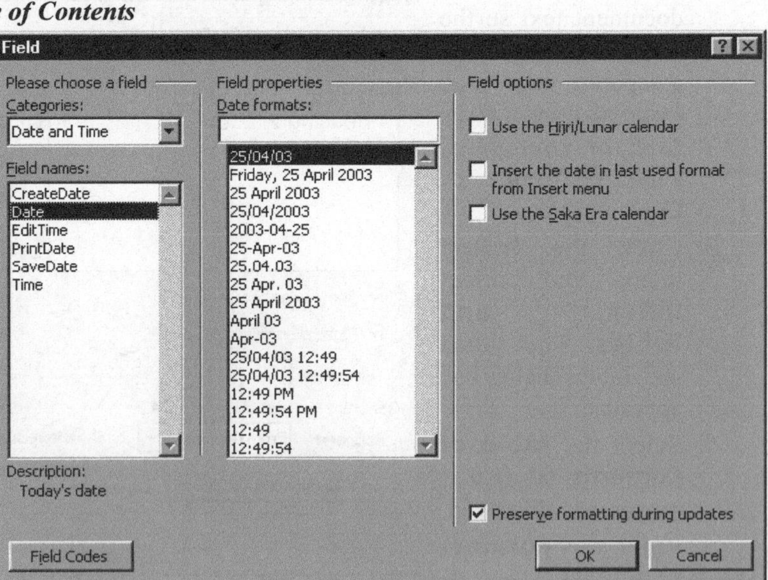

1. Place cursor immediately before the text you want to include in the contents.
2. Click the **Insert** menu and select **Field**. The Field dialog box appears.
3. From the Categories list, select **Index and Tables**.
4. From the Field Names list, select **TC**.
5. Following the TC in the **Field Codes** box, enter the text that you want to appear in the table of contents. The text should be enclosed in double quotes.

6. Choose Ok. A field code is inserted in the document text but is hidden. Choose **Show/Hide** on the Standard toolbar to see the code.

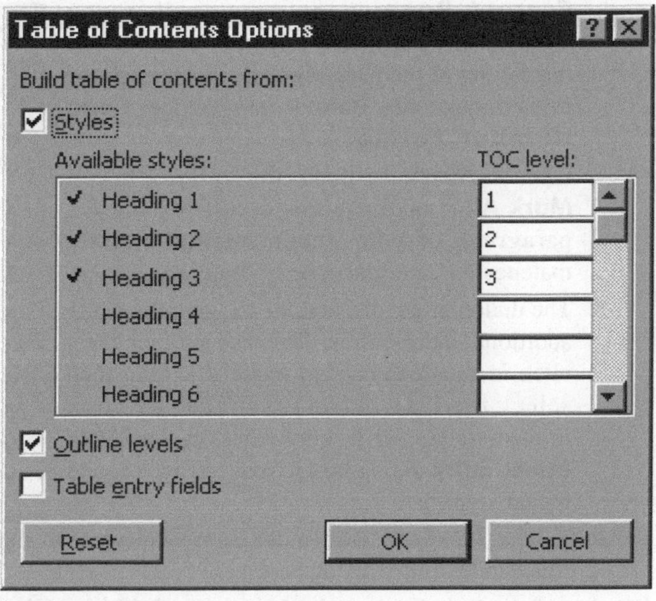

Perform the following steps to generate a table of contents from your marked entries.

7.25.2.2 Generate a Table of Contents from Marked Entries

1. Place the insertion point where you want the table of contents to appear.
2. Click the **Insert** menu and select **Index and Tables**. The Index and Tables dialog box appears.
3. Select the **Table of Contents** tab if it is not already selected.
4. Choose **Options** to open the **Table of Contents Options** dialog box. Click **Table Entry Fields**. Choose Ok to return to the Index and Tables dialog box.
5. Choose Ok to generate the table of contents.

7.25.3 Create an Index

An index usually appears at the end of the book. It contains references to the text which appears in the book alongwith the page number where it appears. It can have multiple entries, e.g., a word can appear at different places in the document at various pages.

To create a topic and page reference in your index, you must mark the words or phrases you want to appear in the index. Doing this provides Word a way to know what and where indexed references appear in your document.

7.25.3.1 Marking Index Entries

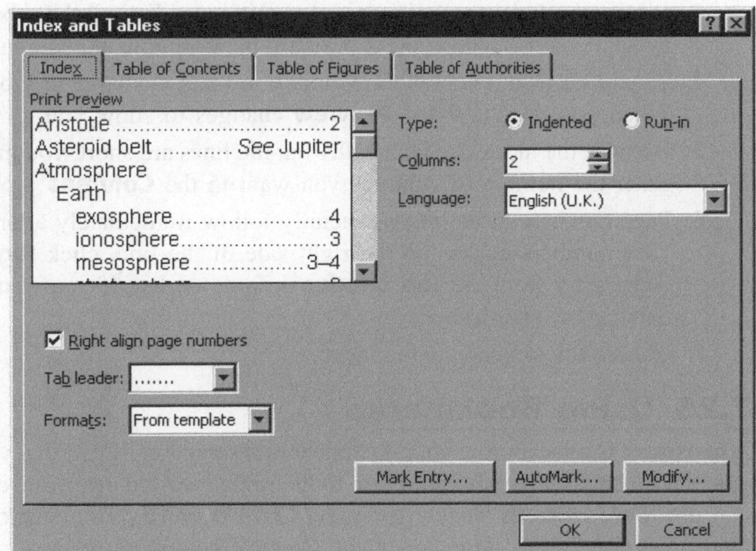

1. Select the text that you want for the index entry.
2. Click the **Insert** menu and select **Index and Tables** to open the Index and Tables dialog box.
3. Select the **Index** tab.
4. Choose **Mark Entry**. The Mark Index Entry box appears.
5. The selected text appears in the **Main Entry** box. Edit that text or enter new text if the selected text is not exactly what you want to display in the index.
6. Under **Options**, select

Current Page as the page number you want cited in the index. If you want to add formatting to the page numbers as they appear in the index, click **Bold** or *Italics* under **Page Number Format**.

7. Choose **Mark** to mark the entry. Choose **Mark All** to mark the first occurrence in each paragraph of your document that exactly matches the text and case of the entry.
8. The dialog box remains open so you may make additional index entries. To make another entry click in the document to make it active, then select the text in the document or click immediately after it, click back in the **Mark Index Entry** dialog box to make it active, and repeat steps 5 to 7.

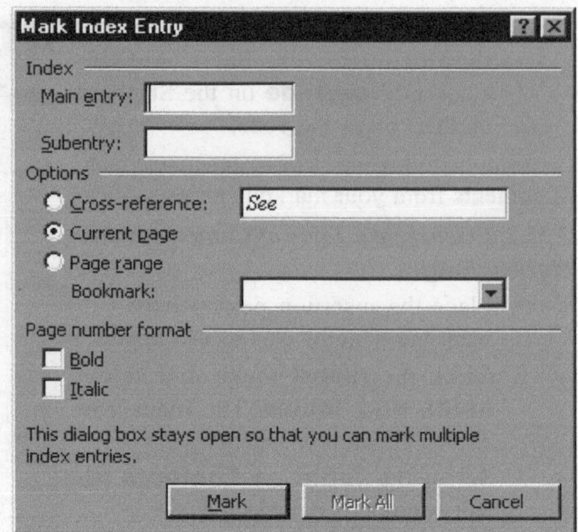

9. Repeat step 7 for each index entry you want to make in this session. Choose **Close** to close the Mark Index Entry dialog box.

Word marks each index entry by inserting a field immediately after the entry text in your document. If the field is not visible, choose **Show/Hide** on the **Standard** toolbar.

After you have all the index entries marked in your document., you are ready to generate the index. You may want to insert a section or page break at the end of the document where you want the index to start so it begins on a new page.

7.25.4 Generate an Index

1. Put cursor at the location in your document where you want the index to appear.
2. Click the **Insert** menu and select **Index and Tables**. When the Index and Tables dialog box appears, select the **Index** tab.
3. Under **Type**, click **Indented** or **Run-In**. An indented index lists the subentries as indented paragraphs under the main topic. A run-in index lists all the subentries in a single paragraph, separated by semicolons. When you choose a type, a sample appears in the Print Preview window.
4. To choose from the predefined index formats available in Word, select one from the **Formats** list. When you do, the **Print Preview** changes to show you an example of that format.
5. Because the index can be lengthy but the lines are short, you may want to set it up to run in columns. Enter the number of columns you want in the **Columns** box.
6. Page numbers in an index generally follow immediately after the topics. If you would rather have your numbers appear on the right side of the line, click **Right Align Page Numbers**. Choose a character from the **Tab Leader** drop-down list, if you want to join the entry text with the page number by a tap leader.
7. Choose Ok to generate the index.

7.26 Using Bookmarks

A bookmark is a location in your document or a selection of text that you name for reference purposes. After you place a bookmark, you can return to the same location again and again by selecting the bookmark when you use Word's **Go To** feature (pressing **Ctrl+G** or **F5**). Bookmarks are especially useful when you are modifying or editing a large document. Create a bookmark when you close the document so on opening it again, you can find where you left. Bookmarks are also useful as reference points for cross-references, index entries, and macros.

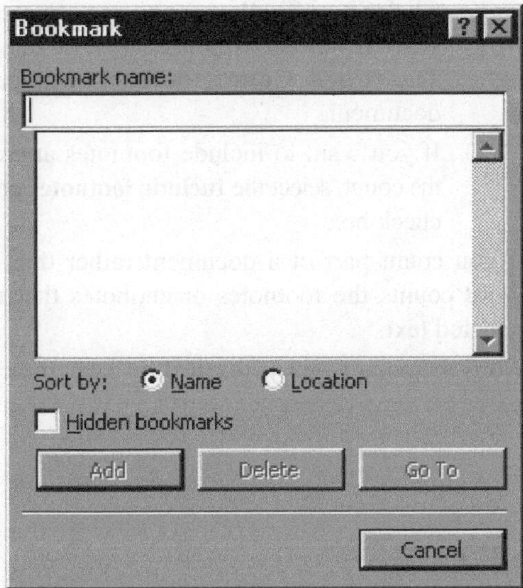

7.26.1 Add a Bookmark

1. Place cursor where you want to insert the bookmark.
2. Click the **Insert** menu and select **Bookmark** to open the Bookmark dialog box.
3. Type a name for the bookmark in the **Bookmark Name** box (do not enter any spaces in the name) or select one from the list. If you select the name of an existing bookmark, it will move the bookmark location to the current position of your cursor.
4. Choose **Add**.

7.26.2 Deleting Bookmark

1. Click the **Insert** menu and select **Bookmark**.
2. Select the name of the bookmark you want to *remove*.
3. Choose **Delete**.
4. Choose **Close**.

7.26.3 Displaying Bookmarks

Bookmarks are not visible in the document. They can be made to appear as square brackets ([]). To see the bookmarks in your document, do the following:

1. Click the **Tools** menu and select **Options**.
2. Select the **View** tab.
3. Under **Show**, click **Bookmarks**.
4. Choose Ok.

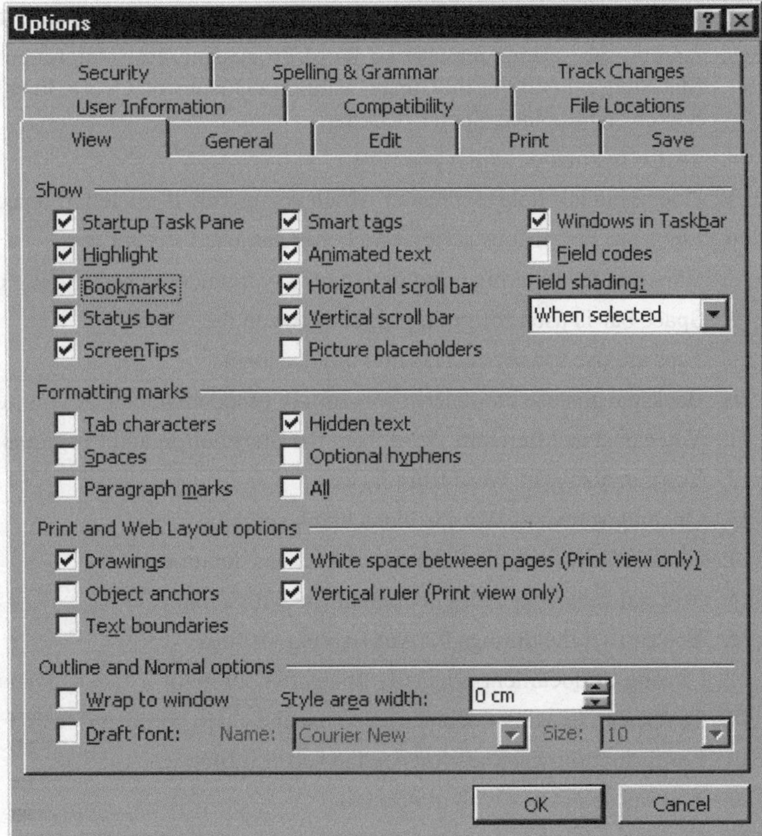

7.27 Count words

You can count the number of words in your document using the option called Word Count.

1. On the **Tools** menu, click **Word Count**. The results of everything Microsoft Word counts are displayed in the **Word Count** dialog box.

2. Click **Show Toolbar** if you want to recount as you make revisions without reopening the dialog box. The **Word Count** toolbar will open in your document.
3. If you want to include footnotes and endnotes in the count, select the **Include footnotes and endnotes** check box

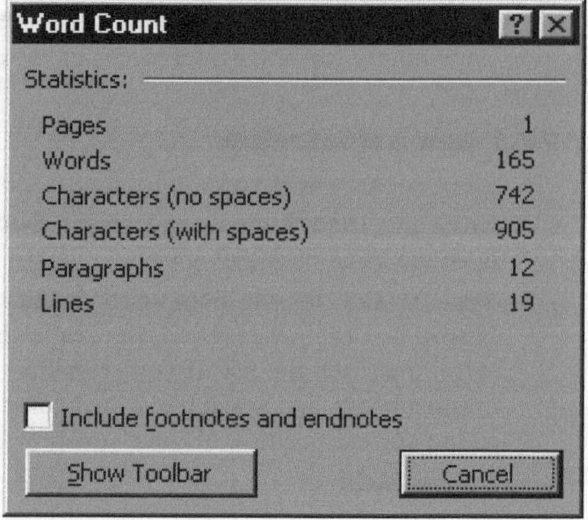

If you count part of a document rather than the whole, Word counts the footnotes or endnotes that refer to the selected text.

Word recounts when you select or clear the check box.

Let us Revise

1. Word processing programs allow you to manipulate text consisting of words.
2. In a word processing program, you can change the various aspects of the text.
3. Among the various features of Word Processing are: Alignment, Deleting Mistakes, Line Spacing, MailMerging, Moving the Cursor, Naming a Document, Overwriting Mistakes, Page Breaks, Page Numbers, Search and Replace, Spell Checking.
4. Text is the matter which you type.
5. Document is whole text matter which you create, like a letter, or a chapter, etc.
6. Fonts are the various styles which you can use for your text.
7. Cursor is the blinking point which tells you where to start typing or what your current position is.
8. Space bar is used for giving space between the words.
9. Tabs are used to set the text into tabular form.
10. Backspace is used to delete the wrongly typed character in your text.
11. You can start Microsoft Word from the Start button and Programs.
12. You can also start Word from its icon.
13. Opening screen of Word is like a blank screen.
14. Click at New from the File menu to create a document.
15. You can save your Word document file with a name.
16. You can set the timings for Auto saving of files.
17. Closing of document is usually done after saving it.
18. To open an existing document, you use the Open command from File menu.
19. For formatting the text, you need to select it first.
20. You can select text with mouse too.
21. You can select text from keyboard too.
22. The various formats supported by Word are: Bold, Italics, Underline.
23. You can also make the text Strikethrough, Double strikethrough, Superscript, Subscript, Shadow, Outline,

Emboss, Engrave, Small Caps, All Caps and Hidden.

24. You can change the size of the text from Formatting bar and Font dialog box.
25. You can change the font of the text too from Formatting bar and Font dialog box.
26. You can change the colour of the text too.
27. Alignment supported by Word are: Left, Right, Center and Justify.
28. Using Paragraph dialog box, you can change the line space and para space among other things.
29. You can put Headers on top of the pages of the document and Footers at the bottom.
30. You can set the page numbers according to your liking.
31. Spell checking is an important aspect of the word processing.
32. You can even add the words which are not there in the dictionary.
33. You can print all or few pages of the document on the printer.
34. You can do all the editing operations like Cut, Copy, Paste, Delete, etc., in Word.
35. You can also have graphics inserted into your Word documents.
36. Word has its own set Clip Arts which can be inserted in the documents.
37. You can have the text wrapped around the graphics in your document.
38. WordArt is an independent program which allows to create text in diffrent formats.
39. You can set the various options of your page using Page Setup.
40. You can highlight your text using Bullets and Numering.
41. You can even Borders around your text.
42. You can have various tabs in your documents to make the text tabular.
43. You can find particular word in Word and replace it with another.
44. You can have a table inserted into your document.
45. You can align your text in the table in any format which you may desire.
46. You can add Rows and Columns in your table.
47. MailMerge is an important feature of Word.
48. You can give page number to each page of the document.
49. You can have header and footer on each page.
50. You can insert a symbol from the hard disk in your document.
51. You can have border with shades around your text in Word.
52. You can have your text in multiple columns.
53. A Table of Contents can be created in Word.
54. You can create an index of the document.
55. You can place a bookmark in your text.
56. You can count the number of words in your text.

Multiple Choice Questions

1. In word processing, you manipulate ________

   (a) numbers (b) text

2. You can set Left, Right and ______ alignment in word processing.

(a) Center (b) Justify (c) Both

3. Can you spell check you text in word processing?

(a) Yes (b) No

4. Can you locate a word in word processing?

(a) No (b) Yes

5. Blinking point which shows your position in the text is called:

(a) Cursor (b) Blinker (c) Position

6. Spacebar is used for :

(a) giving space (b) deleting space

7. You can start Microsoft Word by using ________ button.

(a) New (b) Start (c) Program

8. For creating a document, you use _____ command at File menu.

(a) New (b) Open (c) Document

9. For saving a document, you need to have ________ for it.

(a) Name (b) Surname

10. For opening an existing document, you need to give _____ command.

(a) New (b) Open (c) Close

11. You can select the text by:

(a) Keyboard (b) Mouse (c) Both

12. You click at B to make the text

(a) Bold (b) Italics (c) Underline

13. Can you emboss you text?

(a) Yes (b) No

14. You can change the size of the text from:

(a) Formatting bar (b) Font dialog box (c) Both

15. You click at I to make the text

(a) Bold (b) Italics (c) Underline

16. You can change the font of the text from

(a) Formatting bar (b) Font dialog box (c) Box

17. Colour of the text can be changed:

(a) Yes (b) No

18. You click at U to make the text

(a) Bold (b) Italics (c) Underline

19. Word supports alignments like Left, Right, Center and ______

(a) Justify (b) Up (c) Down

20. You can change the line and para spacing from ______ dialog box.

(a) Font (b) Paragraph (c) Open

21. Header appears at the ______ of the page.

(a) Top (b) Bottom (c) Center

22. Footer appears at the ________ of the page

(a) Top (b) Bottom (c) Center

23. For printing a document you have to have __________ on.

(a) Printer (b) Monitor (c) Scanner

24. Most of the editing tools are available under _____ menu.

(a) File (b) Format (c) Edit

25. You can add picture in your document from the ________ menu.

(a) File (b) Edit (c) Insert

26. Clip Art is

(a) Text (b) Graphics (c) Both

27. Can Text be mingled with Graphics?

(a) Yes (b) No

28. WordArt is a

(a) Text (b) Graphic (c) Independent program

29. You can set margins by using the dialog box:

(a) Font (b) Page Setup (c) Margins

30. Two main orientations are, Potrait and

(a) Landscape (b) Photo (c) Lying

31. Can you shade your text?

(a) Yes (b) No

32. Can you put border across your text in the document?

(a) Yes (b) No

33. Decimal is tab?

(a) Yes (b) No

34. In text you can find a word and replace it with another word using command _____.

(a) Find (b) Replace (c) None

35. You can insert a table from __________ toolbar.

(a) Formatting (b) Standard (c) Drawing

36. You can align data vertically in a table:

(a) Yes (b) No

37. Can you insert more rows in a table?

(a) Yes (b) No

38. Sending of same letter to different people is done by:

(a) Send (b) Letter (c) Mailmerge

39. Headers are put:

(a) at the top (b) at the bottom (c) in the middle

40. You can put page numbers :
    (a) at the top (b) at the bottom (c) both places
41. Footers are put:
    (a) at the top (b) at the bottom (c) in the middle
42. Table of contents has:
    (a) Page number (b) Marked entry (c) both
43. Borders can be shaded:
    (a) Yes (b) No
44. You can have line in between the columns:
    (a) Yes (b) No
45. Index has all marked enteries with page numbers:
    (a) Yes (b) No
46. Word count gives you :
    (a) Numuber of lines (b) Number of words (c) Both

True/False Questions

1. Word processing is to mix words.
2. You can spell check your typed text.
3. You cannot use various fonts available under Windows for your text.
4. Spacebar is used for giving space between words.
5. You use Open to start a new document.
6. You can save your documents with a name.
7. For formatting the text, you need not select it.
8. Keyboard cannot be used for selecting the text.
9. You cannot change the colour of your text.
10. You can change the size of your text.
11. You can change the line spacing from Paragraph option.
12. You cannot number your pages in Word.
13. You can check your grammer too in Word.
14. You can print some selective page too.
15. You can edit the text of your document.
16. You cannot insert graphics in your document.
17. You cannot align text in the table.
18. You can add more rows and columns in the table.
19. You cannot put borders across your text.
20. For mailmerging you have to create two files.
21. Table of Contents does not have page numbers.

22. Index usually appears in the beginning of the book.
23. There is no provision for Bookmark in Word.
24. Clip Art are graphics.

Matching Columns

In the following case, commands are given in the left hand columns and their actions in the right hand column. Match them.

Column A	Column B
A. Header	1. Merging of documents according to data
B. Table	2. Horizontal page
C. Clip Art	3. Used to identify rows
D. Portrait	4. It rows and columns to refer text
E. Justify	5. Display document before printing
F. Next page	6. Changing text to Bold
G Data Source	7. Readymade documents
H. Page break	8. Readymade graphics
I. Save a document	9. Command to help you generate a document
J. Numbers	10. Start new section on new page
K. Print preview	11. Ctrl + S
L. Times New Roman	12. File having data
M. MailMerge	13. Displayed in top margin
N. Wizard	14. Bottom of the page
O. Use B for	15. An alignment
P. Template	16. Vertical page
Q. Footer	17. A font
R. Landscape	18. End of a page and beginning of new page

Fill in the Blanks with appropriate words

a. File	b. Centre	c. Tools	d. Backspace
e. Replace	f. Status	g. Save	h. Font
i. Green	j. Find	k. Insert	l. Standard

1. You can save your document using ______ command.
2. Using ________ command you can find a word.
3. The command used to replace one word with another is _________.
4. The bar which shows your current status in the document is called __________.
5. You can delete one character using _________ key.

6. You can use _____ alignment to centralize your text.
7. Spell check is under ______ menu.
8. Grammatical errors are shown in _______.
9. All open, close icons are there on the _________ toolbar.
10. Text can be styled using _______.
11. You can enter page numbers from _______ menu.
12. You can start a new document using New command which is under _______ menu.

Descriptive Type Questions

1. What is word processing?
2. What are the various features of word processing?
3. Define the following terms:

Text	Document
Fonts	Cursor
Arrow keys	Space bar
Tabs	Backspace

4. Describe the various methods of starting Microsoft Word.
5. Describe the various items on the screen of Word.
6. How would you create a new document?
7. Describe the process of saving a document.
8. How would you set the timing for AutoSave?
9. If you do not save before closing, what will happen?
10. Describe the process of opening an existing document.
11. Describe the various methods of selection of text.
12. Describe the process of making the text, Bold, Italics and Underline.
13. Describe the various options of Font dialog box.
14. How would you change size & font of the text?
15. Describe the process of changing the colour of the text.
16. What is an alignment? Describe the various alignments supported by Word.
17. Describe the various options of Paragraph dialog box.
18. How would you allot page numbers to various pages in your document?
19. How is spell checking ?
20. What are various options of spell checking dialog box?
21. Describe the various options of Print dialog box.
22. Describe the various editing tools of Word.
23. Describe the various shortcuts attached to editing tools.
24. How would you insert graphics into your document?

25. What is a Clip Art? How would you add a clip art in your text.
26. Describe the process of wrapping text around the graphic.
27. What is WordArt? Describe the process of creating a WordArt text.
28. Describe the various options of Page Setup.
29. How are Bullets and Numering used?
30. Describe the various options of Borders and Shading.
31. Describe the various Tabs supported by Word and how they are used?
32. Describe the process of finding a word and replacing it with another.
33. How would you create a table in your document?
34. Describe the various options of table alignments.
35. How would you add rows and columns in a table?
36. Describe the complete process of MailMerge.
37. How would you enter a chart in your document?
38. How would you use Wizard to create your bio-data?
39. What are Headers and Footers and how are they put in the documents?
40. How would you insert a symbol in your document?
41. How would you put border across your text in the document?
42. What is columns command used for?
43. How would you create a Table of Contents?
44. Describe the process of creating the index.
45. What is bookmark used for?
46. How are the words in the document counted?

Answers to Objective Type Questions

Multiple Choice Questions

1. b	2. c	3. a	4. b
5. a	6. a	7. b	8. a
9. a	10 b	11. c	12. a
13. a	14. c	15. a	16. c
17. a	18. a	19. a	20. b
21. a	22. b	23. a	24. c
25. c	26. b	27. a	28. c
29. b	30. a	31. a	32. a
33. a	34. b	35. a	36. a
37. a	38. c	39. a	40. c
41. b	42. a	43. a	44. a
45. a	46. c		

True False Questions

1. T	2. T	3. F	4. T
5. F	6. T	7. F	8. F
9. F	10. T	11. T	12. F
13. T	14. T	15. T	16. F
17. F	18. T	19. F	20. T
21. F	22. F	23. F	24. T

Matching Columns

A. 13	B. 4	C. 8	D. 16
E. 15	F. 10	G. 12	H. 18
I. 11	J. 3	K. 5	L. 17
M. 1	N. 9	O. 6	P. 7
Q. 14	R. 2		

Fill in the Blanks

1. g	2. j	3. e	4. f
5. d	6. b	7. c	8. i
9. l	10. h	11. k	12. a

Spreadsheets 8

8.1 Spreadsheet Concepts

Excel for Windows is a spreadsheet program. A spreadsheet is a graphical representation of rows and columns. Data can be fed into these rows and columns and mathematical and other operations performed on it. An opening screen of Excel is shown here.

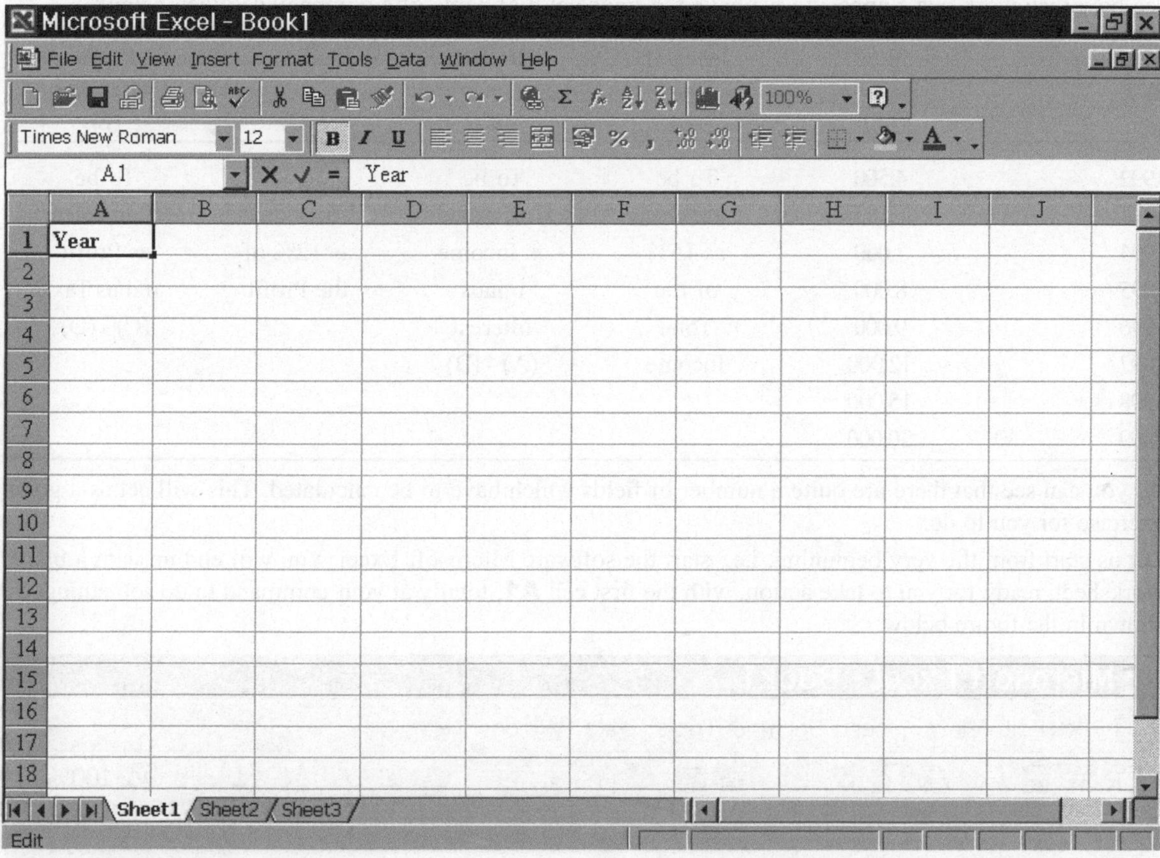

8.1.1 Naming Convention

It is not I have named rows from 1 onwards and columns A onwards on my own but they are so numbered by the software itself. These are the standard way of expressing these columns and rows.

If we have to name a large number of cells or columns, for that too we have the convention which asks us to call them with starting cell address and last cell address with colon in between. For example, see the addressed cells here.

Another convention is of the sheets in the worksheet.

8.1.2 Sheets

These are like pages in a book. Initially there are 16 worksheets in a file. But, you can add more. However, there may be only 6 of them visible on the screen. These sheets are independent but you can transfer data from one sheet to another.

These sheets are very helpful. For example, for a salary spreadsheet, one sheet may belong to one month and there may be a sheet for the total of the year.

8.2 Creating a Spreadsheet

Before we learn the various commands let us create a worksheet and use some commands side-by-side to see how they work out. Supposing we have the financial highlights of a company as given below:

Year	Total Income (A)	Interest Paid (B)	Profit (C)	Tax (D)	Profit After Tax (E)
1992	4,500	To be	To be	To be	To be
1993	5,500	Calculated	Calculated	Calculated	Calculated
1994	7,000	as 15%	as Income	as 12% of	as Profit
1995	8,000	of the	minus	the Profit	minus Tax
1996	9,000	Total	Interest		(C) - (D)
1997	12,000	Income	(A) - (B)		
1998	15,000				
1999	20,000				

As you can see that there are quite a number of fields which have to be calculated. This will act as a good exercise for you to do.

Let us start from the very beginning, i.e., start the software Microsoft Excel. You will end up with a blank worksheet, ready for you to take action, with the first cell **A1**, totally at your command to do something, as shown in the figure below.

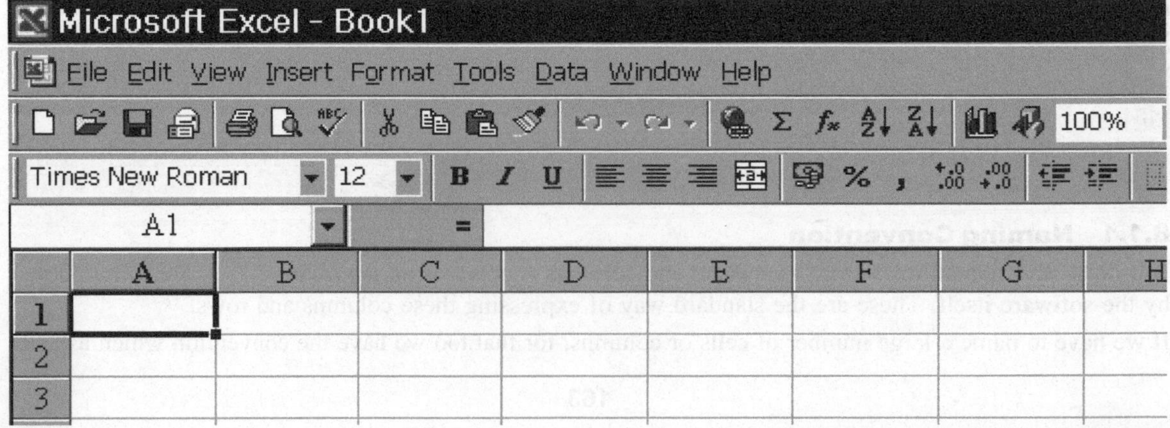

So what we have to do here. We have to type "Year". So just type the word Year and press **Enter**. You will see the word being shown in the formula bar too. This will also take you to the cell **A2**. But, for typing the next heading, you have to go to the cell **B1**. So use the arrow keys right and up to reach **B1**.

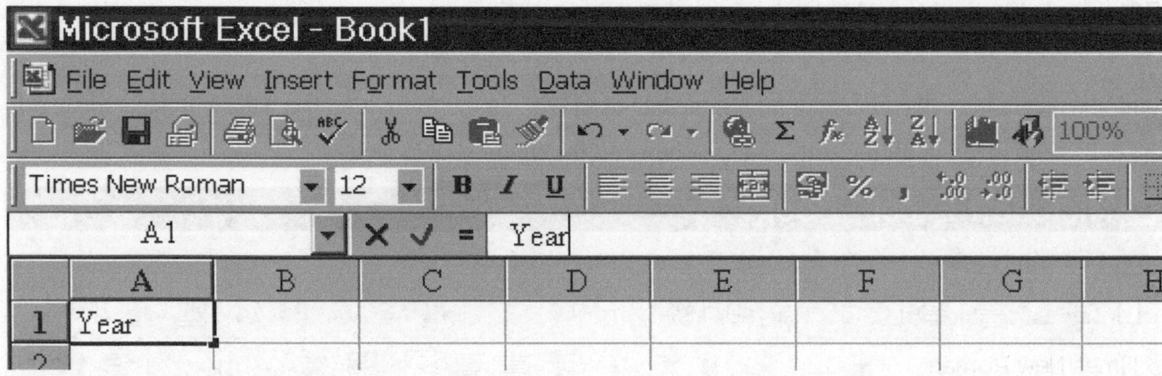

Next we have to type "Total Income". (Please note that for the sake of convenience I had shown this heading in 2 lines, but, if permitted we will type it in one line. Also (A), (B), etc., in the table are just symbolic and are not to be typed).

So for type the next heading, "Total Income" in the cell **B1**, as shown next.

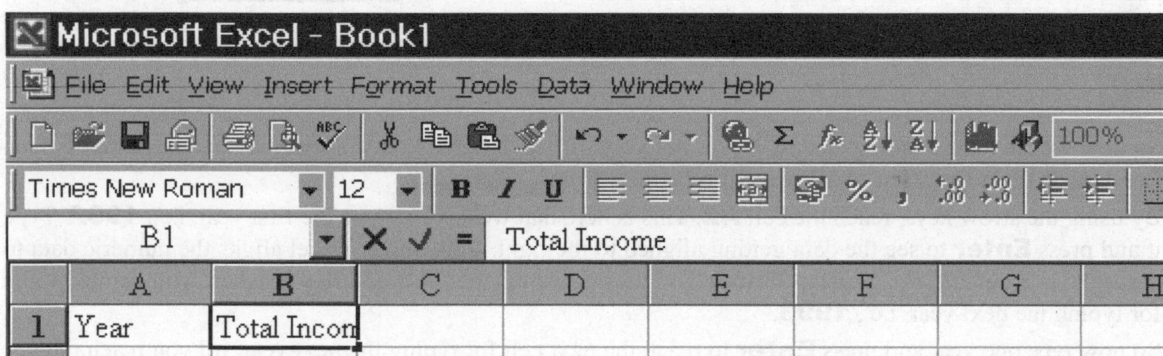

Did you notice anything wrong here? Well, the cell is not big enough to carry your heading. So what will we do? We will increase the width of the column **B**, by using one of the methods mentioned earlier in the chapter.

This way now we will type the complete headings, i.e., all of them, as shown next.

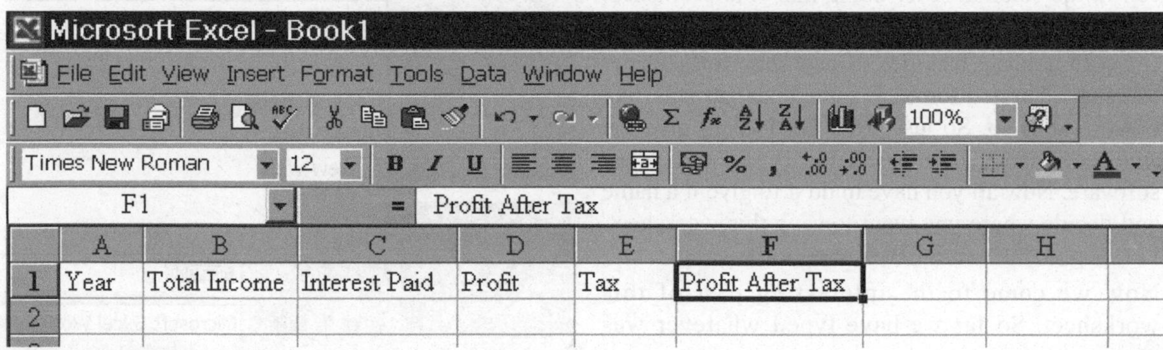

But, since these are headings, and are to be highlighted. We will make them **Bold** and put them in the centre of the cells. This way they will look good.

Highlight all the cells by just clicking at cell **A1** and then while pressing **Shift** key click mouse in the cell **F1**, the whole row gets highlighted.

Now click at B in the formatting bar to make the whole text as Bold.

With the text in the cells remaining highlighted, click at in the formatting bar. This will make the text in the cells centralized in all the cells. This is shown in the figure shown next.

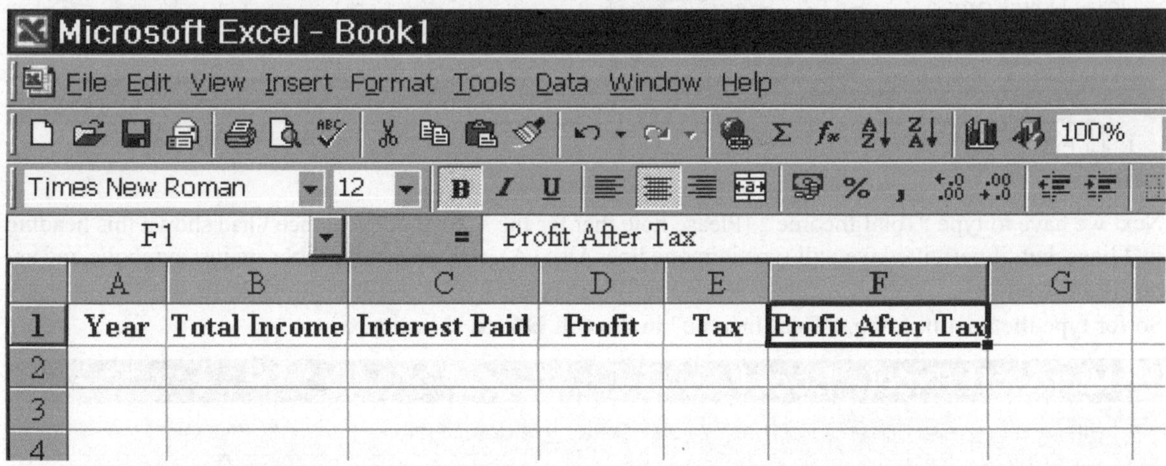

So now we have the headings ready. It was not very difficult, was it? Now all we have is the numeric data. Let us type them too. First of all we will type the various years.

By using the arrow keys, reach the cell **A2**. This is here that we have to type the first year, i.e., **1992**. Type it and press **Enter** to see the data getting aligned to the right. Remember, Excel aligns the numeric data to the right as a default. By pressing **Enter** you must have reached **A3** and this is where you wanted to be for typing the next year, i.e., **1993**.

So now type one year and press **Enter** to reach the next cell for typing the next year, till you reach the last year, i.e., **1999**. At this stage your worksheet will look like the one shown on the next page.

Next step is also easy. You have to just type the numbers in the cells **B2** to **B9**. All these figures are available with you. Just type one figure and press **Enter** to reach the next cell and so on till you reach the last cell in the column. After doing this your worksheet will look like the one shown next on the next page.

It would not be a bad idea to save this worksheet at this stage. For god forbid, if something happens, like power cut or so. So just press **Ctrl+S** to give the save command, as you would give in any other software. Now all you have to do it to give it a name and decide where you want to save this worksheet. Let us give the name **Finance** to it.

Now we come to the interesting part of this worksheet. So far we have typed whatever was

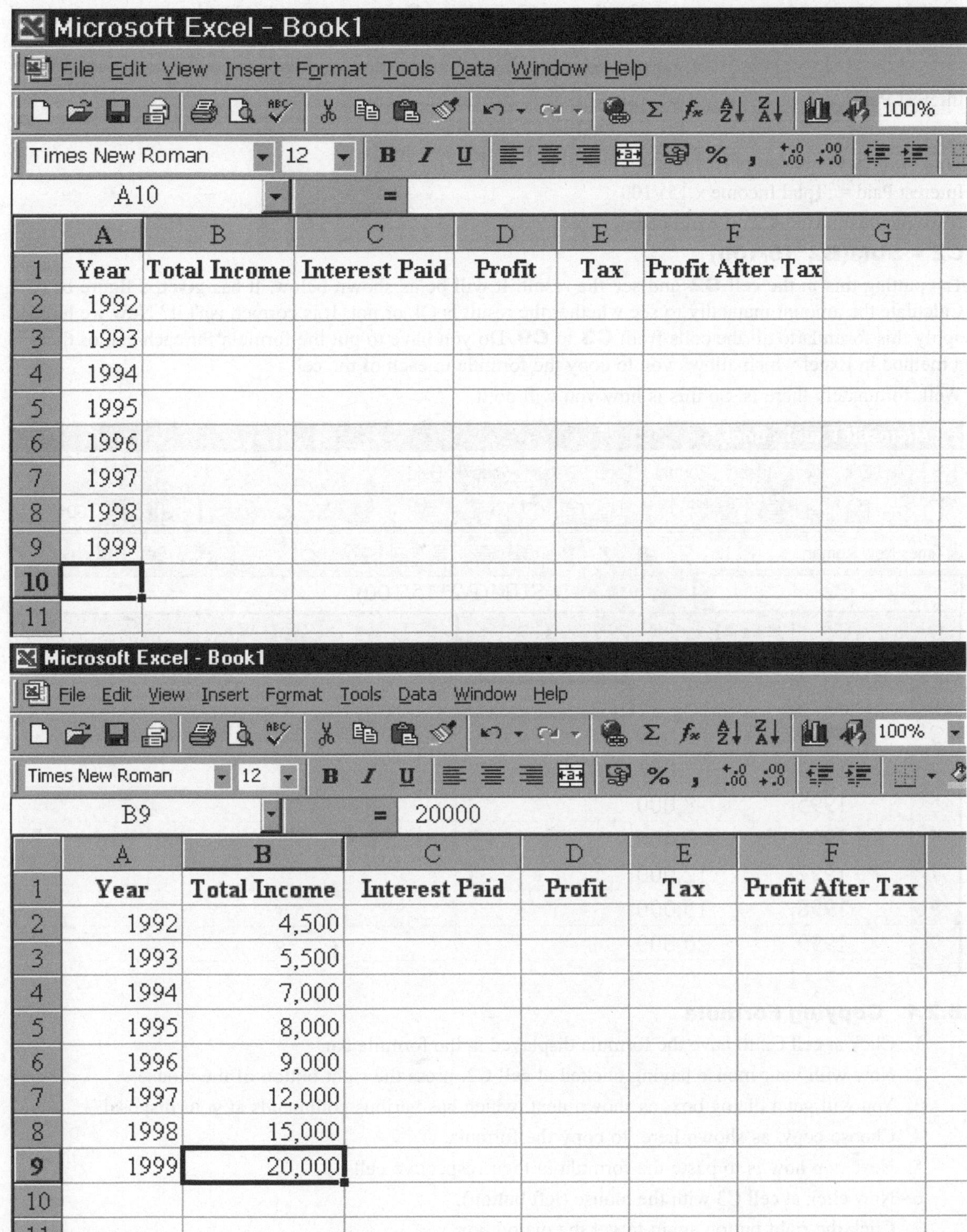

	A	B	C	D	E	F	G
1	Year	Total Income	Interest Paid	Profit	Tax	Profit After Tax	
2	1992						
3	1993						
4	1994						
5	1995						
6	1996						
7	1997						
8	1998						
9	1999						
10							
11							

	A	B	C	D	E	F
1	Year	Total Income	Interest Paid	Profit	Tax	Profit After Tax
2	1992	4,500				
3	1993	5,500				
4	1994	7,000				
5	1995	8,000				
6	1996	9,000				
7	1997	12,000				
8	1998	15,000				
9	1999	20,000				
10						
11						

available. Now we have to generate the figures. The column **C** is of Interest Paid which is to be calculated by using the formula.

$$\text{Interest Paid} = \frac{\text{Total Income} \times 15}{100}$$

Transformed to the computer language it will become:

Interest Paid = (Total Income x 15)/100

If we put this in Cell **C2**, it will become:

C2 = SUM(B2*15/100)

Try putting this in the cell **C2** and see the result. It will be as shown below. It has given a figure of 675. Calculate the amount manually to see whether the result is Ok or not. It is correct, isn't it? Now we have to apply this formula to all the cells from **C3** to **C9**. Do you have to put the formula for each cell or there is a method in Excel which allows you to copy the formula in each of the cell.

Well, fortunately there is. So this is how you will do it.

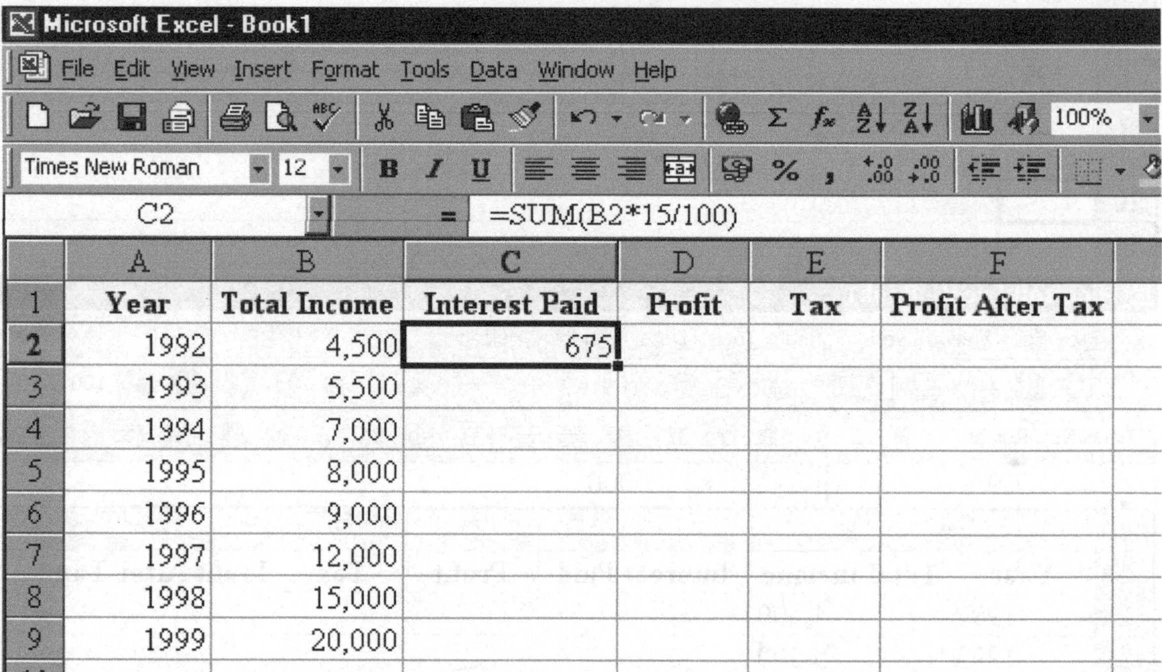

8.2.1 Copying Formula

1. Click at cell C2 to have the formula displayed in the formula bar.
2. Now with your mouse having clicked at cell C2, press the right button of the mouse.
3. You will get a dialog box, as shown next, which has various commands at your disposal.
4. Choose copy, as shown here, to copy the formula.
5. Next step now is to paste the formula in their respective cells.
6. Now click at cell C3 with the mouse (left button).
7. Click the right button again to get the dialog box.

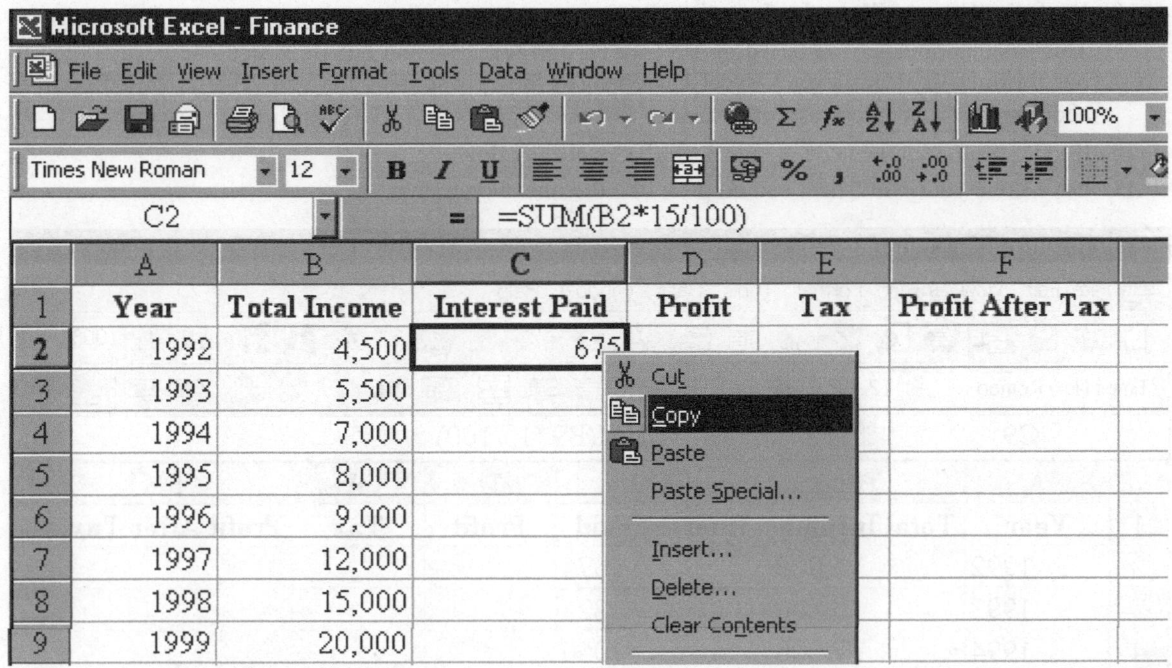

8. This time click at Paste instead, as shown next.

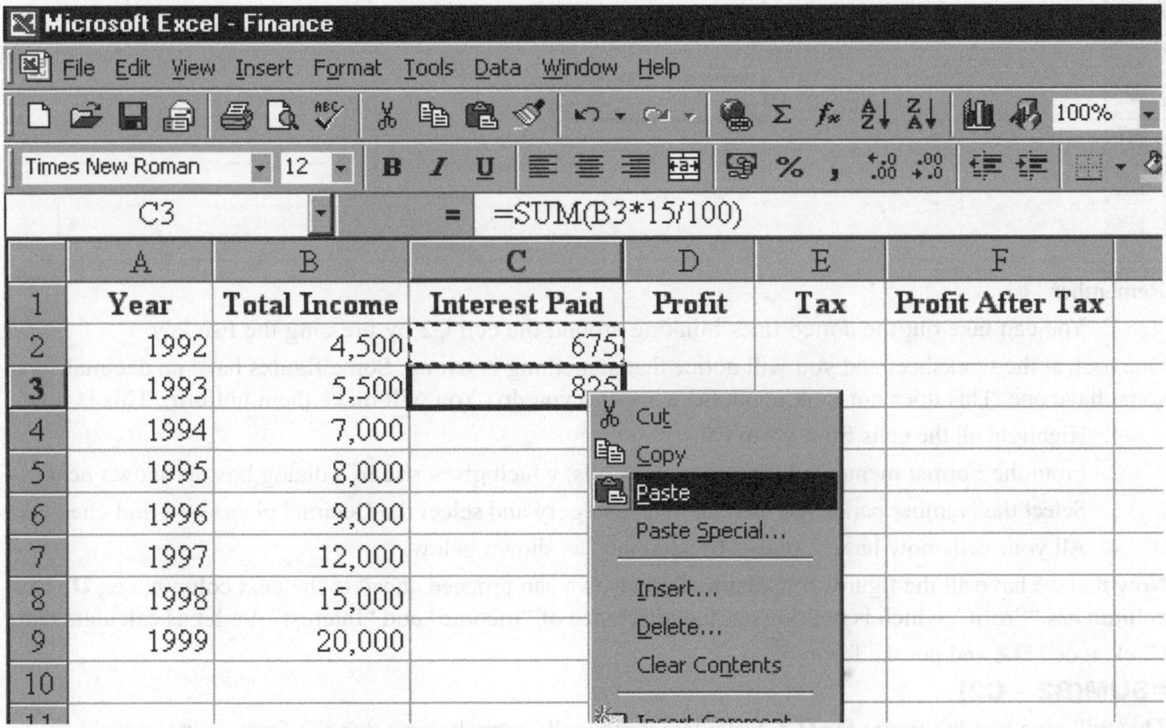

Microsoft Excel - Finance

File Edit View Insert Format Tools Data Window Help

100%

Times New Roman 12

C3 = =SUM(B3*15/100)

	A	B	C	D	E	F
1	Year	Total Income	Interest Paid	Profit	Tax	Profit After Tax
2	1992	4,500	675			
3	1993	5,500	825			
4	1994	7,000				
5	1995	8,000				
6	1996	9,000				
7	1997	12,000				
8	1998	15,000				
9	1999	20,000				
10						

Cut
Copy
Paste
Paste Special...
Insert...
Delete...
Clear Contents
Insert Comment

9. Immediately you will get the figure in cell C3.
   This calculation has been based on B3 (see the formula bar) and not B2 which had been copied in our formula. Is it not great? Excel has changed the cell address for you. This is called relative addressing and is a very useful feature of Excel.
10. Similar pasting in the cells from C4 to C9 can also be done.
11. Once done your worksheet should look like the one shown next.

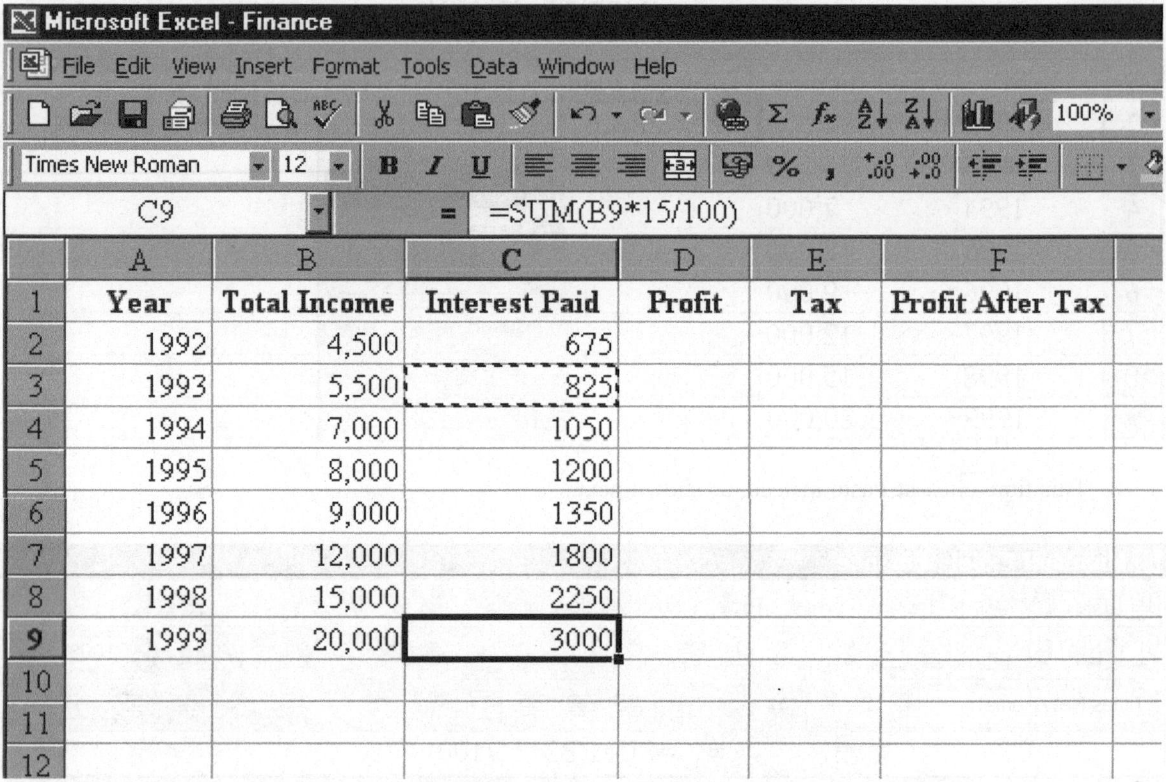

Microsoft Excel - Finance

File Edit View Insert Format Tools Data Window Help

Times New Roman 12 100%

C9 = =SUM(B9*15/100)

	A	B	C	D	E	F
1	Year	Total Income	Interest Paid	Profit	Tax	Profit After Tax
2	1992	4,500	675			
3	1993	5,500	825			
4	1994	7,000	1050			
5	1995	8,000	1200			
6	1996	9,000	1350			
7	1997	12,000	1800			
8	1998	15,000	2250			
9	1999	20,000	3000			
10						
11						
12						

Remember

1. You can take out the dotted lines blinking around the cell C2 by pressing the Esc key.

One look at the worksheet and you will notice that something is wrong. Some figures have no decimals and some have one. This does not look good. So what will you do? You will make them uniform. This is how:

1. Highlight all the cells from C2 to C9.
2. From the Format menu, call the command Cells, which gives rise to a dialog box, as shown next.
3. Select the Number panel and then number Category and select the Decimal places as 2 and click Ok.
4. All your cells now have 2 places of decimals, as shown below.

Now that we have all the figures of Column **C** ready, we can proceed ahead to the next column, i.e., **D**. This column has "Profit", which is nothing but the difference of "Income" and "Interest". So let us calculate that. Click at cell **D2** and put the formula

=SUM(B2 – C2)

This will give you the figure for **D2**. Calculate it manually to make sure that the formula is right.

Now, as we had done in the earlier case of Interest Paid, we will copy the formula and paste it in other cell, as shown below. One by one you would be able to calculate all the figures of Profit and would be able to fill up the whole column **D**. After you have done so, your worksheet would look like the one shown above. These figures have been corrected to 2 places of decimals as was done in the earlier case.

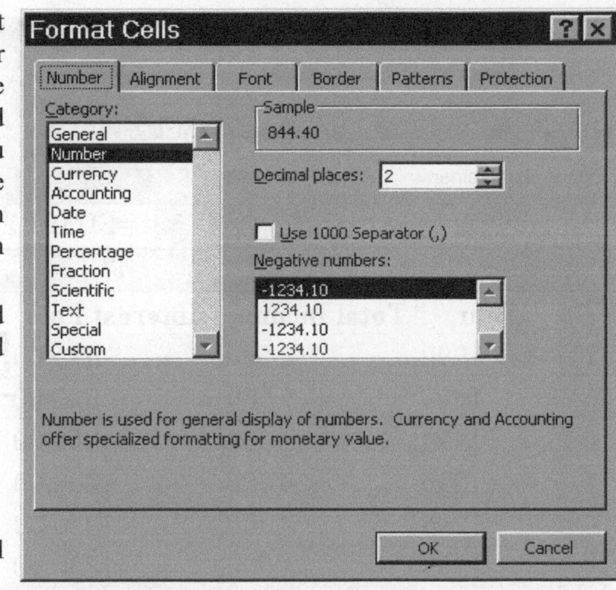

Next in line is the column called Tax. This is as said earlier, 12% of the Profit. So this can be calculated as below:

$$\text{Tax} = \frac{\text{Profit x 12}}{100}$$

Transformed to the computer language it will become:

Microsoft Excel - Finance

File Edit View Insert Format Tools Data Window Help

Times New Roman 12

C9 = =SUM(B9*15/100)

	A	B	C	D	E	F
1	Year	Total Income	Interest Paid	Profit	Tax	Profit After Tax
2	1992	4,500	675.00			
3	1993	5,500	825.00			
4	1994	7,000	1050.00			
5	1995	8,000	1200.00			
6	1996	9,000	1350.00			
7	1997	12,000	1800.00			
8	1998	15,000	2250.00			
9	1999	20,000	3000.00			
10						
11						

Tax= (Profit x 12)/100

If we put this in Cell **E2**, it will become:

E2 = SUM(D2*12/100)

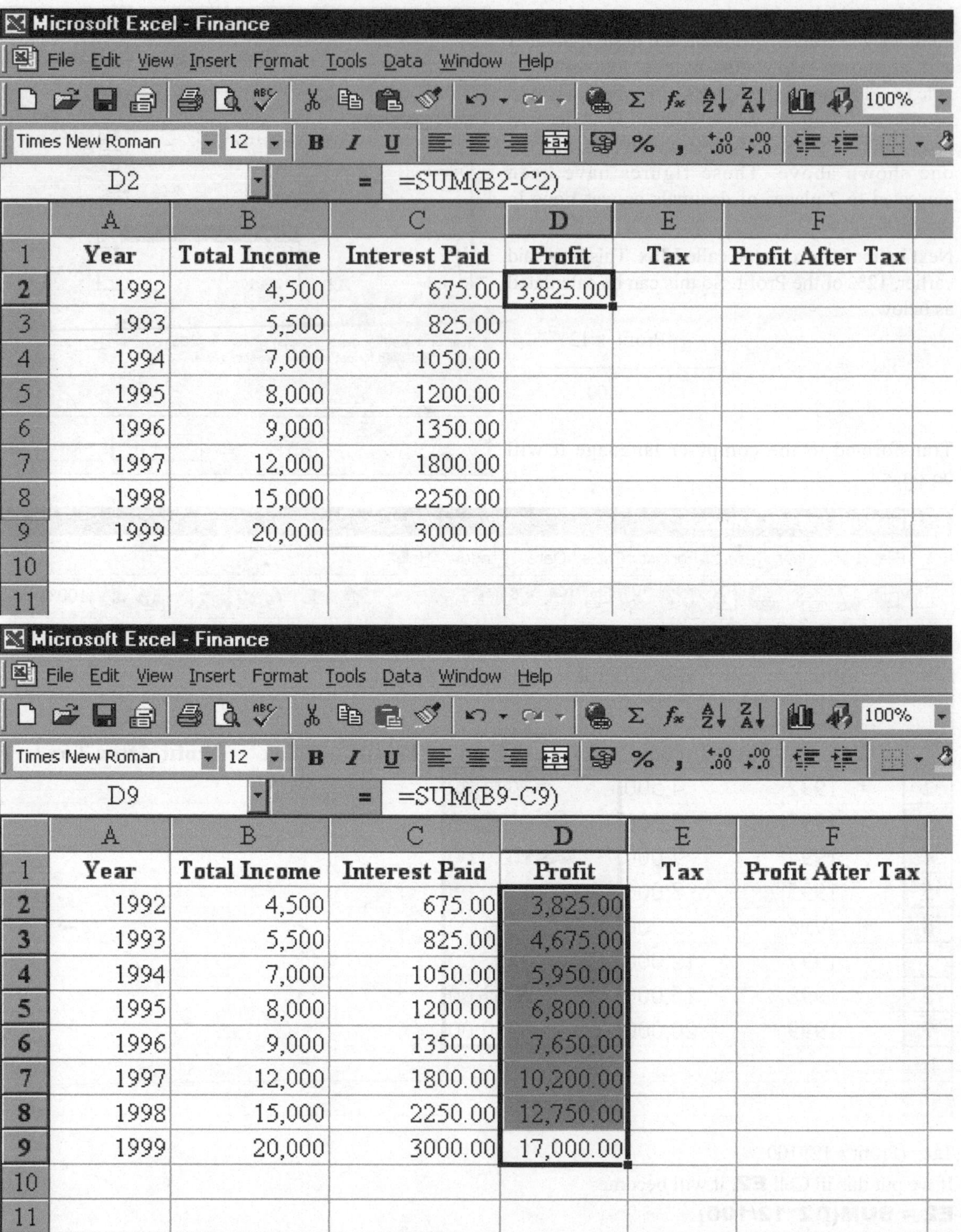
Microsoft Excel - Finance

D2 = =SUM(B2-C2)

	A	B	C	D	E	F
1	Year	Total Income	Interest Paid	Profit	Tax	Profit After Tax
2	1992	4,500	675.00	3,825.00		
3	1993	5,500	825.00			
4	1994	7,000	1050.00			
5	1995	8,000	1200.00			
6	1996	9,000	1350.00			
7	1997	12,000	1800.00			
8	1998	15,000	2250.00			
9	1999	20,000	3000.00			
10						
11						

Microsoft Excel - Finance

D9 = =SUM(B9-C9)

	A	B	C	D	E	F
1	Year	Total Income	Interest Paid	Profit	Tax	Profit After Tax
2	1992	4,500	675.00	3,825.00		
3	1993	5,500	825.00	4,675.00		
4	1994	7,000	1050.00	5,950.00		
5	1995	8,000	1200.00	6,800.00		
6	1996	9,000	1350.00	7,650.00		
7	1997	12,000	1800.00	10,200.00		
8	1998	15,000	2250.00	12,750.00		
9	1999	20,000	3000.00	17,000.00		
10						
11						

Let us apply this formula in **E2** and see what happens. It gives you the result as 459. Copying this formula to the other cells, i.e., from **E3** to **E9**, you can fill up the whole column and make the worksheet look like the one shown next.

Microsoft Excel - Finance

File Edit View Insert Format Tools Data Window Help

Times New Roman 12 B I U % , 100%

E2 = =SUM(D2*12/100)

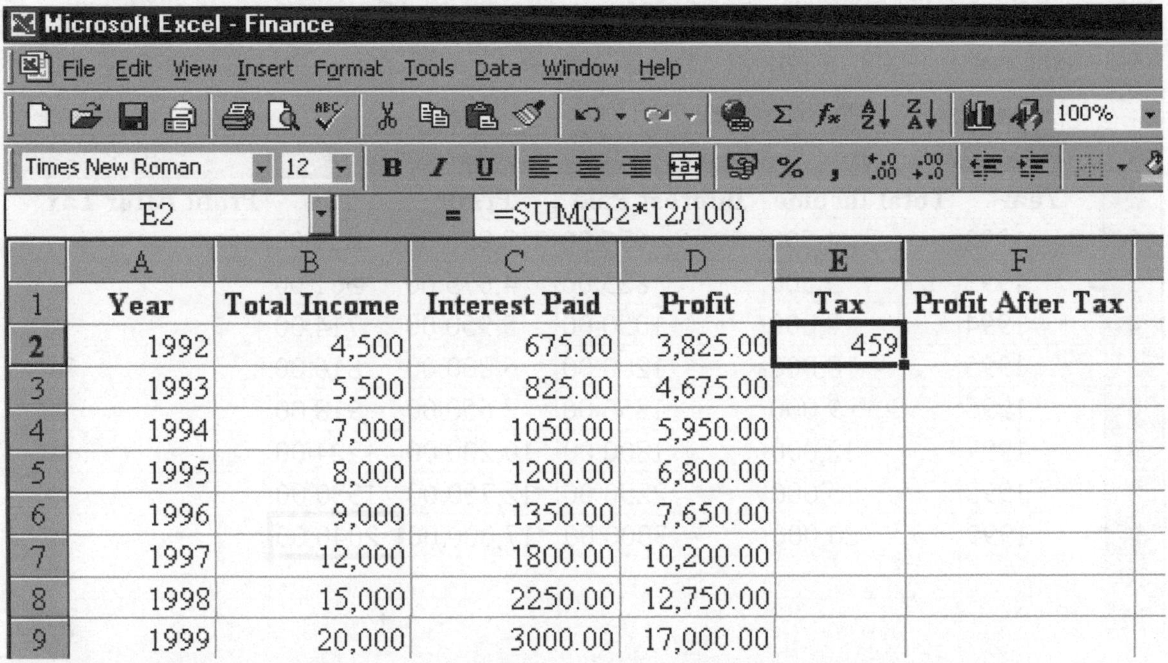

	A	B	C	D	E	F
1	Year	Total Income	Interest Paid	Profit	Tax	Profit After Tax
2	1992	4,500	675.00	3,825.00	459	
3	1993	5,500	825.00	4,675.00		
4	1994	7,000	1050.00	5,950.00		
5	1995	8,000	1200.00	6,800.00		
6	1996	9,000	1350.00	7,650.00		
7	1997	12,000	1800.00	10,200.00		
8	1998	15,000	2250.00	12,750.00		
9	1999	20,000	3000.00	17,000.00		

The last column in this case is the "Profit After Tax", which can be calculated after subtracting "Tax" from the "Profit". This calculation I am not showing here, since I assume that you should be able to do this easily. However, your resultant worksheet should look like the one shown next.

You think the worksheet is complete. No. You still have to do the column totals without which the whole worksheet looks incomplete.

For this follow the following steps.

1. Click at cell B10 to get the total of figures from B2 to B9.
2. Now click at Σ symbol in the Standard toolbar.
3. It will search for the numeric cells above and put the formula for the same and highlight the cells it has selected.
4. It will wait for your Ok in the form of Enter to put the result.
5. Press Enter to get the total in the cell B10, as shown on the next page.

Similarly all the other columns can be summed up showing the result as shown below.

Now you can say that your worksheet is complete. But, supposing we want to make any change. This is done delibrately to show you the main advantage of Excel software.

Supposing, we change the figure of the year 1996 from 9,000 to 9,200, which we can assume that it was wrongly given to us or was a typing mistake. It is shown on next page. Try changing this figure in the cell **B6** and see the resultant effect.

What have you noticed? Well since all the figures are mostly inter-linked, if you change one figure all the relative figures change automatically. This is the main advantage of Excel or for that an electronic spreadsheet.

Microsoft Excel - Finance

File Edit View Insert Format Tools Data Window Help

Times New Roman 12 100%

E9 = =SUM(D9*12/100)

	A	B	C	D	E	F
1	Year	Total Income	Interest Paid	Profit	Tax	Profit After Tax
2	1992	4,500	675.00	3,825.00	459.00	
3	1993	5,500	825.00	4,675.00	561.00	
4	1994	7,000	1050.00	5,950.00	714.00	
5	1995	8,000	1200.00	6,800.00	816.00	
6	1996	9,000	1350.00	7,650.00	918.00	
7	1997	12,000	1800.00	10,200.00	1224.00	
8	1998	15,000	2250.00	12,750.00	1530.00	
9	1999	20,000	3000.00	17,000.00	2040.00	

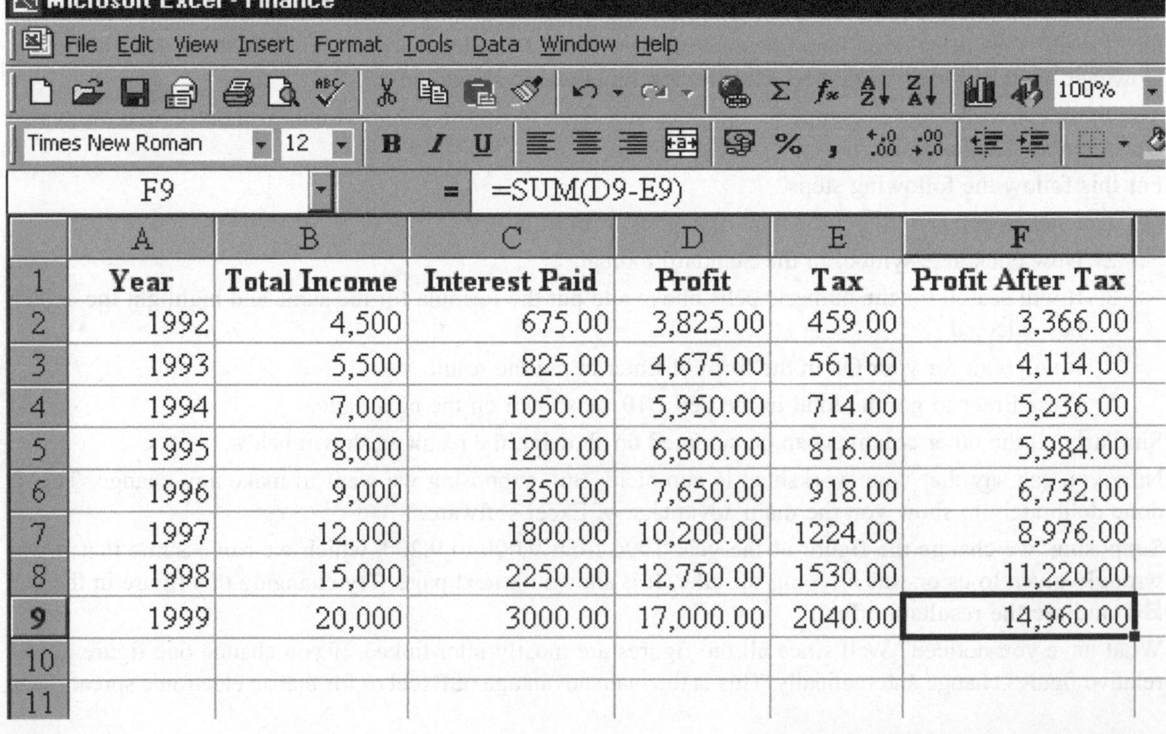

Microsoft Excel - Finance

File Edit View Insert Format Tools Data Window Help

Times New Roman 12 100%

F9 = =SUM(D9-E9)

	A	B	C	D	E	F
1	Year	Total Income	Interest Paid	Profit	Tax	Profit After Tax
2	1992	4,500	675.00	3,825.00	459.00	3,366.00
3	1993	5,500	825.00	4,675.00	561.00	4,114.00
4	1994	7,000	1050.00	5,950.00	714.00	5,236.00
5	1995	8,000	1200.00	6,800.00	816.00	5,984.00
6	1996	9,000	1350.00	7,650.00	918.00	6,732.00
7	1997	12,000	1800.00	10,200.00	1224.00	8,976.00
8	1998	15,000	2250.00	12,750.00	1530.00	11,220.00
9	1999	20,000	3000.00	17,000.00	2040.00	14,960.00

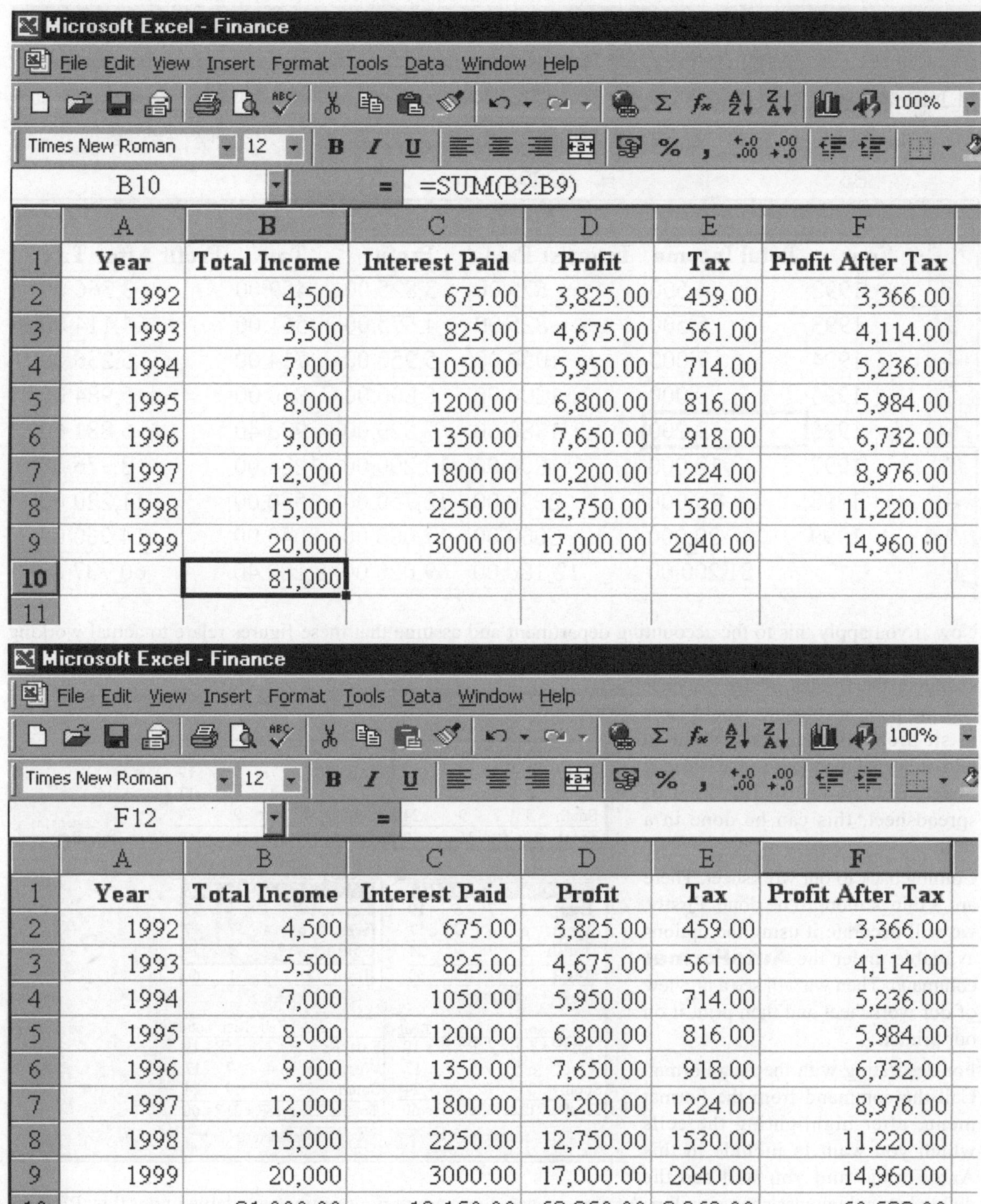

Microsoft Excel - Finance

B10 = =SUM(B2:B9)

	A	B	C	D	E	F
1	Year	Total Income	Interest Paid	Profit	Tax	Profit After Tax
2	1992	4,500	675.00	3,825.00	459.00	3,366.00
3	1993	5,500	825.00	4,675.00	561.00	4,114.00
4	1994	7,000	1050.00	5,950.00	714.00	5,236.00
5	1995	8,000	1200.00	6,800.00	816.00	5,984.00
6	1996	9,000	1350.00	7,650.00	918.00	6,732.00
7	1997	12,000	1800.00	10,200.00	1224.00	8,976.00
8	1998	15,000	2250.00	12,750.00	1530.00	11,220.00
9	1999	20,000	3000.00	17,000.00	2040.00	14,960.00
10		81,000				
11						

Microsoft Excel - Finance

F12 =

	A	B	C	D	E	F
1	Year	Total Income	Interest Paid	Profit	Tax	Profit After Tax
2	1992	4,500	675.00	3,825.00	459.00	3,366.00
3	1993	5,500	825.00	4,675.00	561.00	4,114.00
4	1994	7,000	1050.00	5,950.00	714.00	5,236.00
5	1995	8,000	1200.00	6,800.00	816.00	5,984.00
6	1996	9,000	1350.00	7,650.00	918.00	6,732.00
7	1997	12,000	1800.00	10,200.00	1224.00	8,976.00
8	1998	15,000	2250.00	12,750.00	1530.00	11,220.00
9	1999	20,000	3000.00	17,000.00	2040.00	14,960.00
10		81,000.00	12,150.00	68,850.00	8,262.00	60,588.00
11						

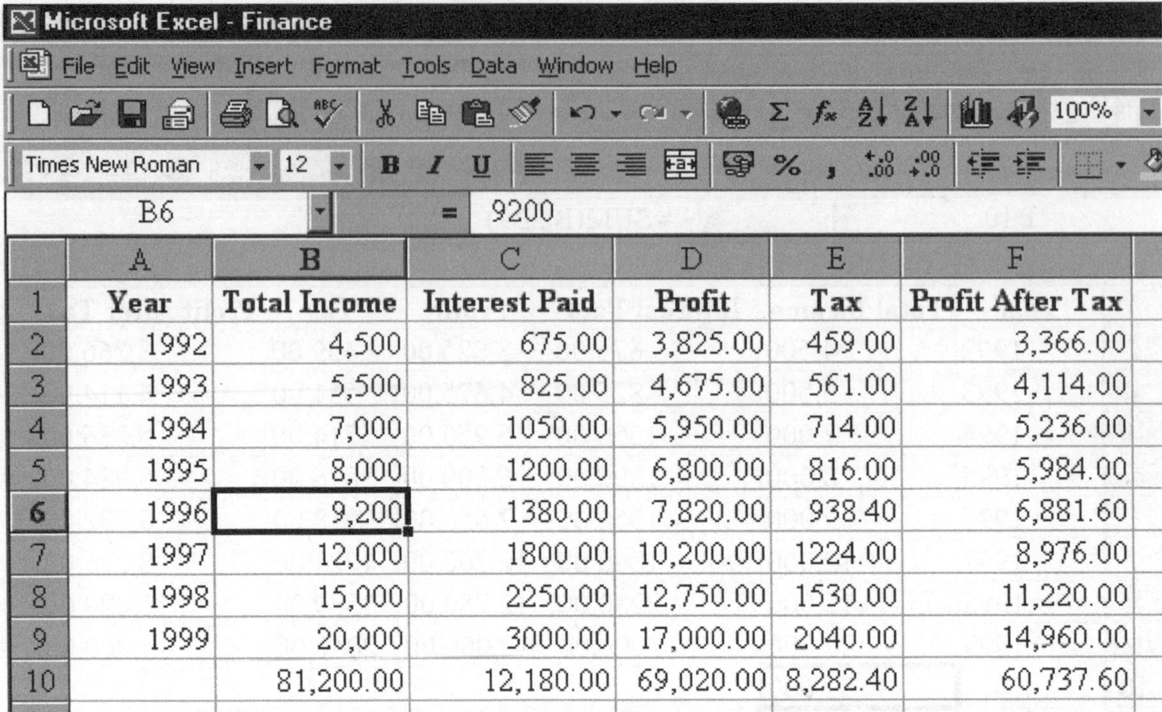

Microsoft Excel - Finance

B6 = 9200

	A	B	C	D	E	F
1	Year	Total Income	Interest Paid	Profit	Tax	Profit After Tax
2	1992	4,500	675.00	3,825.00	459.00	3,366.00
3	1993	5,500	825.00	4,675.00	561.00	4,114.00
4	1994	7,000	1050.00	5,950.00	714.00	5,236.00
5	1995	8,000	1200.00	6,800.00	816.00	5,984.00
6	1996	9,200	1380.00	7,820.00	938.40	6,881.60
7	1997	12,000	1800.00	10,200.00	1224.00	8,976.00
8	1998	15,000	2250.00	12,750.00	1530.00	11,220.00
9	1999	20,000	3000.00	17,000.00	2040.00	14,960.00
10		81,200.00	12,180.00	69,020.00	8,282.40	60,737.60

Now if you apply this to the accounting department and assume that these figures relate to actual working of the finance department. Try changing the figures of one voucher and the poor accountant would have to sit probably the whole night to recalculate all the totals in the Balance Sheet. But, now with this kind of spreadsheet, this can be done in a flash.

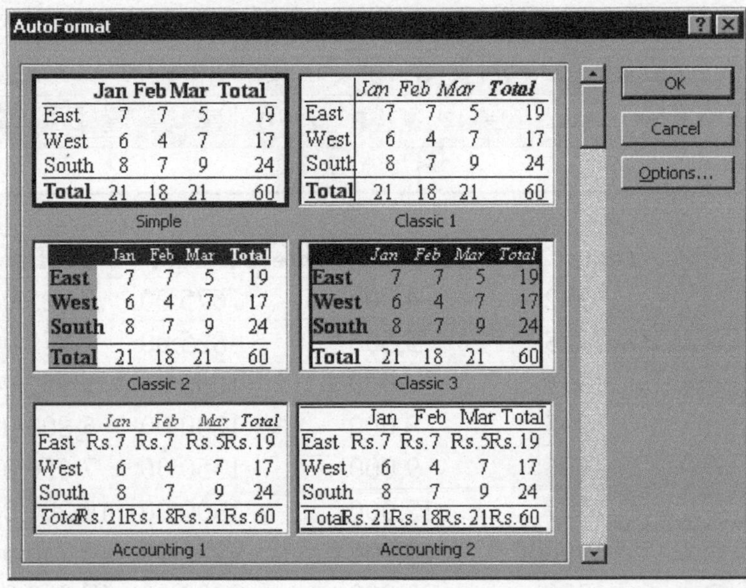

Coming back to our worksheet. There are 3 things more to be done. Firstly, we will decorate it using the options available under the **AutoFormat** command. Then we will see a preview of our worksheet and then print it on our printer.

For decorating with the AutoFormat. Call the command from the Format menu, after highlighting the cells which you want to include in this AutoFormat and you will see the dialog box, which was shown earlier. As you can see, there are various options available under this. Ranging from Simple, Classic, Accounting to 3-D ones. For our worksheet we are going to choose the one called Classic 2.

Microsoft Excel - Finance

File Edit View Insert Format Tools Data Window Help

Times New Roman 12 100%

C18 =

	A	B	C	D	E	F	G
1	**Year**	Total Income	Interest Paid	**Profit**	**Tax**	**Profit After Tax**	
2	**1992**	4,500	675.00	3,825.00	459.00	3,366.00	
3	**1993**	5,500	825.00	4,675.00	561.00	4,114.00	
4	**1994**	7,000	1050.00	5,950.00	714.00	5,236.00	
5	**1995**	8,000	1200.00	6,800.00	816.00	5,984.00	
6	**1996**	9,200	1380.00	7,820.00	938.40	6,881.60	
7	**1997**	12,000	1800.00	10,200.00	1224.00	8,976.00	
8	**1998**	15,000	2250.00	12,750.00	1530.00	11,220.00	
9	**1999**	20,000	3000.00	17,000.00	2040.00	14,960.00	
10		81,200.00	12,180.00	69,020.00	8,282.40	60,737.60	
11							

Just click at this and it would be applied. I am quite sure you would be interested to know the result of this. See the worksheet shown above for the result. I am quite sure that you are impressed with your work. You can make it look more impressive using the features of Borders, Patterns, etc.

Now that you have to print it on your printer to see the final result. But, before that we would like to see its **Preview**. This command is part of the **Print** command which is available under the **File** menu.

There are various other options in the print dialog box, shown on the next page, alongwith the print preview of the worksheet.

Printer You have to specify the various options of your printer. It is usually the printer installed in your Windows.

Print range You specify whether you want to print the whole file or few selected pages.

Print what You can choose to print a selected portion of the worksheet, or a full worksheet or even few selected worksheet.

Preview As said earlier, this gives you the preview of the worksheet which you can see before printing.

Copies You can print number of copies of the worksheet and even collate the various pages of the worksheet.

8.3 Saving

See the section where the above worksheet was saved as Finance.

8.4 Editing a Worksheet

The easiest way to change the text or number in a cell is to click the cell and then type right over the contents.

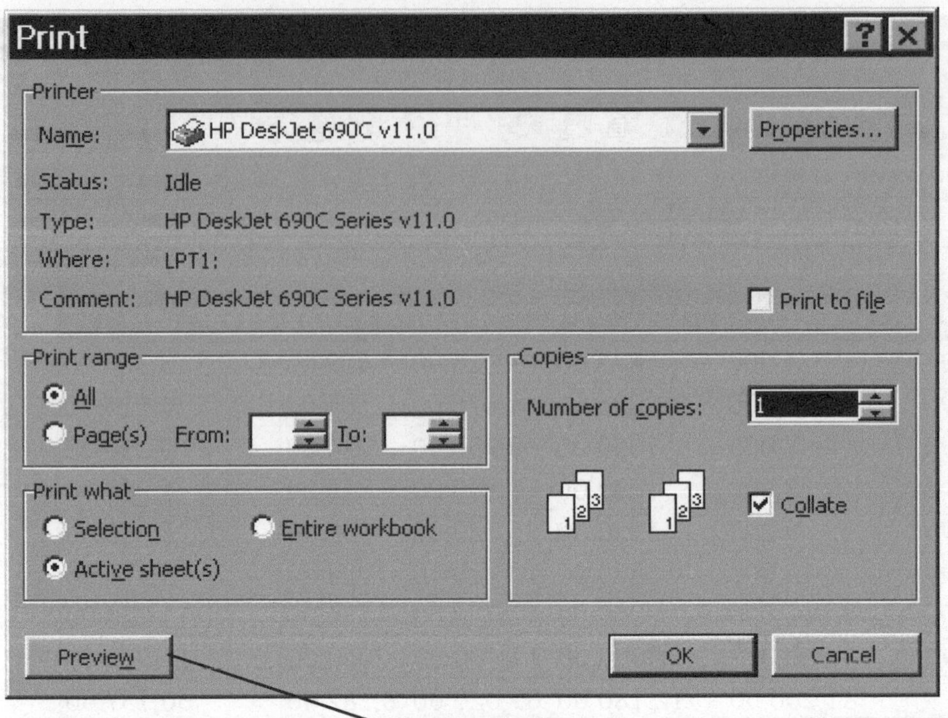

Year	Total Income	Interest Paid	Profit	Tax	Profit After Tax
1992	4,500	675.00	3,825.00	459.00	3,366.00
1993	5,500	825.00	4,675.00	561.00	4,114.00
1994	7,000	1050.00	5,950.00	714.00	5,236.00
1995	8,000	1200.00	6,800.00	816.00	5,984.00
1996	9,200	1380.00	7,820.00	938.40	6,881.60
1997	12,000	1800.00	10,200.00	1224.00	8,976.00
1998	15,000	2250.00	12,750.00	1530.00	11,220.00
1999	20,000	3000.00	17,000.00	2040.00	14,960.00
	81,200.00	12,180.00	69,020.00	8,282.40	60,737.60

But if you have a formula or extensive text in the cell, you might prefer to edit the existing contents to avoid retyping the whole entry.

8.4.1 To edit data in a cell

1. Click the cell and then type over its contents

   Or

   Double click the cell to position an insertion point with the cell contents.
2. Edit the contents as though you were editing text in Word.
3. Press Enter to enter the revised text in the cell.

This is if you have just one cell to edit, But, if you have more than one cell to edit. Then you need to select the various cells.

8.5 Inserting Worksheets

This is easy. Just click at Worksheet in the Insert menu and a new worksheet would be added.

8.6 Deleting Worksheets

Similar to above click at Delete and the current worksheet would be deleted, only after confirming that you really want to delete.

8.7 Entering data in a cell/formula

You can enter text, a number, or a formula into each cell in a worksheet. You enter text to create a label, such as a column heading. You can enter a number to provide information with which you can do calculations.

8.7.1 To Type Data in a Cell

1. Select the cell.
2. Type text, a number, or a formula. A flashing insertion point will appear at the end of whatever you type. You will notice that whatever you type will appear not only in the active cell but also in the Formula bar.
3. Press Enter key to move to the next cell. The cell below will become the new active cell.

Remember

1. You don't have to press Enter after you type the contents of a cell. You can simply press right arrow key to move to the next cell.
2. Excel right aligns the numbers in the cell but left aligns the text.

8.8 Copying and Moving from Selected Cells

Copying puts selected data in a new location. Unlike moved data, copied data also remains in the original location.

1. Select a range of cell. The cells will be highlighted.
2. Click the Copy button.
3. A marquee (running dashes) will appear around your selection.
4. Click in the cell at the top left of the range where you want to place a copy.
5. Click on Paste button.
6. The selected range will appear in both the original location and new location.
7. If you want you can paste the selection at another location too.

The next figure show the result of highlighting, copying of the cells range and copying them at a new location.

Microsoft Excel - Book1

File Edit View Insert Format Tools Data Window Help

Times New Roman 12 B I U % , 100%

A9 = Earnings

	A	B	C	D	E	F	G
1	**Year**	2000	1999	1998	1997	1996	
2	Sales	20,302	14,553	13,404	8,730	7,786	
3	Earnings	4,746	3,318	2,887	1,948	1,752	
4	Depreciation	1,278	855	667	410	337	
5	Taxable Profit	2,403	1,704	1,653	1,323	1,405	
6	Tax	3,719	2,893	3,021	2,490	2,234	
7							
8							
9	Earnings	4,746	3,318	2,887	1,948	1,752	
10	Depreciation	1,278	855	667	410	337	
11	Taxable Profit	2,403	1,704	1,653	1,323	1,405	
12							

8.8.1 Moving data

1. Select a range of cells. The cells will be highlighted.
2. Click on the Cut button. Moving dashes (called a marquee) will appear around your selection.
3. In this case the data does not disappear like text does in a word processor.
4. Click in the cell that will be upper left corner of the new location of the range. The cell will be selected.
5. Click on the Paste button. The data will be pasted in the new location.

8.9 Handling Operators in Formulae

They establish relationships between two or more cells. If you want to add the values in cells **C6** and **C7** and put the result in cell **C8**, move to the cell **C8** and type **=C6+C7** and press **Enter**. The result is displayed immediately in cell **C8**. Another way to achieve the same result is to move to cell **C8** and type **+**, point to cell **C6**, type **+**, then point to **C7**, and press **Enter**. The easiest way to achieve this operation is to point to **C8**, pick up the AutoSum button Σ on the toolbar.

8.10 Formatting a Worksheet

You can format a worksheet for varrious options. You can add/delete cells/rows, change their alignment, change their font, font size, width, height, etc. Some of them are covered here next.

8.11 Formatting Cells

For formatting, the first step, as always is the selection of the cells on which you want to perform some operations.

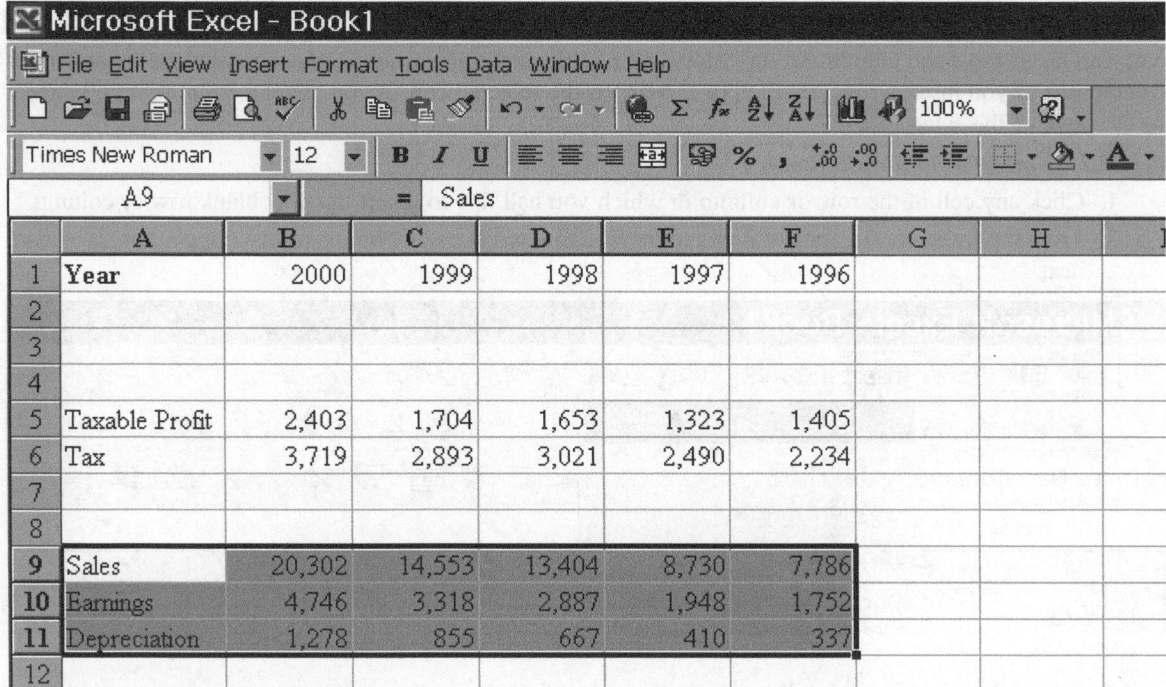

	A	B	C	D	E	F	G	H
1	**Year**	2000	1999	1998	1997	1996		
2								
3								
4								
5	Taxable Profit	2,403	1,704	1,653	1,323	1,405		
6	Tax	3,719	2,893	3,021	2,490	2,234		
7								
8								
9	Sales	20,302	14,553	13,404	8,730	7,786		
10	Earnings	4,746	3,318	2,887	1,948	1,752		
11	Depreciation	1,278	855	667	410	337		
12								

8.11.1 Selecting Cells

You can select a number of consecutive cells called a range by one of the following methods:

1. Click and drag over the selection.
2. Click in one cell, and then hold down the Shift key and click in the opposite corner of the selection.
3. Click on the Select All button, the gray rectangle where the column and row heading meet, to select the entire worksheet.
4. Click in a column or row heading to select the whole column or row.

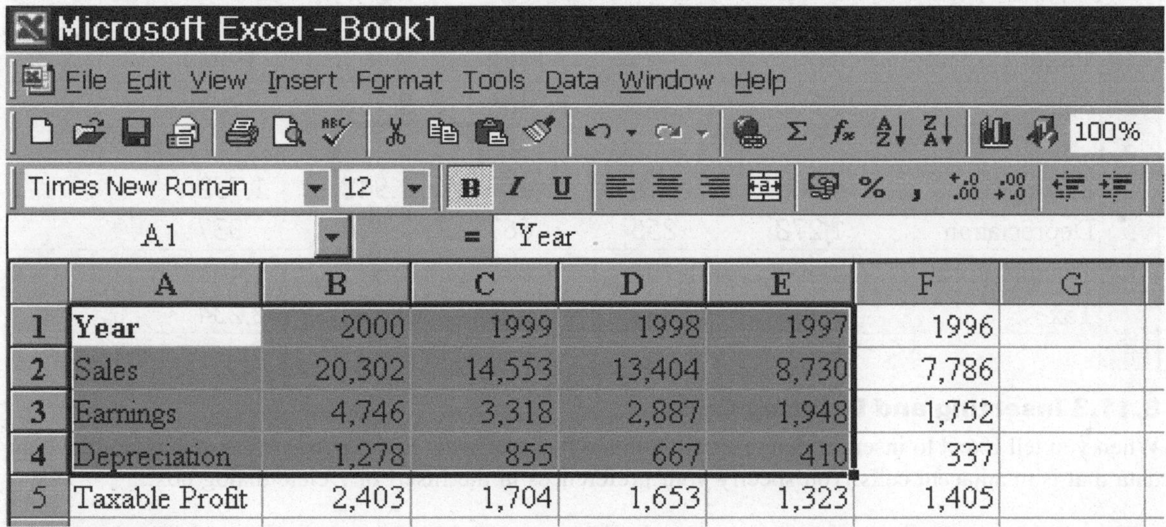

	A	B	C	D	E	F	G
1	**Year**	2000	1999	1998	1997	1996	
2	Sales	20,302	14,553	13,404	8,730	7,786	
3	Earnings	4,746	3,318	2,887	1,948	1,752	
4	Depreciation	1,278	855	667	410	337	
5	Taxable Profit	2,403	1,704	1,653	1,323	1,405	

8.11.2 Inserting Rows and Columns

You can insert rows and columns at any time, and Excel adjusts all formulas to accommodate the new rows or columns. If you insert a row, it will appear **above** the selected cell; if you insert a column, it will appear to the **left** of the selected cell.

8.11.2.1 To insert a row or a column

1. Click any cell of the row or column in which you had like to insert the new blank row or column.
2. From the Insert menu, choose Rows to insert a row or choose Columns to insert a column, as shown next.

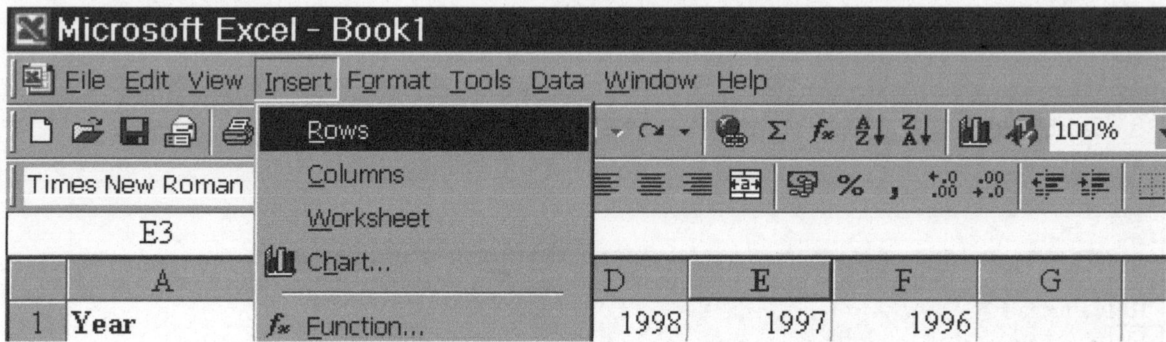

3. A new Row in this case will be inserted, as shown next.

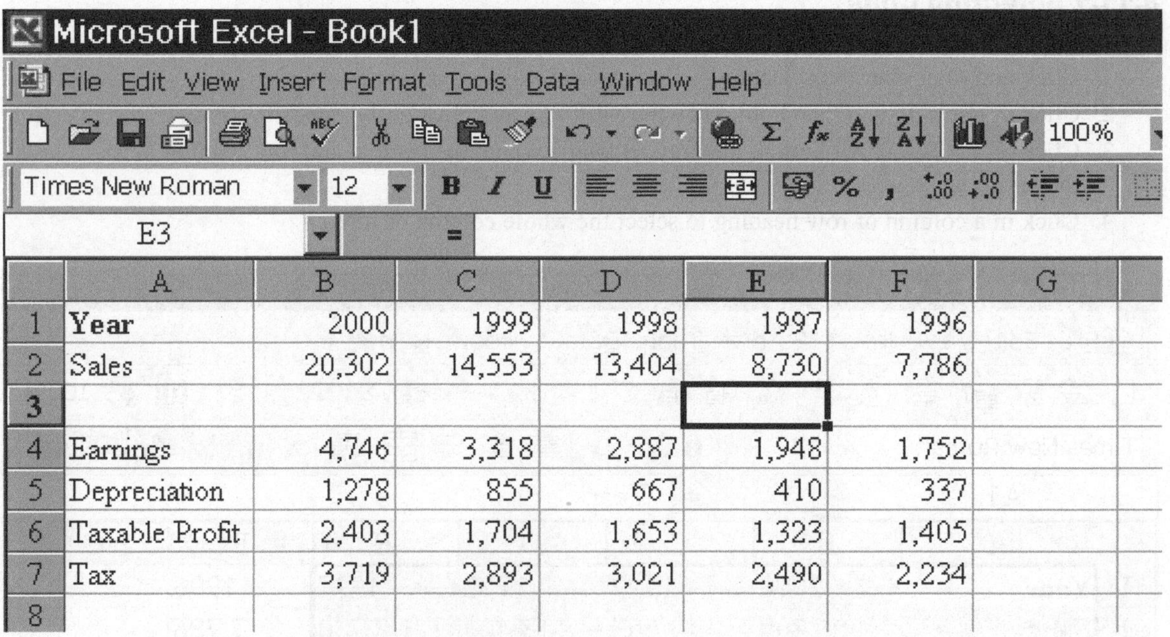

8.11.3 Inserting and Deleting Cells

When you tell Excel to insert or delete a cell within a range of data, Excel needs to know how to move the data that is in adjacent cells. You specify your preferences in the Insert or Delete dialog box.

8.11.3.1 To Insert a Cell

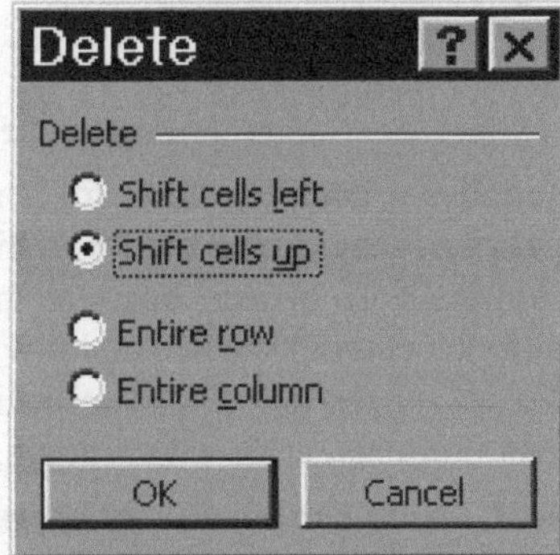

1. Click the destination for the new, blank cell.
2. Choose Cells from the Insert menu.

   Or

   Right-click the cell and choose Insert from the shortcut menu.
3. In the Insert dialog box, select either Shift Cells Right or Shift Cells Down.
4. The new cell appears.

8.11.3.2 To Delete a Cell

1. Click the cell you want to delete.
2. Choose Delete from the Edit menu.

   Or

   Right-click the cell and choose Delete from the shortcut menu.
3. In the Delete dialog box, select either Shift Cells Left or Shift Cells Up.
4. To delete an entire row or column, select at least one cell in the row or column, choose Delete from the Edit menu, and in the Delete dialog box, choose either Entire Row or Entire Column.

8.11.4 Changing Width of a Column

1. Position the mouse pointer on the right edge of the gray column heading button for the column you want to widen.
2. When the mouse pointer changes to a double arrow, drag right or left. While you are dragging, you will see the new width of the column in a ToolTip measured in pixels.
3. You can also select Column from the Format menu and then choose Width from the submenu to open the Column Width dialog box. In this case, you can specify the exact setting.

8.11.5 Changing Height of a Row

Row Height

Row height: 15.75

OK Cancel

1. Position the mouse pointer on the bottom edge of the gray row heading button for the row whose height you want to change.
2. When the mouse pointer changes to a double arrows, drag up and down.
3. You can also select Row from the Format menu and then choose Height from the submenu to open the Row Height dialog box. In this case, you can specify the exact setting.

8.11.6 Formatting Text

You can use formatting to improve the appearance of your worksheet and to make it easier to locate the information you need.

To format selected text

1. Select the cell or cells containing the text to format.
2. Choose formatting options by clicking the text formatting buttons on the Formatting toolbar.

   Or

1. Select the cell or cells containing the text to format.
2. From the Format menu, choose Cells, or right-click and choose Format Cells from the shortcut menu.
3. In the Format Cells dialog box, change the options on the Alignment and Font tabs.
4. Click Ok.

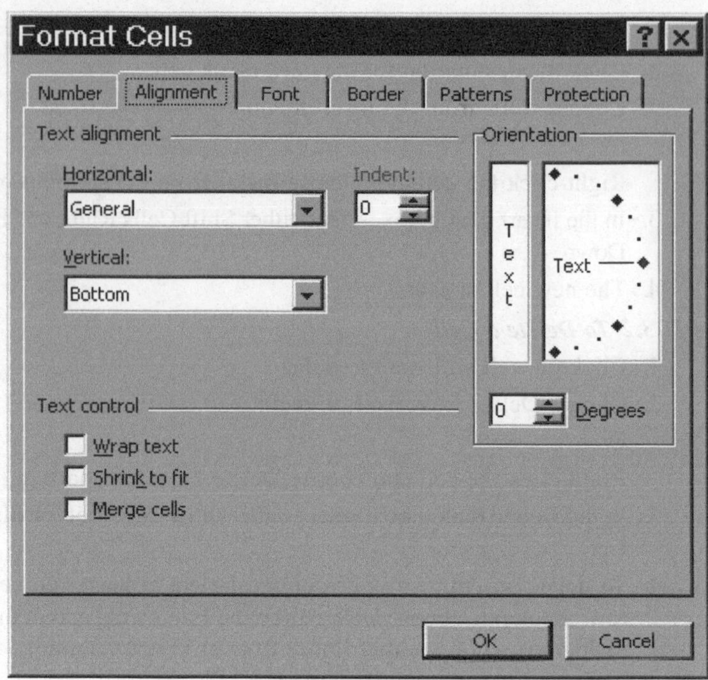

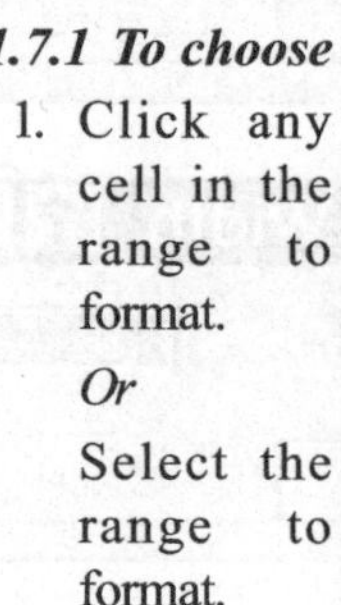

8.11.7 AutoFormat

The fastest and easiest way to make a worksheet presentable is to give an AutoFormat command. **AutoFormat** supplies a complete look for a range of data by changing the font, text alignment, number formatting, borders, patterns, colours, column widths, and row heights. Excel provides a selection of AutoFormats, each with a unique look.

8.11.7.1 To choose an AutoFormat

1. Click any cell in the range to format.

   Or

   Select the range to format.
2. From the Format menu, choose AutoFormat.
3. In the AutoFormat dialog box, select an AutoFormat from the display.
4. Click Ok.

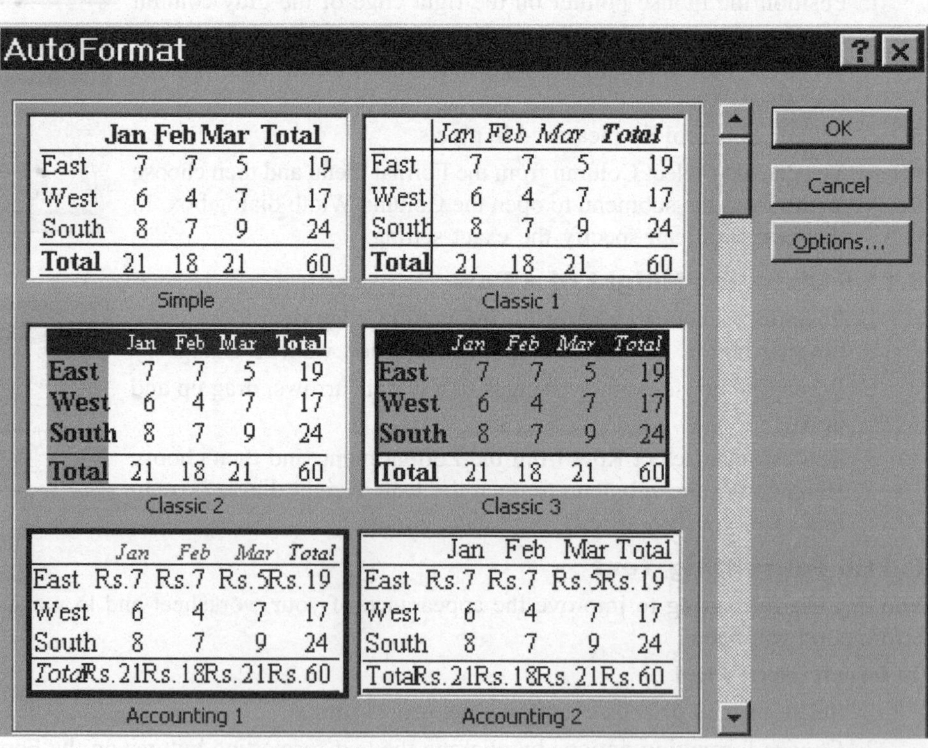

8.12 Changing Data Alignment

Use these options to change the alignment of text in text boxes on selected chart elements. Availability of text box options depends on the chart element that you select.

8.12.1 Text layout

8.12.1.1 Vertical alignment

To specify the vertical position of the text in a shape, select an option from the list.

8.12.1.2 Text direction

To specify the orientation of the text in a shape, select an option from the list.

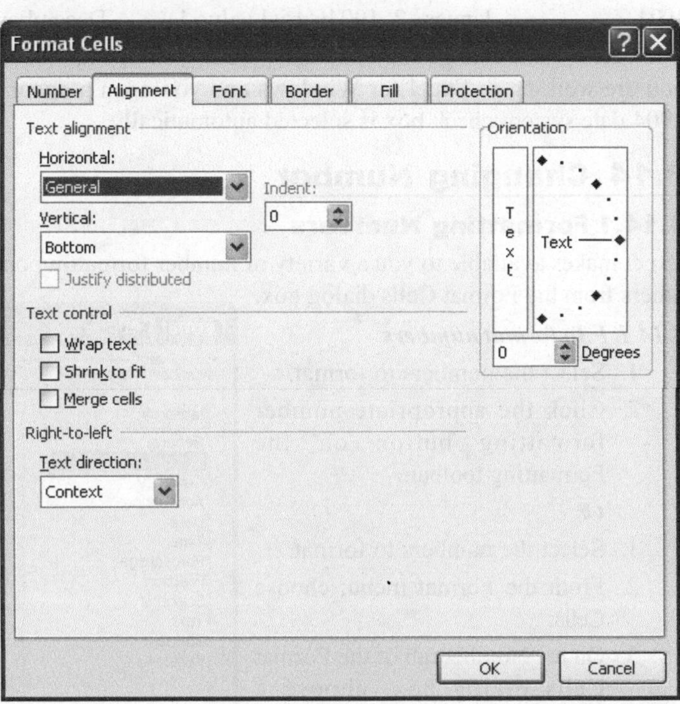

8.12.2 Autofit

Resize shape to fit text To increase the size of the shape vertically so that the text fits inside of it, click this button.

8.12.3 Internal margin

The internal margin is the distance between the text and the outer border of a chart element. You can increase or decrease the amount of this space by using the following options.

8.12.3.1 Left

To specify the distance between the left border of the selected chart element and the text, enter the margin number that you want in the Left box.

8.12.3.2 Right

To specify the distance between the right border of the selected chart element and the text, enter the margin number that you want in the Right box.

8.12.3.3 Top

To specify the distance between the top border of the selected chart element and the text, enter the margin number that you want in the Top box.

8.12.3.4 Bottom

To specify the distance between the bottom border of the selected chart element and the text, enter the margin number that you want in the Bottom box.

8.12.3.5 Columns

To specify the number of columns of text in a chart element and the spacing between the columns, click this button.

8.13 Changing Date

Dates are often a critical part of data analysis. You often ask questions such as: when was a product purchased, how long will a task in a project take, or what is the average revenue for a fiscal quarter? Entering dates correctly is essential to ensuring accurate results. But formatting dates so that they are easy to understand is equally important to ensuring correct interpretation of those results.

Excel supports two date systems: the 1900 and 1904 date systems. The default date system for Microsoft Office Excel for Windows is 1900. The default date system for Microsoft Office Excel for the Macintosh is 1904.

The following table shows the first date and the last date for each date system and the serial value associated with each date.

Date system	*First date*	*Last date*
1900	January 1, 1900(serial value 1)	December 31, 9999(serial value 2958465)
1904	January 2, 1904(serial value 1)	December 31, 9999(serial value 2957003)

The date system changes automatically when you open a document from another platform. For example, if you are working in Excel for Windows and you open a document created in Excel for the Macintosh, the 1904 date system check box is selected automatically.

8.14 Changing Number

8.14.1 Formatting Numbers

Excel makes available to you a variety of number formatting options, some from the Formatting toolbar and others from the Format Cells dialog box.

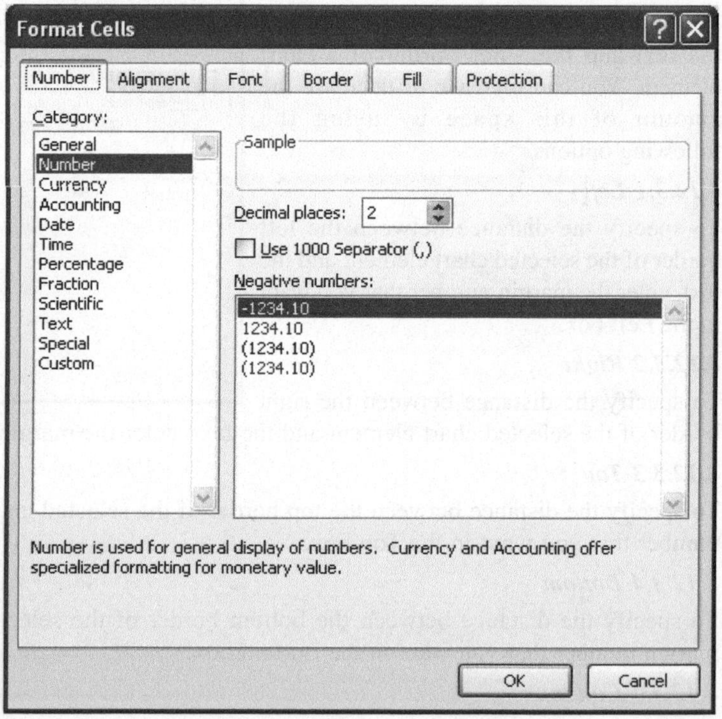

8.14.1.1 To format numbers

1. Select the numbers to format.
2. Click the appropriate number formatting button on the Formatting toolbar.

Or

1. Select the numbers to format.
2. From the Format menu, choose Cells.
3. On the Number tab of the Format Cells dialog box, choose a category and other options.
4. Click Ok.

8.15 Character or Currency Format

Changing the default country/region changes the standard settings for numbers, currencies, time, and date to those most commonly used for that country/region. This setting affects various features in various Microsoft Office programs. Examples of features affected include:

- Calendar in Microsoft Office Outlook.
- Cells formatted with certain date, time, or currency options in Microsoft Office Excel.

8.16 Changing Font

Change the font or font size in a worksheet

Select the cell, range of cells, text, or characters that you want to format.

- To change the font, click the font that you want in the Font box .
- To change the font size, click the font size that you want in the Font Size box , or click Increase Font Size or Decrease Font Size until the size you want is displayed in the Font Size box.

Note:

- Small-caps and all-caps font options are not available in Microsoft Office Excel. For a similar effect, you can choose a font that includes only capital letters, or you can press CAPS LOCK and choose a small-sized font.
- If some of the data that you entered in a cell isn't visible, and you want to display that data without specifying a different font size, you can wrap the text in the cell. If only a small amount isn't visible, you may be able to shrink the text so that it fits.

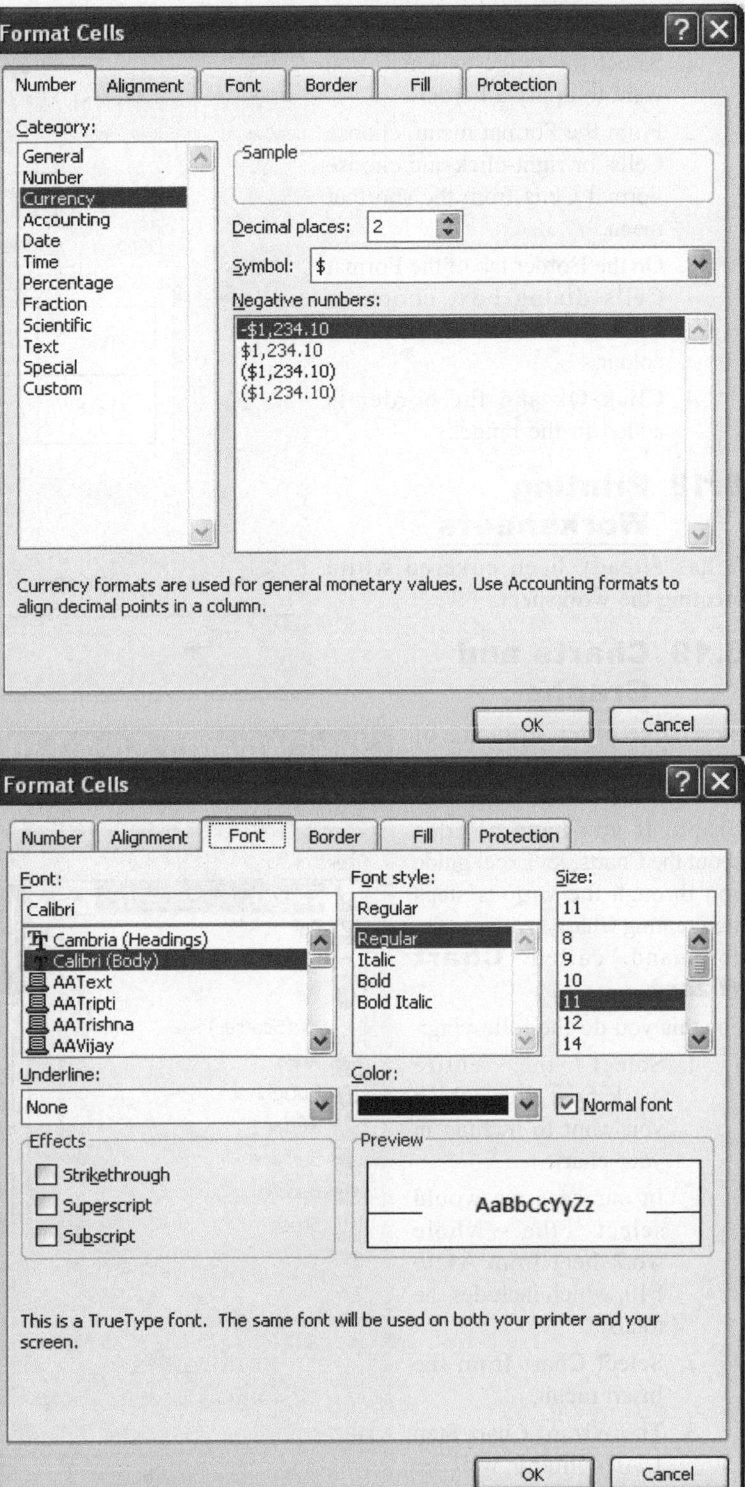

8.17 Adding Borders and Colours

A border is a line at the edge of a cell. You can use borders to divide the information on the sheet into logical regions. Borders appear on the screen and will print when you print the sheet.

8.17.1 To add a border to a cell

1. Select the range to which you want to apply a border.
2. Click the arrow button next to the Borders button to see the full range of border you want for the range

Or

1. Select the range to which you want to apply a border.
2. From the Format menu, choose Cells, or right-click and choose Format Cells from the shortcut menu.
3. On the Border tab of the Format Cells dialog box, choose a border, a border style, and a colour.
4. Click Ok and the border is added to the range.

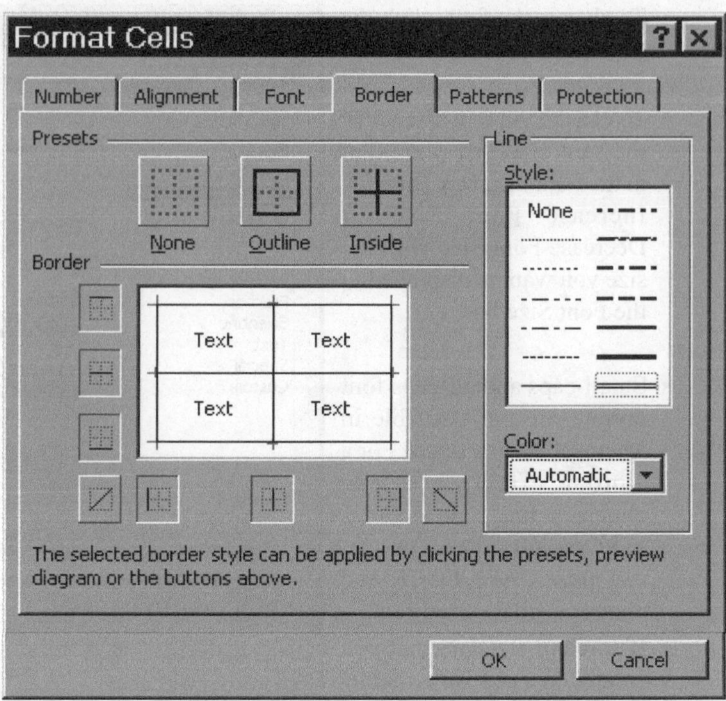

8.18 Printing Worksheets

It has already been covered while creating the worksheet.

8.19 Charts and Graphs

Excel like other software of Microsoft Office, makes use of the software called Microsoft Graph. If you have no idea about the Charts, let Excel guide you through the various steps are creating Charts by using the command called **Chart Wizard**.

For this you do the following:

1. Select the entire worksheet area which you want to include in your chart.

   In our case we would select the whole worksheet from A1 to F10, which includes the totals.
2. Select Chart from the Insert menu.
3. The Wizard Chart Step 1 of 4 menu will be given to you to select

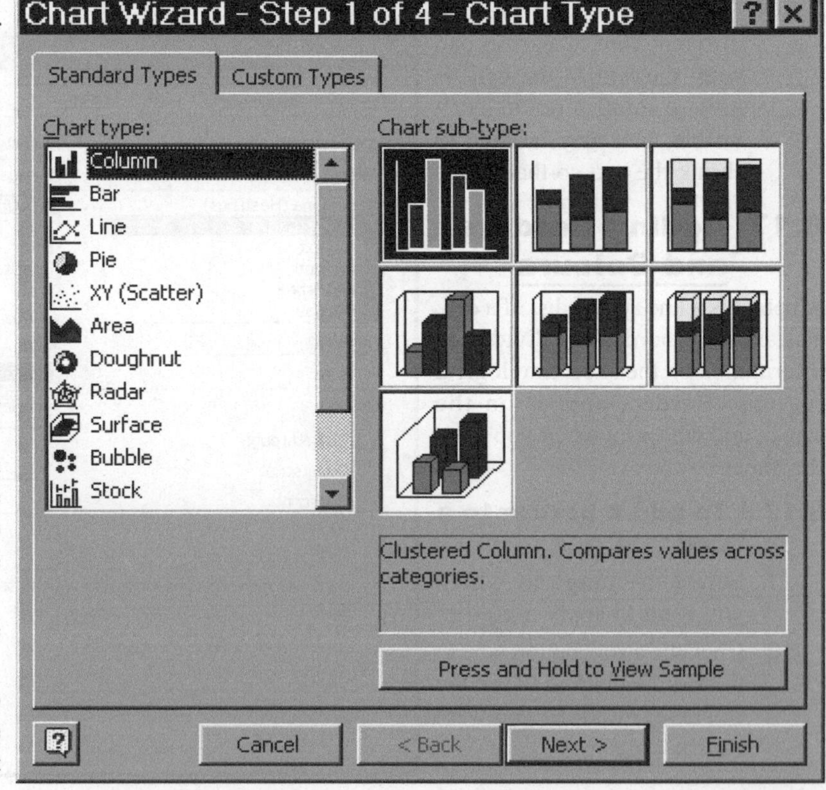

the type of chart you want for your worksheet.

For our worksheet we have selected Column Chart type, as can be seen in the first of the four Chart Wizard dialog box.

Press Next to reach Wizard Chart Step 2 of 4.

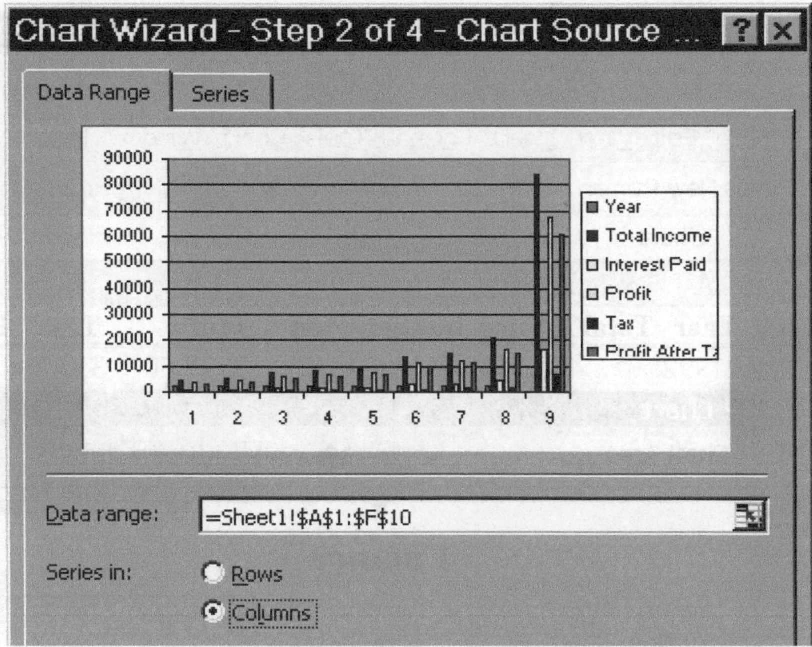

4. In this chart you can opt for different ways of representing your chart, i.e., row wise or column wise.

   For our worksheet we have selected columns.
5. Press Next to reach the next step.
6. Chart Wizard Step 3 of 4 gives you the option of naming the chart and the Y and X-axis. In our case we have named the worksheet as Finance. Press Next to reach the next step.
7. Chart Wizard Step 4 of 4 gives you the option of placing this chart in the worksheet as an object or in the form of a new cell.
8. Once this is over, you can press Finish to end the Chart Wizard routine.
9. A new chart will be placed in your worksheet with the Chart toolbar present for making the changes which you may require to do to your chart.
10. The final Chart is shown next.

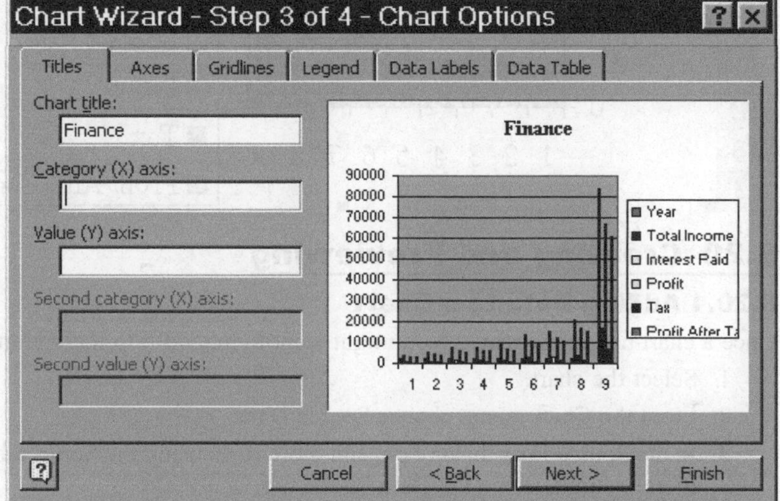

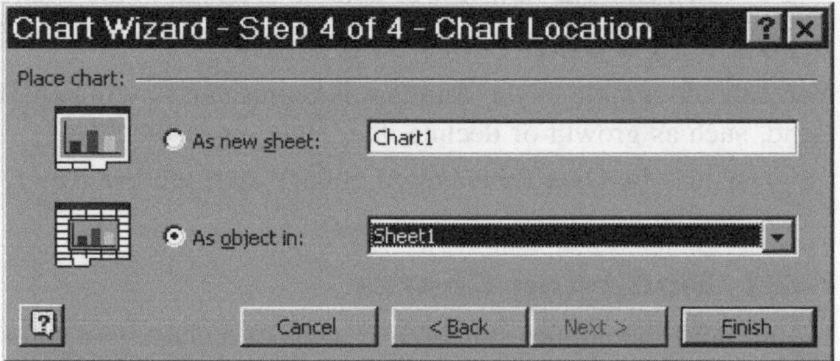

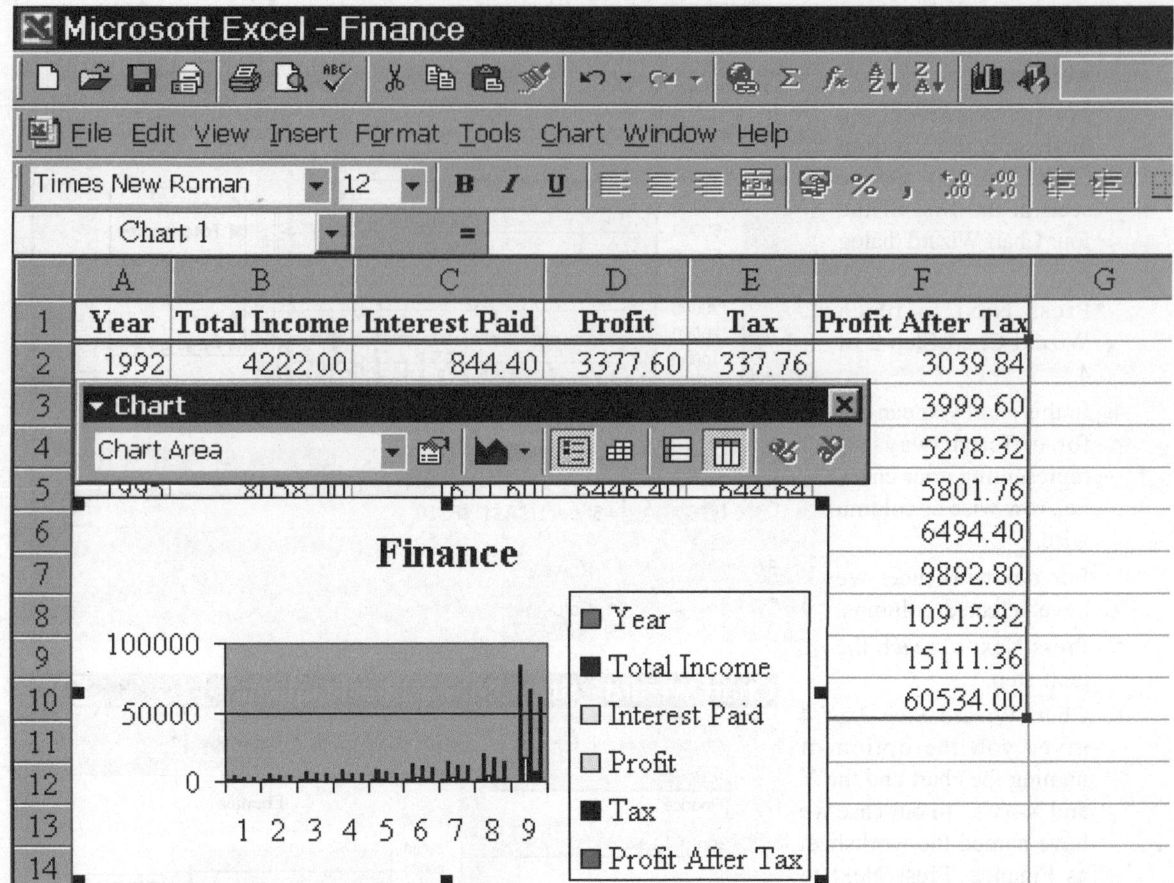

8.20 Creating and Previewing

8.20.1 Adding Data to a Chart

Once a chart has been created, you might want to extend it to include more data. For this do the following:

1. Select the chart.
2. From the Chart menu, choose Source Data.
3. In the Source Data dialog box, add more rows using the Series tab or extend the data range to include more columns using the Data Range tab.
4. Click Ok. The new row or column is added to the Chart.

8.20.2 Add a Data Table to a Chart

You can add a table of the data that is represented by the chart and add a trendline that shows the general trend, such as growth or decline, that emerges in the data.

1. Click the Data Table button on the Chart toolbar. The Data Table appears below the chart, as shown on the next page.

8.21 Modifying Charts

If you move the pointer slowly over areas of a chart, you can see ToolTips identifying the items that make up the chart. Each item can be formatted separately.

8.21.1 To modify a chart

1. Double click a chart object to display the formatting dialog box appropriate for that object.

   Or

   Right-click a chart object, and choose the appropriate formatting dialog box from the shortcut menu.

   Or

   Click a chart object, and click the Chart toolbar's Format button to display the appropriate formatting dialog box

   Or

   Click a chart object, and choose Selected Chart Area from the Format menu to display the appropriate dialog box.

   Or

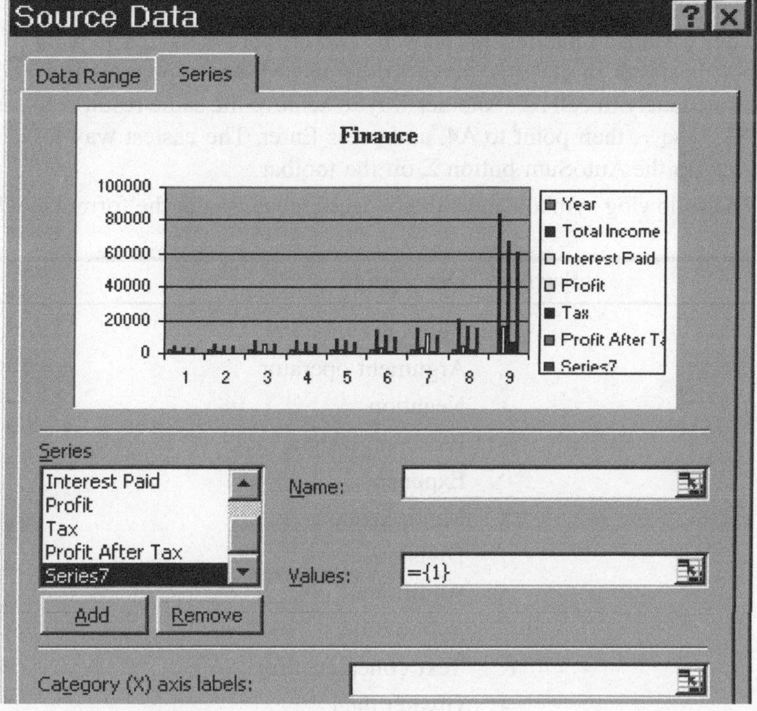

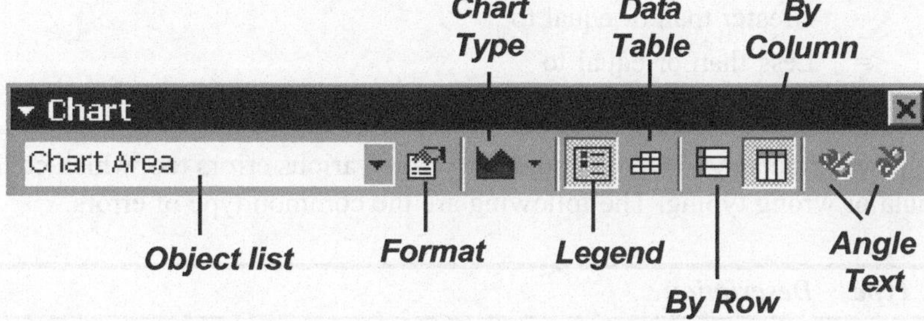

   Choose the object you want to modify from the Chart Objects list on the Chart toolbar, and click the Chart toolbar's Format button to display the dialog box.

Remember

1. To modify several chart elements at the same time, choose Chart Options from the Chart menu and use the various tabs in the Chart Options dialog box.
2. Drag the chart to move it on the sheet, or drag the handles of the chart window to resize the chart.
3. Format the most general elements of the chart first (such as the chart area), and then format individual elements within that area (such as axis labels).
4. Don't be afraid to experiment with options you don't completely understand; you can easily undo almost any change by using the Undo command on the Edit menu or the Undo button on the Standard toolbar.

8.22 Functions

They establish relationships between two or more cells. If you want to add the values in cells A3 and A4 and put the result in cell A5, move to the cell A5 and type =A3+A4 and press Enter. The result is displayed immediately in cell A5. Another way to achieve the same result is to move to cell A5 and type +, point to cell A3, type +, then point to A4, and press Enter. The easiest way to achieve this operation is to point to A5, pick up the AutoSum button Σ on the toolbar.

The following symbols have their specific meaning in the formulae which are used in Excel.

Symbol	*Description*
:	Reference operator
,	Argument operator
–	Negation
%	Percentage sign
^	Exponent
*	Multiplication
/	Division
+	Addition
–	Subtraction
&	Text concatenation
>	Greater than
<	Less than
>=	Greater than or equal to
<=	Less than or equal to
<>	Not equal to

While working with the formulae you would come across the various errors too, which could happen due to wrong use of formula or wrong typing. The following are the common type of errors.

Error Type	*Description*
# # # #	the column is not wide enough to display the number so either widen the column, or reduce the font size or change the numeric format.
# DIV/0!	Dividing by zero is invalid
# N/A	Data is not available. It happens usually when you refer to a function or value where data is not available
# NAME?	The formula references a name that is unknown to Excel
# NUM !	The formula is using an invalid number
# REF !	A cell reference is not available may be because you deleted that cell or moved another cell onto it.
# VALUE !	The formula contains an invalid operator or argument, for example, adding a text value to a numeric value

8.23 Mathematical Functions

ABS Returns the absolute value of a number.

ACOS Returns the arccosine of a number.

ACOSH Returns the inverse hyperbolic cosine of a number.

ASIN Returns the arcsine of a number.

ASINH Returns the inverse hyperbolic sine of a number.

ATAN Returns the arctangent of a number.

ATAN2 Returns the arctangent from x- and y- coordinates.

ATANH Returns the inverse hyperbolic tangent of a number.

CEILING Rounds a number up to the nearest integer or to the nearest multiple of significance.

COMBIN Returns the number of combinations for a given number of objects.

COS Returns the cosine of a number.

COSH Returns the hyperbolic cosine of a number.

DEGREES Converts radians to degrees.

EVEN Rounds a number up to the nearest even integer.

EXP Returns e raised to the power of a given number.

FACT *Returns the factorial of a number.*

FLOOR Rounds a number down, toward zero.

GCD Returns the greatest common divisor.

INT Rounds a number down to the nearest integer.

LCM Returns the least common multiple.

LN Returns the natural logarithm of a number.

LOG Returns the logarithm of a number to a specified base.

LOG10 Returns the base-10 logarithm of a number.

MDETERM Returns the matrix determinant of an array.

MINVERSE Returns the matrix inverse of an array.

MMULT Returns the matrix product of two arrays.

MOD Returns the remainder from division.

MROUND Returns a number rounded to the desired multiple.

MULTINOMIAL Returns the multinomial of a set of numbers.

ODD Rounds a number up to the nearest odd integer.

PI Returns the value of p (pi) to 15 digits.

POWER Returns the result of a number raised to a power.

PRODUCT Multiplies its arguments.

QUOTIENT Returns the integer portion of a division.

RADIANS Converts degrees to radians.

RAND Returns a random number between 0 and 1.

RANDBETWEEN Returns a random number between the numbers you specify.

ROMAN Converts an arabic numeral to roman, as text.

ROUND Rounds a number to a specified number of digits.

ROUNDDOWN	Rounds a number down, toward zero.
ROUNDUP	Rounds a number up, away from zero.
SERIESSUM	Returns the sum of a power series based on the formula.
SIGN	Returns the sign of a number.
SIN	Returns the sine of the given angle.
SINH	Returns the hyperbolic sine of a number.
SQRT	Returns a positive square root.
SQRTPI	Returns the square toot of (number * p).
SUBTOTAL	Returns a subtotal in a list or database.
SUM	Adds its arguments.
SUMIF	Adds the cells specified by a given criteria.
SUMPRODUCT	Returns the sum of the products of corresponding array components.
SUMSQ	Returns the sum of the squares of the arguments.
SUMX2MY2	Returns the sum of the difference of squares of corresponding values in two arrays.
SUMX2PY2	Returns the sum of the sum of squares of corresponding values in two arrays.
SUMXMY2	Returns the sum of squares of differences of corresponding values in two arrays.
TAN	Returns the tangent of a number.
TANH	Returns the hyperbolic tangent of a number.
TRUNC	Truncates a number to an integer.

8.24 Logical

AND	Returns TRUE if all its arguments are TRUE.
FALSE	Returns the logical value FALSE.
IF	Specifies a logical test to perform.
NOT	Reverses the logic of its argument.
OR	Returns TRUE if any argument is TRUE.
TRUE	Returns the logical value TRUE.

8.25 Statistical

AVEDEV	Returns the average of the absolute deviations of data points from their mean.
AVERAGE	Returns the average of its arguments.
AVERAGEA	Returns the average of its arguments, including numbers, text, and logical values.
BETADIST	Returns the cumulative beta probability density function.
BETAINV	Returns the inverse of the cumulative beta probability density function.
BINOMDIST	Returns the individual term binomial distribution probability.
CHIDIST	Returns the one-tailed probability of the chi-squared distribution.
CHIINV	Returns the inverse of the one-tailed probability of the chi-squared distribution.
CHITEST	Returns the test for independence.
CONFIDENCE	Returns the confidence interval for a population mean.
CORREL	Returns the correlation coefficient between two data sets.
COUNT	Counts how many numbers are in the list of arguments.

COUNTA	Counts how many values are in the list of arguments.
COUNTBLANK	Counts the number of blank cells within a range.
COUNTIF	Counts the number of non blank cells within a range that meet the given criteria.
COVAR	Returns covariance, the average of the products of paired deviations.
CRITBINOM	Returns the smallest value for which the cumulative binomial distribution is less than or equal to a criterion value.
DEVSQ	Returns the sum of squared of deviations.
EXPONDIST	Returns the exponential distribution.
FDIST	Returns the F probability distribution.
FINV	Returns the inverse of the F probability distribution.
FISHER	Returns the Fisher transformation.
FISHERINV	Returns the inverse of the Fisher transformation.
FORECAST	Returns a value along a linear trend.
FREQUENCY	Returns a frequency distribution as a vertical array.
FTEST	Returns the result of an F-test.
GAMMADIST	Returns the gamma distribution.
GAMMAINV	Returns the inverse of the gamma cumulative distribution.
GAMMALN	Returns the natural logarithm of the gamma function, G(x).
GEOMEAN	Returns the geometric mean.
GROWTH	Returns values along an exponential trend.
HARMEAN	Returns the harmonic mean.
HYPGEOMDIST	Returns the hypergeometric distribution.
INTERCEPT	Returns the intercept of the linear regression line.
KURT	Returns the kurtosis of a data set.
LARGE	Returns the kth largest value in a data set.
LINEST	Returns the parameters of a linear trend.
LOGEST	Returns the parameters of an exponential trend.
LOGINV	Returns the inverse of the lognormal distribution.
LOGNORMDIST	Returns the cumulative lognormal distribution.
MAX	Returns the maximum value in a list of arguments.
MAXA	Returns the maximum value in a list of arguments, including numbers, text, and logical values.
MEDIAN	Returns the median of the given numbers.
MIN	Returns the minimum value in a list of arguments.
MINA	Returns the smallest value in a list of arguments, including numbers, text, and logical values.
MODE	Returns the most common value in a data set.
NEGBINOMDIST	Returns the negative binomial distribution.
NORMDIST	Returns the normal cumulative distribution.
NORMSINV	Returns the inverse of the standard normal cumulative distribution.

NORMSDIST	Returns the normal cumulative distribution for a value with a mean of 0 and a standard deviation of 1.
PEARSON	Returns the Pearson product moment correlation coefficient.
PERCENTILE	Returns the kth percentile of values in a range.
PERCENTRANK	Returns the percentage rank of a value in a data set.
PERMUT	Returns the number of permutations for a given number of objects.
POISSON	Returns the Poisson distribution.
PROB	Returns the probability that values in a range are between two limits.
QUARTILE	Returns the quartile of a data set.
RANK	Returns the rank of a number in a list of numbers.
RSQ	Returns the square of the Pearson product moment correlation coefficient.
SKEW	Returns the skewness of a distribution.
SLOPE	Returns the slope of the linear regression line.
SMALL	Returns the kth smallest value in a data set.
STANDARDIZE	Returns a normalized value.
STDEV	Estimates standard deviation based on a sample.
STDEVA	Estimates standard deviation based on a sample, including numbers, text, and logical values.
STDEVP	Calculates standard deviation based on the entire population.
STDEVPA	Calculates standard deviation based on the entire population, including numbers, text, and logical values.
STEYX	Returns the standard error of the predicted y- value for each x in the regression.
TDIST	Returns the Student's t-distribution.
TINV	Returns the inverse of the Student's t-distribution.
TREND	Returns values along a linear trend.
TRIMMEAN	Returns the mean of the interior of a data set.
TTEST	Returns the probability associated with a Student's t-test.
VAR	Estimates variance based on a sample.
VARA	Estimates variance based on a sample, including numbers, text, and logical values.
VARP	Calculates variance based on the entire population.
VARPA	Calculates variance based on the entire population, including numbers, text, and logical values.
WEIBULL	Returns the Weibull distribution.
ZTEST	Returns the two-tailed P-value of a z-test.

8.26 Text

CHAR	Returns the character specified by the code number.
CLEAN	Removes all nonprintable characters from text.
CODE	Returns a numeric code for the first character in a text string.
CONCATENATE	Joins several text items into one text item.
DOLLAR	Converts a number to text, using currency format.

EXACT	Checks to see if two text values are identical.
FIND	Finds one text value within another (case-sensitive).
FIXED	Formats a number as text values are identical.
LEFT	Returns the leftmost characters from a text value.
LEN	Returns the number of characters in a text string.
LOWER	Converts text to lowercase.
MID	Returns a specific number of characters from a text string starting at the position you specify.
PROPER	Capitalizes the first letter in each word of a text value.
REPLACE	Replaces characters within text.
REPT	Repeats text a given number of times.
RIGHT	Returns the rightmost characters from a text value.
SEARCH	Finds one text value within another (not case-sensitive).
SUBSTITUTE	Substitutes new text for old text in a text string.
T	Converts its arguments to text.
TEXT	Formats a number and converts it to text.
TRIM	Removes spaces from text.
UPPER	Converts text to uppercase.
VALUE	Converts a text argument to a number.

8.27 Financial

ACCRINT	Returns the accrued interest for a security that pays periodic interest.
ACCRINTM	Returns the accrued interest for a security that pays at maturity.
AMORDEGRC	Returns the prorated linear depreciation for each accounting period.
AMORLINC	Returns the prorated linear depreciation of an asset for each accounting period.
COUPDAYSB	Returns the number of days in the coupon period that contains the settlement date.
COUPDAYSNC	Returns the number of days from the settlement date to the next coupon date.
COUPNCD	Returns the next coupon date after the settlement date.
COUPNUM	Returns the number of coupons payable between the settlement date and maturity date.
COUPPCD	Returns the previous coupon date before the settlement date.
CUMIPMT	Returns the cumulative interest paid between two periods.
CUMPRINC	Returns the cumulative principal paid on a loan between two periods.
DB	Returns the depreciation of an asset for a specified period using the fixed-declining balance method.
DDB	Returns the depreciation of an asset for a specified period using the double-declining balance method or some other method you specify.
DISC	Converts a dollar price, expressed as a fraction, into a dollar price, expressed as a decimal number.
DOLLARFR	Converts a dollar price, expressed as a decimal number, into a dollar price, expressed as a fraction.

DURATION	Returns the annual duration of a security with periodic interest payments.
EFFECT	Returns the effective annual interest rate.
FV	Returns the future value of an investment.
FVSCHEDULE	Returns the future value of an initial principal after applying a series of compound interest rates.
INTRATE	Returns the interest rate for a fully invested security.
IPMT	Returns the interest payment for an investment for a given period.
IRR	Returns the internal rate of return for a series of cash flows.
ISPMT	Returns the straight-loan payment interest.
MDURATION	Returns the Macauley-modified duration for a security with an assumed par value of $100.
MIRR	Returns the internal rate of return where positive and negative cash flows are financed at different rates.
NOMINAL	Returns the annual nominal interest rate.
NPER	Returns the number of periods for an investment.
NPV	Returns the net present value of an investment based on a series of periodic cash flows and a discount rate.
ODDPRICE	Returns the price per $100 face value of a security with an odd first period.
ODDFYIELD	Returns the yield of a security with an odd first period.
ODDLPRICE	Returns the price per $100 face value of a security with an odd last period.
ODDLYIELD	Returns the yield of a security with an odd last period.
PMT	Returns the periodic payment for an annuity.
PPMT	Returns the payment on the principal for an investment for a given period.
PRICE	Returns the price per $100 face value of a security that pays periodic interest.
PRICEDISC	Returns the price per $100 face value of a discounted security.
PRICEMAT	Returns the price per $100 face value of a security that pays interest at maturity.
PV	Returns the present value of an investment.
RATE	Returns the interest rate per period of an annuity.
SLN	Returns the straight-line depreciation of an asset for one period.
SYD	Returns the sum-of-years digits depreciation of an asset for a specified period.
TBILLEQ	Returns the bond-equivalent yield for a Treasury bill.
TBILLPRICE	Returns the price per $100 face value for a Treasury bill.
TBILLYIELD	Returns the yield for a Treasury bill.
VDB	Returns the depreciation of an asset for a specified or partial period using a declining balance method.
XIRR	Returns the internal rate of return for a schedule of cash flows that is not necessary periodic.
XNPV	Returns the net present value for a schedule of cash flows that is not necessarily periodic.
YIELD	Returns the yield on a security that pays periodic interest.
YIELDDISC	Returns the annual yield for a discounted security.

YIELDMAT	Returns the annual yield of a security that pays interest at maturity.

8.28 Date and Time Functions

DATE	Returns the serial number of a particular date.
DATEDIF	Returns the number of months, days, or years between two different dates.
DATEVALUE	Converts a date in the form of text to a serial number.
DAY	Converts a serial number to a day of the month.
DAYS360	Calculates the number of days between two dates based on a 360-day year.
HOUR	Converts a serial number to an hour.
MINUTE	Converts a serial number to a minute.
MONTH	Converts a serial number to a month.
NETWORKDAYS	Returns the number of whole workdays between two dates.
NOW	Returns the serial number of the current date and time.
SECOND	Converts a serial number to a second.
TIME	Returns the serial number of a particular time.
TIMEVALUE	Converts a time in the form of text to a serial number.
TODAY	Returns the serial number of today's date.
WEEKDAY	Converts a serial number to a number that represents a day of the week.
WEEKNUM	Converts a date serial number to a week number in the year.
WORKDAY	Returns the serial number of the date before or after a specified number of workdays.
YEAR	Converts a serial number to a year.
YEARFRAC	Returns the year fraction representing the number of whole days between start_date and end_date.

8.29 Using Function Wizard

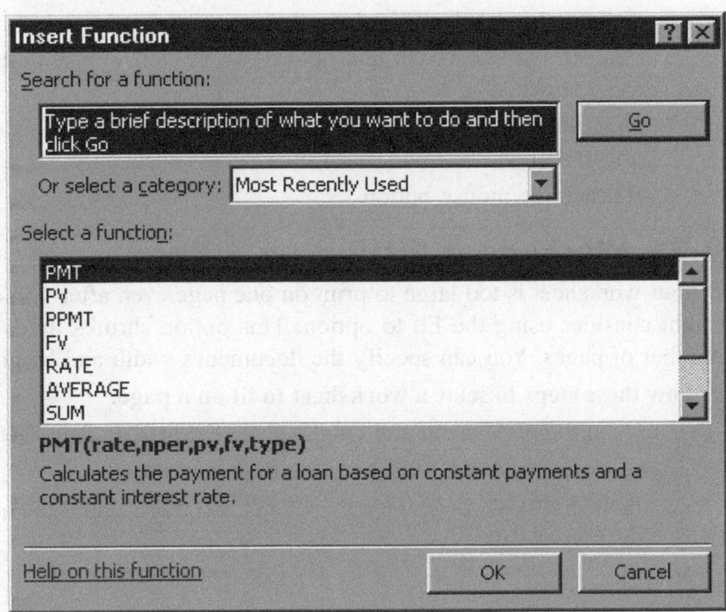

Sum and Average are just two of the most commonly used functions whereas there are lots of them in Excel. You can use them to get the desired results in a flash. To get them click the Paste Function button on the Standard toolbar as your are building the formula. The Paste Function wizard takes you through the steps of building a formula.

1. Click the destination cell for the formula.
2. Click the Paste Function button on the Standard toolbar.
3. In the Paste Function dialog box, select the category and then the function.

4. Click Ok.
5. Use the Paste Function Wizard to guide you in completing the formula.
6. Click Ok when you have finished.

8.30 Working with Workbooks

You can transfer data between two workbooks or compare the information in one workbook with that in another. To compare the two workbooks, lets name them **Book1** and **Book2**.

1. Open Book1 and click at New Workbook button. Excel displays a new workbook called Book2.
2. To see both the workbooks at the same time, choose Arrange from the Windows menu to display a dialog box.
3. Click Ok to accept the default Tiled option. Excel arranges Book2 and Book1 side by side on your screen.

8.30.1 Copying Entries Between Workbooks

The procedure for copying information between workbooks is the same as for copying between sheets in one workbook.

Do the following:

1. Activate Book1 by clicking its title bar.
2. Select a range and click the Copy button.
3. Click A1 cell of Book2 and click the Paste button. The data will be pasted in Book2.
4. Press Ctrl + Home to move to cell A1 and see the full result.

8.30.2 Moving Sheets Between Workbooks

A sheet can be easily moved within a workbook or from one workbook to another. For example, you can move a worksheet from Book1 to Book2.

Do the following:

1. Activate the Book1 window.
2. Activate the Books2 Window.
3. Point to the Sheet1 tab and hold down the left mouse button. The pointer is now an arrow with a sheet attached to it.
4. Drag the sheet pointer until it sits between Sheet2 of the Book1 workbook. Excel indicates with an arrowhead where it will place the selected sheet.
5. Release the mouse button.

8.31 Worksheet Fitting on a Page

If your worksheet is too large to print on one page even after you change the orientation and margins, you might consider using the Fit to option. This option shrinks the worksheet to make it fit on the specified number of pages. You can specify the document's width and height.

Follow these steps to scale a worksheet to fit on a page:

1. Open the File menu and choose Page Setup. The Page Setup dialog box appears.
2. Click the Page tab to display the Page options.
3. In the Fit to XX page wide by XX tall text boxes, enter the number of pages in which you want Excel to fit your data.

4. Click Ok to close the Page Setup dialog box and return to your worksheet. Or click the Print button in the Page Setup dialog box to display the Print dialog box, and then click Ok to print your worksheet.

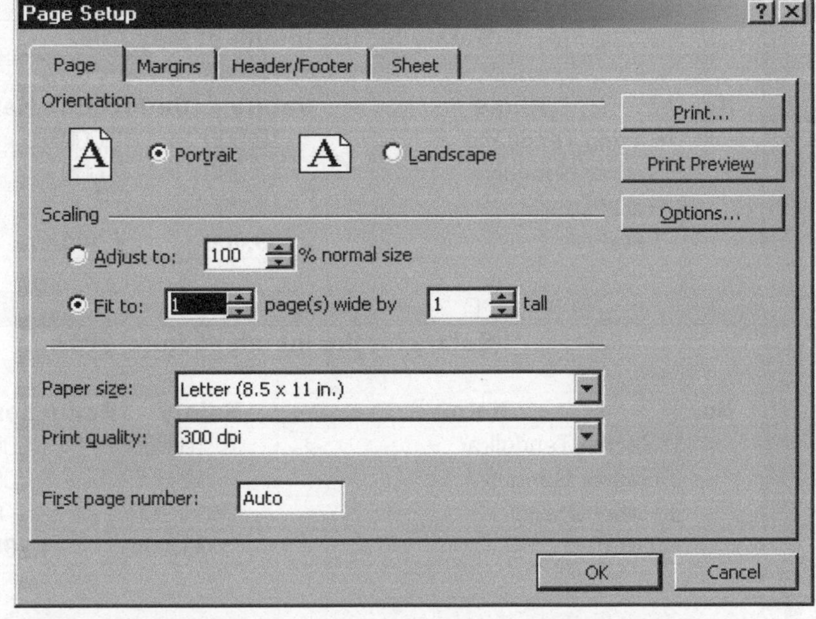

8.31.1 Consolidation of Worksheets

This command as the name sounds is used to consolidate the data of more than one worksheet in a single worksheet. The common data of various worksheets can be combined to create the worksheet to reflect the result of the consolidation.

This consolidation can be effected with the help of various statistical functions like Sum, Count, Average, Max, Min and StdDev. This is vary useful when you have the data availble in the monthly format and you would like to combine the data in a single worksheet to create a total consolidate data for the year.

In a similar example, I have taken the salaries and deductions of 3 moths i.e., April, 2002; May 2002 and June 2002. I have tried to consolidate the data in a new worksheet.

Let us see how this is done.

The following data has been taken for consolidation. This data is various sheets of the same file.

1. Open a blank sheet and type the heading for consolidation, for example, the consolidation results for the month of April, May and June, 2002.
2. Make cell A4 the active cell.

	A	B	C	D	E	F
1	**Salary for the month of April, 2002**					
2						
3	**No.**	**Name**	**Salary**	**Deduction**	**Nett. Payable**	
4	1	Sachin Tendulkar	10,000	2,000	8,000	
5	2	Saurav Ganguly	12,000	1,000	11,000	
6	3	Rahul Dravid	11,000	1,500	9,500	
7		**Total**	**33,000**	**4,500**	**28,500**	

3. From from the Data menu choose the Consolidate command.
4. This gives rise to Consolidate dialog box, as shown on next page.
5. Here the Sum function is there by default. You can choose to have another function like Average, if you want to have average of the fields. In all cases the corresponding cells of each of the ranges that you specify in the next step would take effect.
6. Click the Reference box and then indicate the first reference by choosing the sal-04 tab and selecting

	A	B	C	D	E	F
1		**Salary for the month of May, 2002**				
2						
3	**No.**	**Name**	**Salary**	**Deduction**	**Nett. Payable**	
4	1	Sachin Tendulkar	10,000	1,000	9,000	
5	2	Saurav Ganguly	12,000	2,000	10,000	
6	3	Rahul Dravid	11,000	1,500	9,500	
7		**Total**	**33,000**	**4,500**	**28,500**	

	A	B	C	D	E	F
1		**Salary for the month of June, 2002**				
2						
3	**No.**	**Name**	**Salary**	**Deduction**	**Nett. Payable**	
4	1	Sachin Tendulkar	10,000	500	9,500	
5	2	Saurav Ganguly	12,000	700	11,300	
6	3	Rahul Dravid	11,000	0	11,000	
7		**Total**	**33,000**	**1,200**	**31,800**	
8						
9						
10						

the range of cells to be consolidated. In this case they are from A3 to E6. See how it is reflected in the Reference.

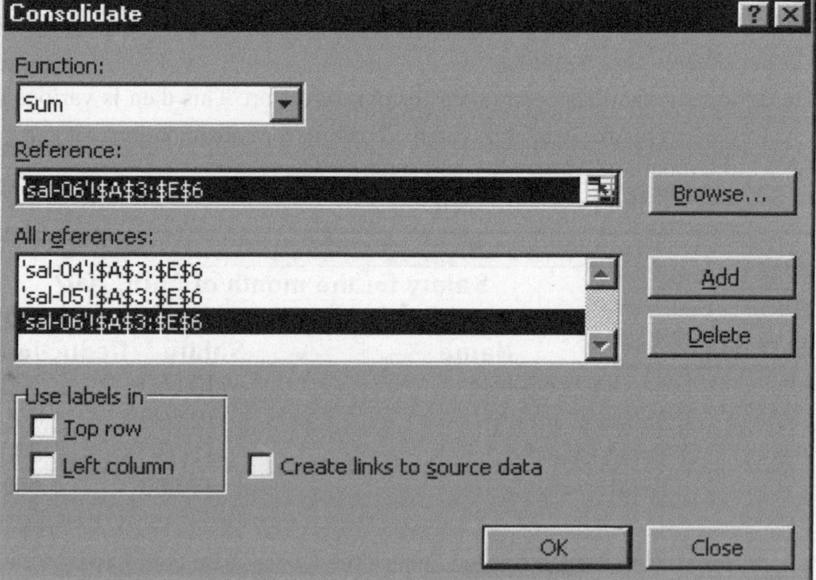

7. After choosing the range, click at Add to register it in the All references box.
8. Similarly do it for all the months and their ranges and have them stored in the All Reference column.
9. If you are using labels, make sure to point them out. In our case they are at the top of all the columns, so we will select the option Top row.
10. Click Ok to have the data consolidated in the worksheet.
11. The consolidated data is shown next.

Microsoft Excel - Book4

A3 = No.

	A	B	C	D	E
1	**Salary for the 1st Quarter - April, May and June**				
2					
3	No.	Name	Salary	Deduction	Nett. Payable
4	3		30,000	3,500	26,500
5	6		36,000	3,700	32,300
6	9		33,000	3,000	30,000
7			99,000	10,200	88,800

8.32 Scenarios Manager

Human mind is made of What-if situations. The same what-if can be applied to your worksheet to see if the results of the selection displays the good or bad results.

Each time you change the data, the previous solution is lost. To address this limitation, the Scenario Manager helps you keep track of multiple what-if models. Using the Scenarios manager, you can create new forecasting scenarios, view existing scenario, run scenario management commands and display consolidated scenario reports. Let us start with creating a worksheet and then apply the scenario to it.

Next a worksheet is shown which has been taken as an example for creating a scenario. Here the figures are

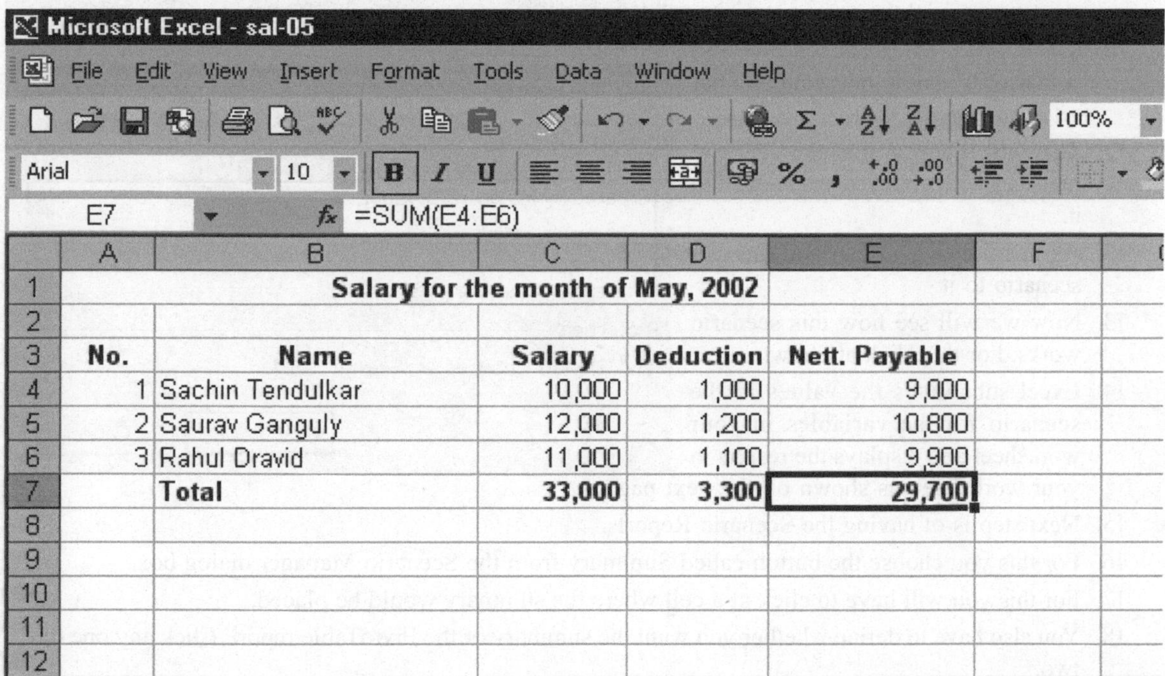
Microsoft Excel - sal-05

E7 =SUM(E4:E6)

	A	B	C	D	E
1		**Salary for the month of May, 2002**			
2					
3	**No.**	**Name**	**Salary**	**Deduction**	**Nett. Payable**
4	1	Sachin Tendulkar	10,000	1,000	9,000
5	2	Saurav Ganguly	12,000	1,200	10,800
6	3	Rahul Dravid	11,000	1,100	9,900
7		**Total**	**33,000**	**3,300**	**29,700**
8					
9					
10					
11					
12					

very simple and calculated. If you want you can use the constant figures too. Next we perform the following steps to create and view the scenario.

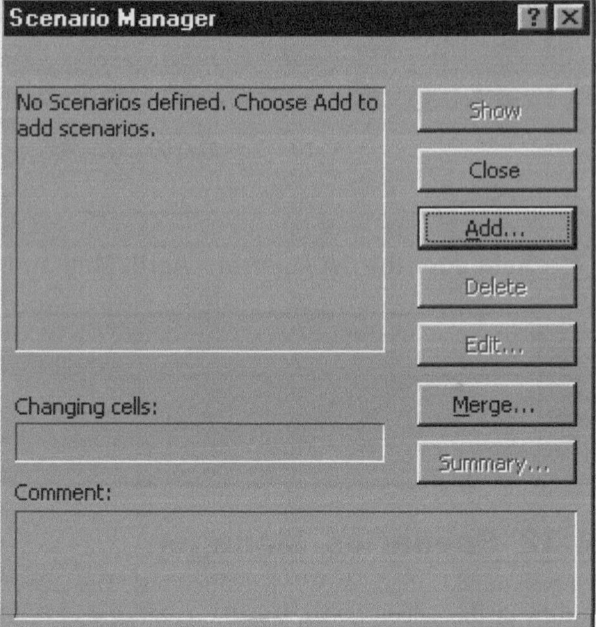

1. Click at Scenarios in the Tools menu.
2. A Scenario manager dialog box would appear on the screen, as shown on the next page.
3. As the dialog box says, click at Add to add a scenario.
4. This gives rise to another dialog box, which is called Add scenario.
5. In this dialog box, you have to firstly name the screnario.
6. I have named it as Good.
7. You can type the cell names or choose them by clicking at those cells. I have chosen cells from E4 to E7.
8. Click OK to add your scenario to the Scenario Manager. You'll see the Scenario Values dialog box, which asks you for your model's variables. The default values are the numbers that were already in the cells.

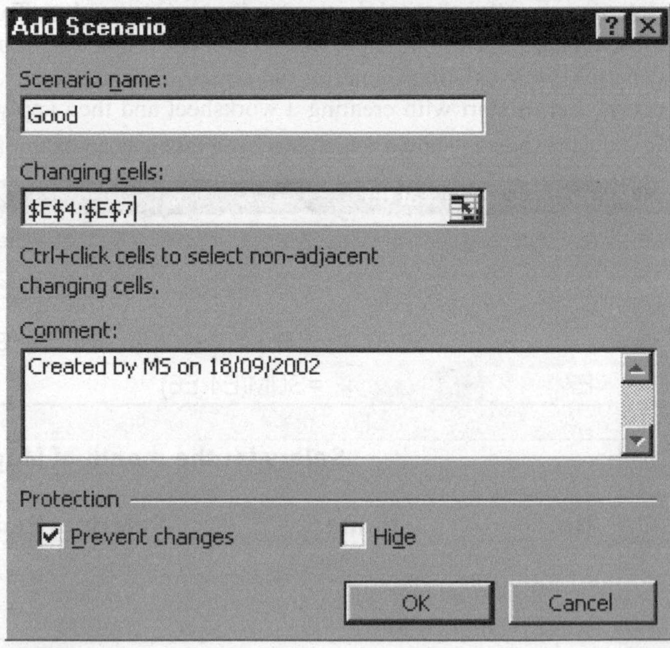

9. Type the various values which you want to see in the scenario.
10. Click Add to create a second scenario. If you do not want another set, just click at Ok.
11. This will return you to the scenario manager with your scenario added to it.
12. As mentioned you can add another scenario to it.
13. Now we will see how this scenario works. For this click at Show.
14. Excel substitutes the values in the scenario for the variables in your worksheet and displays the results in your worksheet, as shown on the next page.
15. Next step is of having the Scenario Reports.
16. For this you choose the button called Summary from the Scenario Manager dialog box.
17. For this you will have to click at a cell where the summary would be placed.
18. You also have to define whether you want the summary or the PivtoTable report. Click any one of the two.

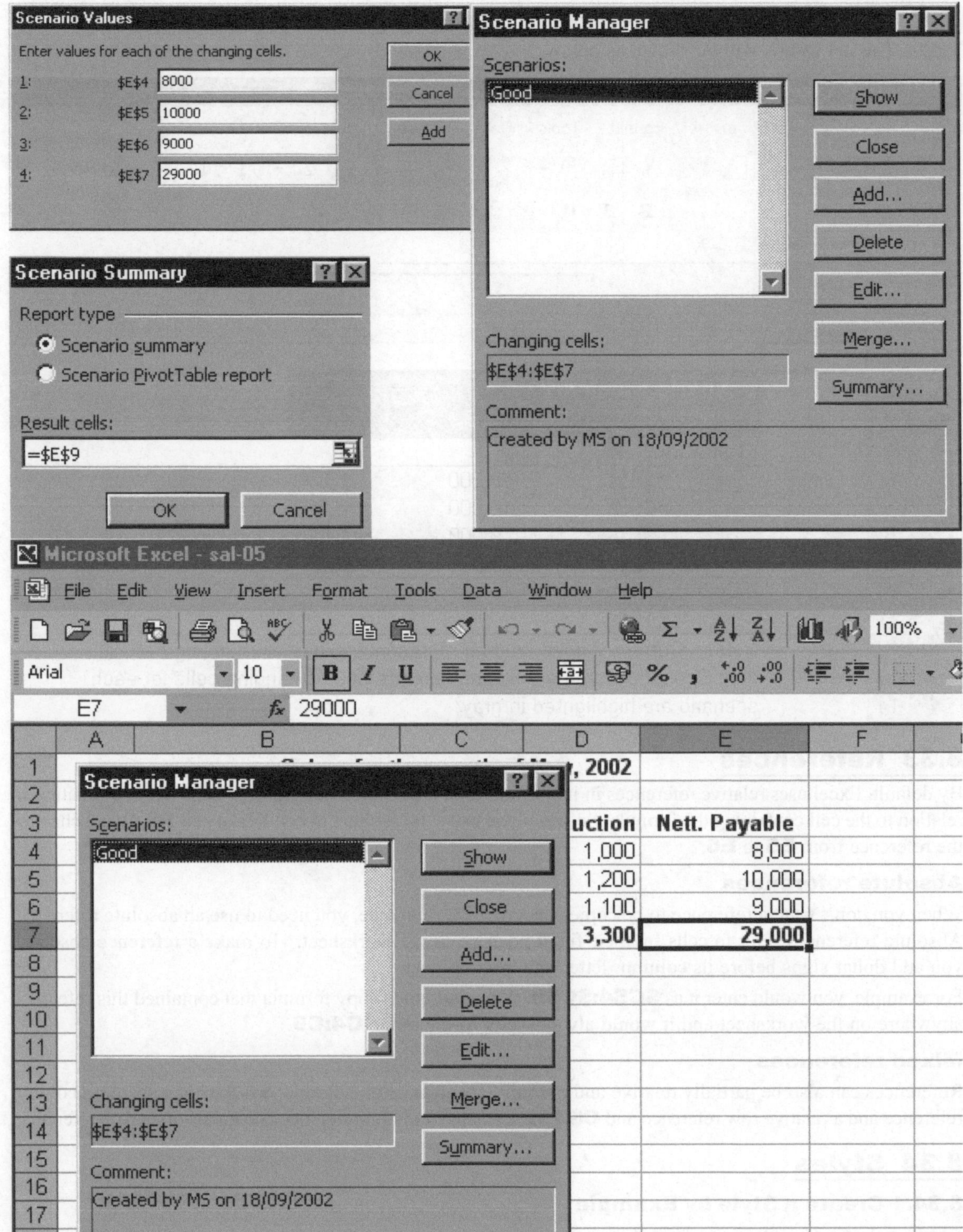
Scenario Values
Enter values for each of the changing cells.
1: $E$4 8000
2: $E$5 10000
3: $E$6 9000
4: $E$7 29000
OK
Cancel
Add
Scenario Manager
Scenarios:
Good
Show
Close
Add...
Delete
Edit...
Merge...
Summary...
Changing cells:
$E$4:$E$7
Comment:
Created by MS on 18/09/2002
Scenario Summary
Report type
Scenario summary
Scenario PivotTable report
Result cells:
=$E$9
OK
Cancel
Microsoft Excel - sal-05
File Edit View Insert Format Tools Data Window Help
Arial 10
E7 29000
, 2002
uction Nett. Payable
1,000 8,000
1,200 10,000
1,100 9,000
3,300 29,000

19. I have taken here Scenario summary and have given E9 as the cell for showing the results.
20. The net results will be shown as below.

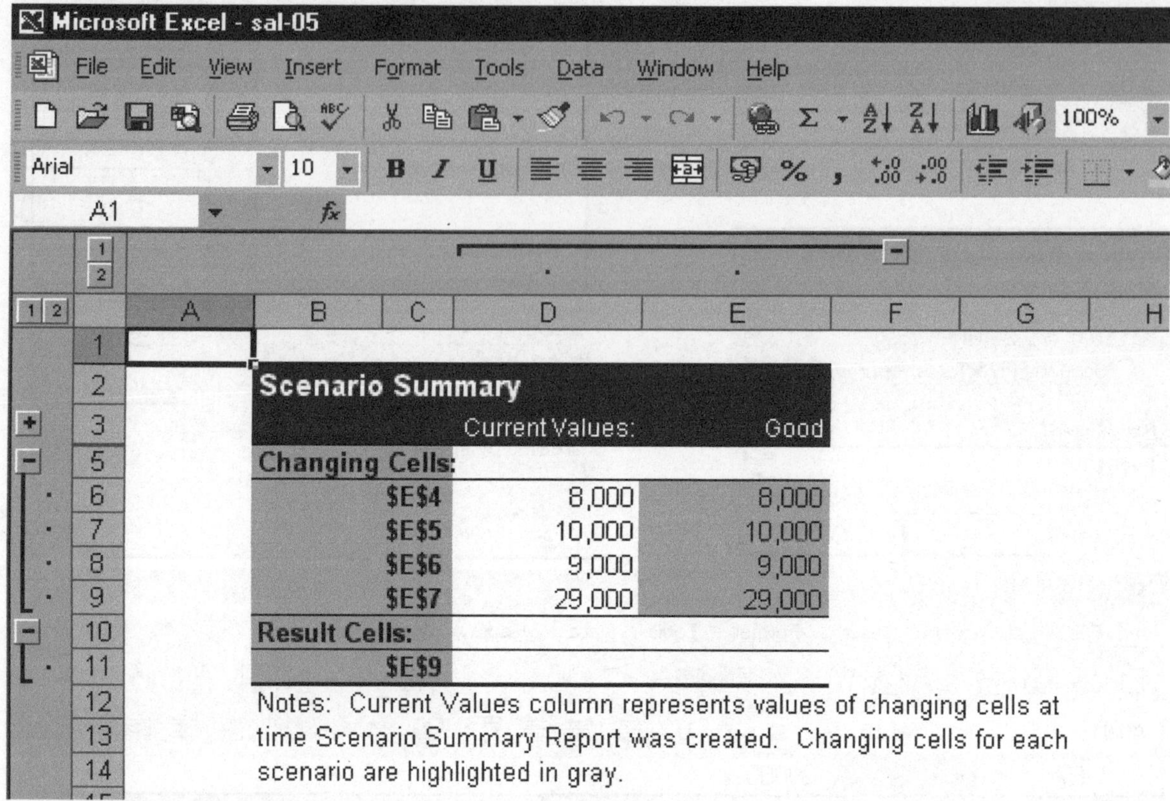

8.33 References

By default, Excel uses relative references in its formulae. Relative references refer to cells by their position in relation to the cell containing the formula. So when you copy the formula in cell **F5** to cell **F6**, Excel changes the reference from **E5** to **E6**.

Absolute references

When you don't want a reference to be copied as a relative reference, you need to use an absolute reference. Absolute references refer to cells by their fixed position in the worksheet. To make a reference absolute, you add dollar signs before its column letter and now number.

For example, you would enter it as **$C$4:$C$9**. You could then copy formula that contained this reference anywhere on the worksheet and it would always refer to the range **C4:C9**.

Mixed references

References can also be partially relative and partially absolute. For example, **$C3** has an absolute column reference and a relative row reference and **C$3** has a relative column reference and an absolute row reference.

8.34 Styles

8.34.1 Create a Style by Example

1. Select cell containing desired formats

2. Click Format menu, Style...
3. Type a name for style in Style Name: The style's formats in Style includes box.

Exclude formats of selected cell from style:

1. Deselect Style Includes (by example) options: Number, Font, Alignment, Border, Patterns, Protection
2. Click Ok.

8.34.2 Create a Style by Defining It

1. Click Format menu, Style...
2. Type a name for style in Style Name.

Exclude formats of selected cell from style:

1. Deselect Style Includes options:
2. Click Modify...
3. Click tab of format category to include
4. Select options for selected tab

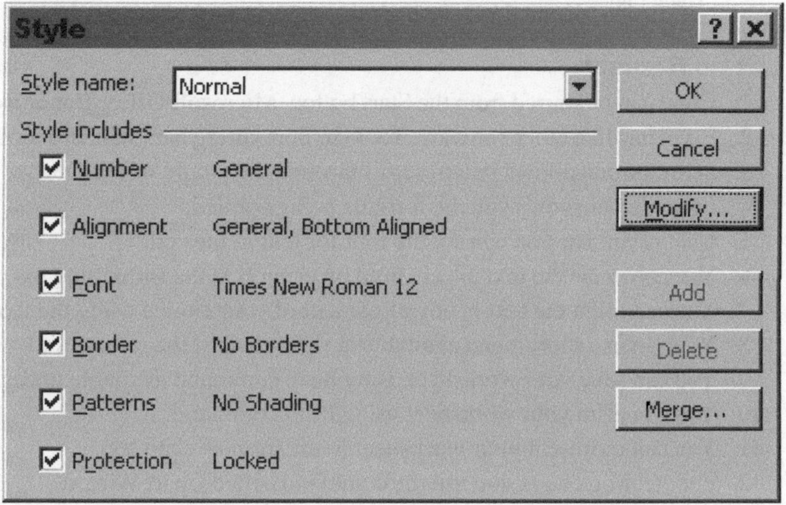

8.34.3 Redefine a Style by example

1. Select cell containing formats to assign to style
2. Click Format menu, Style...
3. Type (do not select) name of style to redefine in Style name.
4. Click Add...

If Redefine prompt appears

1. Click Yes
2. Click Ok

8.34.4 Redefine a Style by Defining It

1. Click Format menu, Style...
2. Select name of style to redefine in Style Name

Exclude format categories from style:

1. Deselect Style Includes options:

Change formats:

1. Click Modify...
2. Click tab of format category to change

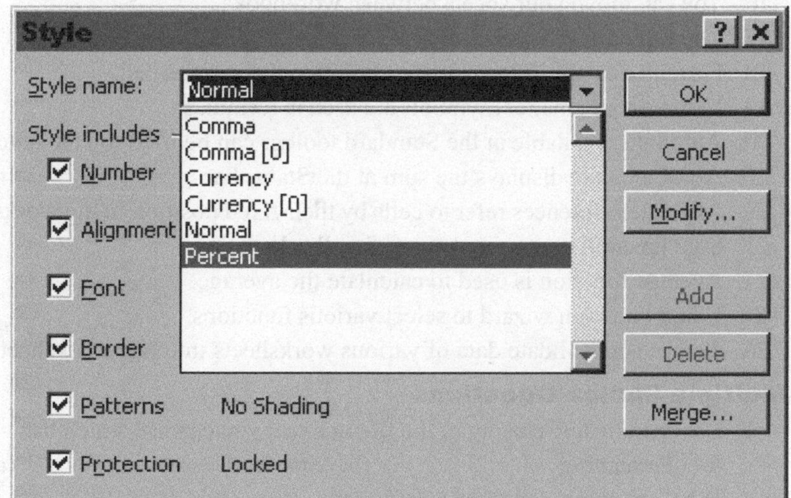

3. Select options for selected tab.
4. Repeat steps for each format category to change
5. Click Ok

8.34.5 Apply a Style

Add the Style box to the Formatting toolbar if you use styles often. Then select or define styles quickly without opening menus.

1. Select cell(s) to which to apply style
2. Click Format menu, Style...
3. Select style name in Style Name
4. Click Ok

Let us Revise

1. Excel can be started from the Start button, Microsoft Office Bar or from Windows Explorer.
2. Excel has like other software, Toolbar, Formatting bar, Standard toolbar, etc.
3. Scroll button allows you to scroll through the whole worksheet.
4. Formula bar shows you the formula being applied.
5. Using Font bar you can set the font for text in the cell.
6. You can make the text in cell, bold by using B at the formatting bar.
7. You can align the text in any alignment of your choice using the icons on the formatting bar.
8. You can use short menu available at right click of the mouse for Cut and Paste.
9. You can save your worksheet using Save command available under the File menu.
10. You can print your worksheet using Print command.
11. You can represent your worksheet in the form of chart too.
12. For creating charts you use the command called Chart Wizard.
13. You can modify the chart made by you by double clicking the chart.
14. You can add data to any chart.
15. You can even add a Pivot Table to your chart.
16. You can move your sheets between workbooks.
17. You can protect a work book.
18. Formulas establish the relations between the various cells.
19. Various mathematical symbols are used in formulas.
20. AutoSum, available at the Standard toolbar can be used to calculate the sum instantenously.
21. AutoCalculate displays the sum at the Status bar.
22. Absolute references refer to cells by their fixed position in the worksheet.
23. Sum function is commonly used for all calculations.
24. Average function is used to calculate the average.
25. Using Function wizard to select various functions.
26. You can consolidate data of various worksheets into one worksheet.

Multiple Choice Questions

1. For opening and closing of the file in Excel you can use which bar.

   (a) Formatting (b) Standard (c) Title

2. What are numbered from A to Z, etc?

   (a) Rows (b) Cells (c) Columns

3. You can move around the worksheet using which buttons?
(a) Scroll (b) Logic (c) Start
4. For making the text bold in the cell, you use B in which bar.
(a) Standard (b) Formatting (c) Title
5. For getting the short menu on the screen, you click which button of the mouse.
(a) Right button (b) Left button (c) Centre button
6. Charts are created using which option.
(a) Chart Wizard (b) Pivot Table (c) Pie Chart
7. For editing the chart, you ____________ the chart itself.
(a) Click (b) Delete (c) Double click
8. In Excel formula starts with ___________.
(a) = sign (b) + sign (c) - sign
9. In Excel worksheets are given _____ extension.
(a) .xls (b) .doc (c) .bmp
10. In Microsoft Excel, you use _______ for calcualtions.
(a) Formula (b) Row (c) Cell
11. Formula which can be used directly from the Standard toolbar is
(a) AutoSum (b) Auto (c) Sum
12. The result of AutoCalculate is shown at ___ bar.
(a) Standard (b) Formatting (c) Status
13. Sum function needs to have ______ before it.
(a) + (b) – (c) =
14. To access to any formula in Microsoft Excel, you need to go through _____
(a) Function Wizard (b) File (c) Formula
15. Anything that is typed in a worksheet appears:
(a) in both the active cell and the formula bar
(b) in the active cell only
(c) none of the above
16. The formatting toolbar
(a) is placed just below the Standard toolbar
(b) is used to apply common formats
(c) both of above
17. The combination of the column letter and row number for a cell in an Excel worksheet is called a
(a) cell identification number (b) cell reference (c) cell identity
18. In Excel the simplest way to move data from one location to another is
(a) by menu commands (b) by mouse (c) by drag and drop method
19. Using borders you
(a) can add lines above, below or to either side of a cell
(b) can add a single line or multiple lines, along one side of a cell or around it.
(c) both a and b above
20. Cell address B$6 in a formula means it is a
(a) relative cell reference (b) absolute cell reference (c) mixed cell reference
21. A function in Excel
(a) is a ready made formula (b) is a shortcut formula (c) both of above

True/False Questions

1. Microsoft Excel is a spreadsheet program.
2. Using Formatting toolbar you can format the data.
3. There is only one worksheet in a spreadsheet.
4. Formula is displayed in the formula bar.
5. You cannot have fonts applied to the data.
6. You cannot align the data in a cell.
7. For cut and paste you can use the shortcut menu available at right click of the mouse.
8. A worksheet cannot be given a name.
9. Before printing you cannot see a preview of the worksheet.
10. You cannot represent your worksheet data in the form of a chart.
11. Chart Wizard is used for creating the chart.
12. Once created a chart cannot be modified.
13. You cannot add a Pivot Table to your chart.
14. You cannot move your data in between the various sheets of the workbook.
15. A password protection can be made of the worksheet.
16. A formula can estabish relation between cells.
17. All mathematical symbols can be used in the formula.
18. AutoSum is used for calculating sum.
19. AutoCalculate displays the sum at Formatting toolbar.
20. Absolute references refer to cells by their fixed position in the worksheet.
21. Average function would calculate the average.
22. You cannot consolidate data of various worksheets.
23. Function Wizard cannot be used for various functions.
24. Data and Time functions would give you the various options of data and time.
25. Text functions would give you the various options of text.
26. A formula can have a mixed reference of the cells.
27. A border cannot be added around the data in the worksheet.

Matching Columns

Match the data in Column A with the data in Column B.

Column A	Column B
A. Formating toolbar	1. Sheets in a workbook
B. Functions	2. A selection of cells
C. Standard toolbar	3. Beginning of a formula
D. Cols	4. Right click of the mouse
E. Rows	5. A combination of column letter and row number of a cell
F. Worksheets	6. Used for performing standard operations
G Active cell	7. Refers to an absolute location of a specific cell
H. Range of cells	8. Mathematical function
I. =	9. Monthly instalment calculator
J. Short cut menu	10. Used for formatting data in cells

K. Cell reference	11. Ready made formula
L. Absolute reference	12. Horizontal row
M. TRUNC()	13. Vertical columns
N. PMT()	14. A selected cell

Fill in the Blanks with appropriate words

a. Chart	b. .xls	c. An active cell	d. AVERAGE
e. Scroll	f. Cell	g. =	h. Columns
i. Sheets	j. Chart Wizard	k. Right button	l. Standard

1. Cross section of a row and column is called _____.
2. In Excel formula starts with ______ sign.
3. For opening and closing of the file in Excel you can use the _________ bar
4. In Excel worksheets are given ______ extension
5. Charts are created using ________..
6. The function ________ is used for calculating average.
7. You can move around the worksheet using _________ buttons.
8. For editing the chart, you double click ________.
9. In Excel ______ are numbered from A to Z.
10. For getting the short menu on the screen, you click ______ of the mouse.
11. A selected cell in Excel is called ________.
12. A workbook can have a number of ________.

Descriptive Type Questions

1. Describe various methods of starting Excel?
2. Describe the various components of the Excel worksheet window.
3. Describe the method of copying formula.
4. Describe the process of saving a worksheet.
5. Describe how would you insert a chart in the worksheet.
6. Describe the working of the Chart Wizard.
7. Describe the process of modifying chart.
8. How would you add data to the chart?
9. Describe the process of creating a Pivot Table.
10. How would you audit a worksheet? Explain.
11. Describe the process of inserting a comment in the worksheet.
12. Describe how the logical functions work in worksheet.
13. Describe how would you put Headers and Footers in a worksheet.
14. How would you merge two worksheets?
15. Describe the method of putting Outlines to worksheets.
16. How would you put labels on your rows and columns of the worksheet?
17. How would you protect your worksheet?
18. How would you name a range of cells?
19. Describe the various type of references.
20. Describe the command Goal Seek.
21. Describe the process of naming sheets.
22. How would you create a style?

23. How would you copy entries between workbooks?
24. Write down the steps to protect the workbook.
25. Which mathematical symbols are used in Microsoft Excel formulas?
26. Which type of errors you get while using formulas?
27. How would you use AutoSum?
28. Describe the process of using AutoCalculate.
29. Describe Absolute and Mixed References.
30. How is the Sum function used?
31. How would you use the AVERAGE function?
32. What is Function Wizard?

Answers to Objective Type Questions

Multiple Choice Questions

1. b	2. c	3. a	4. b	5. a
6. a	7. c	8. a	9. a	10 a
11. a	12. c	13. c	14. a	15. a
16. c	17. b	18. c	19. c	20. b
21. c				

True False Questions

1. T	2. T	3. F	4. T	5. F
6. F	7. T	8. F	9. T	10. F
11. T	12. F	13. F	14. F	15. T
16. T	17. T	18. T	19. F	20. T
21. T	22. F	23. F	24. T	25. T
26. T	27. F			

Matching Columns

A. 10	B. 11	C. 6	D. 13	E. 12
F. 1	G. 14	H. 2	I. 3	J. 4
K. 5	L. 7	M. 8	N. 9	

Fill in the Blanks

1. f	2. g	3. l	4. b	5. j
6. d	7. e	8. a	9. h	10. k
11. c	12. i			

Presentations Software 9

9.1 Creating a Presentation

There are three methods of creating a presentation. They are given here.

9.1.1 Creating a Presentation using Wizard

The Wizard would create for you a complete presentation, just add few graphics and text here and there, your presentation is complete. To create a presentation using AutoContent, do the following:

1. Select New from the File menu.
2. Select AutoContent from the General Panel or Click at From AutoContent Wizard in the Task Pane, as shown above.
3. The first screen of the AutoContent Wizard appears on the screen.
4. Click Next
5. The next screen of the Wizard allows you to choose a type of presentation you want. I have chosen here the Selling a Product or Service from the Sales/Marketing heading.
6. Click Next.
7. The next screen allows you to select the type of output you want. I have selected here the On-screen presentation.

   Various other options are also there which are shown here on the screen.

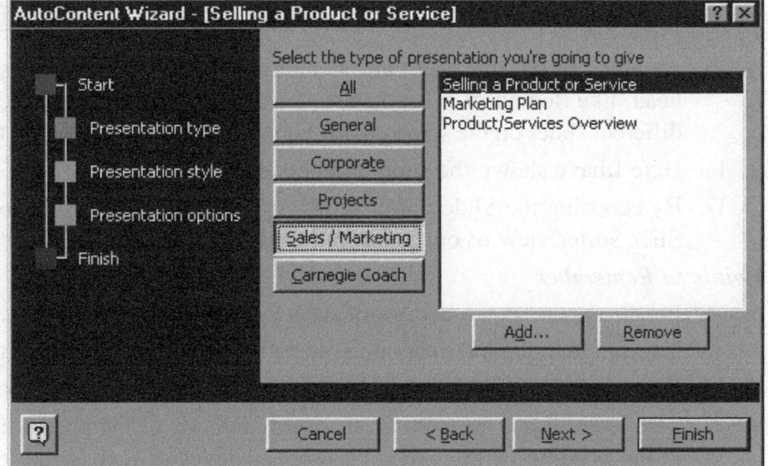

8. Click Next.
9. The next screen asks you to give title of the presentation and the text you want to appear on the footer page. I have put them as Selling of Toothpaste and New Toothpaste in the market. I have also chosen for the Date and Slide number to the displayed. Of course, you can have your own header and footer.
10. Click Next.
11. Click at Finish to end the AutoContent Wizard session.
12. The presentation you have chosen can be seen on the screen.
13. As you can see from the presentation, the left hand side of the screen contains text of the presentation and on the right hand side you can see the presentation.
14. Click at Slide Show to see full screen presentation as it would look on the screen. Press Esc to come back.

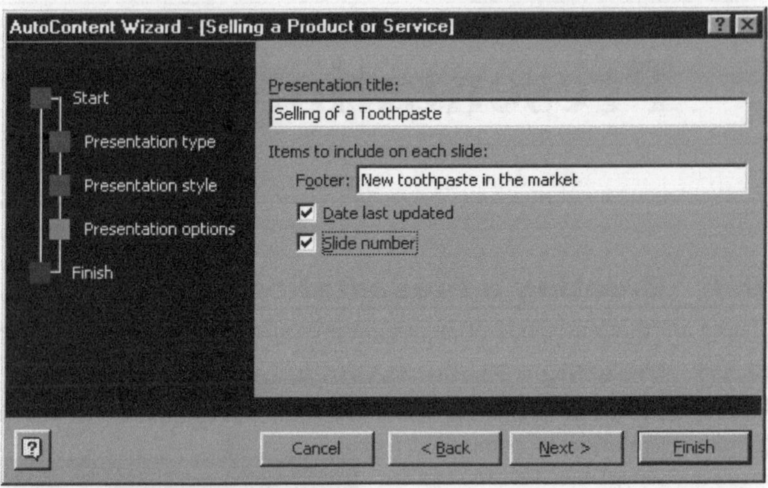

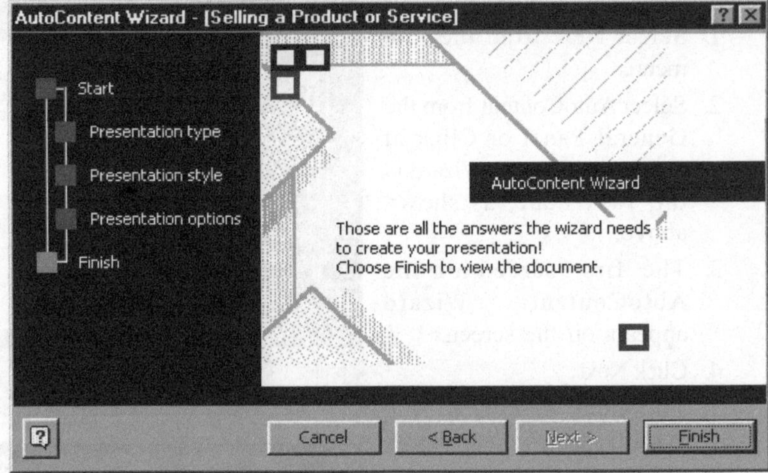

15. As you can see that there are as many as 8 slides in this presentation, each representing different head, like Selling of a Toothpaste, Customer requirements, Meeting the needs, etc. You can see the different slides on the screen when you move the vertical bar on the right hand side of the presentation.
16. Here I have shown the slide numbers 4 and 7.
17. By choosing the Slide Sorter view you can see all the slides on the screen but in very small form. Slide sorter view of our presentation is also shown.

Points to Remember

1. Footer appear at the bottom of each page on the presentation.
2. You can skip the intermediatory steps by clicking at Finish in the first dialog box of the Wizard.
3. Each presentation is given a look which is preset. You can change this according to your liking.
4. Two level of text is given on the left hand side of the presentation. The one with the serial number is the heading of the slide. The second level of text is the text which appears as the part of the presentation.
5. You can change this text about which you will read later.

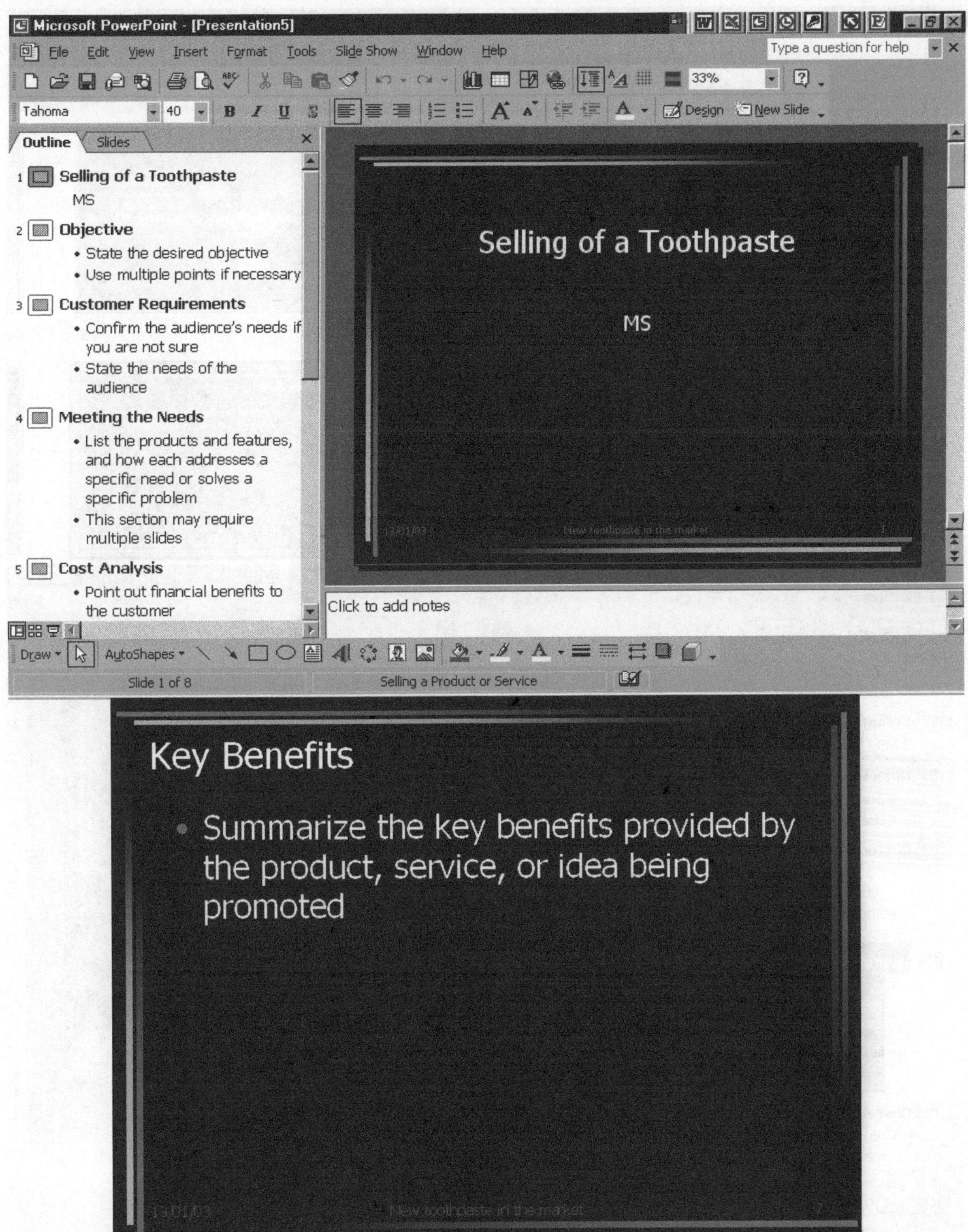
Microsoft PowerPoint - [Presentation5]
File Edit View Insert Format Tools Slide Show Window Help
Type a question for help
Tahoma
40
33%
Design
New Slide
Outline
Slides
1 Selling of a Toothpaste
MS
2 Objective
• State the desired objective
• Use multiple points if necessary
3 Customer Requirements
• Confirm the audience's needs if you are not sure
• State the needs of the audience
4 Meeting the Needs
• List the products and features, and how each addresses a specific need or solves a specific problem
• This section may require multiple slides
5 Cost Analysis
• Point out financial benefits to the customer
Selling of a Toothpaste
MS
Click to add notes
Draw
AutoShapes
Slide 1 of 8
Selling a Product or Service
Key Benefits
• Summarize the key benefits provided by the product, service, or idea being promoted

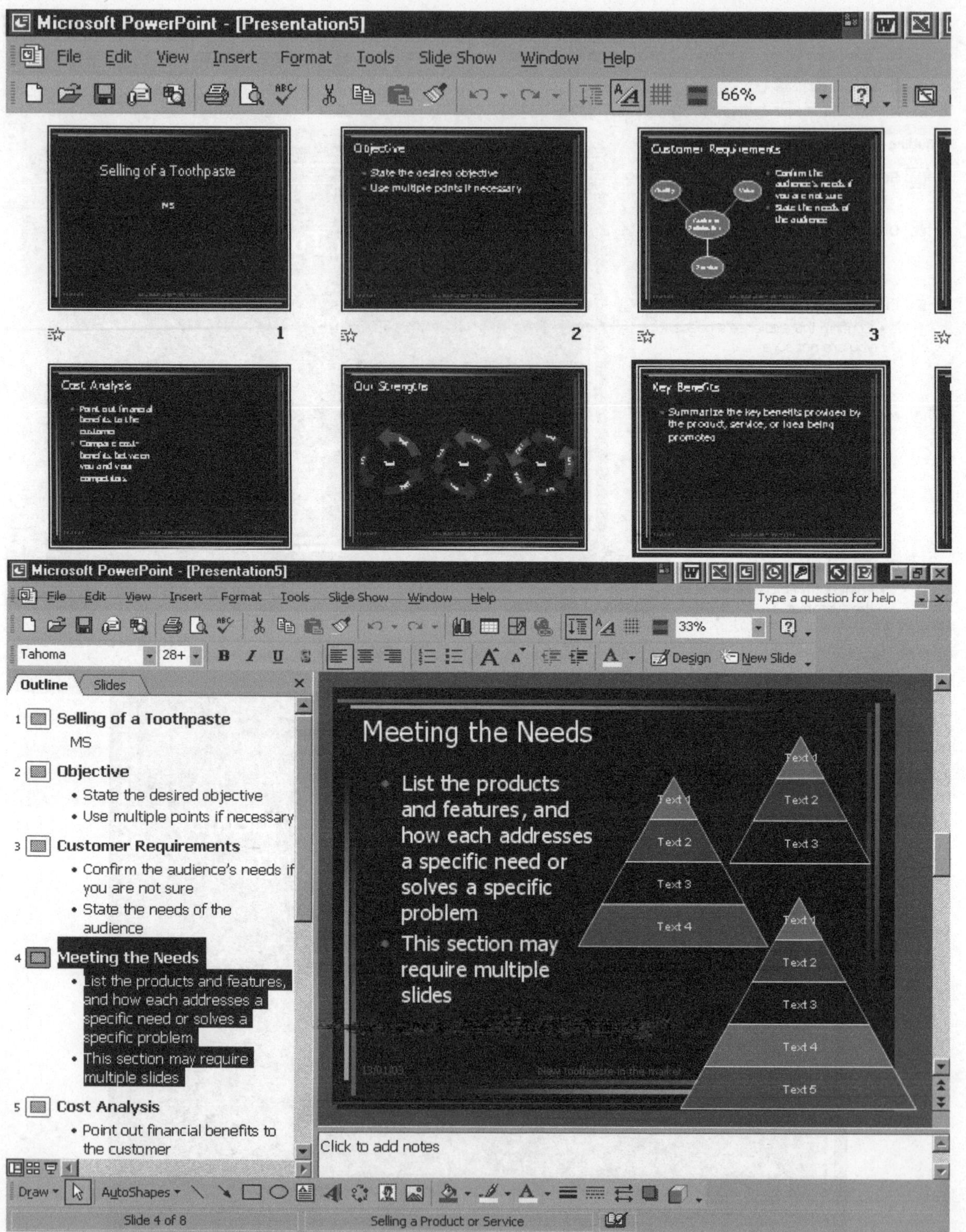
Microsoft PowerPoint - [Presentation5]
File Edit View Insert Format Tools Slide Show Window Help
66%
Selling of a Toothpaste
MS
Objective
State the desired objective
Use multiple points if necessary
Customer Requirements
Confirm the audience's needs if you are not sure
State the needs of the audience
Cost Analysis
Point out financial benefits to the customer
Compare cost benefits between you and your competitors
Our Strengths
Key Benefits
Summarize the key benefits provided by the product, service, or idea being promoted
Microsoft PowerPoint - [Presentation5]
File Edit View Insert Format Tools Slide Show Window Help
Type a question for help
33%
Tahoma
28+
Design
New Slide
Outline
Slides
1 Selling of a Toothpaste
MS
2 Objective
• State the desired objective
• Use multiple points if necessary
3 Customer Requirements
• Confirm the audience's needs if you are not sure
• State the needs of the audience
4 Meeting the Needs
• List the products and features, and how each addresses a specific need or solves a specific problem
• This section may require multiple slides
5 Cost Analysis
• Point out financial benefits to the customer
Meeting the Needs
List the products and features, and how each addresses a specific need or solves a specific problem
This section may require multiple slides
Text 1
Text 2
Text 3
Text 4
Text 5
Click to add notes
Draw
AutoShapes
Slide 4 of 8
Selling a Product or Service

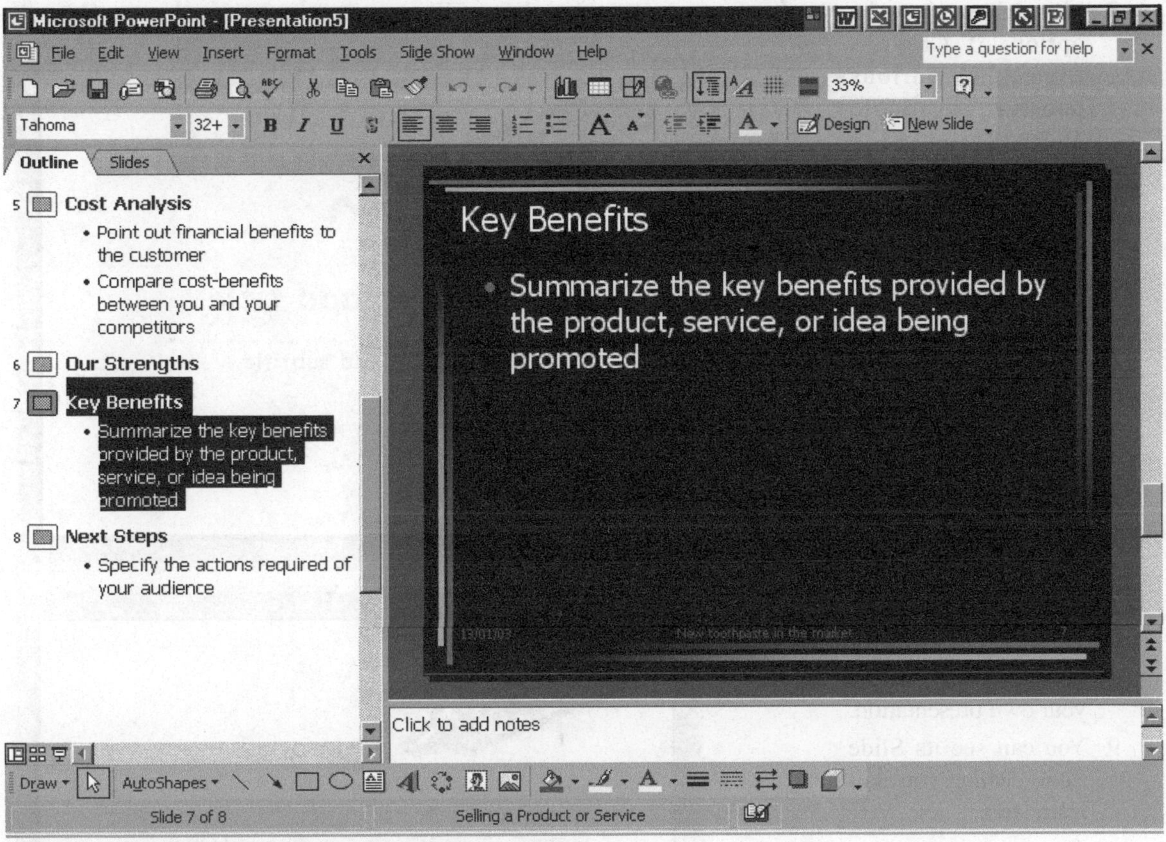

9.1.2 Creating Presentation from Template

As I had mentioned earlier that the software has available presentations, these are called Templates. These can be used for creating your own. Templates can provide either the graphic design and color scheme of a presentation (design template) or suggest content and structure, using a set of slides whose text you can edit.

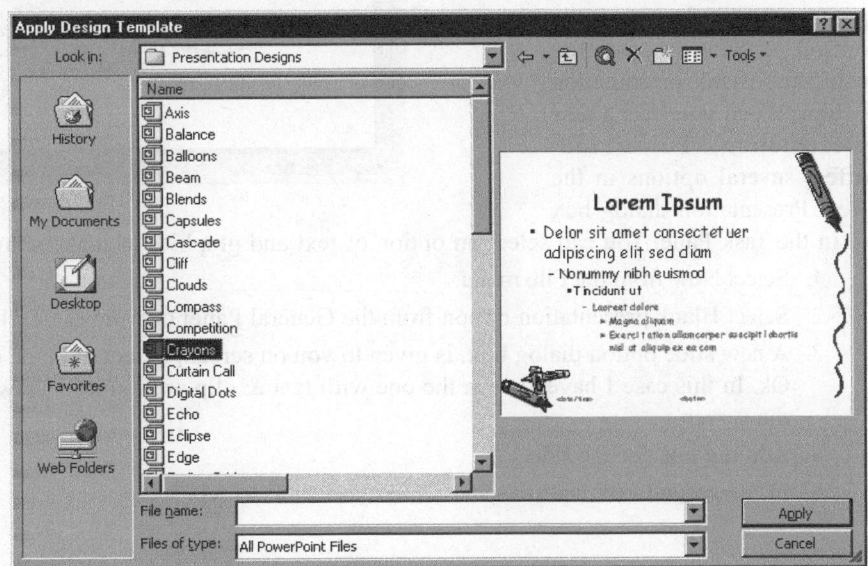

1. Select New from the File menu.
2. Select Design Templates option on the New Presentation dialog box or select From Design Templates from the Task Pane.

3. I have chosen here the option of Crayons from the various options available under Presentation Templates.
4. You would be given a choice to choose the type of slide. Here you can type the title of your choice and then add the subtitle of your choice.
5. I have type some text as shown.
6. From Insert menu, click at New Slide.
7. A new blank slide will appear.
8. This way you can keep adding slides and make your own presentation.
9. You can see its Slide Show, which you will learn later.

9.1.3 Creating a New Presentation

Another method of creating presentation is by using the option of New presentation using the Blank presentation option. When you start a new presentation, PowerPoint offers several options in the New Presentation dialog box or in the Task Pane. You can select an option of text and graphics to make show on the screen.

1. Select New from the File menu.
2. Select Blank presentation option from the General Panel or from the Task Pane.
3. A new slide option dialog box, is given to you on screen. Select the type of slide you want and click Ok. In this case I have chosen the one with text & clip art and it is shown on the small window on the screen.
4. Add the text for the title.
5. In the second box type the text which you want to type.

6. The graphic icon allows you to add graphics of various types, i.e., Table, Chart, Clip Art, Picture, Diagram and Media Clip.
7. I have chosen to add a Picture here and have chosen the picture of Capitol Hill.
8. See how it looks when inserted in the slide on the next page.
9. On the otherhand you can choose a different option of text, graphics and even the type of slide too.

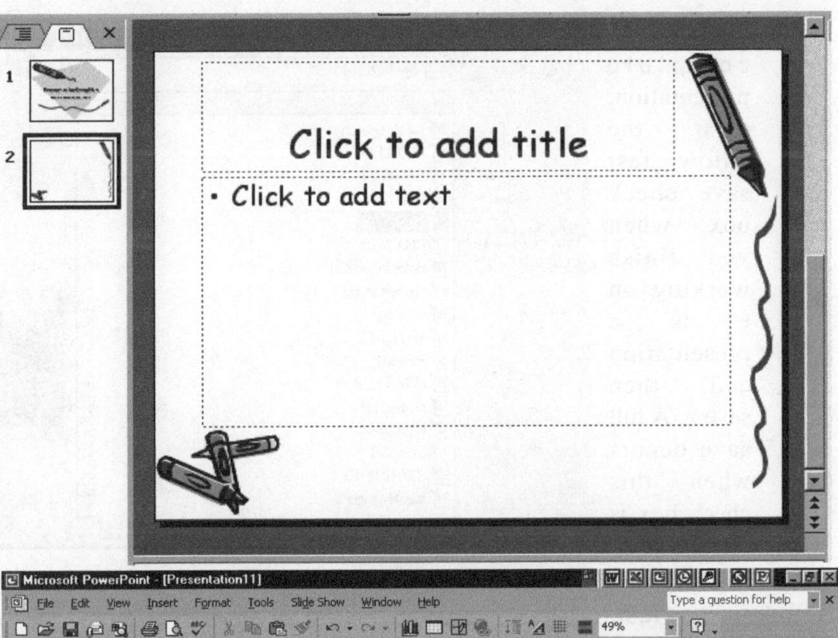

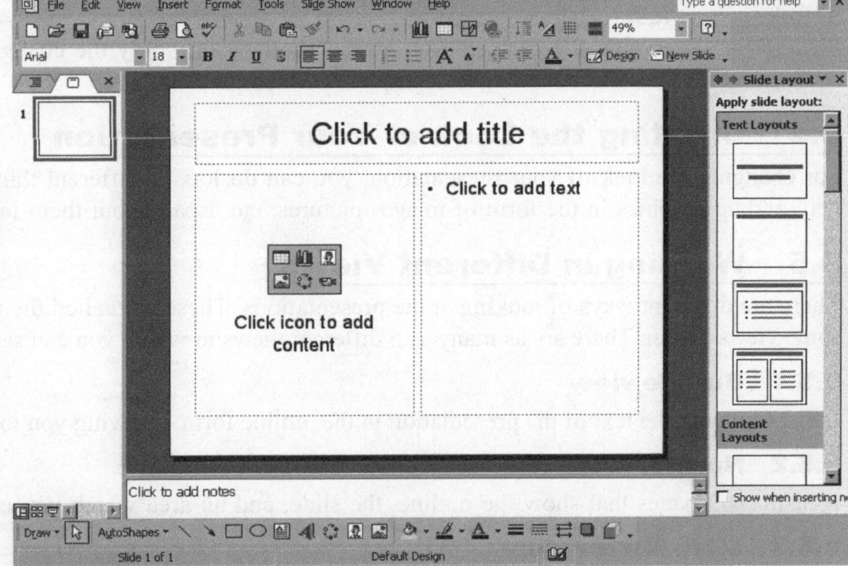

9.2 Opening a Presentation

An existing presentation can be opened by using the Open command from the File menu. The dialog box shows the existing presentation files, select the one which you want to open and press Enter. The presentation would come on the screen and can be worked upon using the various available commands.

9.3 Saving a Presentation

You can save the presentation you are working on by choosing Save Options from File menu or by clicking the Save button on the Standard toolbar. If you are Saving the presentation for the first time, Save As dialog box appears where you have to enter the file name.

Speed up Saving a Presentation

1. On the Tools menu, click at Options to get the options dialog box.
2. Click on the Save panel.
3. To Save only the changes to a presentation, select the Allow fast saves check box and then continue to Save as you work on the presentation.

4. To save a complete presentation, clear the Allow fast save check box when you finish working on the presentation and then save it. A full save occurs when this check box is clear.

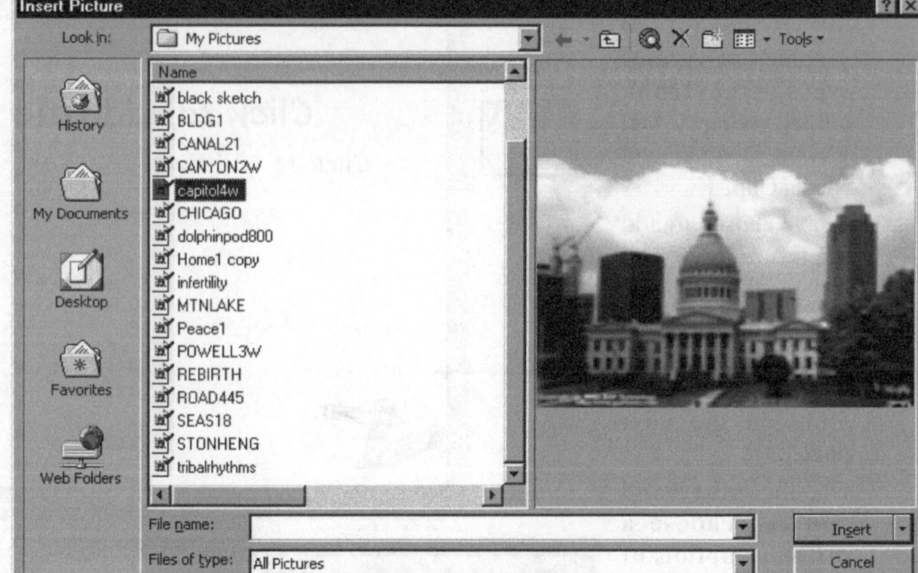

If you select the Allow fast, PowerPoint saves only the changes to a presentation. Saving only the changes takes less time than a full save, in which PowerPoint saves the complete revised presentation.

9.4 Creating the Look of Your Presentation

For changing the look of your presentation, you can do lots of different things on the slides, like adding text, adding graphics in the form of images/pictures, etc. Read about them in subsequent paragraphs.

9.5 Working in Different Views

There are different ways of looking at the presentations. These are called the views. I had mentioned about some views earlier. There are as many as 5 different views in which you can see your presentation. They are:

9.5.1 Outline view

It displays only the text of the presentation in the outline form, allowing you to work easily with the content.

9.5.2 Normal view

It displays 3 panes that show the outline, the slide, and an area which you can enter speaker's notes.

9.5.3 Slide Sorter view

It displays thumbnail views of your slides so that you can reorganize the slides and change the overall look of the presentation. In this view you can also add and edit the transition effects for the slide show.

9.5.4 Slide Show view

It displays the presentation one slide at a time in sequence as an automatic slide show.

9.5.5 Notes Page view

It is available only from the view menu, lets you enter and edit speaker's notes for the presenter.

Points to Remember

1. Each view shows a different aspect of the same presentation.
2. You can switch from one view to another at any time.

3. Right-click in Slide Sorter view or click the button at lower left corner of the current slide to display the Slide Show shortcut menu.

9.6 Working with Slides

Once you have created slides, you can work on them using the various commands given here.

9.6.1 Entering the Text

Let us create another presentation which has more of text. Here, we will add the text as per the following:

1. Create a new presentation which has only text in the slide.
2. Type the name Adobe Corporation in the title bar.
3. In the next box, type the name of the famous software of the company called PageMaker.
4. Pressing enter would lead you to another sub heading.
5. Type here the next heading, Photoshop.
6. Similarly press enter and type Type Manager.
7. At this stage your presentation would like the one shown on the next page.
8. Now we come to adding text in between the main headings, i.e., sub-headings.
9. Place your cursor at the end of the first heading, i..e., after PageMaker and press Enter. A new heading with 2 will appear. Just press Tab to get the bulleted text format. Type here the first line of your tabbed matter, which is Version 6.5.
10. Press enter again to get the new line and type version 7.0.
11. At this stage your presentation will look like, the one shown on the next page.
12. You can thus type the date in the steps required by you.
13. Next obvious step would be change the data, read on.

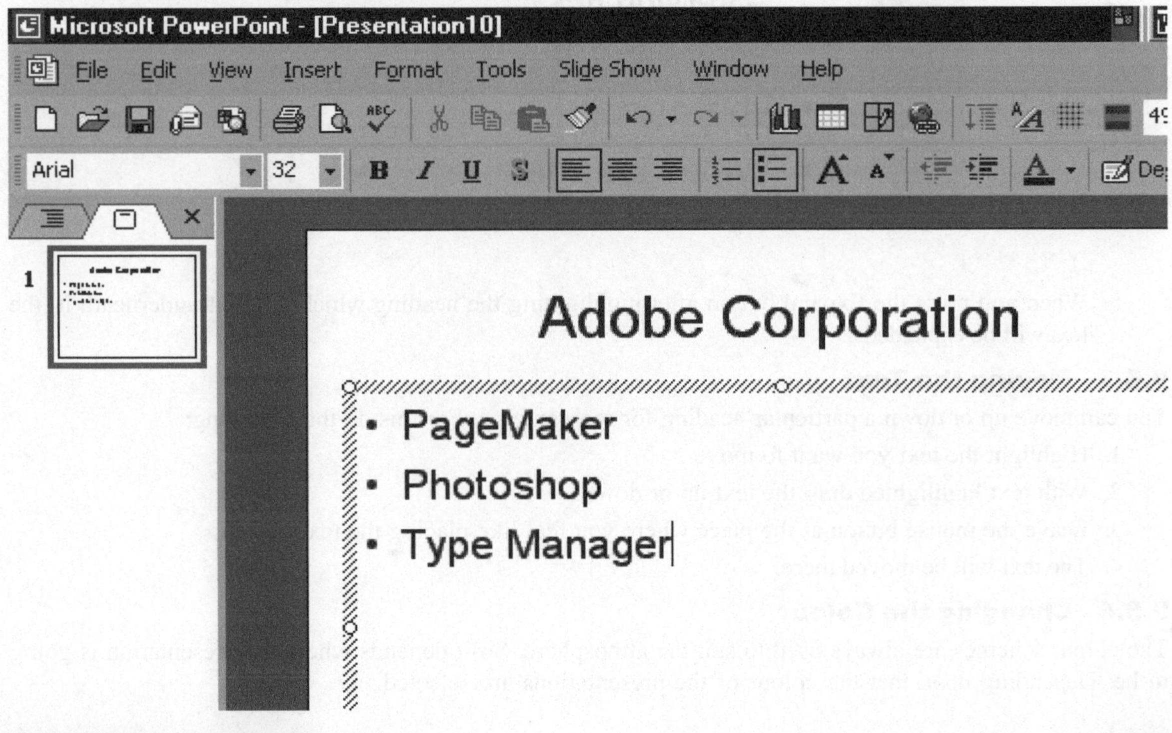

9.6.2 Changing Display

You can hide the text of the bulleted text or the sub-heading and let only the headings remain visible. For this do the following:

1. Highlight the text you want to hide.
2. With text highlighted, click at right mouse button to get another submenu.
3. Select Collapse from here.
3. The text will be hidden and only the heading will remain in view, as shown on next to next page.
4. The heading which has text hidden underneath it is indicated by the text being shown as underlined.

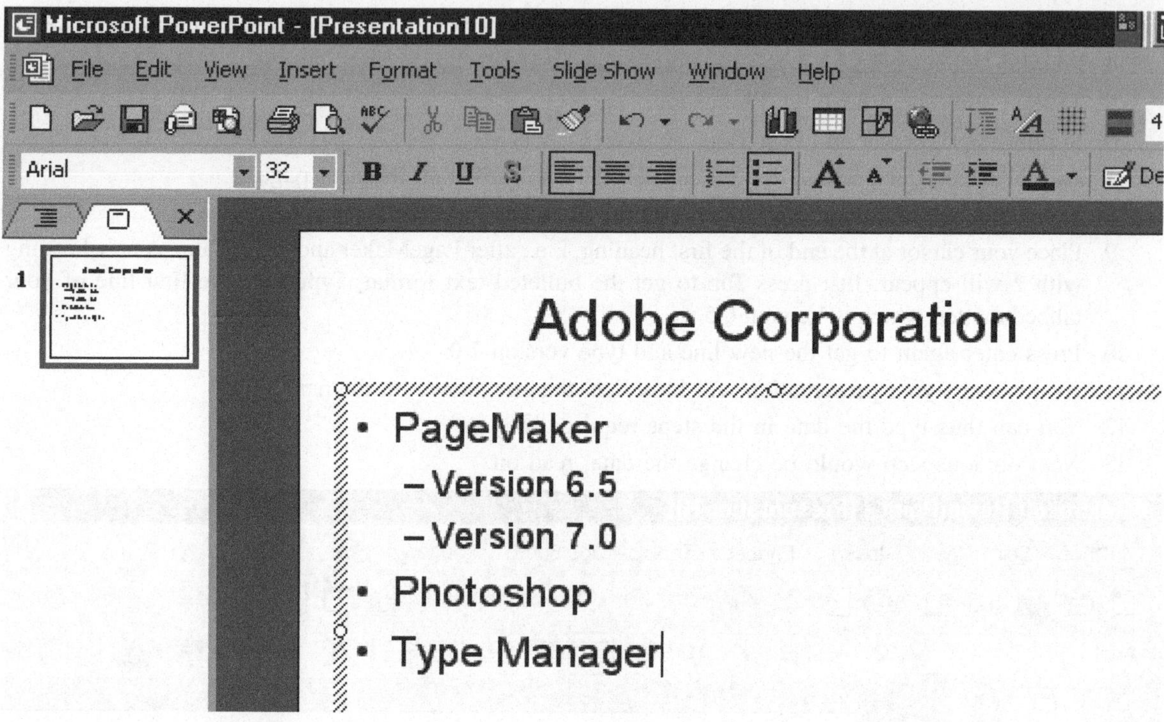

5. When you press the Expand button after highlighting the heading which has text underneath it, the text will be expanded.

9.6.3 Moving the Text

You can move up or down a particular heading for reorganizing. For this do the following:

1. Highlight the text you want to move.
2. With text highlighted drag the text up or down.
3. Leave the mouse button at the place where you feel like placing the text.
4. The text will be moved there.

9.6.4 Changing the Colour

The colour schemes are always used to suit the atmosphere. So it depends where the presentation is going to be. Depending upon that the colour of the presentations are selected.

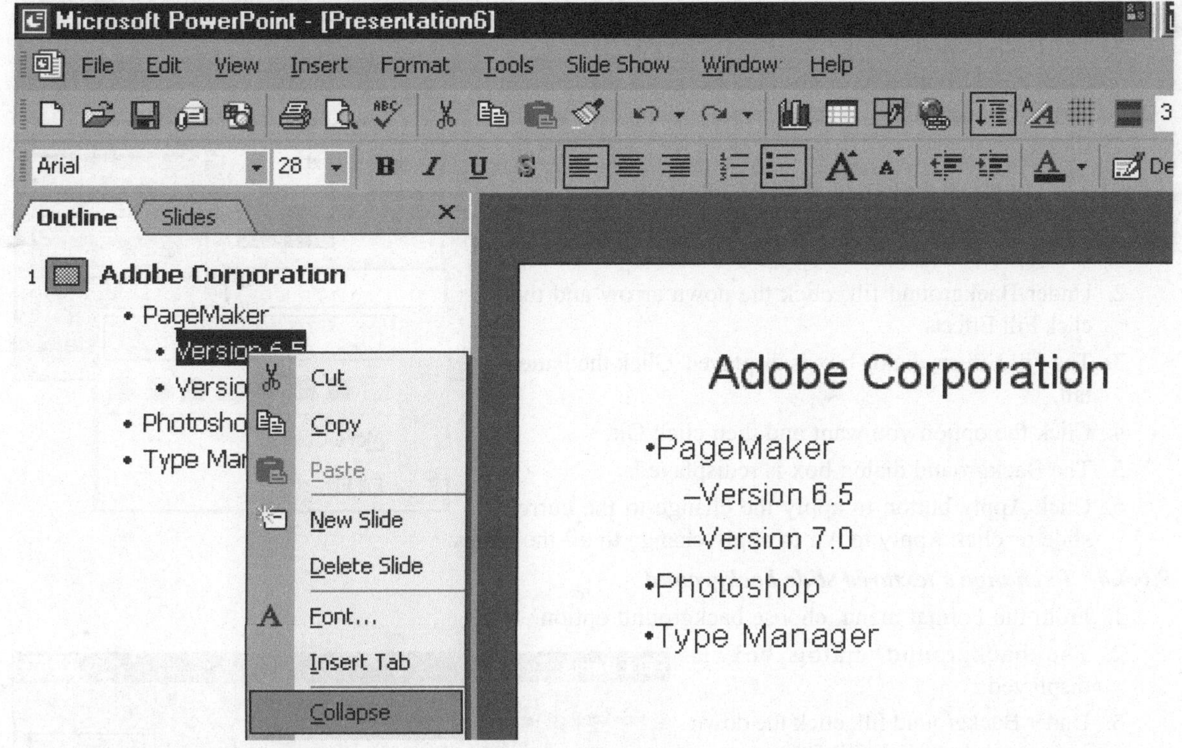

9.6.4.1 To Change the Colours

1. Select Background from Format menu.

   Or

   Right click outside the placeholder areas in Slide or Normal view and choose slide colour scheme from the shortcut menu
2. Background dialog box appears, as shown here.
3. Under Background fill, click the down arrow.
4. To change to a colour in the colour scheme, click one of the eight colours below Automatic.
5. To change to a colour which is not there, click at More colours.
6. Click the colour you want on the standard tab or click the custom tab to mix your own colour and then click Ok.
7. Click Apply button to apply the changed colour to the current slide or click Apply to All, to apply the change to all slides in the presentation.

9.6.4.2 Working with Shaded Background

1. From the Format menu, choose background option. The background dialog box is displayed.
2. Under Background fill, click the down arrow and then click Fill Effects.
3. The Fill Effects dialog box is displayed. Click the Gradient tab.

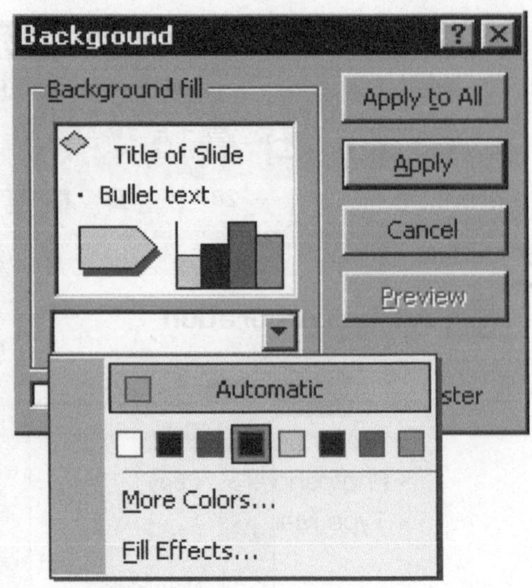

4. Click the options you want and then click Ok.
5. The Background dialog box is redisplayed.
6. Click Apply button to apply the change to the Current slide or click Apply to All to apply change to all the slides.

9.6.4.3 To change a patterned slide background

1. From the Format menu, choose background option. The background dialog box is displayed.
2. Under Background fill, click the down arrow and then click Fill Effects.
3. The Fill Effects dialog box is displayed. Click the Pattern tab.
4. Click the option you want and then click Ok.
5. The Background dialog box is redisplayed.
6. Click Apply button to apply the change to the current slide or click Apply to All to apply change to all the slides.

9.6.4.4 To change a textured slide background

1. From the Format menu, choose background option.
2. The background dialog box is displayed.
3. Under Background fill, click the down arrow and then click Fill Effects.
4. The Fill Effects dialog box is displayed. Click the Texture tab.
5. Click the texture you want and then click Ok.
6. The Background dialog box is redisplayed.
7. Click Apply button to apply the change to the current slide or click Apply to All to apply change to all the slides.

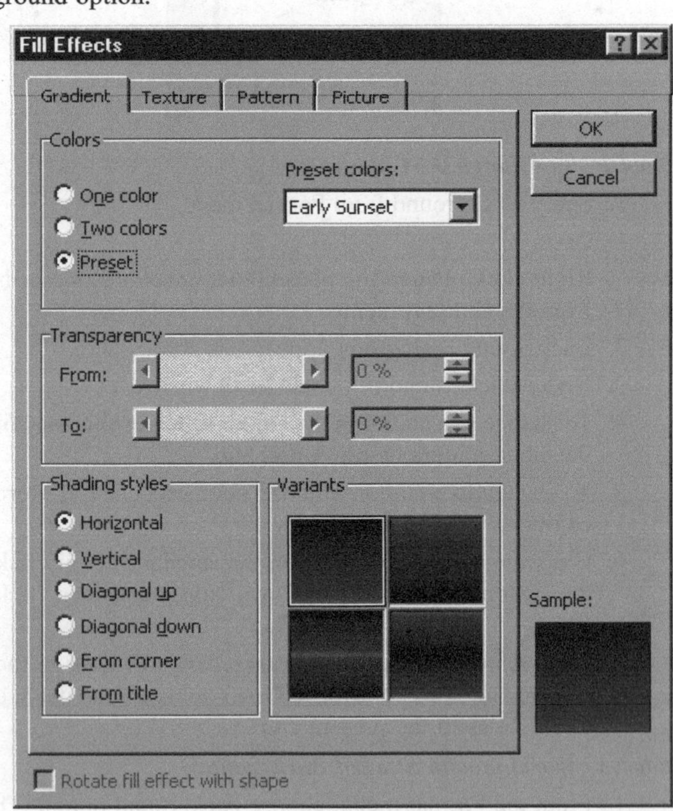

9.6.4.5 To change a slide background picture

1. From the Format menu, choose background option.
2. The background dialog box is displayed.
3. Under Background fill, click the down arrow and then click Fill Effects.
4. The Fill Effects dialog box is displayed. Click the Picture tab.

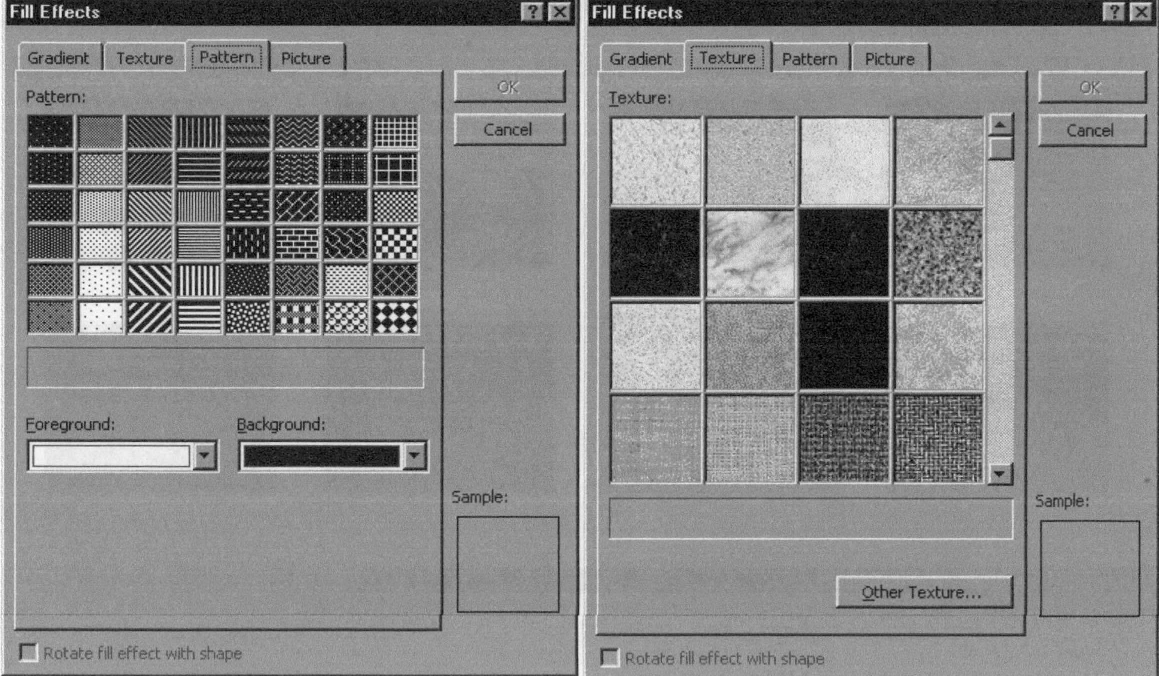

5. Click the Select Picture and find the folder that contains the picture you want. Double click the file name and then click Ok.
5. The Background dialog box is redisplayed.
6. Click Apply button to apply the change to the current slide or click Apply to All to apply change to all the slides.

9.6.5 Reordering Slides

As you see from the view, each slide is numbered. These number belong to their order of display. This order can be changed at any point of time in the presentation.

9.6.5.1 To Change the Order of the Slides:

1. Click with the mouse the slide whose position you want to change.
2. Pressing the mouse button drag the slide to a new position.
3. A vertical line appears to indicate where the slide will drop when you release the mouse button. In the figure on the next page, the slide 6 is being moved to a between position number 3 and 4.
4. Releasing the mouse button will drop the slide at the right place.
5. In the figure on the next page (bottom), you will see that the slide 6 has been placed between the number 3 and 4. The numbering of all the slides has been changed subsequently.

Points to Remember

1. You can select several slides to move by drawing a selection box around the group of slides and then dragging the group to the new position.
2. You can also select several slides by holding down the Shift key and selecting the first and last slides in the series.
3. To gather slides from different parts of a presentation, hold down the Ctrl key as you click each slide.

Drag any one slide in the group to a new point in the presentation. All the selected slides will appear in sequence and in the same relative order at new position.

9.6.6 Duplicating Slides

You can duplicate selected slides in Slide Sorter view and see the effect on the flow of slides immediately.

To Duplicate a slide or slides:

1. Select the slide or slides you want to duplicate.
2. Select Slide number 2 .
3. Press Ctrl + D or click at Duplicate in the Edit menu to duplicate the slide.
4. See the result next.
5. Slide 2 has been duplicated as Slide number 3.

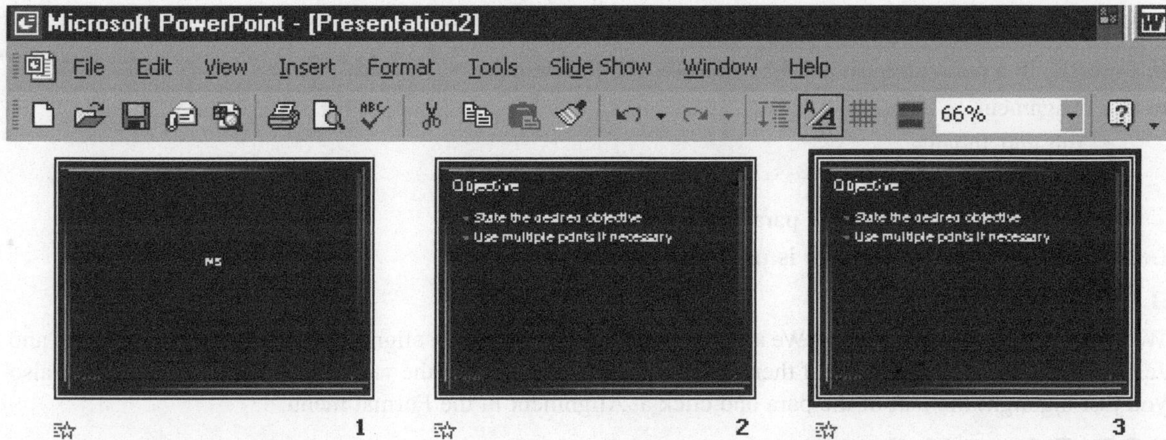

9.6.7 Deleting Slides

You can delete the selected slides in Slide Sorter view and see that the numbering of other slides change immediately.

To delete a slide or slides:

1. Select the slide or slides you want to delete.
2. Supposing we want to delete these new 3 numbered slides.
3. Press Del or Ctrl + X to delete the slides.
4. See the result of the deletion on the next page.
5. Notice the line after the slide number 2 indicating that the slides have been deleted from here.

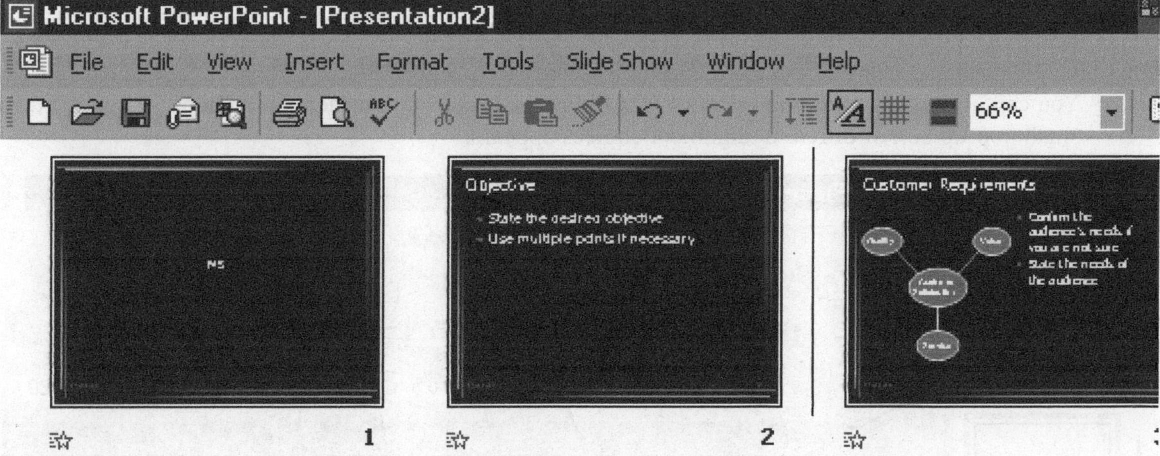

Remember

1. You can also choose Duplicate or Delete Slide from the Edit menu.

9.7 Adding and Formatting Text

See under working with Slides.

9.8 Formatting Paragraphs

In PowerPoint a paragraph can be formatted for the followings:

- Alignment
- Tab and Indents
- Line spacing
- Space before the after the paragraph

Let us see how each one of them is used.

9.8.1 Alignment

We all know about the alignment. We also know that there are 4 main alignments like Left, Right, Centre and Justify. PowerPoint supports all of them. As you would do in any of the word processing software, here also you just highlight the text of the para and click at Alignment in the Format menu.

9.8.2 Tabs and Indents

You would usually set tabs for making the text in the tabular manner. The tab is a small marker and tells the text where you want to stop. PowerPoint gives you the option of choosing four different tab stops: left, right, center and decimal tabs. In PowerPoint tabs are set in the following manner.

1. Choose the type of tab you want by clicking in the tab selection box at the left of the horizontal ruler until the tab type appears.
2. Move the pointer ruler bar and click the point at which you want to add the tab.

   Different types of tab types

Tab Type	*Description*
Left tab	The text left align at the tab
Right tab	The text right align at the tab
Center tab	The text is center align at the tab
Decimal tab	The decimal point where the numbering is aligned

You can also change the alignment of text by opening the Format menu and choose Alignment. A small pop-up box of different alignment choices appears.

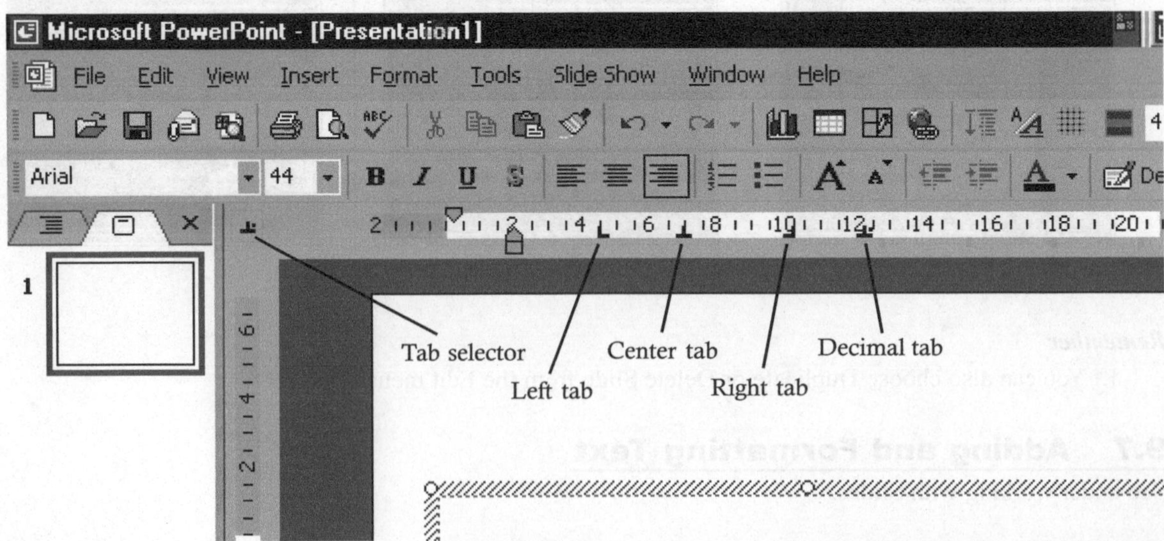

9.8.2.1 Clearing Tabs

1. Select the slide pane, then select the text where you want to set or clear tab stops.
2. To clear a tab stop, drag the tab marker off the ruler.

9.8.2.2 Setting Paragraph Indents

1. In this slide pane, select the text you want to set an indentation for.
2. If the ruler is not displayed, click View menu and choose Ruler.
3. To set the indent for the first line of a paragraph, drag the upper indent marker.
4. To set the left indent for other lines in a paragraph, drag the lower indent marker. The rectangular part of the lower indent marker also moves with it.
5. To maintain the relationship between the first line and the rest of the paragraph, move both markers by dragging the rectangular part of the lower market.

9.8.3 Line spacing

You may not need this for setting the line space but PowerPoint provides you with the option of changing the line space, in case it is required. For this do the following:

1. In the Slide pane, click anywhere in the paragraph you want to add space between lines.
2. Click the Format menu and choose Line Spacing. The Line Spacing dialog box appears as shown here.
3. In the Line spacing section, click up-arrow or down-arrow to increase of decrease the number of lines you want separating text lines.
4. In the Before Paragraph area, you do the same thing.
5. In the Slide pane, click anywhere in the paragraph if you want to add space after.
8. In the spinner box, click up-arrow or down-arrow for adding space after the paragraph.
9. After you make changes in the dialog box click OK.

Line Spacing
Line spacing
1 Lines
Before paragraph
0 Lines
After paragraph
0 Lines
OK Cancel Preview

9.9 Checking Spelling and Correcting Typing Mistakes

If you think you can spell a document in Word only, you are wrong. You can check spelling of the text which you have typed in PowerPoint too. Here also you have the dictionary which takes care of your spelling needs. Like in any word processor, spellings are checked with the dictionary and the wrong ones are pointed out. The spelling checker moves through your presentation one slide at a time and then checks the Notes Pages (if any) before closing the Spelling dialog box.

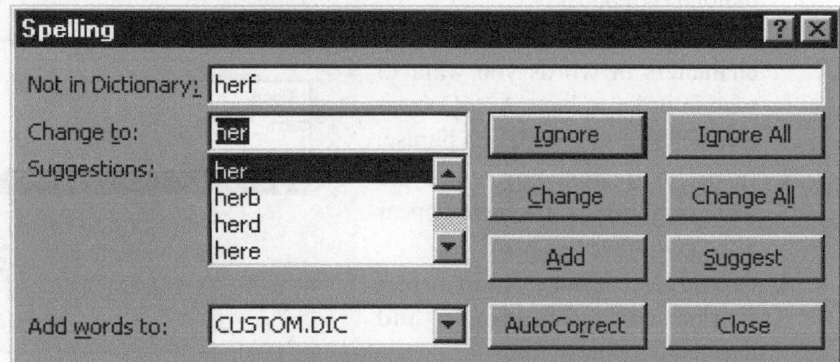

You can stop using the spelling checker at any time by clicking the Close button in the Spelling dialog box.

1. Place the cursor at the beginning of the text in the first slide and click Tools menu and then choose Spelling…

   Or

   Click the Spelling button on the Standard toolbar to display the Spelling dialog box. The spelling checker highlights the first unrecognised word in the presentation file and displays the word in the Not in Dictionary box.
2. Click the appropriate command button, from the following lists:

Ignore	Ignores this word and moves on
Ignore all	Ignores this word every time you find it.
Change	Changes the original word by replacing it with the word in the Change to: box.
Change all	Changes every occurrence of this word to the word in the Change to: box.
Add	Adds this word to the dictionary so the speller does not stop here any more.
Suggest	Searches the dictionary and displays possible replacement words (you choose the one that is correct).

3. The spelling checker takes the indicated action and then highlights the next unrecognized word.
4. Repeat step 2 until the spelling checker displays a message saying that the entire presentation has been checked.
5. Click OK.

9.9.1 Using AutoCorrect

This is another feature which is there in the Word processing. It takes care of all your typing mistakes if know them in advance. For example, as shown here, if you have the bad habit of typing teh instead of the, then say that to the computer and it will take of this error every time it occurs. So Autocorrect will take care of all your commonly made errors.

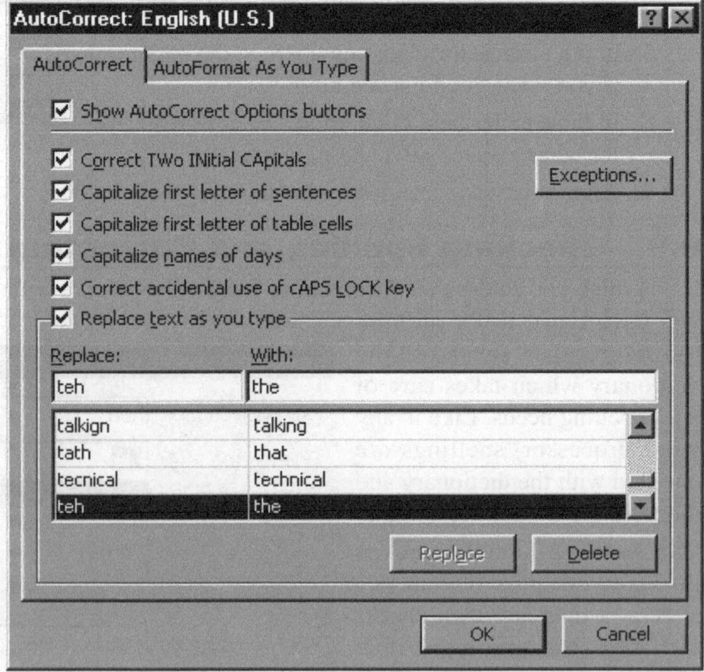

I suggest you just sit with the dialog box and go through it and then add the most common mistakes you make.

For this do the following:

1. Click Tools menu and choose AutoCorrect… the AutoCorrect dialog box appears.
2. In the Replace: text box, enter the characters or words you want to type in order to have AutoCorrect change them to a word or a phrase.
3. In the With: text box, enter the word or phrase you want to appear after you enter the word.
4. Configure the way AutoCorrect works by selecting and deselecting the options.

5. To delete any autocorrections if select the characters in the Replace: box and click delete.
6. Click OK when you have finished configuring the dialog box.

9.10 Making Notes, Pages and Handouts

There are three important tools for your presentation. These tools are:

9.10.1 Notes Pages

These pages are like the script for your presentation. In this script you have an image of slides along with the words you want to deliver for the specific slide.

9.10.2 Handouts

These printed pages are the hard copies of the presentation slides which you can distribute to y or audience.

9.10.3 Master

These are control elements of a slide like the title master which controls appearance of the title on all the slides.

9.10.4 Using Notes Pages

Notes Pages act like a cheat sheet for your presentation. You would write the text you want to read without letting the audience know that you are reading during the course of a presentation for each slide.

9.10.4.1 Creating Notes

PowerPoint offers two ways for preparing Notes Pages. These notes can be prepared while working on slides or after you have finished with all the slides.

To create notes using Notes Pages, do this:

1. Click the View menu and choose Notes Pages.

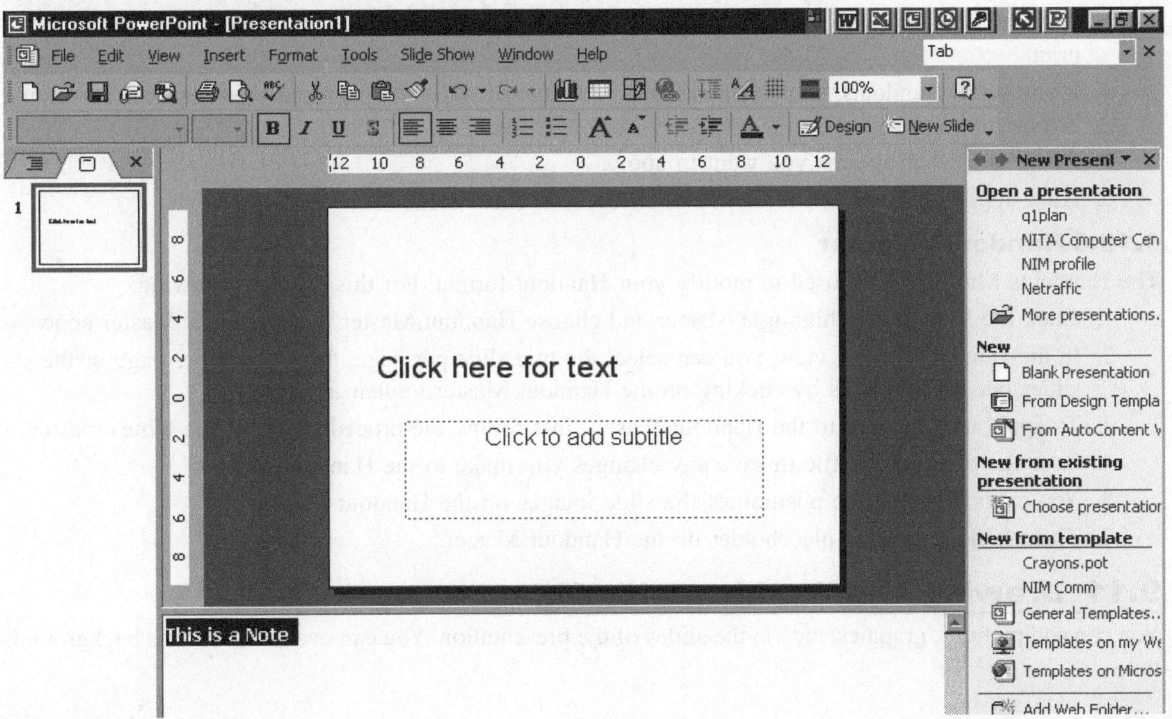

2. In the Notes Page View, you see the entire Notes page as it will print. There is a picture of the slide at the top and a text place holder at the bottom. Click the place holder to begin entering the text for your Note.

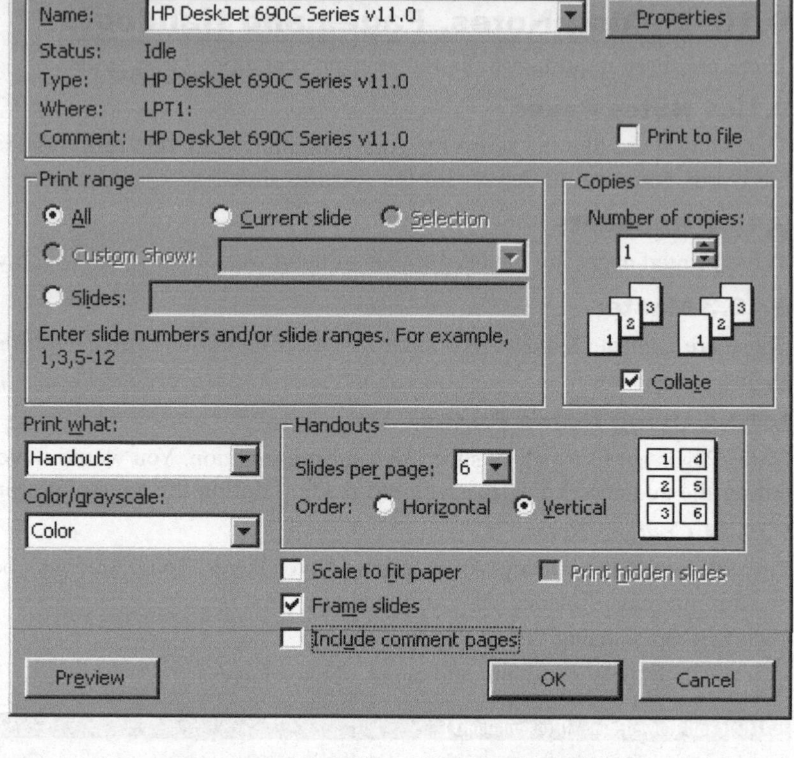

9.10.5 Printing Handouts

You can print your entire presentation in the form of handouts. These handouts are used to distribute among the audience in advance. You can also print specific slides, notes pages or outline pages.

For this do the following:

1. Open the presentation you want to print.
2. Click the File menu and Print. The Print dialog box appears.
3. In the Print what: box, click the item you want to print.
4. If you select Handouts, you can then select a number of slides per page and whether the order should be horizontal or vertical,
5. Select any other options you want to apply.
6. After applying the option in the handouts section, click OK.

9.10.6 Handouts Master

The Handouts Master can be used to modify your Handout format. For this do the following:

1. Click the View menu, highlight Master and choose Handout Master. The Handout Master appears.
2. In the Handout Master view, you can select the two slide per page, three slides per page or the six slides per page formats by clicking on the Handout Master toolbar as shown.
3. To apply any changes to the Handout Master, just follow the procedure as for the Notes master.
4. Save the presentation file to save any changes you make to the Handout Master.
5. You cannot change the position of the slide images on the Handout Master.
6. There is no notes text placeholder on the Handout Master.

9.11 Drawing and Working with Objects

You can add pictures, graphics, etc., in the slides of the presentation. You can even add these as backgrounds too.

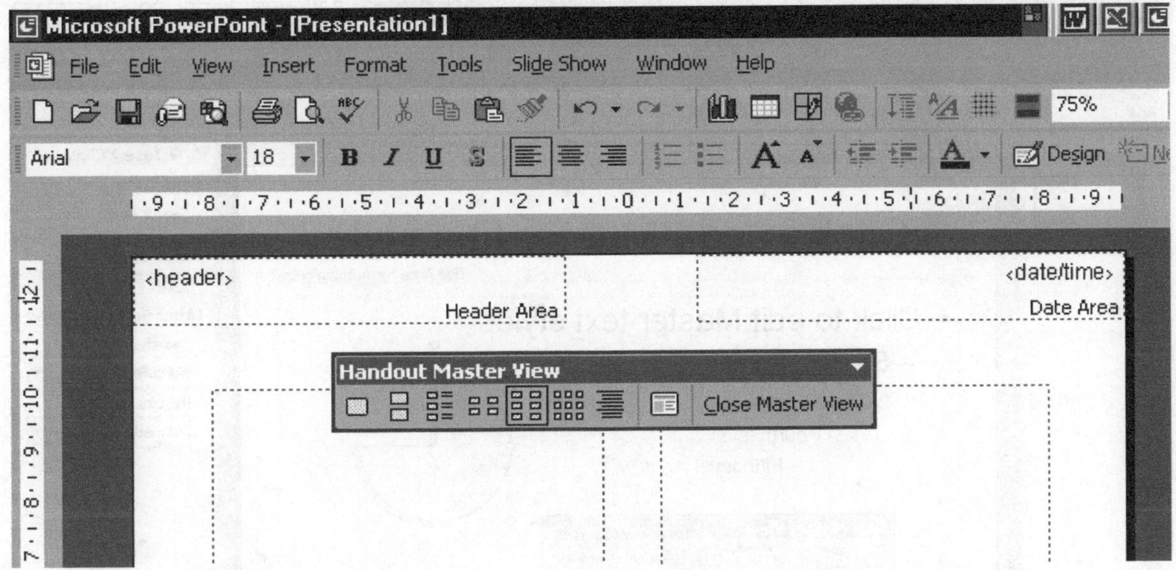

9.11.1 Drawing Shapes and Lines

Using the drawing tools available with PowerPoint you can draw the various figures like squares, circles, etc.

1. In Slide view, click one of the drawing tools or menus on the drawing toolbar.
2. Drag with the mouse pointer to create the shape.
3. Click the shape and choose Colours and Lines from the Format menu.
4. In the Colours and Lines dialog box, choose a fill colour, line colour, and line style. Click Ok.
5. To type text inside the shape, click the shape and then begin typing.
6. To delete a line or shape, click it so that the handles appear, and press Del.
7. To keep a shape regular, i.e., drawing a square instead of a rectangle and drawing a circle instead of an oval, etc., hold down the Shift key while dragging through the area to create the shape.

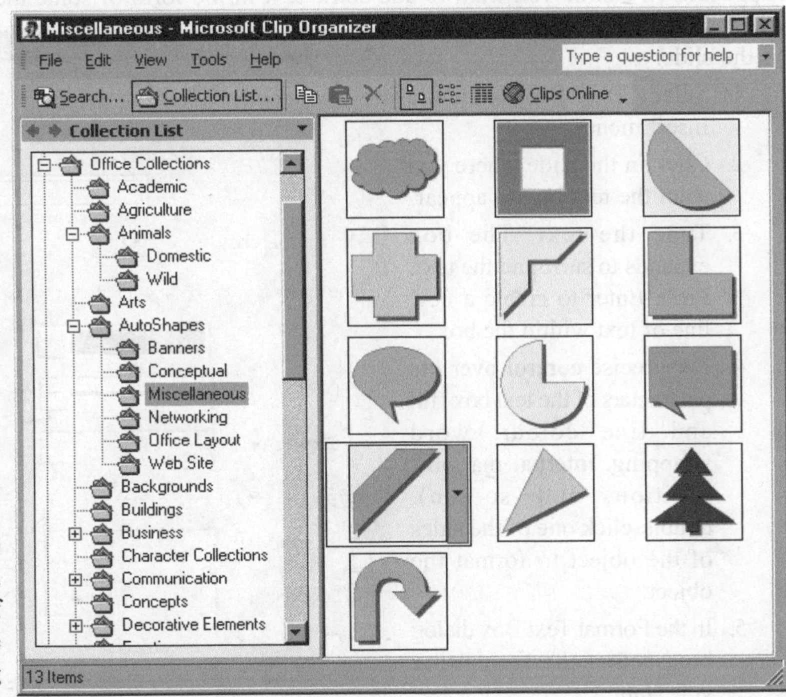

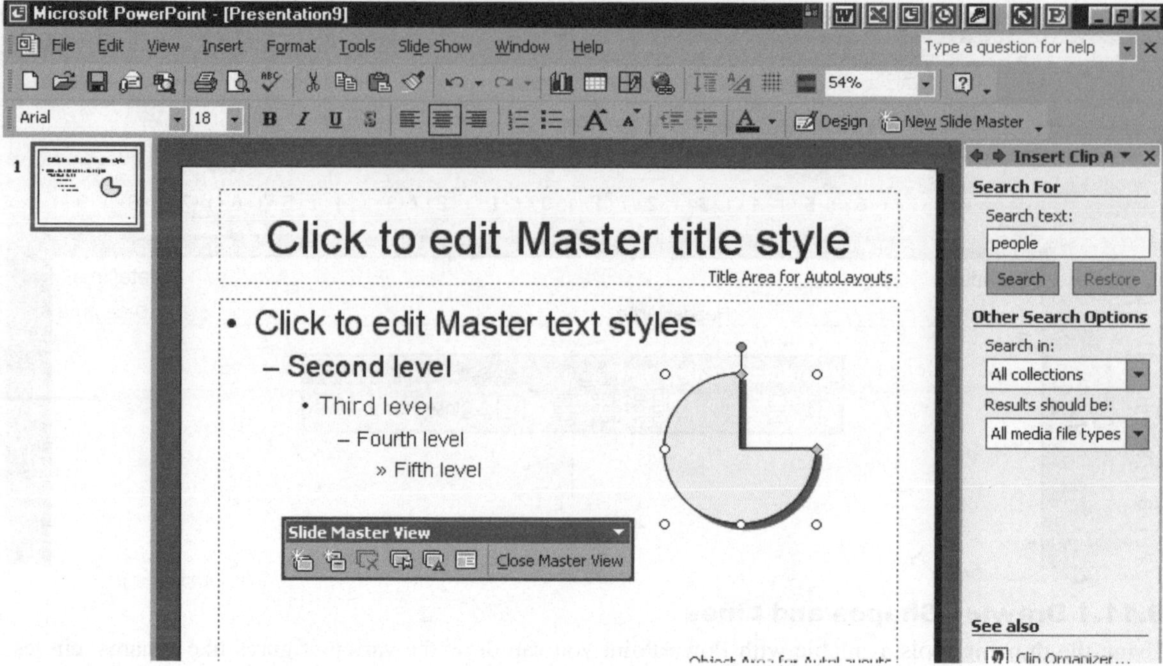

9.11.2 Adding Text Box

Supposing on a slide you want to add some text in the form of some message or an afterthought. You can always do so by adding a text block on the slide.

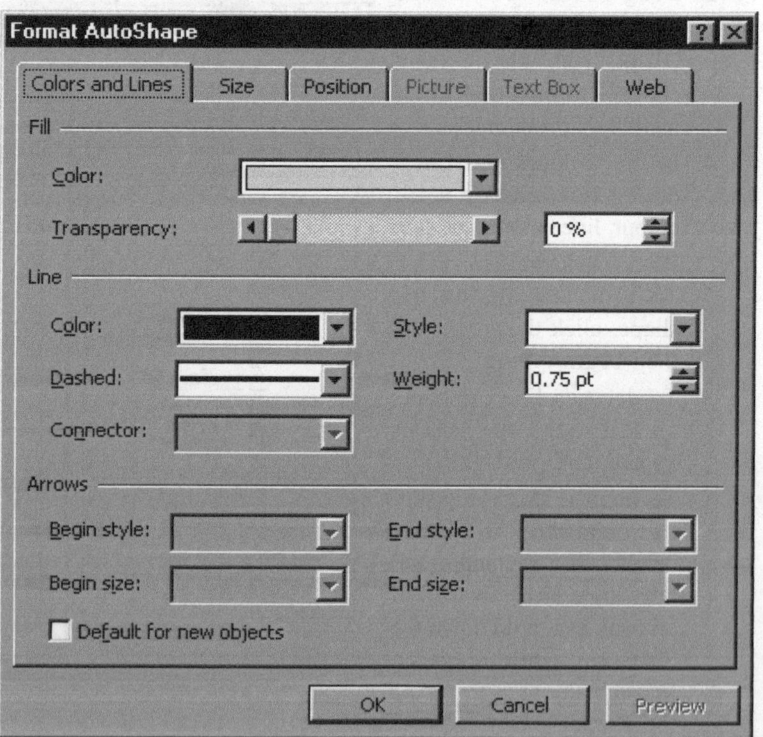

1. Select Text Box from the Insert menu.
2. Click in the slide where you want the text box to appear.
3. Type the text. The box expands to surround the text. Press Enter to create a new line of text within the box.
4. For precise control over the parameters of the text box (fill and line colour, word wrapping, internal margins, position, and so on), double-click one of the sides of the object to format the object.
5. In the Format Text Box dialog box, select the formatting you want.
6. Click Ok.

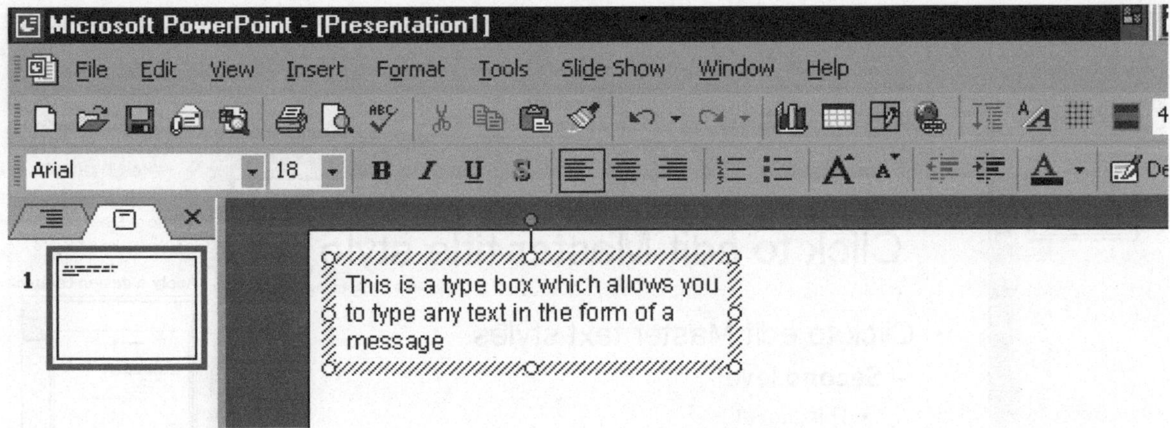

Remember

1. Change the location of the text box by clicking one of the sides (not at a handle) and dragging the box to the new location.
2. You can also add text to any other shape by clicking in the shape and typing.
3. After you have entered the text, you can change the shape of the text box by dragging the side handles.
4. To delete a text box, click one of the sides so that the insertion point inside disappears and press Del.
5. To keep a shape you are drawing regular, hold down the Shift key as your drag to draw the shape.

9.12 Adding Clip Art and other pictures

9.12.1 Adding picture to the Background

A picture can be inserted into any slide. This can be in the form of a logo of a company or any other picture. This picture can be a ready made graphic or a clip art. For this do the following:

1. Select Slide Master from Master command in the View menu.
2. You will get the dialog box.
3. From the Insert menu, select to insert Picture and Clip Art or any other picture which you may want to use.
4. From the clip art menu, select the clip art.
5. The picture will be placed in the centre of the slide. You can increase or decrease its size and place it anywhere on the slide to be reflected at the slides in the presentation.
6. You can copy and paste a graphic from another program onto the slide master.

9.12.2 Adding Predefined Shapes

Autoshapes are the shapes given to you by the software are much more better looking than the usual ones drawn by you. Make the best use of them to highlight the text or that matter anything in your presentation.

1. AutoShapes button is available on the drawing toolbar.
2. Clicking on it will lead to the various other options on the menu, as shown on the next page. It has Lines, Connectors, Basic Shapes, Block Arrows, Flowchart, Stars and Banners, Callouts, and Action Buttons. More AutoShapes will lead you to more shapes.
3. Select one of the menu and then the shape.

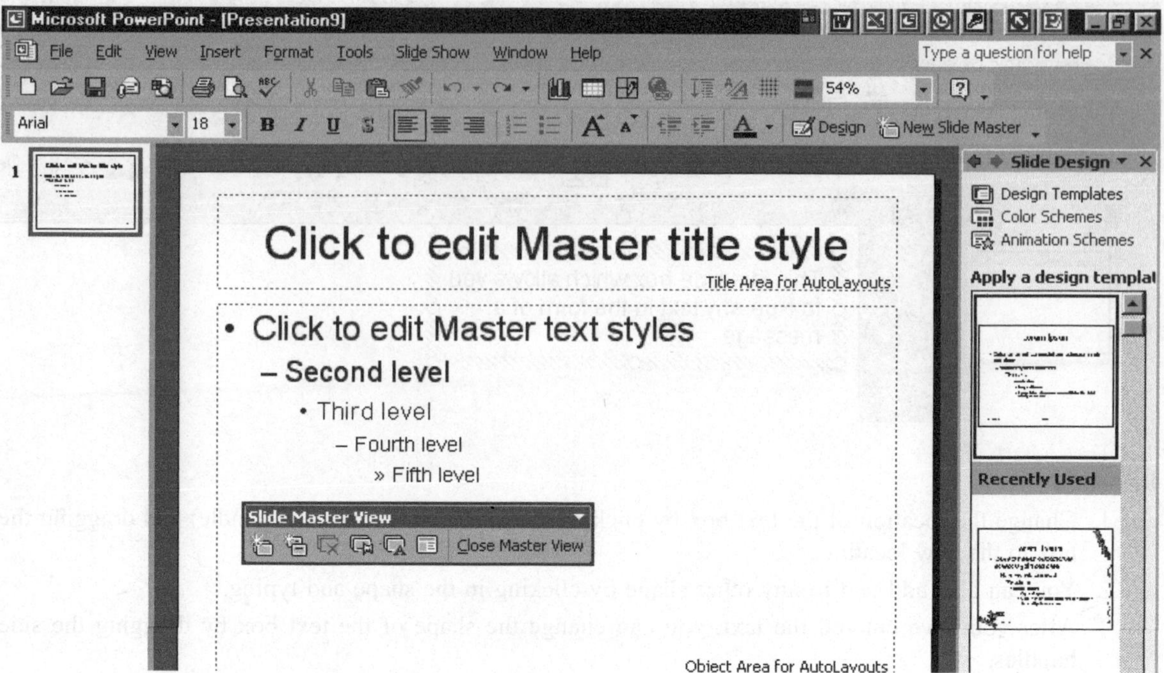

4. The shape would be selected for pasting to the slide.

9.12.3 Adding From WordArt

If you have through the chapter on Microsoft Word thoroughly you would have see the working of WordArt. In a very similar way, as you would enter the WordArt in your document in Word, here too you can enter a WordArt in your presentation.

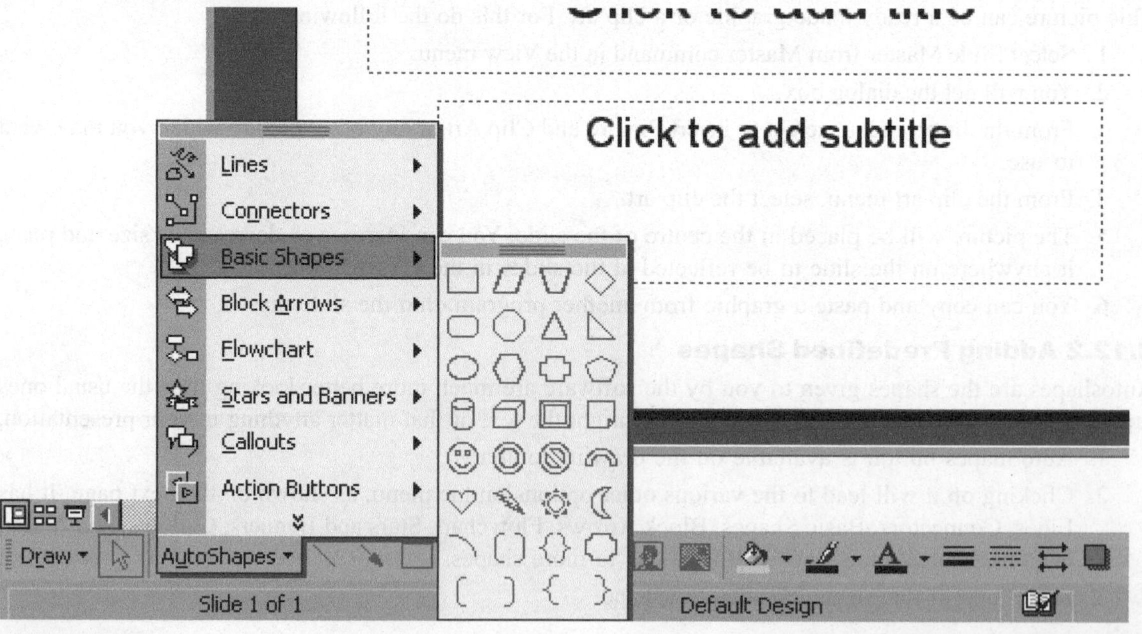

9.13 Designing Slide Shows

This effect shows all the hard work you have put in making the slides. It shows one slide after another, stopping in between for a set time on either the monitor of your screen or on the projector which may have been attached to your computer. It is also possible to add animated effects on the slides and show them in a sophisticated manner. It is also possible to add audio, video, narration, music, etc., to your slides.

9.13.1 Adding Audio

You can add sounds to the transition effects and to the preset animation. You can also add audio to your presentation by inserting files from the Clip Art Gallery or from other folders available to you.

9.13.1.1 To Add an Audio File

1. Select the slide where you want to put this audio and display it in the Slide view.

2. Select Sound from File in the Movies and Sounds command from the Insert menu.
3. Click Ok to add the sound effect, and select a file.
4. Answer Yes to have the sound play automatically or No to have it play when you click it.

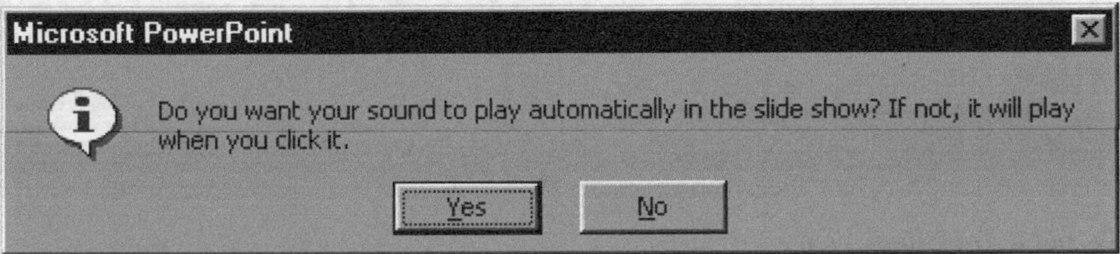

5. The sound icon appears in the middle of the slide. You can move it as you would any object.
6. If you right-click the sound icon, you can choose Play Sound or Edit Sound Object from the shortcut menu.
7. The sound icon as it appears on the slide is shown next.

9.13.2 Adding Video Effect

Like sound, you can add video effects too. The steps are quite similar to the ones used in the case of Audio.

9.13.2.1 To Add an Video File

1. Select the slide where you want to put this video and display it in the Slide view.
2. Select Movies from File in the Movies and Sounds command from the Insert menu.
3. Click Ok to add the video effect.
4. Answer Yes to have the sound play automatically or No to have it play when you click it.
5. The video icon appears in the middle of the slide. You can move it as you would any object.
6. If you right-click the video icon, you can choose Play Video or Edit Video Object from the shortcut menu.

9.13.3 Adding Effects

These effects can be of the form of wipes, splits, dissolves, etc., which you usually see in the film show. For this you have to work in the Slide Sorter view.

9.13.1.1 To Add a Transition View

1. Choose the slide on which you want to put this effect.
2. Click on the arrow next to the transition effect as shown here.
3. This will lead to the Slide Transition dialog box as shown here.
4. In this dialog box, choose a transition effect from the drop-down list, a speed (slow, medium, or fast) and the advance option (on mouse click or after a period of time).
5. Click Apply to All to apply this transition effect to all slides, or click Apply to apply it only to the selected slide.
6. To apply the same transition effect to multiple slides, hold down the Shift key while you click the slides and then choose a transition effect.
7. To preview the transition effect in Slide Sorter view, click the transition icon that appears below each slide that has a transition effect.

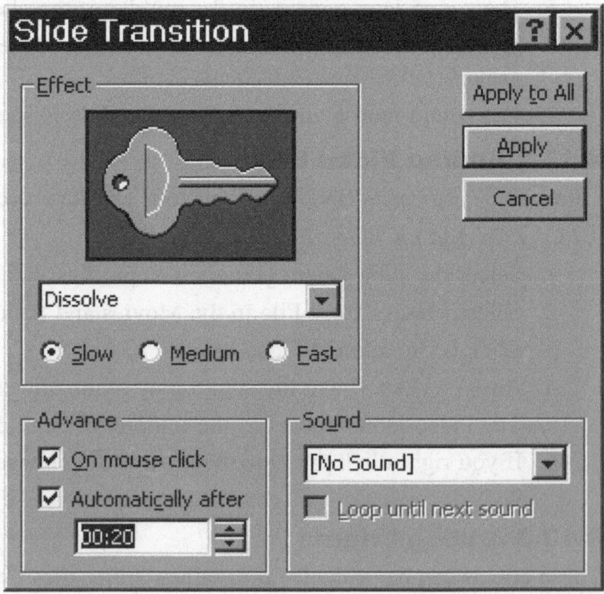

8. A small icon can be seen on all the slides in the Slide Sorter view.

9.13.4 Adding Animation

You can add animation to the slides which are going to displayed. This helps in presenting a slide with special effects. You can choose from the various animations available.

9.13.4.1 To Select an Animation

1. In the Slide Sorter view click at the slide to which you want to add the animation effect.
2. Once it has been applied, you can see the small icon being put under the slide to show that this slide has an animation effect.
3. You can see the preview of this animation effect by clicking at the preview button.
4. If you want you can apply different effects on various slides and see the whole presentation having the different effects.

Remember

1. You can also apply effects using the buttons on the Animation Effects toolbar. Choose Toolbars from the View menu and then choose Animation Effects from the pop-out menu.
2. To apply the same present animation effect to multiple slides, hold down the Shift key and click the slides and then choose an effect.
3. To preview the animation effect in Slide Sorter view, click the animation icon that appears below each slide that has an animation effect.

9.13.5 Creating Your Own Animation

It is possible to have your own animation which can give you more control over the display of the presentation. This can be applied to both text and objects. These can be created only in Slide view.

9.13.5.1 To Create a Custom Animation

1. Select the slide where you want to put this animation and display it in the Slide view.
2. Select Custom Animation from the Animation Effects toolbar.
3. In the Custom Animation dialog box, check the items you want to animate and set the order and timing.
4. Click at Effects panel to select the effects from the drop-down list.
5. Select the options here according to your liking or choose the ones selected in the dialog box shown here.
6. You can also preview an animation by clicking the Animation Preview button on the Animation Effects toolbar.

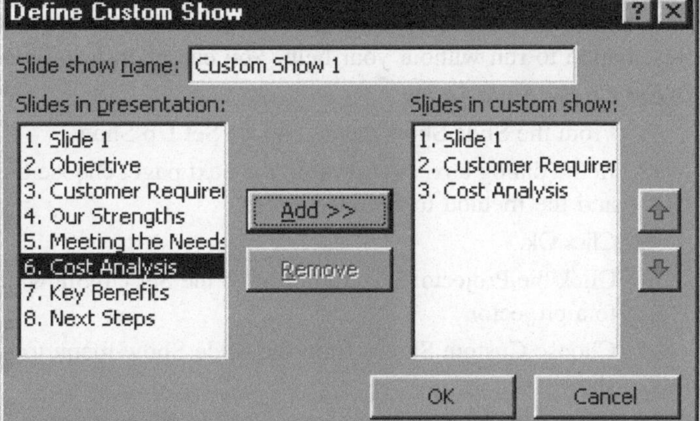

9.13.6 Adding Action Buttons

These buttons allow you to play sound, video at your choice when displaying the presentation.

9.13.6.1 To Add an Action Button:

1. Select the slide to which you want to add this button. This can be done in any view except Slide Sorter view.

2. Select Action buttons from the Slide Show menu.
3. Select a button of your choice.
4. Position the button in your slide at any place of your liking.
5. On clicking the button PowerPoint will give rise to a new dialog box called Action settings.
6. Make the necessary settings and click Ok.
7. You action button is now properly placed in the slide.
8. You can add actions to other objects simply by selecting them and then choosing Action settings from the Slide Show menu.

9.14 Runnng and Controlling a Slide Show

Now comes the most important part of the software where you are going to setup the whole show of presentation to run without your help. You can choose to hide few slides for not displaying.

To Set Up the Slide Show:

1. From the Slide Show menu, choose Set Up Show.
2. In the dialog box, as shown on the next page, choose the type of show, which slides to show or hide, and the method to advance slides.
3. Click Ok.
4. Click the Projector Wizard button in the Set Up Show dialog box for help connecting your computer to a projector.
5. Choose Custom Shows from the Slide Show menu to add slides from this presentation to a custom show.
6. Even though a slide is hidden, you can display it by clicking a hyperlink or an action pointing to it.

9.14.1 Rehearsing the Show

As we see the preview of the page before printing. PowerPoint also allows you to do the same. For this you have what is called the Rehearsing of the Show.

You can run the show from any view.

9.14.1.1 To Rehearse the Slide Show:

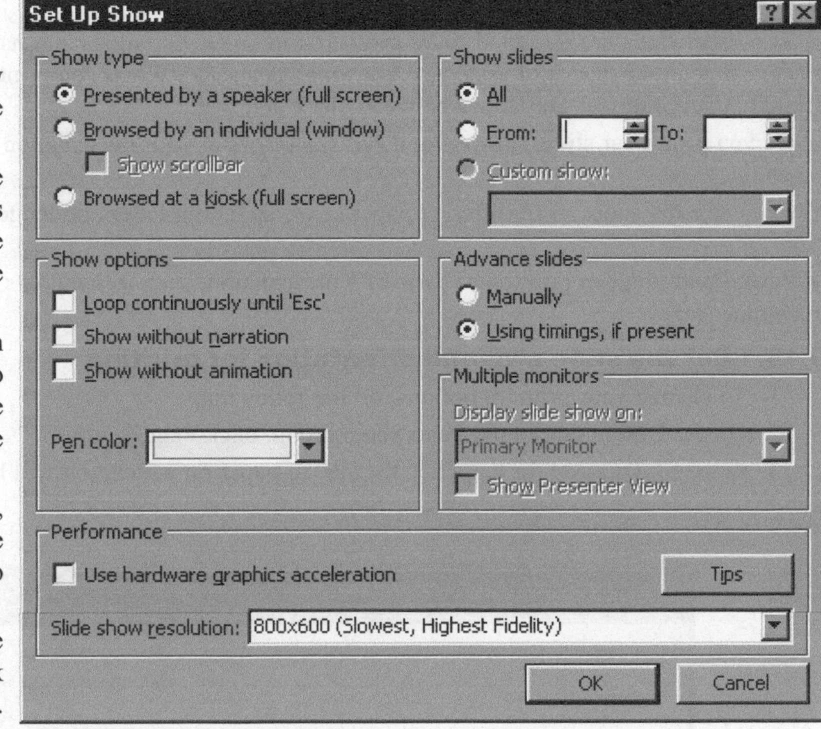

1. From the Slide Show menu, choose Rehearse Timings.
2. You can click the Rehearse Timings button on the Slide Sorter toolbar too in the Slide Sorter view.
3. The show begins with the timer set at the top left hand corner of the screen, as shown on the next page.
4. To use these timings, choose Use Slide Timings in the Set Up Show dialog box.
5. To advance through the slide show, click anywhere on the slide. You can also right-click anywhere and choose as action from the shortcut menu.

9.15 Printing Presentations

Most presentations are designed to be presented in color, but slides and handouts are typically printed in black and white or shades of gray, also known as grayscale. When you print in grayscale, color images are printed in variations of gray tones between black and white.

When you print your slides, PowerPoint sets the colors in your presentation to match the selected printer's capabilities.

You can size the slides to fit different paper sizes, including letter and ledger, or you can specify a custom size.

In PowerPoint you can print other parts of a presentation, such as handouts, notes pages, or a presentation in Outline view.

9.15.1 Set the slide size and orientation for printing

1. To change your printing options, do the following:
2. On the Design tab, in the Page Setup group, click Page Setup.
3. In the Slides sized for list, click the size of paper on which you will be printing.

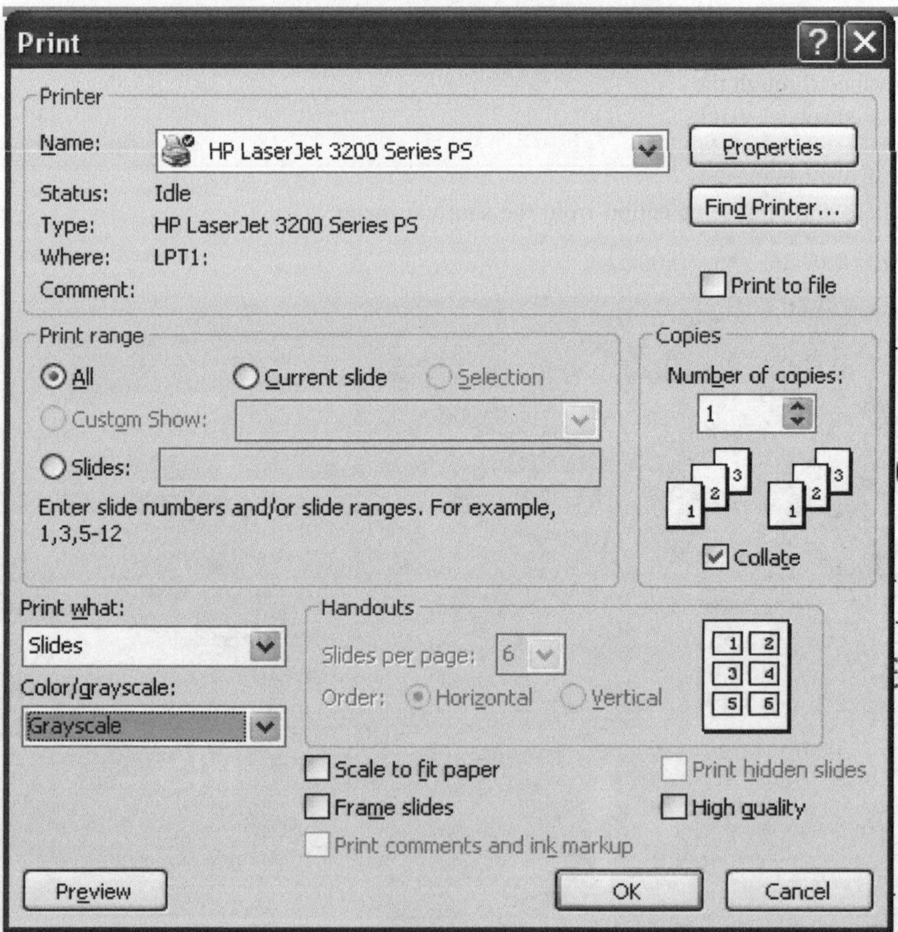

Notes

- If you click Custom, type or select the measurements that you want in the Width and Height boxes.
- To print an overhead transparency, click Overhead.

To set the page orientation for the slides, under Orientation, under Slides, click Landscape or Portrait. All slides in a presentation must be set to one orientation.

9.15.2 Print the slides

1. Click Print in the File menu.
2. In the Page Setup group, in the Print What list, select Slides.
3. Click Options, point to Color/Grayscale, and then click one of the following:
   - Color If you print to a color printer, this option prints in color.
   - Grayscale This option prints images that contain variations of gray tones between black and white. Background fills are printed as white, so that the text will be more legible. (Sometimes grayscale appears the same as Pure Black and White.)
   - Pure Black and White This option prints the handout with no gray fills.
4. Click Print.

Let us Revise

1. AutoContent Wizard creates presentation by asking you just few questions.
2. You can even create a presentation using the Templates given with the software.
3. You can create a presentation using the various optional slides given.
4. You can save your presentation.
5. Various veiws in PowerPoint are: Outline view, Normal view, Slide sorter view, Slide show view and Notes page view.
6. You can enter your text in the slides of your presentation.
7. Using Collapse you can change the view of the slides.
8. You can move the text up and down in the slide.
9. You can change colours of the slides.
10. You can have a patterend background of the slide.
11. A slide with textured background can also be created.
12. You can have picture in the background of a slide.
13. You can format text paragraphs for Alignment, Tabs, Indents and Line Spacing.
14. Like Word processing, you can check spelling of your text.
15. Using Autocorrect, you can preset corrections for your wrongly spelled words.
16. You can have charts in your presentations.
17. You can various types of charts like bar charts, pie charts, etc.
18. You can change the various elements of the charts.
19. Organization charts are used to represent organizations.
20. You can have pictures in the background of slide.
21. You can draw various shapes to put in the presentation slides.
22. You can add a text box in your slide.
23. You can add text from Word Art in your presentation slide.

24. You can change the order of the slides.
25. You can duplicate a particular slide.
26. You can delete a slide.
27. You can makea slide show to show all the slides one by one.
28. Audio clips can be added to the slides.
29. Video clips can also be added to the slides.
30. You can add actions in your slides.
31. Even animations can be added to the slides.
32. Notes Pages are used to have the text on the slides but it is not shown.
33. Handouts can be printed for all your slides.
34. You can create your own animation and add to the slide.

Multiple Choice Questions

1. PowerPoint is used for:
   (a) Word processing (b) Spreadsheets (c) Presentations
2. Overhead projections can be created using PoerPoint:
   (a) Yes (b) No
3. AutoContent Wizard creates a
   (a) Document (b) Presentation (c) Spreadsheet
4. There is no need to use templates in PowerPoint:
   (a) True (b) False
5. You can view your presentation through various views :
   (a) Yes (b) No
6. You can move your text in the slide, up and down:
   (a) Yes (b) No
7. A slide with background picture can be created in PowerPoint:
   (a) Yes (b) No
8. You can even have textured patterns in the background of a slide:
   (a) Yes (b) No
9. You can add organization format in the form of a :
   (a) Table (b) Chart (c) Graphic
10. You can use a picture as a background for a slide:
    (a) Yes (b) No
11. Various alignments available for text formatting in PowerPoint are Left, Right, Center and :
    (a) Justify (b) Natural (c) Reverse
12. Various tabs available in PowerPoint are, Left, Right, Center and :
    (a) Comma (b) Decimal (c) Full stop
13. Optional command which allows you to preset your errors is called:
    (a) Autoset (b) Autoplay (c) Autocorrect

14. Notes pages have on them:

(a) text (b) graphic (c) pictures

15. You can view all slides continuously by using:

(a) Show (b) Slide show (c) Slides

16. You can set tabs using

(a) Ruler (b) Scale (c) Footer

True/False Questions

1. PowerPoint helps in creating charts, graphs, slides, handouts, overheads, and various other formats of presentations which any office would require.
2. PowerPoint cannot be started from Start button.
3. AutoContent Wizard creates presentation by asking you just few questions.
4. There are no templates in PowerPoint.
5. You can create a presentation using the various optional slides given.
6. The presentations cannot be saved.
7. You can use different views to see various positions of the slides.
8. You can enter your text in the slides of your presentation.
9. Using Collapse you can change the view of the slides.
10. You cannot move the text of your slides.
11. You can change colours of the slides.
12. There is no provision for background colour of the slides.
13. A slide can have a textured background too.
14. You can have picture in the background of a slide.
15. You can format text of the slides like that of a paragraph in word processing.
16. There is no provision for spell checking of the text in PowerPoint.
17. Using Autocorrect, you can preset corrections for your wrongly spelled words.
18. You cannot have charts in your slides.
19. You can change the various elements of the charts.
20. Organization charts are used to represent organizations.
21. You can have pictures in the background of slide.
22. You cannot add a text box in your slide.
23. You can add text from Word Art in your presentation slide.
24. You cannot reorder all the slides.
25. You cannot duplicate a particular slide.
26. You cannot delete a slide.
27. It is not possible to see all the slides continuously.
28. Audio and video clips cannot be added to the slides.
29. Actions and animations can be added to the slides.
30. Notes Pages are used to have the text on the slides but it is not shown.
31. Handouts can be printed for all your slides.
32. You can create your own animation and add to the slide.

Matching Columns

Match the text of the column A with the action of Column B.

Column A	Column B
A. AutoContent Wizard	1. Adding text box on the slide
B. Template	2. It can be changed
C. Oragnization chart	3. Changes the view
D. AutoCorrect	4. To check spelling of the text of the slides
E. Alignment	5. Ready made presentation
F. Background colour	6. Making a copy of the slide
G Text box	7. Printed format of presentation slides
H. Notes Pages	8. A chart to represent an organization
I. Collapse	9. To give space between lines of the text
J. Slide Show	10. Aligning text of the slides
K. Spell checking	11. Can be inserted in the slides
L. Reordering slides	12. Self generating presentation
M. Duplicating slides	13. Can be set from the Ruler
N. Handouts	14. To run slides one by one
O. Line spacing	15. A utility to correct your wrong words
P. Drawing shapes	16. Pages´to contain notes
Q. Tabs	17. Can be added to the slide
R. Customized animation	18. Changing the order of slides

Fill in the Blanks with appropriate words

a. Organization chart	b. Decimal	c. AutoCorrect	d. Video
e. Audio	f. Notes pages	g. AutoContent	h. Handouts
i. Ruler	j. Template	k. Collapse	l. Slide Show

1. A presentation can be created easily using __________ or __________
2. You can run all the slides one by one using __________.
3. You can add clips of types __________ and __________ to the slides.
4. Besides Left, Right and Centre the other Tab in PowerPoint is __________.
5. A chart which is used to represent the various levels of office, etc., is called __________.
6. For correcting the words which are often misspelled you use __________.
7. While presenting a presentation, the speaker looks at its __________.
8. Speech, etc., which is printed beforehand for distribution is called __________.
9. To change view of a presentation, you use the __________ command.
10. Tabs are set using _______.

Descriptive Type Questions

1. Describe the process of creating a presentation using AutoContent Wizard.
2. Describe the method of creating a presentation using Tempaltes.
3. How would you create a presentation using the various slide options?
4. Describe the various views of looking at presentations in PowerPoint.
5. Describe the process of entering text into slides.
6. What is the function of Collapse?
7. Describe the various type of backgrounds which you can have in your slides.
8. How would you change the alignment of the text of the slides?
9. How would you make sure that there is no misspelled word in your text.
10. How would you set the various options of AutoCorrect?
11. Describe the process of adding an audio clip to the slide.
12. How is a video clip added to the slide?
13. What is a Note Page?
14. What is a Handout?
15. How are actions and animations added to the slides?
16. How is a chart added to the slide?
17. Describe the process of changing the chart style.
18. Describe the process of adding graphics, pictures, etc., in the slide.
19. What is an organization chart?
20. What is a text box?
21. How would you create a slide show?
22. Describe the use of reheasing the slide show.
23. Describe the process of duplicating the slides.
24. How would you change the background colour of a slide?
25. How would you insert text created from WordArt into a slide?
26. What happens when you delete a slide?

Answers to Objective Type Questions

Multiple Choice Questions

1. c	2. a	3. b	4. b
5. a	6. a	7. a	8. a
9. b	10 a	11. a	12. b
13. c	14. a	15. b	16. a

True False Questions

1. T	2. F	3. T	4. F
5. T	6. F	7. T	8. T
9. T	10. F	11. T	12. F
13. T	14. T	15. T	16. F
17. T	18. F	19. T	20. T

21. T	22. F	23. T	24. F
25. F	26. F	27. F	28. F
29. T	30. T	31. T	32. T

Matching Columns

A. 12	B. 5	C. 8	D. 15
E. 10	F. 2	G. 1	H. 16
I. 3	J. 14	K. 4	L. 18
M. 6	N. 7	O. 9	P. 17
Q. 13	R. 11		

Fill in the Blanks

1. g, j	2. l	3. d, e	4. b
5. a	6. c	7. f	8. h
9. k	10. i		

10 Databases

10.1 Data Manipulation Concepts

Each office has to maintain details of its several employees. It may, for example, maintain the files of the followings:

Personal File
Accounts File
Leave Record File

Details of these files can be worked out (it may be different from office to office) as follows:

Personal File

- ☐ Name
- ☐ Address
- ☐ Telephone number
- ☐ Joining Date
- ☐ Designation
- ☐ Qualifications

Accounts File

- ☐ Name
- ☐ Basic Salary
- ☐ HRA
- ☐ DA
- ☐ I Tax
- ☐ PF

Leave Records File

- ☐ Name
- ☐ Casual Leave
- ☐ Privileged Leave
- ☐ Sick Leave
- ☐ Accumulated Leaves

If you notice all these files have one field in common which is **Name** and this is called the **Primary** key and is the link between all the 3 files. A look at the fields of the Personal file will give us an idea about the database to be created for it.

Personal File

Name	Alphanumeric
Address	Alphanumeric
Telephone number	Numeric
Joining Date	Date
Designation	Alphanumeric
Qualifications	Alphanumeric

Once we create all these tables the **office database** will be created. A database therefore comprises of tables. Tables in turn contain records. If we are to decide what tables should be part of the office database, we have to ask ourselves what is the information which needs to be stored in the database. Once we have this information we can decide about the tables.

A Database is a collection of all the required information pertaining to a particular subject. Thus, all the data pertaining to a office is put together in a database.

Two things should be borne in mind while storing data.

- The data is to be stored in a single database since it pertains to a single subject.
- The distinction between the various groups should be maintained since different types of details are stored for each group.

To satisfy these conditions, the data for each category is stored in a separate table. All the tables are part of a single database. Thus, in the Office Database we have 3 tables as follows:

Office Database

- Personal Table
- Accounts Table
- Leave Record Table

The point to note here is that data in this database is stored in the form of tables, is also known as relations.

10.2 Database and Relational Database Management Systems

It would definitely make things easy for the user if software that enables the user to create a database also allows the user to maintain it. Maintaining a database would involve performing the various data manipulation operations on the tables in the database.

These operations are:

- Adding Records
- Querying
- Modifying Records
- Deleting Records

These operations enable the user to store, retrieve and update data in the database. In addition to this the system should also allow the user to create relationships between the various tables. The system that provides all these facilities is called a **Relational Database Management System** (RDBMS).

Examples of Relational Database Management Systems are:

- Microsoft Access
- Oracle
- Sybase

But, it is Access which is more popular, since it works equally well on both **Personal Computers** (PCs) and on mainframe computers. Whereas Oracle is more popular with bigger computers where you have more than one computer networked together.

Each RDBMS will facilitate the following:

Tables Containing data

Queries Selected information is displayed on the screen

Reports Formatted printed information

Forms Screen created to add, modify and delete records

Let us consider the tasks that have to be performed when we are working with each one of the entities given above.

10.2.1 Tables

In the case of tables, the tasks involved are as follows:

Creating a table

- Specifying the field names

- ☐ Specifying the data names
- ☐ Specifying the field sizes
- ☐ Specifying a field in the table that will have unique value

Adding records to the tables

Modifying data in the table

Deleting records from the table

Creating relationships between tables

The RDBMS will provide the facility to perform all these tasks. For example, using an RDBMS we can create the Office database. We can create the 3 tables described in the case of Office database. We can also create the relationships between the tables.

10.2.2 Queries

In the case of queries, the tasks involved are as follows:

Creating queries to obtain information

- ☐ Specifying the conditions on the basis of which the data is fetched from one or more tables
- ☐ Specifying the fields on the basis of which the data is to be sorted

Creating queries to update data

- ☐ Specifying the conditions to determine which records are to be updated

Creating queries to delete data

- ☐ Specifying the conditions to determine which records are to be deleted

For example, the RDBMS allows us to create a query to obtain the names and designation of all the employees working in the office. We can also have the records sorted in the ascending order by their names.

A report is data presented in an easy-to-understand, good-to-look-at manner. This data can be taken directly from a single table. Or we can use the relationships between tables to fetch the data from more than one table via a query.

10.2.3 Reports

In the case of reports the tasks involved are as follows:

Creating a report

- ☐ Specifying the table or query from which the report is to be created
- ☐ Specifying the fields from the above that are to be included in the report
- ☐ Formatting the data

For example, we can use the query created above. Using the facility provided by the RDBMS, we can highlight the records of employees who have salary over Rs. 10,000. A bold typeface can be used for these records.

10.2.4 Forms

The easiest way to understand forms is to think of them as paper forms. The only difference being that these forms are available on the computer and not on paper. They are used to data entry or to view the data in the table. They can also be used to print the reports created in the above example.

In the case of forms the tasks involved are as follows:

Creating Forms

- ☐ Specifying the table or query from which the form is to be created
- ☐ Specifying the fields from the above that are to be displayed in the form
- ☐ Formatting the form

For example, using the facility provided by the RDBMS, we can create forms to enter data in all the above 3 tables.

10.2.5 Advantages of using RDBMS

There are various advantages of using RDBMS, some of them are listed here.

1. It can handle very large data tables, and also provide tools to safeguard and inspect the data.
2. It provides with a set of powerful tools for sorting, retrieving, and presenting data.
3. Its strong organizational concept helps managing databases very efficiently.
4. Multiple databases can be linked together to give rise to a pyramid structure of database system.
5. Queries can be made on user's request on the basis of select criteria's either from single or multiple database files.
6. Reports can be generated by grouping some fields with suitable headings from a single or multiple databases.
7. Its wizards, like those in other Microsoft products, make it easy to create tables, queries, reports, mailing labels, and other types of information.
8. It also adds advanced features such as object oriented programming and database scheme, making it a more powerful tool for application developers.
9. It has its own menu builder to design customized menu system for organizing the whole program. It also provides customized windows for the display of suitable messages and screen activities.

10.3 Relational Database Example

Database means base of the data. It is based on the information given by you. It can be catalogued, stored and used. For all this information, database is used. Any collection of related information grouped together as a single item is a database. A metal filling cabinet containing customer records, a card file of names and phone numbers, and notebook containing a listing of a store inventory, all are databases.

However, a file cabinet or a notebook does not itself make a database. Containers, like cabinets, notebooks, or computer programs like FoxPro, are only aids in organizing information.

Database uses the table format of **rows** and **columns** to store the information, as shown here. A database, or a FoxPro database file, may consist of one such table or several ones.

In the example shown next you will notice that each row contains a name, an address, a phone number and a customer number. *Each row is related to the others because they all contain the same type of information in the same places.*

A mailing list, for example, containing a similar type of data about various people, is a good example of a database.

Name	Address	City	State	Pin	Ph. No.	Cust.No.
R.Dayal	F-19, Sec-20	Noida	UP	201301	8531642	0005
Sachin	G-478, Sakurpur	Delhi	Delhi	110034	2454312	0001
Rahul	12, Asaf Ali Road	Delhi	Delhi	110002	3255582	0002
Saurav	14, Asaf Ali Road	Delhi	Delhi	110002	3266698	0004
Anil	21, Kinari Bazar	Delhi	Delhi	110006	3280816	0006
Yuvraj	345, Surya Nagar	Ghazi	UP	201204	8876543	0003

The figure here illustrates this idea by comparing a simple one-table database to an address filling system kept on 3x5 file cards. Each **category** of information on a card is a field.

Fields can contain any type of information, as long as each field always contains the same type of information. In the card box, each record contains six fields: a name, address, city, PIN code, and phone number. Since every card in the box has the same type of information, the card box is a database.

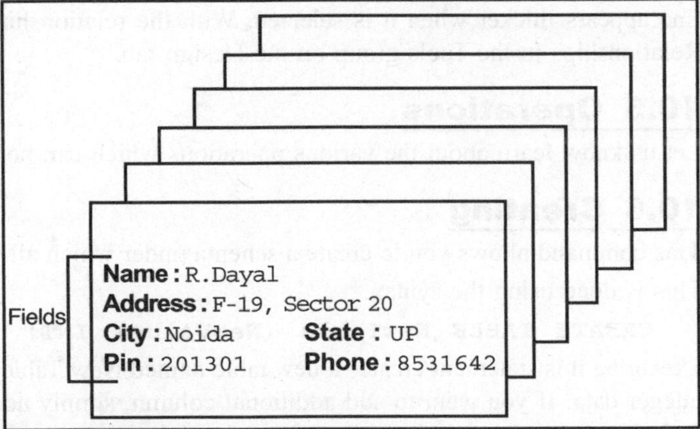

Databases and database technology are having a major impact on the growing use of Computers. It is fair to say that databases play a critical role in almost all areas where computers are used, including business, electronics, commerce, engineering, medicine, law, education, and library science, to name a few.

The preceding definition of database is quite general; for example, we may consider the collection of words that make up this page of text to be related data and hence to constitute a database. However, the common use of the term database is usually more restricted.

A database has the following implicit properties:

- A database represents some aspect of the real world, sometimes called the miniworld or the universe of discourse (UoD). Changes to the miniworld are reflected in the database.
- A database is a logically coherent collection of data with some inherent meaning. A random assortment of data cannot correctly be referred to as a database.
- A database is designed, built, and populated with data for a specific purpose. It has an intended group of users and some preconceived applications in which these users are interested.

10.4 Integrity

The purpose of using referential integrity is to to prevent orphan records and to keep references synchronized so that you don't have any records that reference other records that no longer exist. You enforce referential integrity by enabling it for a table relationship. Once enforced, Database rejects any operation that would violate referential integrity for that table relationship. Database rejects updates that change the target of a reference, and also deletions that remove the target of a reference.

10.4.1 Create a table relationship

You can create a table relationship by using the Relationships window, or by dragging a field onto a datasheet from the Field List pane. When you create a relationship between tables, the common fields are not required to have the same names, although it is often the case that they do. Rather, those fields must have the same data type. If the primary key field is an AutoNumber field, however, the foreign key field can be a Number field if the FieldSize property of both fields is the same.

For example, you can match an AutoNumber field and a Number field if the FieldSize property of both fields is Long Integer. When both common fields are Number fields, they must have the same FieldSize property setting.

10.4.2 Change a table relationship

You change a table relationship by selecting it in the Relationships window and then editing it. Carefully position the cursor so that it points at the relationship line, and then click the line to select it. The relationship line appears thicker when it is selected. With the relationship line selected, double-click it or click Edit Relationships in the Tools group on the Design tab.

10.5 Operations

Let us know learn about the various operations which can be performed on the databases.

10.6 Creating

This command allows you to create a schema under which all the controls will be mentioned.
This is done using the syntax.

```
CREATE TABLE NewTable (NewValue) INT)
```

Executing this statement creates a new table named New Table with a column named New Value that takes integer data. If you want to add additional column, simply add the additional column names followed by their data type so that each pairing of name and data type between the parentheses is separated by a comma, as follows:

```
CREATE TABLE NewTable (NewValue INT, NextValue VARCHAR(6))
```

Since creating a table entails creating columns and creating columns requires the use of data types, it's useful to review the data types available. The following table provides a way of reacquainting yourself with the data types which are available with SQL.

Name	*Storage*
binary	Up to 8,000 bytes of binary data
bit	Integers 0 or 1
char	A fixed-length string of characters not encoded as Unicode
datetime	Date and time values from 1/1/175 to 12/31/9999
decimal	Numbers containing decimal fractions from -10^ 38-1 to 10^38-1
float	Floating-point decimals from -1.79E+308 to 1.79E+308
image	A variable-length string of bits (binary data) with a maximum size of 2^31
int	Integers from -2^31-1 to 2^31-1
money	Numbers representing monetary values from -2^63 to 2^63-1
nchar	A fixed-length string of characters encoded as Unicode
ntext	A variable-length string of characters not encoded as Unicode with a maximum size of 2^31-1
nvarchar	A variable-length string of characters encoded as Unicode
numeric	Same as decimal
real	Floating-point decimals from -3.40E+38 to 3.40E+38
smalldatetime	Date and time values from 1/1/1900 to 6/6/2079
smallint	integers from -2^15-1 to 2^15-1
smallmoney	Numbers representing monetary values from -214,748.3648 to 214,748.3647
text	A variable-length string of characters not encoded as Unicode with a maximum size of 2^31-1
timestamp	A unique number in the database
tinyint	Integers from 0 to 255-failed copy
verbinary	A variable-length string of bits (binary data) with a maximum size of 8,000 bytes

varchar	A variable-length string of characters not encoded as Unicode
uniqueidentifier	A globally unique identifier (GUID), that is, a number in the world.

One thing that you have to consider is the ultimate size of your database and to certain extent, its speed. In general, you want to plan your tables by choosing table names and column names that are descriptive and self-documenting. People have to remember how to use your tables and columns and table names and column do not take up large amounts of space. This statement should not suggest, however, that 256-character column names are a good idea. The data type for a blank occurrence of that column. Many SQL databases require on database creation that you set the maximum file size for the database. Under these circumstances, you want to choose your data types wisely so that you do not bump up against that maximum size too quickly.

In choosing data types, therefore, apply the following suggestions:

- ❑ Choose varchar over char whenever possible. Char (256) sets aside 1 filled byte and 255 blank bytes for the value "A." Varchar (256), while it does incur slight overhead to allow variable-length strings, only uses the number of bytes it requires for the string.
- ❑ If you absolutely know that you will never ever need to store a Unicode string, use the standard data types (like char) instead of the data types that begin with "n" (line nchar). Storing Unicode incurs some additional storage, because you are not using a character set that can be represented by a single byte. However, you need to be absolutely certain that you will need to store Unicode, because you won't be able to if you try.
- ❑ Use a tiny data type or a small data type whenever it makes sense to do so. For example, you can use tinyint, smallint or int. The int data type takes the most storage, because it has to be prepared to store very large integers. The smallint data type restricts the possible range of integers and takes less storage. The tinyint type takes the least storage but has a maximum value of 255.
- ❑ Avoid the binary and next data types whenever possible. If you need to store a collection of binary large objects (BLOBs), such as a collection of pictures, consider storing the path to the graphics file in the database and the BLOB in a folder set aside for holding the BLOB files. Your database will be smaller, storage for the BLOBs will actually be less, because you won't have the overhead the database wraps around the BLOB to keep track of it and response time for queries will be faster. The same is true for large chunks of text.

In addition to planning data types, you need to consider default value and nullability when planning column layouts in tables. The default value is what is placed in the column when a row is created if no value for the column is provided. To provide a default value, you use the default keyword as follows:

```
CREATE TABLE NewTable (NewValue INT DEFAULT 0)
```

The column NewValue now takes a value of 0 if no other value is provided for it by an INSERT statement. A default value of 0 is somewhat redundant for any numeric data type, because the data type itself usually defaults the column to 0.

However, there are many instances where 0 is not the appropriate default, such as when you want to specify a guaranteed interest rate for a life insurance contract. In addition, you need to specify whether the column can be null, that is, whether it can contain no data at all. You do so using the following syntax:

```
CREATE TABLE NewTable (NewText CHAR(6) NULL)
```

This table definition states that the column NewText can be null, which will be its value if an INSERT does not supply another value. You can also specify a default value for a nullable column as follows:

```
CREATE TABLE NewTable (NewText CHAR(6) NULL DEFAULT 'ABCDEF')
```

Here, an INSERT that does not provide a value for this column creates a row that contains 'ABCDEF' in the column NewText. However, another INSERT statement could later set the value of this column to NULL if we so desired. If your database supports filenames or filegroups that represent the files that containing the data on the disk, you can usually specify which files to use in creating a table using the ON keyword. You should check you database's documentation for the exact conventions to use, because they can differ. Most tables have more than one or two columns, so let's take a brief look at a table definition:

```
CREATE TABLE Friends
(
    friend_id char(4)  NOT NULL,
    friend_name varchar(40) NULL,
    city             varchar(20) NULL,
    state            char(2)          NULL,
    country          varchar(30) NULL,
                          DEFAULT("INDIA")
)
```

Things to note here are:

- The use of identification to make the statement more readable.
- Each column has its own line.
- Any additional lines necessary for a given column are indented well underneath that column name.

In addition, note that you can use NOT NULL to indicate that a column absolutely cannot contain NULL as a value.

10.7 Dropping

You can also delete tables with the DROP statement. The syntax is straightforward:

```
DROP TABLE [dbo].[friends]
```

Keep in mind that DROP needs a keyword to identify what you want to delete, in this case a table. Following this keyword is the table name. DROP is final and does not prompt you to have your sanity checked before you carry through the deletion. Make sure you have the names right. If there is data in the table, it will be deleted along with the table.

10.8 Manipulating Table Strucutre

There are many things you have to take into consideration when modifying existing columns of a table. Common rules for modifying columns are:

- The length of a column can be decreased only if the largest value for that column in the table is less than or equal to the new length of the column.
- The number of digits for a number data type can always be increased.
- The length of a column can be increased to the maximum length of the given data type.
- The number of digits for a number data type can be decreased only if the value with the most number of digits for that column is less than or equal to the new number of digits specified for the column.
- The data type of a column can normally be changed.
- The number of decimal places for a number data type can either be increased or decreased.

The command for modifiying would be as mentioned below:

```
ALTER TABLE TABLE_NAME [MODIFY]  [COLUMN COLUMN_NAME];
```

10.9 Manipulation of Data

Data Manipulation Language (DML) allows a database user to actually propagate changes among data in a relational database. With it the user can populate tables with new data, update existing data and delelte the data from the tables.The three basic DML statements are:

INSERT
UPDATE
DELETE

Let us read about them in details.

10.9.1 INSERT Statement

This statement as it may sound is used to insert new data into an existing table. The syntax is:

```
INSERT INTO SCHEMA.TABLE_NAME VALUES {'VALUE1', 'VALUE2', [ NULL ]};
```

Each value in the statement has to be separated by commas. Every coloumn in the table must be mentioned in the INSERT statement. Quotation marks are not required for numeric data types or NULL values using the NULL keyword. A value should be present for each column in the table.

Supposing you have a table called STUDENT_TBL with the following structure:

COLUMN NAME	NULL?	DATA Type
ROLL_NO	NOT NULL	VARCHAR2(10)
FIRST_NAME	NOT NULL	VARCHAR2(25)
MARKS	NOT NULL	NUMBER(3)

Now we add data using INSERT statement.

```
INSERT INTO STUDENT_TBL VALUES ('1033', 'SACHIN', 66);
```

In this example, you insert three values into a table with three columns. The inserted values are in the same order as the columns listed in the table. The first two values are inserted using quotation marks, because data types of the corresponding columns are of character type. The third value's associated column, MARKS, is a numeric data type and does not require quotation marks, although they can be used.

10.9.1.1 Inserting New Rows with Null Values

In the above example, you can have NULL values for the various fields. This means that the value is not given at this stage but at present it is NULL. For example, we change the above statement to:

```
INSERT INTO STUDENT_TBL VALUES ('1033', ' ', 66);
```

With everything else remaining the same the above record will be added with the values given. The only difference here would be that the FIRST_NAME column would be NULL.

10.9.1.2 Inserting Date Values

You can enter the special values into the table. For example, if you want to insert a new student in the students record table STUDENT_TBL, then it can be done as follows:

```
INSERT INTO STUDENT_TBL VALUES('HARBHJAN', '1066', '55')
```

A new entry with student name: Harbhajan, roll no: 1066 and marks: 55 will be inserted.

10.9.1.3 Copying Rows from Another Table

You can insert data from another table to an existing table. For this you would use a combination of INSERT and SELECT statements. By combining the INSERT and SELECT statement, you are able to insert the data received from a query into a table. The syntax for this is:

```
INSET INTO SCHEMA.TABLE_NAME [{'COLUMN1', 'COLUMN2}] SELECT
[*|('COLUMN1', 'COLUMN2')] FROM TABLE_NAME [WHERE CONDITION(S)]
```

The following example would make it more clear.

```
INSERT INTO PRODUCTS_TMP SELECT * FROM PRODUCTS_TBL;
```

Now if you list out the details from the PRODUCTS_TMP you would find that all the data of PRODUCTS_TBL is there in it.

10.9.2 Update Statement to Change Existing Data of a Table

Nothing is perfect. You may need to change the data which is there in the table at any stage of time. For this we have the command called UPDATE. The UPDATE command does not add new records to a table, nor does it remove records, it simply updates the existing data. You can update multiple columns of a table but cannot update multiple tables. An individual row of data in a table can be updated, or numerous rows of data can be updated in a single statement, depending on what's needed.

10.9.2.1 Updating Rows/Columns in a Table

The common use of UPDATE is to update a single column data. Similary a single row of data or numerous records can be updated when updating a single column in a table. The syntax for updating a single column is as follows:

```
UPDATE TABLE_NAME SET COLUMN_NAME = 'VALUE' [WHERE CONDITION];
```

To understand it better look at the following example:

```
UPDATE ORDERS_TBL SET QTY = 1 WHERE ORD_NUM = '2316';
```

This would update quantity to 1 for record(s) where order number is 2316.

10.9.2.2 Updating Multiple Rows/Columns

Using a single UPDATE command, you can update a number of rows/columns. The syntax for this is:

```
UPDATE TABLE_NAME SET COLUMN1 = 'VALUE', [COLUMN2 = 'VALUE',] [COLUMN3
= 'VALUE'] [WHERE CONDITION]
```

Using one SET you can give multiple conditions.If used in an example, the above command would then become:

```
UPDATE ORDERS_TBL SET QTY = 1, CUST_ID = '1033' WHERE ORD_NUM = '2316'
```

Here for the order number 2316, it is not only setting the quantity to 1 but also setting the customer identification to 1033.

10.9.2.3 Updating Rows based on Another Table

It is possible to update the contents of a table based on the contents of several other tables using a FROM clause. The syntax for this is:

```
UPDATE TABLE_NAME SET COLUMN1 = VALUE1 [, COLUMNAME2 = VALUE2]...
FROM TABLE_LIST WHERE SEARCH_CONDITION
```

Look at the following example to understand it more.

```
UPDATE COLLECTION SET WORTH = WORTH * 0.05 FROM INVENTORY WHERE COST
= 300
```

Depending upon the item from INVENTORY whose cost is 300, the items worth is increased by 5% in the COLLECTION table. This syntax is useful when the contents of one table need to be updated following the manipulation of the contents of several other tables.

10.9.3 Delete statement/Removing Row/Rows from a Table

When you can add data to the tables, then there must be a method to delete data too. The DELETE statement does the same. The syntax for this is:

```
DELETE FROM TABLENAME WHERE CONDITION
```

The various options of SQL statement, you can do either of the following, using the DELETE statement:

Delete single row

Delete multiple rows

Delete all rows

Delete no rows

While using DELETE must remember the following:

DELETE cannot delete the value of the field

DELETE cannot delete the complete table

DELETE can delete only records

Using this in an example. Follow the example given below:

```
DELETE FROM STUDENT_TBL WHERE ROLL_NO = '1033'
```

The record with roll number 1033 would be deleted.

If you do not give the WHERE command and stop at just giving the DELETE statement and the table name, then all the records will be deleted.

For example,

```
DELETE FROM STUDENT_TBL
```

In this case all the records of the table would be deleted.

10.9.3.1 Deleting Rows based on condition from another Table

You can also use the sub-queries to DELETE the rows from a table. Supposing you have two tables, STUDENT_TBL and MARKS_TBL. Now if you want to delete the rows in STUDENT_TBL where the student has marks less than 30 in table MARKS_TBL. For this we will give the command as:

```
DELETE FROM STUDENT_TBL WHERE MARKS [SELECT MARKS_TBL WHERE MARKS <
"30"];
```

When the above statement is executed it will delete the records of the students whose marks are less than 30, i.e., they have failed.

10.9.4 Making Data Manipulation Permanent (COMMIT)

COMMIT command is the command used to save changes invoked by a transaction to the database. The COMMIT command saves all transactions to the database since the last COMMIT or ROLLBACK command. The syntax for this is:

```
COMMIT [ WORK ];
```

The word COMMIT is the only mandatory part of the syntax, along with the character or command used to terminate a statement according to each implementation. WORK is a keyword that is completely optional; its only purpose is to make the command more user-friendly.

So usually whenever you give the DELETE command to delete records, follow it up with COMMIT command. This will make the changes permanent. So the commands should be as:

```
DELETE FROM STUDENT_TBL WHERE ROLL_NO = '1033'
```

and it should be followed by:

```
COMMIT
```

There is no need to give the table name here, since there is only one table you are working on. The result of this is:

```
Commit Complete
```

10.9.5 Undo Data Manipulation Changes (ROLLBACK)

The ROLLBACK command is the transactional control command used to undo transactions that have not already been saved to the database. The ROLLBACK command can only be used to undo transactions since the last COMMIT or ROLLBACK command was used. The syntax for this is:

```
ROLLBACK [ WORK ];
```

As earlier, WORK is just optional.

So if you make changes and then suddenly remember that the changes were not required, then give this command immediately and you are returned to the original table.

10.9.5.1 Use of Substitution Variable to Insert Values

SQL allows you to use substitution variables in the INSERT statement that allows the user to add values into the table.

```
INSERT INTO STUDENT_TBL VALUES('&T_ATTN', '&BUS')
```

This statement when executed would allow you to enter the attendance and bus number of each student in the existing data table. At each record the data would be asked for.

10.9.6 The UNION clause

You can combine multiple queries by using UNION clause. But the condition to apply union clause is that both the tables should have same structure and specify the column name of both the tables in the same sequence. The syntax for this is:

```
SELECT [STATEMENT] UNION SELECT [STATEMENT]
```

For example,

```
SELECT NAME, ROLL_NO FROM STUDENT_TBL UNION NAME, ROLL_NO FROM MARKS_TBL;
```

The above statement would display name and roll number from two tables, mainly, STUDENT_TBL and MARKS_TBL. The duplicate rows would be automatically deleted by the UNION clause.

10.9.7 Multiple Row Sub-Query

A multiple row sub query returns more than one row and uses the multiple row comparision operators. The multiple row operator returns more than one value.

For example,

```
SELECT NAME, ROLL_NO FROM STUDENT_TBL WHERE MARKS IN [SELECT MAX[MARKS]
FROM MARKS_TBL
```

In the above example the inner query of having the maximum marks would be solved first. The main query would then be executed.

10.10 Query

A subquery is a query whose results are passed as the argument for another query. Subqueries enable you to bind several queries together. Since subquery is a query within another query, it is thus also known as Nested Query. A subquery is used to return data that will be used in the main query as a condition to further restrict the data to be retrieved. Subqueries are used with the SELECT, INSERT, UPDATE and DELETE statements.

10.10.1 Sub Query to Solve a Problem

A subquery can be used in some cases in place of a join operation by indirectly linking data baetween the tables, based on one or more conditions. When a subquery is used within a query, then the subquery is resolved first, and then the main query is resolved according to the conditions as resolved in the subquery. The subquery can either be used in the WHERE clause or the HAVING clause of the main query.

Logical and relational operators such as =, >, <, IN, NOT IN, AND, OR, and so on, can be used within the subquery as well to evaluate a subquery in the WHERE or HAVING clause.

10.10.2 Guidelines for Using Sub Queries

There are few guidelines which you must follow for using subqueries.

- A subquery can have only one column in the SELECT clause, unless multiple columns are int the main query for the subquery to compare its selected columns.
- Subqueries that return more than one row can only be used with multiple value operators, such as the IN operator.
- Subqueries must be enclosed within parenthesis.
- The SELECT list cannot include any references to values that evaluate to a BLOB, ARRAY, CLOB, or NCLOB.
- An ORDER BY cannot be used in a subquery, although the main query can use an ORDER BY. The GROUP BY can be used to perform the same function as the ORDER BY in a subquery.
- The BETWEEN operator cannot be used with a subquery; however, the BETWEEN can be used within the subquery.
- A subquery cannot be immediately enclosed in a set function.

10.10.3 Types of Sub-Queries—Single Row and Multiple Row

There is no limitation on subquery as far as the number of rows are concerned. You can have your subquery based on single rows or multiple rows.

A simple subquery can be shown in the form of syntax as follows:

```
SELECT COLUMN_NAME [, COLUMN_NAME ] FROM TABLE1 [, TABLE2] WHERE
COLUMN_NAME OPERATOR (SELECT COLUMN_NAME [, COLUMN_NAME ] FROM TABLE1
[, TABLE2 ] [WHERE ])
```

For example in a common payroll file of a company the following subquery can be given:

```
SELECT E.EMP_ID, E.LAST_NAME, E.FIRST_NAME, EP.PAY_RATE FROM
EMPLOYEE_TBL E, EMPLOYEE_PAY_TBL EP WHERE E,EMP_ID = EP.EMP_ID AND
EP.PAY_DATE > (SELECT PAY_RATE FROM EMPLOYEE_PAY_TBL WHERE EMP_ID =
'2003');
```

This would give you the following result based on the content of the tables.

```
LAST_NAME        FIRST_NAME     PAY_RATE
TENDULKAR        SACHIN         15
DRAVID           RAHUL          14
```

10.10.4 Single Row Sub-Query and its Execution

Here we will use the various statements and use them in generating subqueries. First among them is the INSERT statement.

Subqueries with the INSERT Statement

Here the INSERT statement uses the data returned from the subquery to insert into another table. The selected data in the subquery can be modified with any of the character, data, or number functions.

The syntax for this is:

```
INSERT INTO TABLE_NAME [ (COLUMN1 [, COLUMN2 ]) ] SELECT [ * [COLUMN1
[, COLUMN2 ] FROM TABLE1 [, TABLE2 ] [ WHERE VALUE OPERATOR]
```

The following is an example of the INSERT statement with a subquery:

```
INSERT INTO RICH_EMPLOYEES SELECT E.EMP_ID, E.LAST_NAME, E.FIRST_NAME,
EP.PAY_RATE FROM EMPLOYEE_TBL E, EMPLOYEE_PAY_TBL EP WHERE E,EMP_ID =
EP.EMP_ID AND EP.PAY_RATE > (SELECT PAY_RATE FROM EMPLOYEE_PAY_TBL
WHERE EMP_ID = '2003');
```

The INSERT statement inserts the EMP_ID, LAST_NAME, FIRST_NAME and PAY_RATE into a table called RICH_EMPLOYEES for all records of employees who have a pay rate greater than the pay rate of the employee with indentification 2003.

10.10.5 Subquries with the UPDATE Statment

The subquery can be used in conjunction with the UPDATE statement. Either single or multiple columns in a table can be updated when using a subquery with the UPDATE statement. The syntax is:

```
UPDATE TABLE SET COLUMN_NAME [, COLUMN_NAME) ] = [SELECT ]COLUMN_NAME
[, COLUMN_NAME) ] FROM TABLE [WHERE]
```

Using this is the example is shown below:

```
UPDATE EMPLOYEE_PAY_TBL SET PAY_RATE = PAY_RATE * 1.1 WHERE EMP_ID IN
(SELECT EMP_ID FROM EMPLOYEE_TBL WHERE CITY = 'MUMBAI';
```

The result would be:

```
4 rows updated
```

One very important thing to notice here is that this subquery returns multiple rows of data. This is so because you expect multiple rows to be returned, you have used the IN operator instead of the equal sign. Remember the IN is used to compare an expression to values in a list. If the equal sign was used, an error would have been returned.

10.10.6 Subquries with the DELETE Statment

The subquery also can be used in conjunction with the DELETE statement. The syntax is:

```
DELETE FROM TABLE_NAME [WHERE OPERATOR [VALUE ] (SELECT COLUMN_NAME
FROM TABLE_NAME) [WHERE]
```

Using this is the example is shown below:

```
DELETE FROM EMPLOYEE_PAY_TBL WHERE EMP_ID = (SELECT EMP_ID FROM
EMPLOYEE_TBL WHERE LAST_NAME = 'SHARMA' AND FIRST_NAME = 'RAHUL');
```

The result would be:

```
2 rows deleted
```

10.11 Data Entry Form

One area of the system that could stand improvement is data entry. Currently, the system relies on the APPEND command. With the @ command and the SAY, GET, and READ options, you can display the prompts more neatly than you can with the APPEND command, while still storing the data to the fields of the database.

Let's create a new command file called ADDER that will be used whenever you want to add a record to the database. Enter MODIFY COMMAND ADDER, and type the following instructions:

```
USE MEMBERS
CLEAR
@ 0, 5, 14, 60 BOX
APPEND BLANK
@ 1, 10 SAY " Social Sec. " GET SOCIAL
@ 2, 10 SAY " Lastname: " GET FRISTNAME
```

```
@ 4, 10 SAY " Firstname : " GET FIRSTNAME
@ 4, 10 SAY " Address : " GET ADDRESS
@ 5, 10 SAY " City: " GET CITY
@ 6, 10 SAY " State: " GET STATE
@ 7, 10 SAY "PIN Code: "GET PINCODE
@ 8, 10 SAY "Telephone: " GET PHONE
@ 9,10 SAY "Birth date: " GET BIRTHDAY
@ 10, 10 SAY "Expiration DAte: " GET EXPIREDATE
@ 11, 10 SAY "Tape limit: " GET TAPELIMIT
@ 12, 10 SAY " Beta? : " GET BETA
READ
MODIFY MEMO PREFERENCE
RETURN
```

Examine this command file before saving it. After opening the file with USE, clearing the screen, and using the @...BOX command to draw a box, it then uses the BLANK option of the APPEND command. Whenever FoxPro sees APPEND BLANK as a command, it adds a blank record to the end of the database, and the record pointer is positioned at this new last record.

Each @-SAY command displays a query, such as "Birth Date:". The GET option not only displays the contents of each field listed, but it displays them in reverse video, in dimensions corresponding to the field's width. Since the record pointer is referencing the last record, which is empty, only the reverse video is displayed. The READ command toward the end of the command file activates the full-screen entry and editing specified by the GET statements. When data entry or editing has been completed for the last field, you will return to the main menu section of the program.

Press C+s to save the command file, then close the window with C+$. Now you'll need to make one change in the main menu command file to integrate the new ADDER command file into the system. Enter MODIFY COMMAND MENU1 to change the program. Delete the USE MEMBERS line directly underneath CASE CHOICE = 1, and change APPEND in the command file to DO ADDER. Then, press C+s to save the file, and close the window with C+$.

Try out the new command file by entering DO MENU1. Choose the first option on the menu, and try entering a new member of your own choosing.

10.12 Reports

You can coax much flexibility out of your reports and labels by using various expressions within the entry window of the Expression Builder. You usually enter a field in this window, but you can use any valid expression, including memory variables, field names, fields with alias names for related database files, and combinations of fields with or without spaces added. Combinations of character fields are routinely used; as an example, consider a database with fields called Lastname, Firstname, and Midname (containing middle initial). With such a database, the expression

```
TRIM (FIRSTNAME) + " " +LEFT(MIDNAME, 1) +". "+TRIM(LASTNAME)
```

would yield a name like Ram Kumar Sinha. This expression uses the LEFT function to get the leftmost character of a field and the TRIM function to trim excess spaces from the Firstname and Lastname fields. (In this example, if there wee no entry in the middle initial field, you would get an unwanted space and a period. However, this can be prevented by including the IIF function in the Expression for Field text box of the Expression Builder window. Combine names like this to save space in the report.

You can also combine various expressions of different types by converting the noncharacter portions of the expressions to characters. This is done with string functions. For example, you would enter an expression like

```
STR(AMOUNT) + " " + DTOC(DATASOLD)
```

to combine a numeric amount and a date field in a single column. This example uses the STR function, which converts a numeric value into a string of characters, along with the DTOC function, which coverts a valid date into a string of characters.

10.12.1 Using the IIF Function in Expressions

The Immediate IF function, IIF, is also quite useful as part of an expression within reports or labels: Use it when you want to display one set of data when a condition is true and another set when a condition is false. In a personnel report, for example, you may want to indicate the number of weeks of vacation that an employee gets; the company gives two weeks to employees with fewer than five years employment, and three weeks to all others. Assuming five years is equivalent to 365 days multiplied by 5, plus 1 for at least one leap year, any employee whose hire date is at least 1826 days earlier than the date on the computer's clock gets three weeks' vacation. This is simple enough to calculate; for a given record in the personnel database with a date field called Hire_Date, the expression

```
IIF ((DATE()-HIRE_DATE) < 1826, "two weeks", "three weeks")
```

would return the character string "two weeks" if fewer than 1826 days have passed since the date of hire, and 'three weeks" if 1826 or more days have passed since the date of hire. You could place the entire expression into the Expression Builder window for a field within the report, and the report would display the appropriate number of weeks of vacation for that employee.

As an example of another use of the IIF function, recall the first example in this chapter. That report expression produces an unwanted period if no initial is entered in the middle-initial field. To solve this problem, you could use an expression like the following:

```
TRIM(FIRSTNAME) +" " + IIF(LEFT (MIDNAME) <> " ",
LEFT(MIDNAME, 1)) + ". ", ""+ TRIM(LASTNAME)
```

If the leftmost character of the Midname field is a space (indicating no middle initial), a space appears instead of a middle initial and period.

Yet another common use for the IIF function within a report is to blank out numeric amounts that are equivalent to zero. For example, to display hyphens in place of zero if a numeric field called Balance in a sales database contains a zero, you could use the following expression:

```
IIF(BALANCE=0, " —", STR(BALANCE, 7,2))
```

The results are shown in this example report:

Credit Sales
Account Report

CUSTNAME	CUSTNUMB	HIGHCREDIT	BALANCE
Sharma, A.	1001	2000.00	788.50
Jadav, L.	1002	1200.00	675.00
Jain, C.	1003	900.00	350.00
Jain, J.L.	1004	2000.00	1850.00
Akhtar, L.	1005	2000.00	312.00
Verma, B.	1006	1300.00	1167.00
Kureshi, S.	1007	2000.00	0.00
Aqib, K.	1008	1200.00	0.00
Sharma, A.M.	1009	2000.00	220.00
Verma, V.	1010	2000.00	0.00
Jain, J.	1011	2000.00	875.00

Again, if the precise syntax for these functions is unfamiliar, consult Chapter 14 for more information.

10.12.2 Other Useful Functions

A few additional functions and one system variable that may come in handy with reports and labels are shown here.

_PAGENO This is a special system memory variable that FoxPro interprets as the current page number. To add page numbering to a report, use it at the top or bottom of each page. Simply click the Field tool in the Toolbox, and click and drag to size and place the new filed where desired in the Page Header band (for page numbers at the top of the page) or in the Page Footer band (for page numbers at the bottom of the page). Then click the Expression button in the dialog box to open the Expression Builder, and double-click _PAGENO in the Variables list box of the window. Select OK twice to close both dialog boxes and place the page numbers in the report.

DATE TIME These functions place the current date or the current time, respectively. You can place them anywhere within a report or label by clicking the Expression button to bring up the Expression Builder, and then choosing DATE() or TIME() from the Date list box in the Expression Builder.

CMONTH/DAY/YEAR These functions can be combined with the DATE function to produce the current month, day, or year as determined by the PC's clock. For example, the expression

```
CMONTH(DATE())
```

produces the spelled-out name of the current month, while the expression

```
YEAR (DATE())
```

results in the current year. (Note that the YEAR function yields a number; to combine it with character data, you must use it with the STR function.) You can place these functions as expressions within text in a report to produce the full current date.

10.12.3 Designing form Letters

Designing a report as a form letter lets you generate form letters for names and addresses within a database. You can do this by exporting a file for use with a word processor, but the following method has the advantage of letting you create the form letters without leaving FoxPro.

To design a report that will serve as a form letter, increase the size of the Detail band and place the text of the form letter, along with the necessary fields for the name and address, within this band, Add fields as desired at appropriate locations within the letter. Add a Summary band at the bottom of the report and turn on the New Page option for the Summary band, so that each record in the report prints on a separate page.

To see how this works, create a form letter for the MEMBERS database. Open the database with USE MEMBERS, and create a new report by entering CREATE REPORT LETTER. Maximize the window so you will be able to see more of your work area. Click the rectangle just to the left of the Page Header band, and drag it upwards to the top of the window. Then, click the rectangle just to the left of the Page Footer band and drag it downwards to the bottom of the window. In the resulting report, all visible space is used by the detail band, as shown in next figure.

Click the Text tool in the Toolbox, then click at the gridline that is 1 inch down from the top of the window, at a point roughly 1/2 inch in from the left margin. Enter

```
July 20, 1996
```

and click anywhere outside the text to deselect it. Then select the Field tool and click and drag just below the date until the box formed by the dotted line is roughly 1/4 inch high and 1 inch long (exact size and placement do not matter for now). When you release the mouse, the Report Expression dialog box appears. Click the Expression button to open the Expression Builder. In the Expression for Field on Report text box, enter

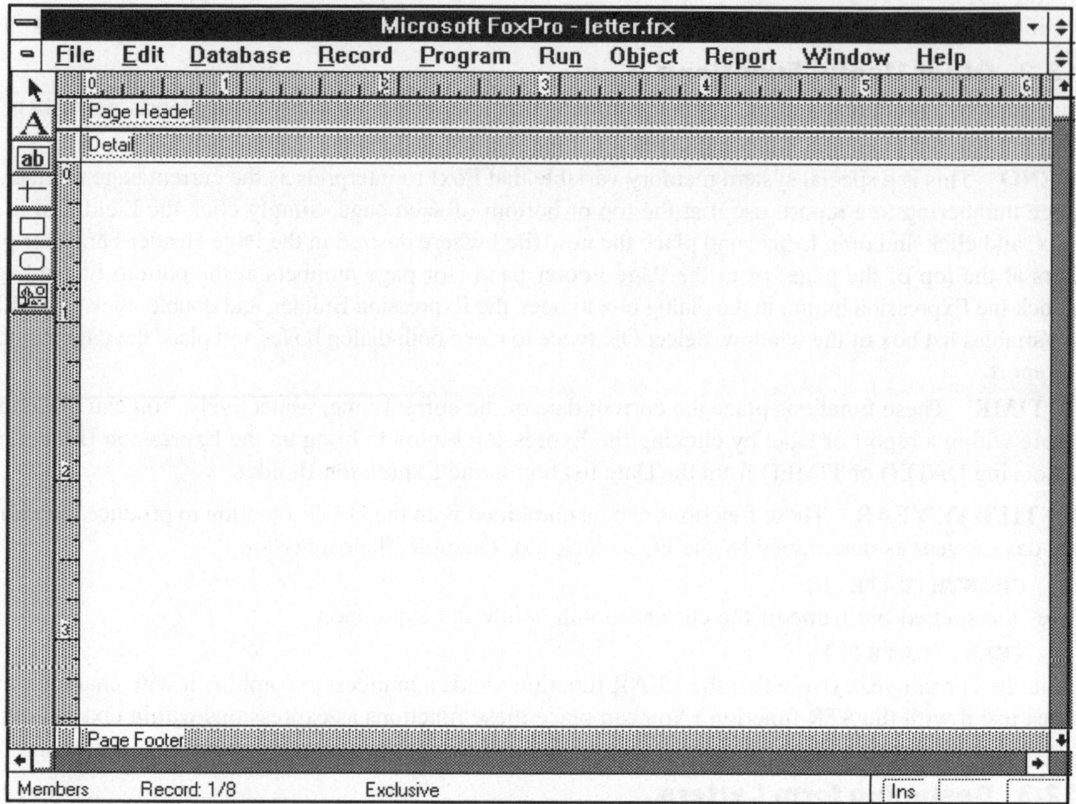


```
TRIM(FIRSTNAME) + " " + LASTNAME
```

This expression causes the contents of the Firstname field (trimmed of extra blanks) to appear, followed by one space and the contents of the Lastname field. Click OK twice to close both dialog boxes. Click and drag the new field until it is aligned with the typed text, roughly 1/4 inch below the typed text. (You can judge distances by examining the horizontal and vertical rulers that appear at the top and left edges of the window.) Next, you need to place the Address field in the report. Select the Field tool, then click and drag just below the name fields until the box formed by the dotted line is roughly 1/4 inch high and 2 inches long (again, exact size and placement do not matter for now). When you release the mouse, the Report Expression Builder, then double-click the Address field in the Fields list box to place it in the Expression for Field text box. Click OK twice to close the dialog boxes. After the new field appears, click and drag the field until it is directly under the name fields.

To place the city, state, and Pincode fields, you'll use an expression much like that used earlier to combine the first and last names on a single line. Select the Field tool in the Toolbox, then click and drag below the address field to place a field roughly 1/4 inch high and 2 inches in length. When you release the mouse, the Report Expression dialog box appears. Click the Expression button to open the Expression Builder. In the Expression for Field on Report text box, enter

```
TRIM(CITY) + ", " + STATE + " " +ZIPCODE
```

This expression causes the contents of the City field (trimmed of extra blanks) to appear, followed by a comma and space, the State field, a space, and the Pincode field. Click OK twice to close both dialog boxes, then click and drag the new field until it is directly underneath the Address field.

To fill in the rest of the Detail band, you use the Text tool to place a text cursor below the existing name and address, and then you simply type the text of the form letter. The Report Writer does not have the automatic word-wrap capabilities of a word processor, so you must press E at the end of each line. Click the Text tool now (remember, it's the icon containing the letter A), then click roughly 1/2 inch below the left edge of the last field you placed. Type the text shown pressing E after each line.

```
Dear Member:
We have been pleased to have you as a member of Dayal
Videos movie club during the past year. Because you are a
valued member, we would like to extend to you the chance to
renew your membership now at a special reduced rate.
```

Due to an internal memory limit, FoxPro will not let you place more than roughly 255 characters in a single text object. To complete the text of our sample letter, you need to place the second paragraph of text in another text object.

Click anywhere outside of the existing text, then select the text tool in the Toolbox again. Click roughly 1/2 inch below the existing paragraph, at the left edge. Then, type the second paragraph:

```
If you return the enclosed form within 30 days, you will
save an additional 33% off the regular membership rate.
```

Keep in mind that you can intermix fields within the text of the form letter. Although it is not necessary in this case, you might find such a technique helpful in your own applications. For example, if you had a database with a numeric field containing a customer's past-due amounts, you could have the past-due amount appear within a sentence in the letter. To do this, you would use the Field tool of the Toolbox to add a new field at the point in the letter where the data is to appear. Then, you would enter the field name in the Expression text box or click the Expression button to bring up the Expression Builder and choose the desired name from the list, and finally click OK to place the field.

If you insert numeric fields into the body of your form letters, you will want to get rid of any leading blanks. You can do this by converting the numeric value into a character string, and then using the LTRIM function to trim leading blanks. For example, if you wanted to insert the Tapelimit field into the text of the letter and trim and leading blanks, you could use the Field tool of the Toolbox to add a new field at the desired location, click the Expression button to bring up the Expression Builder, and enter an expression like

```
LTRIM(STR (TAPELIMIT)
```

to accomplish such a task.

One item is still needed: A Group band containing a New Page option must be added, so that each record will print on a separate page. Open the Report menu an choose the Data Grouping option. Click Add, then click Group. Double-click the Social field in the scroll box, then click OK to close the Expression Builder dialog box. Turn on the New Page option by clicking it. Finally, click OK in the dialog box to place the Group band in the report. Choose OK from the resulting dialog box. At this point, your screen should resemble the example shown in next figure.

Save the completed report by choosing File/Save. When prompted to save the environment information, answer Yes. Then, close the report design window by pressing C+$.

```
REPORT FORM LETTER TO PRINT
```

to print a letter for every record in the database. Or, in the interest of saving paper, you may want to limit the scope of your printing by using a command such as

```
REPORT FORM LETTER NEXT 5 TO PRINT
```

In either case, the result should resemble the sample shown on the next page.

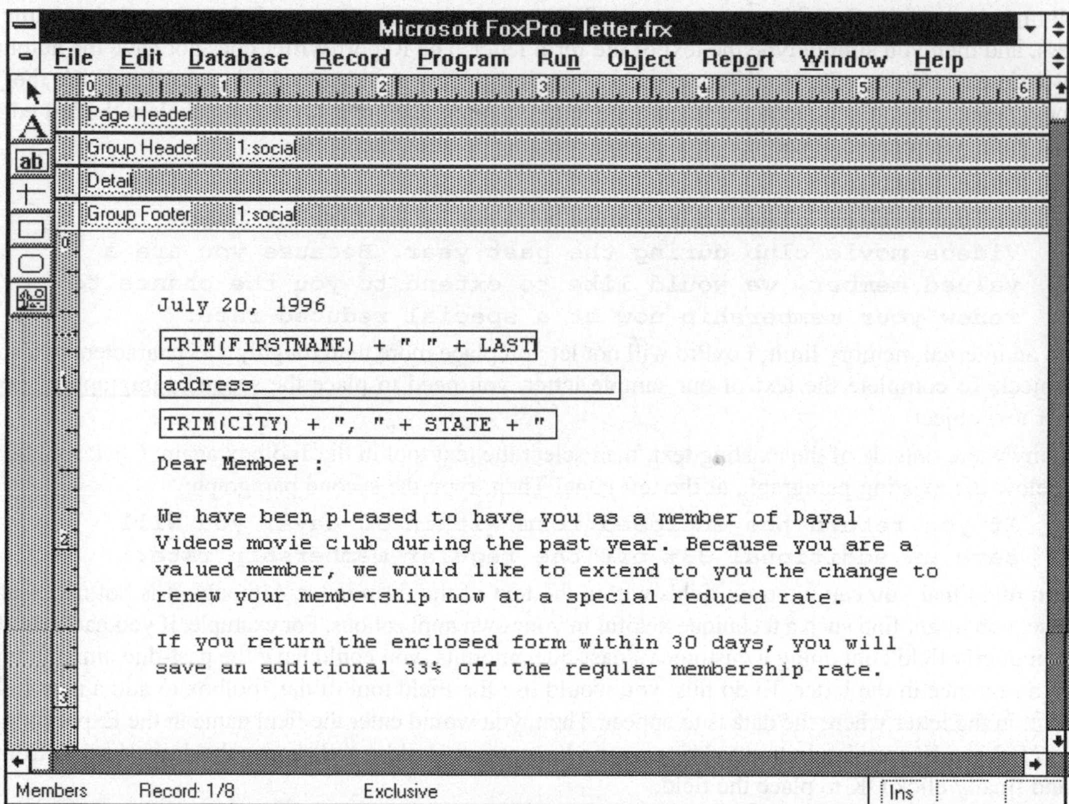

You can add more text by placing additional Detail lines as needed; in this example, a closing salutation could have been added in the lines following the last paragraph. Window size does not limit the number of Detail bands you can place in the report; as you reach the bottom of the window, use the scroll bars or drag

> July 20, 1996
>
> Rakesh Modi
> 270, Mori Gate
> O.D, Delhi 110006
>
> Dear Member;
>
> We have been pleased to have you as a member of Dayal Videos movie club during the past year. Because you are a valued member, we would ike to extend to you the chance to renew your video membership now at a special reduced rate.
> If you return the enclosed form within 30 days, you will save an additional 33% off the regular membership rate.

the box in the vertical ruler down to cause the top of the report's layout to scroll off the screen as more of the bottom comes into view.

You can also change the size of the text used in your reports. If you click a text object you've placed in a report to select it and then choose Object/Font from the menus, the font dialog box appears as shown in next figure.

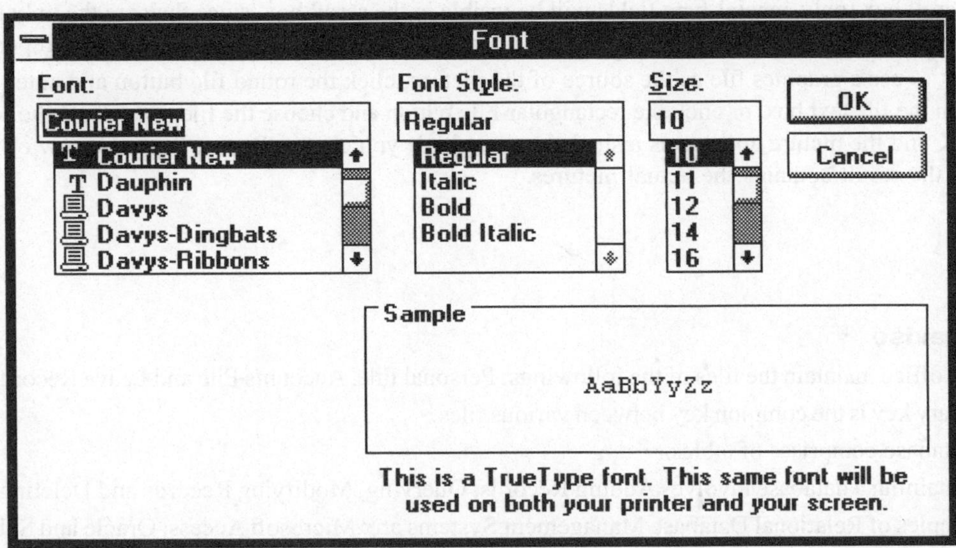

Choose the desired font, font style, and font size from the dialog box, then click OK. Keep in mind that you may want to apply the same kind of font and style changes to the fields used in your report; if you change the fonts for text but not for the field used, the result may be a report with a bizarre combination of character sizes and styles.

10.12.4 Adding Pictures to a Report

You can add pictures to a report, using the Picture tool in the Toolbox. To add pictures contained in a general field to a report, begin designing the report in the manner outlined earlier. When you are ready to add the general field, click the Picture tool in the Toolbox. Then, click at the desired starting location in the report and drag until the frame that is to contain the picture reaches the desired size. When you release the mouse, the Report Picture dialog box appears on the screen, as shown in figure here.

You can use the options

within this dialog box to identify the source of the picture (the picture can come from a database field, or from a graphics file), and to tell FoxPro how to handle the display of the picture if the picture and the frame you've placed in the report are of different sizes.

If you want to use the contents of a general field as a picture, click the round Field button and enter the name of the field in the Field text box, or click the rectangular Field button and choose the desired field name from the scroll box (only general-type fields will be visible in the scroll box, since they are the only fields that can contain pictures). Click OK and the picture will appear as a shaded rectangle within the report.

If you want to use a graphics file as the source of the picture, click the round file button and enter the name of the file in the file text box, or click the rectangular File button and choose the file name from the scroll box. Choose OK and the picture appears as a shaded rectangle. If you choose Report/Page Preview or you print the report, the result contains the actual pictures.

Let us Revise

1. Each office maintain the files of the followings: Personal File, Accounts File and Leave Record File.
2. Primary key is the common key between various files.
3. A database comprises of tables.
4. Maintaining a database involves Adding Records, Querying, Modifying Records and Deleting Records
5. Examples of Relational Database Management Systems are: Microsoft Access, Oracle and Sybase
6. Tables contain data in rows and columns called fields.
7. Queries are used to get result from the database.
8. Reports are generated to print information from tables.
9. Forms are created on screen to fill in the data.
10. Using RDBMS you can handle large volume of data.
11. A subquery is a query whose results are passed as the argument for another query.
12. A subquery can be used in some cases in place of a join operation by indirectly linking data baetween the tables, based on one or more conditions.
13. You can have your subquery based on single rows or multiple rows.
14. The subquery can be used in conjunction with the UPDATE statement.
15. The subquery also can be used in conjunction with the DELETE statement.

Multiple Choice Questions

1. Common field to various tables in the database is called :

   (a) Key (b) Common (c) Same

2. Forms are :

   (a) Displayed on screen (b) Printed on printer (c) Outputted on plotter

3. A database consists of various :

   (a) Tables (b) Chairs (c) Stools

4. Full form of RDBMS is :

   (a) Relational Database Management System

(b) Regional Database Management System

(c) Relational Database Making System

5. For deleting the data from the records we use :

(a) INSERT (b) UPDATE (c) DELETE

6. For changing the data in a number of rows/columns you can use :

(a) INSERT (b) UPDATE (c) DELETE

True/False Questions

1. Primary key is the common key between various files.
2. A database comprises of forms.
3. Maintaining a database involves Adding Records, Querying, Modifying Records and Deleting Records
4. Tables contain data in rows and columns called fields.
5. Queries are not used to get result from the database.
6. Reports are generated to print information from tables.
7. Forms are created on screen to fill in the data.

Matching Columns

Match the text in Column A with the text in Column B.

Column A	Column B
1. Database	a. Displaying on screen to fill in the data
2. Table	b. Common key to various tables in database
3. Query	c. Relational Database Management System
4. Report	d. To extract information from table
5. Form	e. A collection of data in rows and columns
6. RDBMS	f. Printing information from table
7. Primary key	g. A collection of tables pertaining to a kind of data

Fill in the Blanks with appropriate words

a. Tables b. Query c. Forms d. Table

e. Report

1. ________ are displayed on screen to fill in the data.
2. A database consists of various ________.
3. A _______ is printed based on information from the tables.
4. A ______ can be generated to get results based on the data in the tables.
5. ________ contains data in rows and columns.

Descriptive Type Questions

1. What is a database?
2. What is Relational Database Management System?

3. What all you need for creating Tables?
4. What sort of queries you can generate from the table?
5. What sort of report can you generate from the table?
6. What are the forms used for?
7. What are the advantages of using RDBMS?
5. Describe what do you understand by Sub-query.
6. Describe the guidelines for using sub-quries.

Answers to Objective Type Questions

Multiple Choice Questions

1. a	2. a	3. a	4. a
5. c	6. b		

True/False Questions

1. T	2. F	3. T	4. T
5. F	6. T	7. T	

Matching Columns

1. g	2. e	3. d	4. f
5. a	6. c	7. b	

Fill in the Blanks with Appropriate Words

1. c	2. a	3. e	4. b
5. d			

Information Technology and Society 11

11.1 Indian IT Act

An Act to provide legal recognition for the transactions carried out by means of electronic data interchange and other means of electronic communication, commonly referred to as "Electronic Commerce", which involve the use of alternatives to paper based methods of communication and storage of information, to facilitate electronic filings of documents with the Government agencies and further to amend the Indian Penal Code, Indian Evidence Act, 1872.

The Bankers' Books Evidence Act, 1891, and the Reserve Bank of India Act.1934 and for matters connected therewith or incidental thereto. Whereas the General Assembly of the United Nations by resolution A/RES/51/162, dated the 30th January, 1997 has adopted the Model Law on Electronic Commerce adopted by the United Nations Commission on International Trade Law; and whereas the said resolution recommends inter *alia that all* State's give favorable consideration to the said Model Law when they enact or revise their laws, in view of the need for uniformity of the law applicable to alternatives to paper-based methods of communication and storage of information; and whereas it is considered necessary to give effect to the said resolution and to promote efficient delivery of Government services by means of reliable electronic records.

India has enacted the first I.T. Act, 2000 based on the Unciral model recommended by the general assembly of the united nations by a resolution dated 30th Jan 1997. The preamble to this Act gives a very clean picture in this regard. The various offences which are provided under this chapter are:

- Tampering with Computer source documents
- Hacking with Computer systems
- Access to protected system
- Access to protected system
- Misrepresentation
- Breach of Confidentiality and Privacy
- Fraud

The elementary problems, which are associated with cyber-crimes are:

1. Jurisdiction is the highly debatable issue as to the maintainability of any suits which has been filled. Today with the growing arms of cyberspace the growing arms of cyberspace the territorial boundaries seems to vanish thus the concept of territorial jurisdiction as envisaged under S.1 of C.P.C and S.2. of the I.P.C. will have to give way to alternative method of dispute resolution.
2. Loss of evidence is a very common & expected problem as all the data are routenly destroyed. Further collection of data outside the territorial extent also paralyzes this system of crime investigation.
3. Cyber Army-There are also an imperative need to built a high technology crime & investigation infrastructure, with highly technical staff a the other end.
4. A law regulating the cyber-space which India has done.

5. Though S.75 provides for extra-territorial operations of this law, but they could be meaningful only when backed with provision recognizing orders and warrants for Information issued by competent authorities outside their jurisdiction and measure for cooperation for exchange of material and evidence of computer crimes between law enforcement agencies.
6. Use of incepted messages, virtually private networks etc. also create a big problem to trace the activities of cyber criminals.
7. Cyber savvy judges are the need of the day. Judiciary plays a vital role in shaping the enactment according to the order of the day. One such stage, which needs appreciation, is the P.I.L., which the Kerela High Court has accepted through an email.
8. The procedural obligation which have to be fulfilled as lettertrography U/s 166A & 166B of the Cr. P.C. and bar in case of crimes committed outside India. (i.e. prior approval of the central government.)

'Perfect' is a relative term. Nothing in this world is perfect. The persons who legislate the laws & by-laws also are neither perfect. The laws therefore enacted by them cannot be perfect. This law has emerged from the womb of globalization. It is at the threshold of development. In due course of exposure through varied & complicated issues it will grow to be a piece of its time legislation. The Information and Technology Act 2000 seeks to introduce some sort of control over the use of encryption for communication in India.

The use of the cryptography and encryption in India is a relatively new phenomenon. The use of this technology for the purposes of communication has begun only over the last 15-20 years in India. According to a recent report in India there are very few companies involved in the development of cryptography. Further, cryptography remains within the domain of the defense sector. It is only as late as 1995 that India introduced a list of items that required licensing before export. The list only included encryption software for telemetry systems in specific and did not relate to encryption software in general.

The information and Technology Act 2000 makes the publishing of information which is obscene in electronic form punishable as under:

"Whoever publishes or transmits or causes to be published in the electronic form, any material which is lascivious or appeals to the prurient interest or if its effect is such as to tend to corrupt persons who are likely, having regard to all relevant circumstances, to read, see or hear the matter contained or embodied in it, shall be punished on first conviction with imprisonment of either description for a term which may extend to five years and with fine which may extend to one lakh rupees and in the event of a second or subsequent Conviction, with imprisonment of either description for a term which may extend to ten years and also with fine which may extend to two lakh rupees."

This new law will operate upon anyone who is within its jurisdiction net. Any one within the country or the area of operation of the law who is carrying on a business of cyber porn will liable under section 67 of the above mentioned Act. Apart from this, a multi-layered governance program should be ushered in.

This will mainly include a mixture of national and international legislations and self imposed regulations by internet service providers and users like parents for their children, hotlines and special organizations to report pornographic content. In this way the balance between the freedom of the individual and the greatest good of the society can be maintained.

11.2 Intellectual Property Right - Issues

Today whenever you visit a site and want to get yourself to he part of that web site, let it be any site like e-mail account, business online, enjoyment site, etc. you have to register yourself on that site by entering your personal information like name, your address, telephone number, your hobbies and like information. Many companies make money of that information by selling it to other companies or firms online so as they further can use information for their own business sake. These credit companies and other organizations collect this data on millions of citizens daily. Much of the data is created while interacting with government and private organizations. Exactly, these thing organizations know about you.

- Credit history
- Income
- Personal data (Social security number, age, family history, ethnicity, religion, etc.)
- Reading material (magazines, books, etc.)
- Reading material (magazines, books, etc.)
- Listening preferences
- Motor vehicle information
- Federal, state, and private loans
- Telephone calls
- Medical information
- Insurance information
- Schools records
- Employment history
- Legal hearing and judgments
- Marital history

Sometimes consumers supply data knowingly, but do not realize how the data may be used later. Unlike the government, private organizations depend on information for profit. This personal information ends up being recorded in many different places as businesses sell information to other private organizations.

The federal government is about the biggest data collector of all and information collected on an individual can be retrieve by keying in the person's social security number. Does the government really need so much data on individuals?

Some of the hottest buzz about the Internet is the issue of privacy. Everyone on the Internet deserves privacy. Concerns about privacy are the leading reason non-Internet users stay off the Web.

Inset Systems, Inc. v. Instructions Set, Inc., 937 F. SUPP 161.

The Court held that advertising over the Internet was purposefully directed towards the Forum State.

Invasion of privacy can take various forms on the Internet:

- Spam-unwanted e-mails
- Cookies-lead web sites back to your computer
- Hackers-access computer stored information

Electronic mail is a wonderful way of communicating but it is often abused. The constant filing of their e-mail boxes with unwanted information usually annoys people.

Depending on what you do when visit a site, you may provide information about your visit to the web site's owner. It is important to know what a site's privacy policies are. If the site does not say, then perhaps you should ask. As web sites for major companies need to be secured against hackers or persons with malicious intent.

The Internet is a huge technological issue, but due to the privacy issue some people are afraid to make purchases on the net, government needs to make laws to protect these privacy issues. In the US, the law is not doing much to protect your privacy. But in Europe, legislators have passed a law called the "European Union Protection Initiative for the same".

Martiz, Inc. v. Cyber gold, Inc., 947 Supp. 1328.

Finding that it had jurisdiction over a California defendant in a trade mark infringement case where the defendant's only contact with the state was through its California-based web site, which was accessible in Missouri.

11.3 Application of Information Technology in Railways

Railways were among the first to go in for computerization. The first step in this direction was to keep the track of the wagons and their movements. This was perhaps the first but later on most of the operations of railways were taken up for computerization. The final being the booking, which is now done throught India and is completely on line.

Indian Railways has a vast network. Both in terms of number of trains per day and the number of passengers. The computerization has indeed helped both the commuters and the organization too. Now you can book your ticket in advance from any station to any station while standing on a third station. All the bookings are interconnected. So you even see the position of the trains too.

The latest in this line is the concept of Internet. You can now book your tickets on the net too. The payment in this case has to be made using credit cards. So far there is no method of paying by cash.

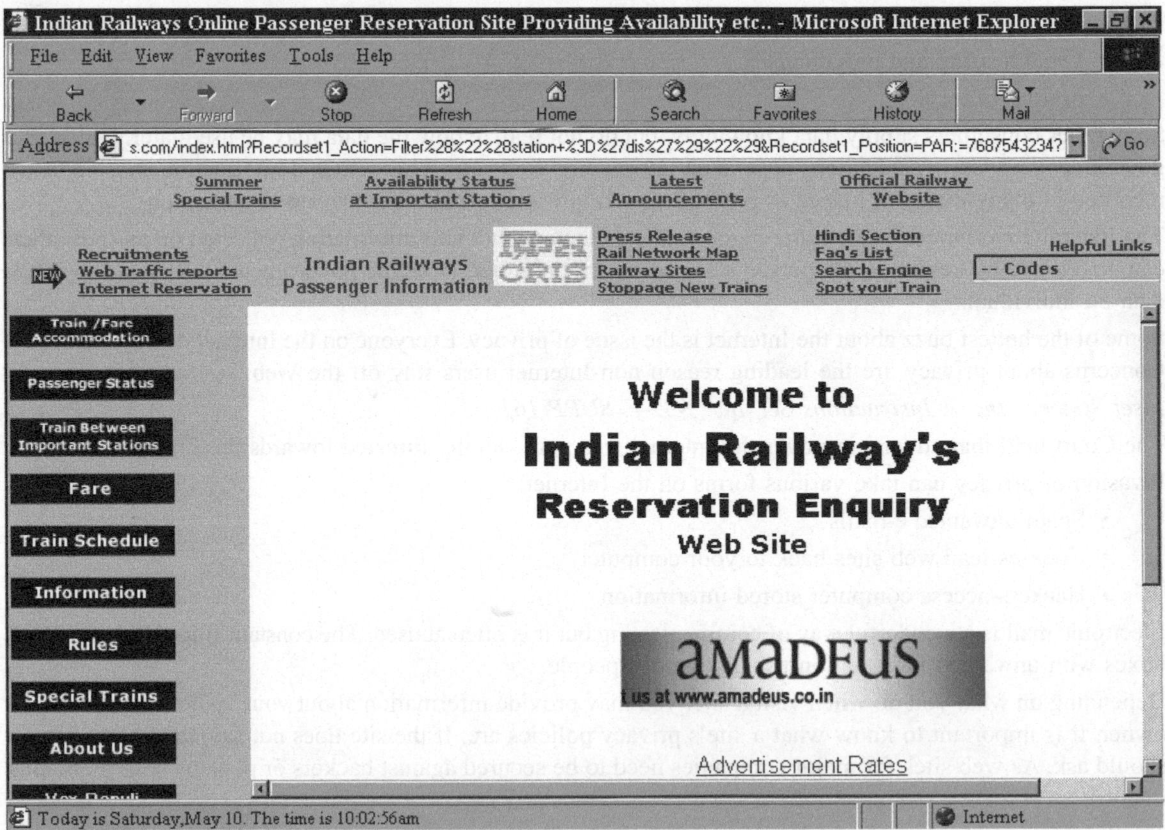

11.4 Airlines

The best part of airline booking is that it is on line throughout the world. Now it is possible for a person living in USA to book his ticket to London on a flight originating from USA and then onward journey to various airlines which do not even touch USA. He can even book a seat from Delhi to Bombay while sitting

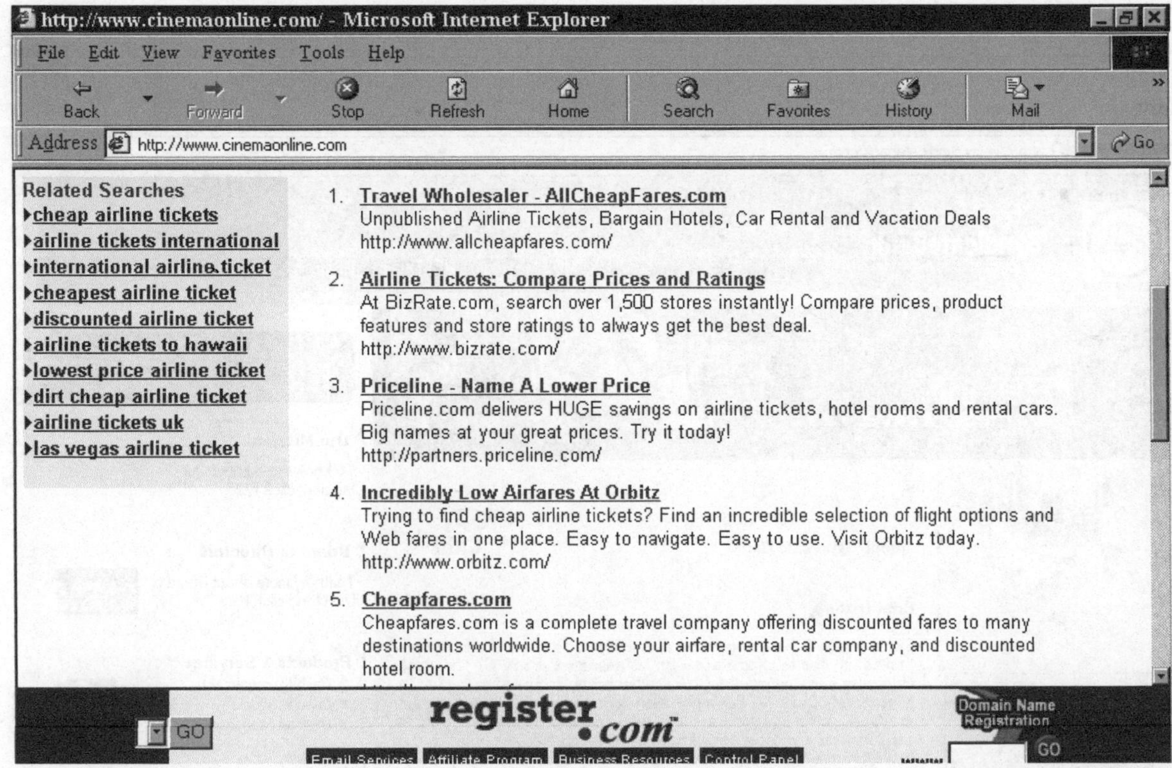

over there. Not only that you can book your seat in advance for so many years to come. For example, you can book your seat for 31st December, 2010.

This is as far as the users are concerned. On the other hand the Airlines have been using the computers for their other work too. For example, the pilots are trained in a cubicle which is exactly like the cockpit of the aeroplane. Here he learns how to handle the plane theoritically and practically before he actually flies the one. The cubicle in this case is totally computer simulated.

11.5 Banking

This one had the stiffest oppositions. Most of the Banks unions were against computerization in the banks. The reason; this would lead to loss of jobs for employees. Well, nothing like this happened and most of the urban banks are now computerized. Lots of banks encourage you to withdraw money from their ATMs so that there is less pressure on their staff. Even the pass books are all computerized. No more making manual entries in them.

Another banking related application is Credit Card. The whole system of credit card is computerized. When you go to a shop to buy something and pay by credit card. The shopkeeper would put your card through a machine and ask for acceptance. The acceptance is given in the form of a slip based on the credit money available in your account. You just have to sign, the bill would come to you in due course and the bank would allow you to pay in its own terms.

11.6 Insurance

Since the opening of insurance sector to the private parties, there are lots of insurance companies have come in. Previously, there was one for life insurance by the name of Life Insurance Corporation of India and

Syndicate BANK - Microsoft Internet Explorer
File Edit View Favorites Tools Help
Back Forward Stop Refresh Home Search Favorites History Mail
Address http://www.syndicatebank.com
Go
सिंडिकेटबैंक
SyndicateBank
CMD's Message | NRI Services | Branch Network | News | Citizens Charter
Reliable
Responsive.
NET BANKING
>> Retail >> Corporate
>> Corp. Admin >> Biller
Our Mission
To know more about Our Mission, click here.
CUSTOMER CARE
about Syndicate Bank
Board of Directors
To know more about Board of Directors, click here.
Brief History
Syndicate Bank was established in 1925 in Udupi, the abode of Lord Krishna in coastal Karnataka with a capital of Rs.8000/- by three visionaries - Sri Upendra Ananth Pai, a businessman, Sri Vaman Kudva, an engineer and Dr.T M A Pai, a physician - who shared a strong commitment to social welfare. Their objective was primarily to extend financial assistance to the local weavers who were crippled by a crisis in the handloom industry through mobilising small savings from the community. The bank collected as low as 2 annas daily at the doorsteps of the depositors through its Agents under its Pigmy Deposit Scheme started in
Products & Services
» Cash Management
» Loan Products
» Deposit Products
Syndicat-e-banking
Done
Internet
Address http://www.insuranceindia.com
Go
insuranceindia.com
CASINO ON NET
Play Now!
888casino.com
Win Real money!!!
Home
Sat, 10 May 2003 GMT
Top Searches
• Debt Reduction
• Hosting
• Home Equity Loans
• Refinance
• Home Mortgages
• Viagra
• Term Life Insurance
• Mortgages
• Bad Credit
• Auto Insurance
• Online Gambling
• Health Insurance
• Auto Loans
• Domain Hosting
Finances
Debt Reduction, Refinance, Home Mortgages, Bad Credit, Auto Loans, Loans, Credit Reports, Fundraising, Cash Advance, Credit
Homes
Home Equity Loans, Refinance, Mortgages, Air Purifiers, Home Improvements, Blinds, Renters Insurance, Home Insurance, Rugs, Humidifiers
Health
Insurance
Term Life Insurance, Auto Insurance, Health Insurance, Dental Insurance, Home Insurance, Travel Insurance, Business Insurance
Business
Payrolls, Fundraising, MBA, Incorporate, Home Based Business, POS, Brochures, Packaging, Ecommerce, Franchises
Autos
Auto Insurance, Auto Loans,
Internet
Hosting, Domain Hosting, Domain Registrations, Dedicated Servers, Affiliate Programs, Ecommerce, Web Sites, Web Site Promotions, Internet Businesses, Shopping Carts
Computers
Toner, Inkjet Cartridges, Shrink Wrap, Security Software, Business Software, Help Desk, Backups, Disaster Recovery, Laptops, Conference

the other 4 for various type of insurance like Home, Vehicle, Factory, etc., for these we had insurance companies like, National Assurance, Oriental Insurance, New India Assurance, General Insurance.

Each insurance company floats various schemes for insurance and each one of them has either the instalments or reducing balances benefits. All these calculations are made on computers. Add to that the various correspondence and printing of literature is also done on the computers. Various reminders for the premium amounts are also prepared by computers.

11.7 Inventory Control

This is a very interesting application of computers. Since it involves the volume of data, the computers prove to be very useful to main the inventory of various parts used in any factory. Without computers it becomes very difficult to know which part is available and how much. Depending upon the minimum stock level of the part, the fresh stock can be ordered.

On the other hand you can always get an idea of how much worth of stock you have in your stores. Some companies even get bank loans on the basis of stocks they have. For this all you have to do is to keep up-to-date the movement of spare parts going out and being consumed. Well if one goes deep into it one can do lots of analysis like the fast moving parts, slow moving parts, high value parts, low value parts, and so on.

11.8 Financial Systems

Accounting is an important part of any company's computerization. This is so because this is the department which effects everyone from employees to employers. A well maintained accounting setup with capabilities of the quick production of reports and summaries is an asset to any business activity in that the management is aware of the latest up to date financial standing of the business thereby facilitating right decision making. Using computerization, the accounts are mostly up-to-date and finalization at the end of the year does not take much time.

Accuracy is the most important as regards accounting data is concerned which is often lost in a manual system. Also the type of accounting data are of simple numerical in nature involving large volumes and laborious calculations. Using computerized accounting, it has become possible to prepare profit and loss figures monthly or if necessary even on a daily basis. To understand a computerized accounting system it is imperative that one should have a clear background to this field of study as otherwise when talking to the accounting personnel, he would be faced with terminologies like debits and credits which would be rather incoherent to a software personnel.

11.8.1 Computerization

The first step in computerizing an accounting system is to identify the heads of accounts required and code them as appropriate. In an actual business environment there would be many more heads of accounts and these should be studied in detail and classified into major and minor groups, such as Fixed Assets and within fixed assets, Land and Buildings, Plant & machinery, etc. A suitable coding structure should then be designed. A typical coding structure is given below.

The account heads in a business can generally be classified as follows:

Balance Sheet Heads

Within this major grouping, we can have various subgroups as under.

1. ASSETS
2. LIABILITIES

Within ASSETS, minor grouping can be done as

1. FIXED ASSETS: Within which sub grouping can be done as

1. Land
2. Building
3. Plant & Machinery
4. Furniture etc.

2. CURRENT ASSETS: sub groups within as
    1. Stocks
    2. Cash
    3. Bank
    4. Debtors etc.

Similarly within liabilities, there can be Capital a/c and Current liabilities with in which Creditors, Loans, etc., can be classified.

11.9 Hotel Management

The benefits of computer and its applications stretch till upto Hotel industry. In today's information world you can use computers and Internet for inquiring availability of rooms in a particular hotel, can make reservation and even pay fares online. Now it is possible to enter basic queries and gather information different regions, countries, people to equip themselves to serve the needs of customers.

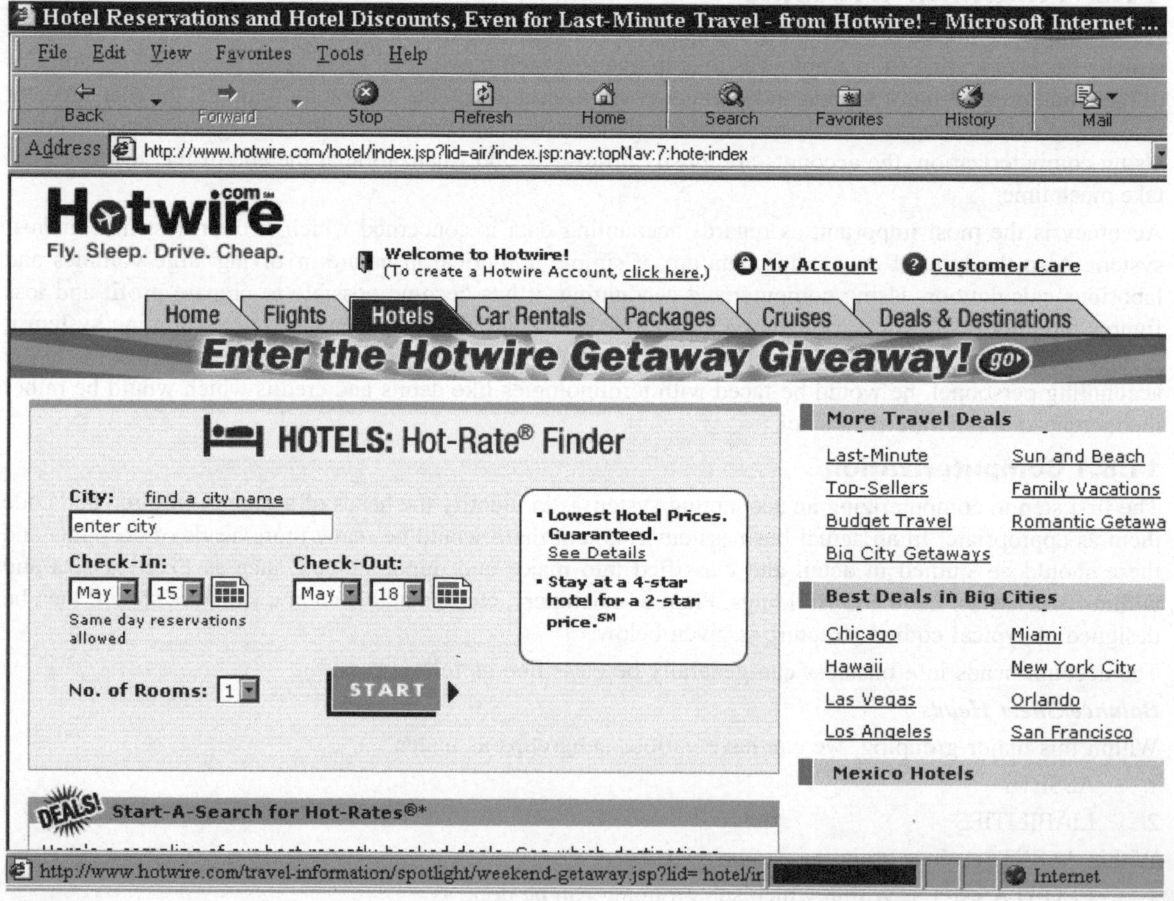

11.10 Education

Most of us have used the services on the Internet such as e-mail, chatting, free MP3 music etc. The other aspect of Internet, which most of us are unfamiliar with is education. This can be done by 4 methods: Knowledge-based e-Learning; Online Support-based e-Learning; Synchronous-based e-Learning and Asynchronous-based e-Learning.

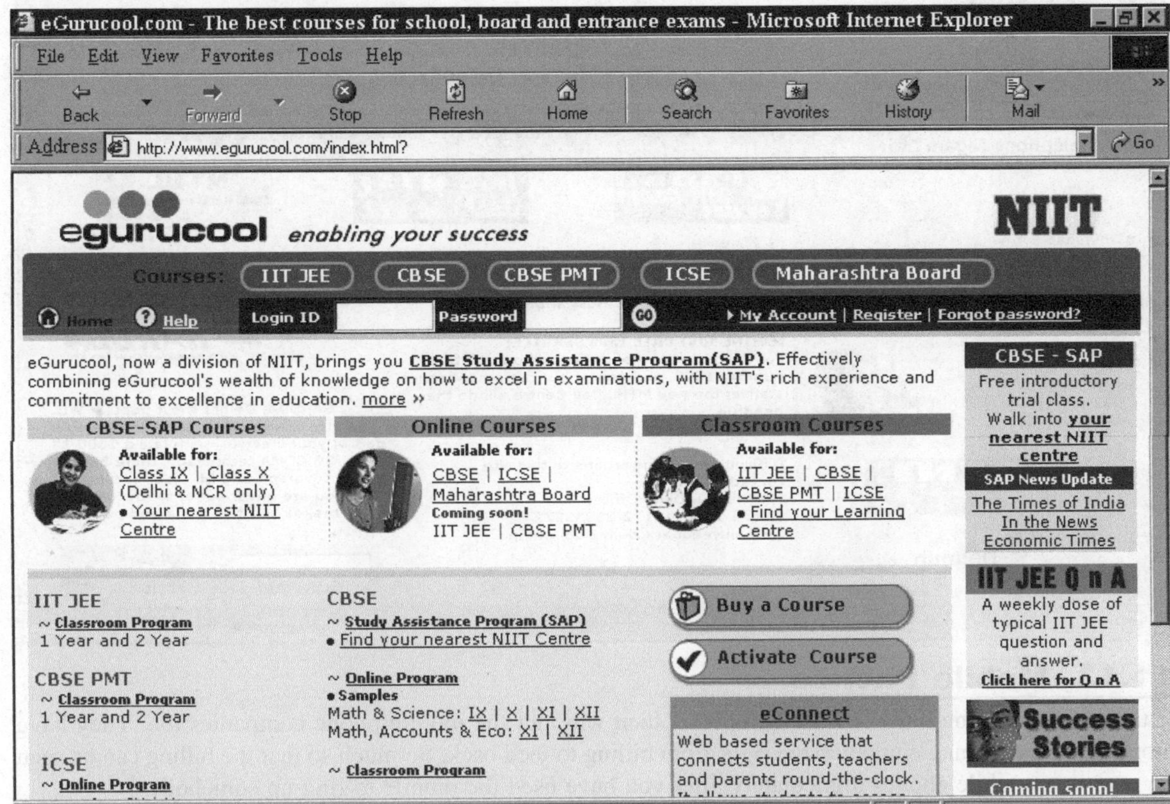

11.11 Video Games

I have yet to see a computer user who does not play games. This is why the computer gaming industry is in such a advanced stage. Lots of new games are introduced worldwide. Even there are games on the Internet which you can access and down load games from there. The gaming zone is one of the most popular sites for people to chat and play game at the same time. The site features mainly board games and card games, which you play online with other users.

11.12 Telephone Exchanges

I was involved at the initial level of computerization of telephone billing through computers. At that time the bills were being made manually and the gap between the closing period and bills used to be more than 2 months. This resulted in huge losses to the telephone department. Once we took over the billing on computer, the gap was reduced to 1 week and now the bills are made and the payments received within 1 month. Now Mahanagar Telephone Nigam Limited not only does the billing through computers but also the fault repair, telephone enquiry, billing reconciliation, etc., are done through using computers.

11.13 Mobile Phones

If the main telephone lines can use computers then why not the mobile phone companies too. They have more or less everything computerized right from billing to feed back. So much so that the billing can be seen on your own mobile phones immediately after you have used the mobile to ring up somebody.

11.14 Information kiosks

The first application that an office would take up for computerisation is Financial Accounting. No doubt it is the crucial aspect of the office. With most of the accounts on computers, the owner may not ask accountant to show him the books each time, he has to just look at his own computer to know where the company stands. In the next phase the company can take up applications like Inventory, Billing/Invoicing, Personel Management, Payroll, etc. With the advent of Microsoft Office software, most of the offices have their records maintained through this software which not only takes care of its documents but also of the finance too. What's if the boss wants to see the presentation, he can see that being prepared in no time.

11.15 Special Effects in Movies

Motion pictures have been using the animation techniques since the time of good old black and white cinema. Now the computers are used for total animation. In fact, a film called Toy Story was completely made by computers. The animation films are totally made on computers. There are software available which not only help you in doing this in minimum time but also help you in doing it fast. Most of the film's editing is also done on computers.

Like the tracks of the audio, the video films are also now-a-days made in tracks. This is the trick they use when the actor plays a double role. They shoot one track with one actor and the other track with another actor and then using the computer, they superimpose them to form a new image where both the actors and seen together.

Let us Revise

1. Internet usage is possible only because of computers.
2. Computers have negative effects too.
3. Initially computers were used for bulk jobs which were difficult to finish in time manually.
4. Computers are used for typesetting pages of the books, magazine, etc.
5. All reservations etc., of Railways is done through computers.
6. In Hospitals each patient's record is kept on computer.
7. Bookings of all the airlines of the world are linked through computers.
8. In banks all transactions are now done through computers.
9. With the arrival of Microsoft Office a small office's complete record can be kept on the computer.
10. In cinema most of the editing work is done on computer. Even animations created with the help of computers are widely used in cinema.

11. Video games are another example of computer usage.
12. Students of the various classes can get feed back from the various sites which are loaded with sample papers, notes, tip and tricks, etc.
13. Hotel bookings are all done through Internet and computers.
14. Most of insurance companies use computers for all their work.
15. Companies maintain their stock inventory through computers.
16. Most of the telephone billing is done through computers.
17. Mobile phones have everything computerized.
18. The new cars are designed on computers.
19. Using computers you can keep the track of the project completion.
20. Among the negative effects of the computers are: computer crimes, computer addiction and loss of jobs.

Multiple Choice Questions

1. The first film made completely using computers was
   (a) Toy Story (b) Toy Game (c) Toy Computer
2. Computers have negative effects too
   (a) Yes (b) No
3. Railways used computers first for:
   (a) wagon locations (b) reservations (c) financial accounting
4. Hotels get their bookings now using:
   (a) Internet (b) Postage (c) Telephone calls
5. Banks use computers for
   (a) all transactions (b) personnels (c) printing
6. For a company the most important application of computer is:
   (a) Inventory control (b) Correspondence (c) Both
7. New cars are designed on computers using:
   (a) Computer Aided Manufacturing
   (b) Word Processing
   (c) Desk Top Publishing
8. For creating pages of the books, magazines, the application used is:
   (a) Spreadsheet (b) Word Processing (c) Accounting

True/False Questions

1. Internet is the most important application of computer.
2. There are no negative effects of using computers.
3. Computers were first used for bulk jobs.
4. Computers are not used for creating pages of books, magazines.
5. All railway reservations are done through computers.
6. Most of the small offices use Microsoft Office software.
7. New cars are made using Word Processing.
8. Telephone bills are made using computers.
9. Stock inventory is not done using computers.

10. In Hospitals, computers are not used.
11. You cannot book a room in a hotel using computer and internet.
12. You cannot get addicted to computers.

Matching Columns

Match the text of the column A with the action of Column B.

Column A	Column B
A. Computer addiction	1. Computer Aided Manufacturing
B. Inventory Control	2. First computer job of Railways
C. Designing of cards	3. Patients records
D. Toy Story	4. A complete software for small office
E. Wagons placements	5. Negative effect of computer
F. Microsoft Office	6. First film made totally by computer
G Computers in Hospitals	7. Taking stock of the inventory through computers

Fill in the Blanks with appropriate words

a. Microsoft Office b. Inventory Control c. Wagon locations d. Computer Crime
e. Internet f. Toy Story g. Computers
h. Computer Aided Manufacturing

1. In Hospitals, patient records are kept using __________.
2. Designing of new cars is done using ____________.
3. Companies use computer for ______________.
4. First film made by computers was called ____________.
5. A small office can use ____________ for all its work.
6. ___________ is one of the negative aspect of computer.
7. Railways used computers first for _________.
8. Hotel booking is usually done using ________.

Descriptive Type Questions

1. How has Internet revolutionized computers?
2. What are the negative effects of computers?
3. Why was computer used for bulk jobs initially?
4. How is computer used in books and magazines?
5. How is computer used in Railways?
6. How is computer used in hospitals?
7. How is computer used in airlines industry?
8. Describe how the computers have helped banks.
9. Which is the best software for small office?
10. How are the computers used in cinema?
11. How are the computers used in education?
12. Describe how computers are used in hotels.
13. Why companies maintain inventory using computers?

14. How are computers used in telephones?
15. What is Computer Aided Manufacturing?
16. How would you use computers in project management?

Answers to Objective Type Questions

Multiple Choice Questions

1. a	2. a	3. a	4. a
5. a	6. a	7. a	8. b

True False Questions

1. T	2. F	3. T	4. F
5. T	6. T	7. F	8. T
9. F	10. F	11. F	12. F

Matching Columns

A. 5	B. 7	C. 1	D. 6
E. 2	F. 4	G. 3	

Fill in the Blanks

1. g	2. h	3. b	4. f
5. a	6. d	7. c	8. e

Sample Paper - 1

S1

Part A

Answer all questions, each of them carries one mark

Multiple Choice Questions

1. Computer uses ____________ number system.
   (a) Decimal (b) Binary (c) Octal
2. Binary system numbers are usually ________.
   (a) short (b) long (c) zeros
3. RAM stands for:
   (a) Random Allowed Memory (b) Ready Access Memory (c) Random Access Memory
4. For seeing the output, you use:
   (a) Monitor (b) Keyboard (c) Mouse
5. You can work with how many media in multimedia?
   (a) 1 (b) 2 (c) Many
6. Which is the most popular hardware for the multimedia creations?
   (a) PCs (b) Mini Computers (c) Mainframe Computers
7. A software package for creating printing artworks is called:
   (a) Word Processing (b) DTP (b) Spreadsheet
8. Which command is used to shift the command from one directory to another?
   (a) CD (b) MD (c) RD
9. Date and Time are available on the desktop at
   (a) Taskbar (b) My Computer (c) Recycle Bin
10. Network Neighborhood is a permanent icon on the desktop:
    (a) True (b) False
11. For accessing your networks you will use the icon
    (a) Recycle Bin (b) My Computer (c) Network Neighborhood
12. Amnong the 2 types of calculators, one is standard and the other one is?
    (a) Ordinary (b) Scientific (c) Physical
13. For sound recorder, what is necessary?
    (a) Speaker (b) Microphone (c) Mouse

14. Cost of Linux operating system is:

(a) $100 (b) $480 (c) Its FREE

15. In word processing, you manipulate ________

(a) numbers (b) text

16. For saving a document, you need to have ________ for it.

(a) Name (b) Surname

17. You can change the size of the text from:

(a) Formatting bar (b) Font dialog box (c) Both

18. You can change the line and para spacing from ________ dialog box.

(a) Font (b) Paragraph (c) Open

19. You can add picture in your document from the ________ menu.

(a) File (b) Edit (c) Insert

20. In text you can find a word and replace it with another word using command ________.

(a) Find (b) Replace (c) None

21. What are numbered from A to Z, etc?

(a) Rows (b) Cells (c) Columns

22. In Excel worksheets are given ______ cxtension.

(a) .xls (b) .doc (c) .bmp

23. PowerPoint is used for:

(a) Word processing (b) Spreadsheets (c) Presentations

Part B

Answer all questions, each of them carries one mark

True False Questions

1. ROM is used to store only the mathematical functions.
2. Files in DOS have 6 + 2 format.
3. A footer is printed at the bottom of the page.
4. A single word can be selected by double click.
5. A new paragraph is created by pressing Enter.
6. A word not be found while spell checking can be added to dictionary.
7. Date can be inserted in the header.
8. You do not have tables in Word.
9. Click at a cell to make it active.
10. You can move or copy a number of cells.
11. There are no 3D charts.
12. You can save a presentation with a name.

Part C

Answer all questions, each of them carries one mark

Matching Questions

A.	Directory listing page wise	1.	REN
B.	Font	2.	Combination of text and optional data
C.	Preview	3.	2D chart with values
D.	Merge	4.	Word processing program
E	Absolute reference	5.	DIR/P
F.	XY chart	6.	Looking before printing
G	Rename a file	7.	Output device
H.	MS Word	8.	Text style
I.	Laser printer	9.	Central Processing Unit
J.	CPU	10.	Refers to an absolute location of a specific cell

Part D

Answer all questions, each of them carries one mark

Fill in the Blanks with Appropriate Words

(a)	Modem	(b)	LOGO	(c)	Presentations
(d)	Cursor	(e)	Justify	(f)	10
(g)	Paint	(h)	Paragraph	(i)	Taskbar
(j)	=Sign	(k)	Standard	(l)	Function keys

1. For connecting to Internet, ________ is a must.
2. Word supports alignments like Left, Right, Center and ______ .
3. Decimal systems have the base __________.
4. For creating drawings, you would use ____________.
5. Sum function needs to have ______ before it.
6. A computer language which is used for drawing pictures on the screen is ________.
7. Blinking point which shows your position in the text is called ___________.
8. In programming, you use the __________ keys.
9. You can insert a table from _________ toolbar.
10. Date and Time are available on the desktop at __________.
11. You can change the line and para spacing from ______ dialog box.
12. PowerPoint is used for ______________.

Part E

Answer any 10 questions, each of them carries five marks

Descriptive Type Questions

1. Which are the various number systems in use?
2. How would you convert a Binary number to its Decimal counterpart?
3. How would you convert an Octal number to Hexadecimal number?
4. Describe the various functions of CPU.
5. Describe the various type of keys on the keyboard.
6. What is multimedia?
7. Describe the various language translators.
8. Describe the Rename command.
9. What is the command to display a directory pagewise?
10. How would you start Windows 98?
11. What is Recycle Bin used for?
12. What is the function of Windows Explorer?
13. How would you access the various accessories of the Windows?
14. If you have a Video CD, how would you run it on your computer?
15. What is Linux?
16. What are the feautes of Linux?
17. What is word processing?
18. Describe the process of saving a document.
19. Describe the process of making the text, Bold, Italics and Underline.
20. How would you allot page numbers to various pages in your document?
21. How would you insert graphics into your document?
22. How are Bullets and Numering used?
23. Describe the various options of table alignments.
24. Which are the various methods of starting Excel?
25. Describe the process of modifying chart.
26. Describe how the logical functions work in worksheet.
27. How would you protect your worksheet?
28. How would you copy entries between workbooks?
29. How would you start PowerPoint?

Part F

Answers to Objective Type Questions

Multiple Choice Questions

A.1.	b	A.2.	a	A.3.	c	A.4.	a
A.5.	c	A.6.	a	A.7.	b	A.8.	a
A.9.	a	A.10	a	A.11	c	A.12	b
A.13	a	A.14.	c	A.15.	b	A.16	a
A.17.	c	A.18	b	A.19	c	A.20	b
A.21.	c	A.22.	a	A.23	c		

True False Questions

B.1.	F	B.2.	F	B.3.	T	B.4	T
B.5.	T	B.6.	T	B.7.	T	B.8	F
B.9.	T	B.10.	T	B.11.	F	B.12.	T

Matching Questions

C.A.	5	C.B.	8	C.C.	6	C.D.	2
C.E.	10	C.F.	3	C.G	1	C.H.	4
C.I.	7	C.J.	9				

Fill in the Blanks with appropriate words

D.1.	a	D.2.	e	D.3.	f	D.4.	g
D.5.	j	D.6.	b	D.7.	d	D.8.	l
D.9.	k	D.10.	i	D.11.	h	D.12.	c

This page left blank for rough work

Sample Paper - 2

S2

Part A

Answer all questions, each of them carries one mark

Multiple Choice Questions

1. Hexadecimal system has a base of ________.

   (a) 2 (b) 8 (c) 16

2. Octal number system uses numbers from 0 to ____________.

   (a) 8 (b) 16 (c) F

3. RAM consists of binary numbers 1s and :

   (a) 0s (b) 2s (c) 3s

4. In programming, you use the following keys:

   (a) Arrow keys (b) Function keys (c) Alpha keys

5. A multimedia project can be active?

   (a) Yes (b) No

6. Can you create a multimedia project alone?

   (a) Yes (b) No

7. Computer language used on Internet is

   (a) PASCAL (b) JAVA (c) BASIC

8. Which command would you use to create a new directory?

   (a) CD (b) MD (c) RD

9. All the deleted files go to

   (a) Taskbar (b) My Computer (c) Recycle Bin

10. Various programs can be accessed from the ________ button.

    (a) Start (b) End (c) Taskbar

11. You keep your personal files/folders in

    (a) My Folder (b) My Documents (c) My Files

12. Which accessory would you use to schedule you tasks?

    (a) Disk Cleanup (b) Disk Defragmenter (c) Task Scheduler

13. For Phone dialer, what extra equipment you need to have in your computer?

    (a) Mouse (b) Printer (c) Modem

14. Windows version of Linux is:
    (a) L Windows (b) X Windows (c) M Windows
15. You can set Left, Right and ______ alignment in word processing.
    (a) Center (b) Justify (c) Both
16. For opening an existing document, you need to give _____ command.
    (a) New (b) Open (c) Close
17. You click at I to make the text
    (a) Bold (b) Italics (c) Underline
18. Header appears at the ______ of the page.
    (a) Top (b) Bottom (c) Center
19. Clip Art is
    (a) Text (b) Graphics (c) Both
20. You can insert a table from _________ toolbar.
    (a) Formatting (b) Standard (c) Drawing
21. You can move around the worksheet using which buttons?
    (a) Scroll (b) Logic (c) Start
22. Formula which can be used directly from the Standard toolbar is
    (a) AutoSum (b) Auto (c) Sum
23. AutoContent Wizard creates a
    (a) Document (b) Presentation (c) Spreadsheet

Part B

Answer all questions, each of them carries one mark

True False Questions

1. CD ROM cannot be used as output.
2. Operating system is a must for computer.
3. Headers are printed on top of the page.
4. You can make the text Bold and Italics in Word.
5. You can see more text by scrolling.
6. You cannot have columanar text.
7. You cannot find a word in a Word document.
8. A page can be previewed before printing.
9. Standard width of a column is 18.43.
10. In Excel text is aligned to the left.
11. Charts once made cannot be changed.
12. Slide show allows you to see the presentation.

Part C

Answer all questions, each of them carries one mark

Matching Questions

A.	Directory listing width wise	1.	An easy way to create document
B.	Header	2.	Horizontal set of cells
C.	Menu	3.	Combination of cols letter and row number of cell
D.	Wizard	4.	Line tracing progress
E.	Row	5.	DIR/W
F.	Cell reference	6.	Spreadsheet program
G	Trendline	7.	Output device
H.	MS Excel	8.	To be put at top of document
I.	Dot Matrix Printer	9.	Arithmetic and Logical Unit
J.	ALU	10.	Containing a list of commands

Part D

Answer all questions, each of them carries one mark

Fill in the Blanks with Appropriate Words

(a)	My Documents	(b)	Icons	(c)	Presentations
(d)	101	(e)	8	(f)	Red Hat
(g)	Monitor	(h)	Character Map	(i)	= sign
(j)	Chart Wizard	(k)	Top	(l)	Its FREE
(m)	COBOL				

1. A computer program used for Business applications is ______.
2. Popular distributor of Linux is __________.
3. In Excel formula starts with ___________.
4. Various applications and documents are represented on the Windows desktop by _____.
5. Charts are created using which option __________.
6. Keyboard has ________ number of keys.
7. For seeing how the various fonts look, you would use ___________.
8. Octal number system uses numbers from 0 to ___________.
9. You keep your personal files/folders in ___________.
10. Header appears at the ______ of the page.
11. For seeing the output, you use ___________.
12. Cost of Linux operating system is _________.
13. PowerPoint is used for ______________.

Part E

Answer any 10 questions, each of them carries five marks

Descriptive Type Questions

1. What is the base of Decimal system?
2. Which steps are used in Decimal number addition?
3. What is hexadecimal system?
4. What does CPU consist of ?
5. Describe the various types of mouse available.
6. How would you assemble a multimedia project?
7. Which are the various popular software packages?
8. What is the command to remove all files in a directory?
9. What is the command to display a directory widthwise?
10. Describe the various items on the desktop of Windows 98.
11. What is the significance of Network Neighborhood?
12. Describe the various components of a Windows dialog box.
13. Describe the various Internet tools.
14. How would you see the shape of various fonts?
15. How was Linux developed?
16. What is meant by Linux distribution?
17. What are the various features of word processing?
18. How would you set the timing for AutoSave?
19. Describe the various options of Font dialog box.
20. How is spell checking ?
21. What is a Clip Art? How would you add a clip art in your text.
22. Describe the various options of Borders and Shading.
23. How would you add rows and columns in a table?
24. Describe the various components of the Excel worksheet window.
25. How would you add data to the chart?
26. Describe how would you put Headers and Footers in a worksheet.
27. How would you name a range of cells?
28. Write down the steps to protect the workbook.
29. Describe the process of creating a presentation using AutoContent Wizard.

Part F

Answers to Objective Type Questions

Multiple Choice Questions

A.1.	c	A.2.	a	A.3.	a	A.4.	b
A.5.	a	A.6.	b	A.7.	b	A.8.	b
A.9.	c	A.10	a	A.11	b	A.12	c
A.13	c	A.14.	b	A.15.	c	A.16	b
A.17.	b	A.18	a	A.19	b	A.20	a
A.21.	a	A.22.	a	A.23	b		

True False Questions

B.1.	F	B.2.	T	B.3.	T	B.4	T
B.5.	T	B.6.	F	B.7.	F	B.8	T
B.9.	T	B.10.	T	B.11.	F	B.12.	T

Matching Questions

C.A.	5	C.B.	8	C.C.	10	C.D.	1
C.E.	2	C.F.	3	C.G	4	C.H.	6
C.I.	7	C.J.	9				

Fill in the Blanks with appropriate words

D.1.	m	D.2.	f	D.3.	i	D.4.	b
D.5.	j	D.6.	d	D.7.	h	D.8.	e
D.9.	a	D.10.	k	D.11.	g	D.12.	l
D.13.	c						

This page left blank for rough work

Sample Paper - 3

S3

Part A

Answer all questions, each of them carries one mark

Multiple Choice Questions

1. Decimal system uses the numbers from 0 to ______.
   (a) 8 (b) 9 (c) 16
2. Hexadecimal number system uses numbers from 0 to ____________.
   (a) 8 (b) 16 (c) F
3. CPU contains Primary Storage, Arithmetic Logic Unit and
   (a) Control Unit (b) Data Unit (c) Alpha Unit
4. Keyboard has ________ number of keys.
   (a) 100 (b) 88 (c) 101
5. Which software is usually used for making overhead presentations?
   (a) Microsoft Frontpage (b) Microsoft Powerpoint (c) Microsoft Word
6. A computer language which is used for drawing pictures on the screen is:
   (a) LOGO (b) COBOL (c) BASIC
7. You can share a printer with Networking.
   (a) Yes (b) No
8. The main directory of the hard disk is:
   (a) Main directory (b) Root directory (c) Final directory
9. Help menu is available at which button:
   (a) Taskbar (b) Start (b) End
10. How many recent documents are shown in the documents window:
    (a) 14 (b) 15 (c) 16
11. Title bar is part of
    (a) Taskbar (b) Windows dialog box (c) Desktop
12. For fragmenting you hard disk which accessory you would use:
    (a) Disk Fragmenter (b) Tools (c) Fragmenter
13. For seeing how the various fonts look, you would use:
    (a) Font (b) See (c) Character Map

14. Linux can be loaded on PC:

(a) Yes (b) No

15. Blinking point which shows your position in the text is called:

(a) Cursor (b) Blinker (c) Position

16. You can select the text by:

(a) Keyboard (b) Mouse (c) Both

17. You can change the font of the text from

(a) Formatting bar (b) Font dialog box (c) Box

18. Footer appears at the ________ of the page

(a) Top (b) Bottom (c) Center

19. WordArt is a

(a) Text (b) Graphic (c) Independent program

20. You can align data vertically in a table:

(a) Yes (b) No

21. For getting the short menu on the screen, you click which button of the mouse.

a. Right button b. Left button c. Centre button

22. The result of AutoCalculate is shown at ________ bar.

(a) Standard (b) Formatting (c) Status

23. You can view your presentation through various views :

(a) Yes (b) No

Part B

Answer all questions, each of them carries one mark

True False Questions

1. Printers are input devices.
2. DIR and Directory commands are some.
3. You cannot have graphics in word processing program.
4. A file can be saved by clicking at Save button on the formatting bar.
5. You can change text with Find and Replace.
6. Fonts are part of MS Word.
7. There are no templates in MS Word.
8. Print button is on formatting bar.
9. You cannot move the active cell within a selected range.
10. Width of column cannot be changed.
11. It is not possible to preview a chart.
12. Text cannot be inserted in presentation slides.

Part C

Answer all questions, each of them carries one mark

Matching Questions

A.	Make directory	1.	A series of rows and columns
B.	Footer	2.	Vertical set of cells
C.	Dialog box	3.	A combination of rows and columns
D.	Table	4.	To be put at the bottom
E.	Columns	5.	Working with one presentation slide at a time
F.	Range	6.	Operating system
G	Normal view	7.	MD
H.	MS Windows	8.	Storage device
I.	Hard disk	9.	A box displaying options
J.	DOS	10.	Disk Operating System

Part D

Answer all questions, each of them carries one mark

Fill in the Blanks with Appropriate Words

(a)	Italics	(b)	CD/	(c)	Status
(d)	CD ROM	(e)	Control unit	(f)	Mailmerge
(g)	Speaker	(h)	Recycle Bin	(i)	Printer
(i)	.lx	(j)	Windows Media Player	(k)	Dialog box
(l)	Random Access Memory				

1. Most popular media for multimedia packaging is ________.
2. For viewing Video CDs you would use ________.
3. Sending of same letter to different people is done by ________.
4. The command ________ transfers to the root directory.
5. For printing a document you have to have ________ on.
6. CPU contains Primary Storage, Arithmetic Logic Unit and ________.
7. Title bar is part of ________.
8. The result of AutoCalculate is shown at ________ bar.
9. All the deleted files go to ________.
10. You click at I to make the text ________.
11. RAM stands for ________.
12. For sound recorder, ________ is necessary.
13. In Excel worksheets are given ______ extension.

Part E

Answer any 10 questions, each of them carries five marks

Descriptive Type Questions

1. What is the base of Binary system?
2. What is an Octal system?
3. What is a Subscript?
4. What are Registers? What function do they play?
5. Describe the various types of optical recognition devices.
6. Describe the process of planning a multimedia project.
7. What are assembly and machine languages?
8. Is it possible to remove the root directory of your hard disk by using the RD command? If yes, how?
9. What is the root directory?
10. What type of icons are there on the desktop?
11. Describe the various features of Taskbar.
12. What is the purpose of Disk clean up?
13. Which all games are there in Windows?
14. If you have to dial from your computer, what would you use?
15. How can you use Linux as an operating system?
16. What are the minimum requirements for Linux working on PC?
17. Describe the various methods of starting Microsoft Word.
18. If you do not save before closing, what will happen?
19. How would you change the size and font of the text?
20. Describe the various options of Print dialog box.
21. Describe the process of wrapping text around the graphic.
22. Describe the various Tabs supported by Word and how they are used?
23. Describe the complete process of MailMerge.
24. Describe the method of copying formula.
25. Describe the process of creating a Pivot Table Report.
26. How would you merge two worksheets?
27. Describe the various type of references.
28. Which mathematical symbols are used in Microsoft Excel formulas?
29. How would you create a presentation using the various slide options?

Part F

Answers to Objective Type Questions

Multiple Choice Questions

A.1.	b	A.2.	b	A.3.	a	A.4.	c
A.5.	b	A.6.	a	A.7.	a	A.8.	b
A.9.	b	A.10	b	A.11	b	A.12	a
A.13	c	A.14.	a	A.15.	a	A.16	c
A.17.	a	A.18	b	A.19	c	A.20	a
A.21.	a	A.22.	c	A.23	a		

True False Questions

B.1.	F	B.2.	T	B.3.	F	B.4	T
B.5.	T	B.6.	F	B.7.	F	B.8	T
B.9.	F	B.10.	F	B.11.	F	B.12.	F

Matching Questions

C.A.	7	C.B.	4	C.C.	9	C.D.	1
C.E.	2	C.F.	3	C.G	5	C.H.	6
C.I.	8	C.J.	10				

Fill in the Blanks with appropriate words

D.1.	d	D.2.	j	D.3.	f	D.4.	b
D.5.	i	D.6.	e	D.7.	k	D.8.	c
D.9.	h	D.10.	a	D.11.	l	D.12.	g
D.13.	i						

This page left blank for rough work

Sample Paper - 4 S4

Part A

Answer all questions, each of them carries one mark

Multiple Choice Questions

1. Decimal systems have the base ________.
   (a) 8 (b) 10 (c) 16
2. Subscript to signify the type of number system is put at the ________ of the number.
   (a) Right (b) Left (c) Center
3. System software controls:
   (a) Hard disk (b) Internal computer system (c) Floppy disk
4. With CD you can:
   (a) Read (b) Write (c) Both
5. What is usually used for displaying information at public places?
   (a) Monitors (b) Overhead projections (c) Touch screen kiosks
6. Computer program which controls the operations of computer is called:
   (a) Assembler (b) Operating System (c) Interpreter
7. Local Area Network cannot be used within the city:
   (a) Yes (b) No
8. Which command will always transfer to the root directory?
   (a) CD\ (b) CD/ (c) CD
9. Various applications and documents are represented on the Windows desktop by:
   (a) Symbols (b) Labels (c) Icons
10. For searching various files, folders, etc., on the hard disk, you use
    (a) Search (b) Find (c) Locate
11. Which accessory allows you to see the items in bigger size in Windows?
    (a) Mirror (b) Bigger (c) Magnifier
12. For creating drawings, you would use:
    (a) Drawing (b) Paint (c) Painter
13. A small word processing program available in Accessories is called:
    (a) Word (b) Processing (c) Word Pad

14. Database available on Linux is known as:
    (a) mSQL (b) lSQL (c) Not available
15. You can start Microsoft Word by using ________ button.
    (a) New (b) Start (c) Program
16. You click at B to make the text
    (a) Bold (b) Italics (c) Underline
17. You click at U to make the text
    (a) Bold (b) Italics (c) Underline
18. For printing a document you have to have ________ on.
    (a) Printer (b) Monitor (c) Scanner
19. You can set ________ by using the dialog box.
    (a) Font (b) Page Setup (c) Margins
20. Can you insert more rows in a table?
    (a) Yes (b) No
21. Charts are created using which option.
    (a) Chart Wizard (b) Pivot Table (c) Pie Chart
22. Sum function needs to have ______ before it.
    (a) + (b) – (c) =
23. A slide with background picture can be created in PowerPoint:
    (a) Yes (b) No

Part B

Answer all questions, each of them carries one mark

True False Questions

1. Spell checking is part of word processing.
2. Deleted objects go to Recycle Bin.
3. To highlight the complete paragraph, you double click.
4. Backspace key can be used to remove character.
5. As you type the cursor also moves.
6. Character spacing cannot be changed.
7. You can use Wizards to create documents.
8. Mail merge is an application of word processing.
9. Last coloumn of a worksheet in IV.
10. You can copy formatting from one cell to another.
11. You can print a worksheet in landscape mode.
12. You can add a clipart in a slide.

Part C

Answer all questions, each of them carries one mark

Matching Questions

A.	Change directory	1.	Cell ready to accept data
B.	For making bold face	2.	An Excel function
C.	Insertion point	3.	CD
D.	Portrait	4.	Allows you to enter, cut, copy text
E.	Active cell	5.	Its the point from where you can enter text
F.	AVG	6.	Output device
G	Outline view	7.	Ctrl + B
H.	MS Powerpoint	8.	Magnetic Ink Character Reader
I.	Monitor	9.	Vertical page
J.	MICR	10.	Presentation software

Part D

Answer all questions, each of them carries one mark

Fill in the Blanks with Appropriate Words

(a)	Right	(b)	Scientific	(c)	Run
(d)	Binary	(f)	15	(g)	Operating System
(h)	Columns	(i)	Landscape	(j)	Open
(k)	16	(l)	Bold	(m)	Text and Pictures

1. A scanner scans ________ and ________.
2. You can also run applications from the _____ dialog box.
3. Two main orientations are, Potrait and __________.
4. Computer program which controls the operations of computer is called _______.
5. You click at B to make the text ______.
6. Hexadecimal number system uses numbers from 0 to ____________.
7. You can see _________ recent documents in the documents window.
8. For getting the short menu on the screen, you click _____ button of the mouse.
9. For opening an existing document, you need to give _____ command.
10. Computer uses ____________ number system.
11. Among the 2 types of calculators, one is standard and the other one is _________.
12. The _________ are numbered from A to Z, etc.

Part E

Answer any 10 questions, each of them carries five marks

Descriptive Type Questions

1. What is the drawback of Binary system?
2. How would you convert an Octal number to Decimal number?
3. How is a Hexadecimal number converted to Decimal number?
4. What happens inside ALU?
5. What is a trackball?
6. Describe what all you need for a multimedia project in terms of Hardware, Software?
7. What is Internet?
8. Type the command to remove a directory. Where must the cursor be to remove a directory or subdirectory?
9. What does the symbol \(backslash) stand for?
10. What all is available on the Start button?
11. How would you change the features of Taskbar?
12. For what purpose do you use Disk Defragmenter?
13. How would you schedule various tasks for maintainance?
14. If you have to create a drawing, which program would you use?
15. Is Linux a multiuser operating system?
16. How does Linux support the file system?
17. Describe the various items on the screen of Word.
18. Describe the process of opening an existing document.
19. What is an alignment? Describe the various alignments supported by Word.
20. Describe the various editing tools of Word.
21. What is WordArt? Describe the process of creating a WordArt text.
22. Describe the process of finding a word and replacing it with another.
23. How would you enter a chart in your document?
24. Describe the process of saving a worksheet.
25. How would you audit a worksheet? Explain.
26. Describe the method of putting Outlines to worksheets.
27. Describe the command Goal Seek.
28. How would you use AutoSum?
29. Describe the various views of looking at presentations in PowerPoint.

Part F

Answers to Objective Type Questions

Multiple Choice Questions

A.1.	b	A.2.	a	A.3.	b	A.4.	c
A.5.	c	A.6.	b	A.7.	b	A.8.	a
A.9.	c	A.10	b	A.11	c	A.12	b
A.13	c	A.14.	a	A.15.	b	A.16	a
A.17.	c	A.18	a	A.19	c	A.20	a
A.21.	a	A.22.	c	A.23	a		

True False Questions

B.1.	T	B.2.	T	B.3.	F	B.4	T
B.5.	T	B.6.	F	B.7.	T	B.8	T
B.9.	T	B.10.	T	B.11.	T	B.12.	T

Matching Questions

C.A.	3	C.B.	7	C.C.	4	C.D.	9
C.E.	1	C.F.	2	C.G	5	C.H.	10
C.I.	6	C.J.	8				

Fill in the Blanks with appropriate words

D.1.	m	D.2.	c	D.3.	i	D.4.	g
D.5.	l	D.6.	k	D.7.	f	D.8.	a
D.9.	j	D.10.	d	D.11.	b	D.12.	h

This page left blank for rough work

Sample Paper - 5

S5

Part A

Answer all questions, each of them carries one mark

Multiple Choice Questions

1. A Binary system number can be represented as 0 and ________.
   (a) 1 (b) 8 (c) 16
2. Binary 1111 1111 1111 can be represented as __________ in Octal system.
   (a) 7777 (b) FFFF (c) 0101
3. Data stored in ROM cannot be changed:
   (a) Yes (b) No
4. A scanner scans
   (a) Pictures (b) Text (c) Both
5. Which is the most popular media for multimedia packaging?
   (a) Floppy disk (b) CD-ROM (c) Hard disk
6. A computer program used for Business applications is:
   (a) LOGO (b) COBOL (c) BASIC
7. For connecting to Internet, which is a must:
   (a) Modem (b) Telephone line (c) Both
8. The files in DOS are named in which format ?
   (a) 9+2 (b) 10+1 (c) 8+3
9. Which version of Windows is discussed in this book:
   (a) 95 (b) 2000 (c) 98
10. You can also run applications from the _____ dialog box.
    (a) Start (b) End (c) Run
11. For setting up your modem to access for using Internet, you would use which accessory?
    (a) Dial up networking (b) Monitor (c) CDPlayer
12. For viewing Video CDs you would use:
    (a) CD Player (b) Windows Media Player (c) Video
13. Solatire is a :
    (a) System tool (b) Game (c) Internet tool

14. Popular distributor of Linux is:
(a) Red Hat (b) Blue Hat (c) Green Hat

15. For creating a document, you use _____ command at File menu.
(a) New (b) Open (c) Document

16. Can you emboss you text?
(a) Yes (b) No

17. Word supports alignments like Left, Right, Center and ______
(a) Justify (b) Up (c) Down

18. Most of the editing tools are available under ______ menu.
(a) File (b) Format (c) Edit

19. Two main orientations are, Potrait and
(a) Landscape (b) Photo (c) Lying

20. Sending of same letter to different people is done by:
(a) Send (b) Letter (c) Mailmerge

21. In Excel formula starts with ___________.
(a) = sign (b) + sign (c) - sign

22. To access to any formula in Microsoft Excel, you need to go through _____
(a) Function Wizard (b) File (c) Formula

23. You can even have textured patterns in the background of a slide:
(a) Yes (b) No

Part B

Answer all questions, each of them carries one mark

True False Questions

1. Light pens and joysticks are both pointing devices.
2. Networking is not supported by LINUX.
3. Margins are the distances between text and corners of paper.
4. You cannot UNDO your operation in MS Word.
5. Normal view of the text is 100%.
6. You can use any point size for the font.
7. Different cells can have different heights.
8. Word Art creates text in presentable form.
9. Date and Time is not numeric data in Excel.
10. Functions are not part of Excel.
11. Presentation can be seen in various views.
12. An organizational chart is used to represent an organization.

Part C

Answer all questions, each of them carries one mark

Matching Questions

A.	Remove directory	1.	Giving a new name to a sheet
B.	For making italics	2.	A button to calculate sum
C.	Spelling button	3.	Displays multiple slides
D.	Landscape	4.	Ctrl + I
E	Sheet renaming	5.	Operating system
F.	AutoSum	6.	Input device
G	Slide sorter view	7.	Programming language
H.	LINUX	8.	To check spelling of the document
I.	Keyboard	9.	RD
J.	COBOL	10.	Horizontal page

Part D

Answer all questions, each of them carries one mark

Fill in the Blanks with Appropriate Words

(a)	Presentation	(b)	JAVA	(c)	Start
(d)	Insert	(e)	9	(f)	Bottom
(g)	X Windows	(h)	Edit	(i)	1
(j)	Root directory	(k)	Windows 98	(l)	Network Neighborhood
(m)	Internal computer system				

1. A Binary system number can be represented as 0 and ___________.
2. Popular version of Windows is ______.
3. Most of the editing tools are available under _____ menu.
4. System software controls ________.
5. You can start Microsoft Word by using __________ button.
6. Decimal system uses the numbers from 0 to ______.
7. The main directory of the hard disk is __________.
8. Footer appears at the ________ of the page.
9. Computer language used on Internet is __________.
10. Windows version of Linux is __________.
11. AutoContent Wizard creates a __________.
12. For accessing your networks you will use the icon _________.
13. You can add picture in your document from the _______ menu.

Part E

Answer any 10 questions, each of them carries five marks

Descriptive Type Questions

1. How would you convert a Decimal number to its Binary counterpar?
2. How would you convert an Octal number to Binary number?
3. How is a Hexadecimal number converted to Decimal number?
4. Describe the various characteristics of computers?
5. What is the difference between Impact and Non-impact printers?
6. What are the different type of system software?
7. Describe the process of connecting to Internet.
8. What are the different options of the DIR command?
9. What display does your monitor show when you type CD?
10. What all is there in My Computer?
11. How can you run an application in Windows?
12. Which accessory would you use to connect computers?
13. How would you control the volume of the CDPlayer?
14. How would you connect various computers?
15. How can Linux be obtained?
16. What is X Windows?
17. How would you create a new document?
18. Describe the various methods of selection of text.
19. Describe the various options of Paragraph dialog box.
20. Describe the various shortcuts attached to editing tools.
21. Describe the various options of Page Setup.
22. How would you create a table in your document?
23. How would you use Wizard to create your bio-data?
24. Describe how would you insert a chart in the worksheet.
25. Describe the process of inserting a comment in the worksheet.
26. How would you put labels on your rows and columns of the worksheet?
27. Describe the process of naming sheets.
28. Describe the process of using AutoCalculate.
29. Describe the process of entering text into slides.

Part F

Answers to Objective Type Questions

Multiple Choice Questions

A.1.	a	A.2.	b	A.3.	a	A.4.	c
A.5.	b	A.6.	b	A.7.	c	A.8.	c
A.9.	c	A.10	c	A.11	a	A.12	b
A.13	b	A.14.	a	A.15.	a	A.16	a
A.17.	a	A.18	c	A.19	a	A.20	c
A.21.	a	A.22.	a	A.23	a		

True False Questions

B.1.	F	B.2.	F	B.3.	T	B.4	F
B.5.	T	B.6.	F	B.7.	F	B.8	T
B.9.	F	B.10.	F	B.11.	T	B.12.	T

Matching Questions

C.A.	9	C.B.	4	C.C.	8	C.D.	10
C.E.	1	C.F.	2	C.G	3	C.H.	5
C.I.	6	C.J.	7				

Fill in the Blanks with appropriate words

D.1.	i	D.2.	k	D.3.	h	D.4.	m
D.5.	c	D.6.	e	D.7.	j	D.8.	f
D.9.	b	D.10.	g	D.11.	a	D.12.	l
D.13.	d						

This page left blank for rough work

Glossary

G

Abort To exit a function or application midway and without saving any data that has been changed. It is also, in DOS commands, the option for cancelling a command that cannot be implemented (for example, trying a DIR of A: without a floppy in it). The key combination - Ctrl+Break or Esc also abort commands.

Accept This command is used to accept the character string from the screen.

Active window The open window in respect of Microsoft Windows programs which a program is being executed. In respect of Clipper debugger, window to which all key strokes (except those valid in the command window) apply.

Add button This button moves the highlighted field from the available fields list box to the selected fields list box.

Add All button This button moves the highlighted field from the available fields list box to be selected fields list box.

Address (1) Number of a particular memory or peripheral storage location. Each byte of memory and each disk sector have its own unique address. Programs are compiled into machine language, which references actual addresses in the computer. (2) As a verb, to mange or work with. For example, "The computer can address 2MB of memory."

Alphanumeric Use of alphabetic letters mixed with numbers and special characters as in name, address, city and state. The text you are reading is alphanumeric.

AND A conjunction. It gives the result as True if both the conditions are true, otherwise false.

Append To add data to the end of an existing structure. For example, the dBASE APPEND commands starts the data entry mode and allows users to add records to the end of the file. Also refers to adding a text block at the end of a file in word processing applications. In DOS, a text file can be attached (appended) to the end of another text file.

Argument In programming, a value that is passed between programs; subroutines or functions. Arguments are independent items or variables, that contain data or codes. When an argument is used to customize a program for a user, it is typically called a parameter.

Arithmetic operators Symbols for arithmetic functions: + for 'add', - for 'subtract', * for 'multiply', / for 'divide'.

AArray Ordered arrangement of data elements. A vector is a one dimensional array, a matrix is a two-dimensional array. Most programming languages have the ability to store and manipulate arrays in one or more dimensions. Multi-dimensional arrays are used extensively in scientific simulation and mathematical processing; however, an array can be as simple as a pricing table held in memory for instant access by an order entry program.

ASCII (American Standard Code for Information Interchange) Pronounced "ass-key." It is a binary code for data that is used in communications, mostly in minicomputers and all personal computers. ASCII is a 7-bit code providing 128 possible character combinations, the first 32 of which are used for printing and transmission control. Since the common storage unit is an 8-bit byte (256 combinations) and ASCII uses only 128, the extra bit is used to hold a parity bit or special symbols. For example, the PC uses the additional values for foreign language and graphics symbols. In the Macintosh, the additional values can be user-defined to enhance a font.

Attribute In many word processing and graphics

programs a character emphasis, such as boldface and italic and other characteristics such as typeface and type size. In MS-DOS and Microsoft Windows 95, information about a file that indicates whether the file is a read-only file, a hidden file or a system file.

Auxiliary storage Same as secondary shortage.

Backup Additional resources or duplicate copies of data on different storage media for emergency purposes.

Backup files To make a duplicate copy of a file or disk for safe keeping. A spare copy of data used for when things go wrong and to avoid the disaster which can follow the damaging or corruption of disks or data. All users should have at least one duplicate copy or backup of their program or data though more would be advisable. The ancestral file method offers additional security for data. Back-up copies may or may not be working copies of the original file.

Band (1) Range of frequencies used for transmitting a signal. A band call can be identified by the difference between its lower and upper limits as well as by its actual lower and upper limits, for example, "a 10MHz band in the 100 to 110MHz range." (2) Contiguous group of tracks that are treated as a unit. (3) Printing element in a band printer.

Bar code A set of lines of varying widths which can be read by passing a light pen across them. On house hold goods there may be 30 lines giving a unique 13-digit code number to each product. When the cashier records this price from memory and is able to register that there is now one less of that item in stock. Library cards and library books sometimes have bar codes, though with more lines. The borrowing of books during the day is recorded on to tape by means of a light pen and the data is transferred to the computer at the end of the day.

Batch processing Processing a group of transactions at one time. Transactions are collected and processed against the master files (master files updated) at the end of the day or some other time period. Contrast with transaction processing.

Block A group of related items (records, characters, etc.) handled as a unit during input and output. A section of program coding treated as a unit.

Browse To View and possibly edit a file on screen like text in a word processing document. Browse commands let the user scroll through the data horizontally by the field and vertically by row or screen to view and edit the class hierarchy of the objects in an object-oriented programming language.

Bubble memory A form of static memory which uses impregnated garnet as the storage medium. It is a garnet chip enclosing one or more thin layers of magnetic film. A bubble represents the presence of a bit and the lack of a bubble represented the absence of a bit.

Buffer Reserved segment of memory used to hold data while it is being processed. In a program, buffers are created to hold some amount of data from each of the files that will be read or written. A buffer may also be a small memory bank used for special purposes.

Cache memory A high-speed temporary storage area in the CPU for storing parts of program or data during processing. This is used to hold another copy of data which has recently been accessed by the microprocessor in anticipation of its use again in the near future. When next needed the data can be accessed very quickly, though the least accessed data in cache memory is replaced by newly accessed data.

Call by value In programming, a call to a subroutine that passes the actual data of the parameters used in the subroutine.

Candidate It is like a primary key index, except that you can have more than one candidate index per table.

Case sensitive Distinguishing lower case from upper case. In a case sensitive language, 'a' is treated differently than 'A'.

Clause A class of commnds that have a specific goal. A clause may control the format of displayed or printed information, or the structure of a table.

Clipboard A temporary storage location used to transfer data between documents and between applications. Typically, you transfer data to the Clipboard by using an application's Copy or Cut command and you insert data from the Clipboard by using the application's Paste command. You use Clipboard Viewer to the view the contents of the Clipboard. Clipboards usually produce ASCII text files and can store graphics files.

Command A word or phrase usually found in a menu that you choose in order to carry out an action. You choose a command from a menu or type a command at the MS-DOS prompt. You can also type a command in the run dialog box in File Manager or program Manager. An instruction given to the CPU rather by a software application, for example: a database package initiating the creation of a new file, or directly by the computer via the operating system. For example, on a VAX machine the command DIR lists the currently available files. In either case the command (if it is valid) will be converted to machine code and acted upon by the CPU.

Command file A series of instructions, or commands, that you can use to perform a repetitive task.

Command scope A condition that specifies the general set of tables records to which a command applies.

comment A brief line of commentary embedded into a computer program. Comments aim to provide a "road-map" through a program, enabling programmers, including the original writer, to follow the overall logic of the program. Since comment occupy a line of code it is best to be brief, rather then verbose in commentary.

Compound index file An index file containing multiple index entriess, called tags.

Concatenated key In the Hierarhical model, a physical record is a hierarchicaal arrangement of segments, each segment having a sequence filed. To pick out a unique segemnt in the record, the sequence fields of aall segments above it in the hierarchy are concatenated to the segment's own sequence field. This forms the concatenated key for the segment.

Connector symbol A flowcharting symbol used to represent a junction in a line of flow. A small circle, possibly containing some identifier, connects broken paths in the line of flow on the same page. A pentagonal shape connects the flow on different ages of the same flowchart.

Constant In programming any data with fixed values within the program. Minimum and maximum amounts, dates, prices, headlines and error messages are examples of constants.

Context-senstive Able to perceive the situation in which an event occurs. For example, an application program might present help information specific to the particular task you are performing, rather than a general list of commands, such help would be content-sensitive.

Control break Change of category used to trigger a subtotal.

Control program Software that controls the operation of and has highest priority in a computer. Operating systems, network operating systems and network control programs are examples. Contrast with application program.

CRT Cathode Ray Tube - Vacuum tube used as a display screen in a video terminal or TV. The term often refers to the entire terminal.

Cycle time Time interval between the start of one cycle and the start of the next cycle.

DASD Direct Access Storage Device - Pronounced "dazdee." Peripheral device that is directly addressable, such as a disk or drum.

Data (1) Technically, raw facts and figures which are processed into information. However, in common usage, both data and information are used synonymously the amount of data kept in the computer versus the amount of information is a tradeoff. Data can be processed into different forms of information, but it takes time to sort and sum transactions. Data is "processed". Software is "run", (2) Any form of information whether on paper or in electronic form. In electronic form, data refers to data fields, records, files and databases, word processing documents, graphic images and digitally-encoded voice and video. (3) Data items in data files and databases in contrast with text, graphics, voice and video files.

Data level model A data model concerned only with stored data, and not with its interpretation or the physical structure of data.

Data communications system A system consisting of computers, terminals and communications links.

Data file A collection of data records stored on a disk.

Data Flow Chart A flow chart showing the path of the data step in a problem solution or though a system.

Data flow diagram A graphic diagramming tool which was a few simple symbols to illustrate the flow of data among external entities, processing activities and data storage elements.

Data Grouping Categorizing data in groups in a report corresponding to a sepecified order. Headers and footers can be defined to print every time the value for a group changess.

Data hiding A property whereby the internal data structure of an object is hidden from the rest of the program. The data can be accessed only by the functions declared within the class of that object.

Data processing Capturing, storing, updating and retrieving data and information. It may refer to the entire computer industry, to only datacenter operations or to only data processing activities, in contrast with word processing and office functions.

Data processing system The network of data processing hardware, software, people and procedures capable for accepting information, processing it according to a plan and producing the desired results.

Data processor A digital device that processes data.

Data transfer rate The rate, in kilobytes or megabytes per second, at which data can be read/ written from/to CDROM, disk, tape etc.

Data type Category of data Typical data types are numeric, alphanumeric (character), dates and logical (true/false). Programming languages allow for the creation of different data types. When data is assigned a type, it cannot be treated like another type, For example, character data cannot be calculated and digits within numeric data cannot be isolated. Data types can only contain valid dates.

Database (1) Set of interrelated files that is created and managed by a DBMS. (2) Any electronically-stored collection of data. A collection of logically related records of files. A database consolidates many records previously stored in separate files so that a common pool of data records serves as a single central file or data bank for many data processing applications. About data and database, it holds the name, type, range of values, source and authorization for access for each data element in the organization's files and databases. It also indicates which application programs use that data so that when a change in a data structure is contemplated, a list of affected programs can be generated.

Database administrator Person responsible for the physical design and management of the database and for the evaluation, selection and implementation of the DBMS. In smaller organizations, the database administrators are one in the same; however, when the two responsibilities are managed separately, the database administrator's function is more technical.

DBMS DataBase Management System - Software that controls the organization, storage, retrieval, security and integrity of data in a database; It accepts requests from the application and instructs the operating system to transfer the appropriate data. DBMSs let information systems be changed more easily as the organization's requirements change. New categories of data can be added to the database without disruption to the existing system.

Database sever Computer in a LAN dedicated to database storage and retrieval. Contrast with the server which stores many kinds of files and programs for shared use.

Debug To correct a problem in hardware or software. Debugging software is finding the errors in the program logic. Debugging hardware is finding the errors in circuit design.

Delete Marks records for deletion.

Delimiter Character or combination of characters used to separate one item or set of data from another. For example: in comma delimited records, a comma is used to separate each field of data.

Dialog box A type of communications connection established using a modem and POTS (Plain Old Telephone Service) to connect another computer, network, or the Internet.

Dimension One axis in an array. In programming, a dimension statement defines that array and sets up the number of elements within the dimensions.

Direct access processing The same as direct processing and random processing. Contrast with sequential processing.

Disk A generic name for magnetic storage media, using flat, circular platters. It is a flat circular plate covered in magnetic material which is able to store data on concentric tracks. As the disk spins a read/write head travels from edge to middle selecting only the required tracks. Each track is divided into sectors. A format program is used to lay down the tracks and sectors on a blank disk and this has to be done on every disk before it can be used. Disks allow fast direct access time compared to the much slower sequential access tapes.

Distributed data processing System of computers connected together by a communications network. The term is loosely used to refer to any computers with communications between them. However, in true distributed processing, each computer system is chosen to handle its local workload and the network has been designed to support the system as a whole. Contrast with centralized processing and decentralized processing.

Dock The act of minimizing a window and placing it in the lower right corner of the screen.

Document file Files created in a work processor such as MS Word which contain formatting information.

Document reader An optical input device that is used to read document printed in a special type font.

Documentation A collection of documents or information that describes a computer program, information system or required data processing operations. Written explanations of the development, design, coding and operation of a program or system is known as documentation.

Double-click Drag To double click without releasing the mouse button, move the mouse and then release the mouse button.

Edit The task of changing and improving a program by adding or removing instructions or by modifying the data. This is sometimes done with the help of a special program called an editor. EDIT is also a text-editor that comes with MS-DOS 5.0 and above for creating and editing text files.

Embedded command Command inserted within text or other codes. In word processing, proprietary codes inserted into the text that commands the printer to change fonts, print underline, boldface, etc. They may be partially or totally invisible on screen, but usually can be revealed when necessary. When a document is printed, the text is copied to a temporary file and the embedded commands are converted into printer commands for specific printer. When printing is finished, the temporary file is erased.

Error message When an error occurs it may be possible for the program to indicate what has gone wrong by putting a message on the screen. Such word wording is known as an error message and helps the user find the fault quickly. For example, 'cannot divide by zero at line 230' is an error message which tells the operator that the value of the denominator is zero at instruction number 230 in the program.

Escape character Control character often used in conjunction with other codes. In ASCII, escape is decimal 27, hex 1B; in EBCDIC, it is hex 27.

Execution error An error detected during the execution of a program, e.g., division by zero or insufficient data values to be read into main memory.

execution time Time in which a single instruction is executed. It makes up the last half of the instruction cycle.

Expression builder It is a dialog box that contains menus, field names and variables from the active database(s), and an area where an expression appears as you are building it.

Extended memory In Intel 286s and up, standard memory above one megabyte used for RAM disks, disk caches and applications using DOS extenders. Windows also uses extended memory. Contrast with expanded memory (EMS) which is specialized memory above one megabyte. Memory boards can usually be set up as a mix of the two.

field Physical unit of data that is one or more bytes in size. A collection of fields make up a record. A field also defines a unit of data on a source document, screen or report. The field is the common denominator between the user and the computer. When you interactively query and update your database, you reference your data by field name. Technically, a field is the physical unit of storage, whereas a data. Element or data item refers to the data itself. For example, it is correct to say, "these data elements are stored in this field." the terms field, data element, data item and variable refer to the same unit of data and are often used interchangeably.

Field Object It represents the data that will appear in the printed report. Field objects can be actual fields from a table or calculated fields resulting from calculations of the data.

File A collection of related records. Also, a document, table, program, or similar entity that has filename, a beginning, and an end. It consists of discrete records having a length of from one to 4,000 characters or bytes.

File management program A program that enables you to manage files, directories and disks by displaying a disk's directory structure and listing existing files. Commands available on the program's menus are used to move and copy files, create directories and perform other housekeeping tasks that help improve disk performance and protect your data. The Windows Explorer and XTree Gold are popular file management programs.

Floppy disk Removable storage medium. Also called a diskette, the medium is a single round disk of flexible, tapc-likc material housed in a square envelope or cartridge. The disk drive grabs II the disk at its center and spins it inside its envelope. Like tape, floppy disks can be recorded and erased over and over. Older floppies were recorded on only one side (single sided); however, most are recorded on both sides (double sided).

Flowchart A graphical representation in which symbols are used to represent operations, data flow, logic equipment and so on. A program flowchart illustrates the structure and sequence of operations of a program, while a system flowchart illustrates the components and flows of information systems. You can call a flowchart as a pictorial representation of program logic using a set of standard symbols. It is used to plan the logic of program as well as to document a completed program.

Footer The text that appears on all (or almost all) pages of a document or book at the bottom of the page. In the case of a document it may be the company name in books it may simply be the number.

Form feed A command built into the control panel of most printers. A Form Feed command advances the paper one page length for example from one perforation line to the text.

Format Physical structure of an items. A screen format is that layout of fields on the screen. A report format is that layout of the printed page including print columns, page headers and footers. A record format is the layout of fields within the record. A file or database format is the layout of fields and records within a data file, layout codes within a word processing document or display lists (vector) or bitmaps (raster) within a graphics file. It also includes the structure of header data or identification data that is typically affixed to the beginning of the file.

Function In programming, a routine that does a particular task. When the program passes control to a function, it performs the task and returns control to the instruction following the calling instruction. It may perform a stand-alone task, such as printing a message, or it may accept values (arguments) from the calling instruction process them and pass the results back. Programming languages generally provide a set of standard functions and allow programmers to define their own. C is built entirely around functions. Contrast with command which is a fundamental instruction within the language. Though in programming, the term is specific, outside of programming, it is used to describe any operation such as the data entry function."

Function keys Set of keyboard keys used to command the computer (labeled Fl, F2, etc.). The commands associated with these keys are defined by the program Function keys are also used with the control, alt and shift keys, allowing 40 functions to be per-formed with 10 keys. Software packages that make extensive use of these keys come with plastic templates that fit around them for visual identification. PC and AT keyboards have 10 function keys in a cluster on the left (Fl-Fl 0). On the Enhanced keyboard, all function keys were relocated across the top of the keyboard (Fl-F12).

Graphics Objects These are lines and boxess that you draw to enhance a report. Graphic objects also include pictures.

Hard copy The printed output usually on paper which can be taken away and studied. A data medium or data record that has a degree of permanence and that can be read by people off the machine.

Hashing A file-organization technique based on the ide of calculating rather than searching for the Address of Records in a file.

Index (1) In data management, the most common

method for keeping track of data on a disk. Indexes are directory listings maintained by the OS, DBMS or the application. An index of files contains an entry for each file name and the location of the file. (2) In programming, a method for keeping track of data in a table.

Input/Output Pettaining to the techniques, media, and devices used for man machine interaction.

Indexed file A file that includes an index directory to facilitate random access.

Indexed Sequential Access Method A method whereby records are organized in a sequential order and can be referenced directly through an index based on some key or characters.

Indexing (1) Creating indexes based on key data fields or key words. (2) Creating timing signals based on detecting a mark, slot or hole in a moving medium.

Information Summarization of data. Technically, data are raw facts and figures that are processed into information, such as summaries and totals. But since information can also be raw data for the next job or person, the two terms cannot be precisely defined. Both terms are used synonymously and interchangeably. As office automation and data processing merge, it may be more helpful to view information the way data is defined and used, namely: data, text, spread-sheet, pictures, voice and video. Data are discretely defined fields. Text is a collection of words. Spreadsheets are data in matrix (row and column) form. Pictures are lists of vectors or frames of bits. Voice is a continuous stream of sound waves. Video is a sequence of frames. Future databases will routinely integrate all these forms of information.

Information hiding Keeping details of a routine private. Programmers only know what input is required and what outputs are expected.

Information technology IT – Hardware, software, telecommunications, database management and other information processing technologies used in computer-based information system.

Input The items of data needed by a computer program to perform its operations. Pertaining to a device, process or channel involved in the insertion of data into a data processing system.

Input device Any hardware, such as a keyboard, scanner, digitiser, barcode reader, light pen, mouse, ATM, remote sensing equipment etc, that generates computer compatible input.

Interface Connection and interaction between hardware, software and the user. Hardware interfaces are the plugs, sockets and wires that carry electrical signals in a prescribed order. Software interfaces are the languages. Codes and messages programs use to communicate with each other. User interfaces are the keyboards, mice, commands and menus used for communication between you and the computer. Hardware "communicates to" other hardware. All this is interfacing. The software "communicates to" the hardware and other software. Users "communicates to" the software. All this is interfacing.

Join In relational database management, to match one file against based on some condition creating a third file with data from the matching files. For example, a customer file can be joined with an order file creating a file of records for all customers who purchased a particular product.

K An abbreviation for the prefix "Kilo". It is used to indicate the capacity of computer storage, 1K=210=1024 characters. Example: 64K=65,536 characters of storage.

Key Keyboard button. Data item that identifies a record. As an identifier, each key value must be unique in each key record. Numeric code used by an algorithm to create a code for encrypting data for security purposes.

Key field A unique field in a record used to distinguish one record from another.

Key word Word used in a text search. Word in a text document that is used in an index to best describe the contents of the document. A Reversed word in a programming or command language.

Label In data management, a made-up name that is assigned to a file, field or other data structure. In spreadsheet descriptive text that is entered into a cell. In programming a made up name used to identify a variable or a subroutine. In computer operation, a self-sticking form attached to the outside of a disk or tape in order to identify it. In magnetic tape files a record used for identification at the beginning or end of the file.

Label object They are any text that you type on the report, such as titles, labesl, or column headings.

Label record A machine readable record that is used to identify a data file. It is the first record of the file.

LAN Local Area Network – Communications network that serves users within a confined geographical area. It is made up of servers, workstations, a network operating system and a communications link. Servers are high-speed machines that hold programs and data shared by all network users. A workstation is a user's machine which can also function as stand-alone personal computer. Diskless workstations or floppy only workstations retrieve all software and data from the server. A printer can be attached to the workstation or it can be attached to a server and be shared by network users.

Language processor Language translation software. Programming languages, command languages, query languages, natural languages and foreign languages are all translated by software.

Layout window The work area is which you design and define the look and content of a report or label.

light pen Light - sensitive styles wired to a video terminal used to draw pictures or select menu options. The user brings the pen to the desired point on screen and presses the pen button to make contact. Screen pixels are constantly being refreshed. When the user presses the button, allowing the pen to sense light, the pixel being illuminated at that instant identifies the screen location.

literal In programming, an unchanging item written into the program, such as a message displayed on screen. It is translated into machine language without conversion.

Local variable A variable whose value is controlled by a program module, such as a subroutine. The variable may or may not be accessible to the main program and/or other modules, however only the module containing the "local variable" can alter its value. This is a useful programming technique as it allows compartmentalisation and therefore safeguarding, of different program variables.

Logical Database A schmea that describes the database as seen by one user. Different users of Applications may have different views of the same database.

Logical error An error that occurs when the actual logic of a program is different from the desired logic.

Logical operator One of the Boolean logical operators (AND, OR and NOT).

Logical record Reference to a data record that is independent of its physical location. It may be physically stored in two or more locations.

Looping It allows user to execute one or more lines of code as many times as necessary.

Macro Series of menu selections keystrokes and/or commands that have been recorded and assigned a name or key combination. When the name is called or the key is pressed, the macro is executed from beginning to end. It is used to shorten long menu sequences into one keystroke as well as to create miniature programs within an application. Macro languages often included programming controls (IF THEN, GOTO, WHILE, etc.) that automatic sequences like any programming language. In assembly language a prewritten subroutine that is called for throughout the program. At assembly time, the macro calls are substitute with the actual subroutine or instructions that branch to it. The high level language equivalent is a function. In dBASE programming a variable which reference another variable that actually contains the data. At runtime, the macro variable is substitute with the data variable.

Macro instruction Instruction that defines a macro. In assembly language, MACRO and ENDM are examples that define the beginning and end of a macro.

Magnetic Ink Character Recognition (MICR) An input device that can read cards and paper documents printed with a special magnetic ink.

Magnetic tape Sequential storage medium used for data collection, backup and historical purpose. Like videotape, computer tape is made of flexible plastic with one side coated with a ferromagnetic material. Tapes come in reels, cartridges and cassettes of many sizes and shapes. As with any tape, locating a specific item requires reading everything before it. There is no way to fast forward. Data bits are usually recorded on parallel recording tracks that run the length of the tape. For example, 9-track tape holds one byte of data across the tape's width (8 bits plug parity). Data is recorded in blocks of contiguous bytes, separated by a space called an inter record or inter block gap. Tape is often used to exchange data between minis and mainframes, since ½" open-reel tape provides a common standard. Storage capacity is measured in bits per inch (bpi). Since tape is laid out in parallel tracks, bpi is equivalent to bytes per inch. Common ½" recording densities are 1650 and 6250 dpi; early densities were 200, 556 and 800 dpi. Tape drive speed is measured in inches per second (ips), thus transfer rate is computed as :ips X bpi.

Magneto-optical (MO) drive A data storage device that uses laser technology to heat an extremely small spot on a magneto-optical (MO) cartridge so that the magnetic medium used in the MO disk becomes capable of having its magnetic orientation changed by the read/write head. Though magneto-optical drives are slow (average seek time of 30 ms, compared to about 15 ms for hard drives) and expensive (the average internal drive costs about $750, including disk), they are highly suitable for backup storage and for storing large programs or data that's accessed infrequently.

Many to many relation A situation in which one or more records in on table are related to one or more records in another.

Many to one relation A situation in which one or more records in one table are related to just one record in another.

Mass storage Secondary storage device with extra large storage capacities such as magnetic or optical disks.

Master file Collection of records pertaining to one of the main subjects of an information system. Master files contain descriptive data as well as summary information.

Megabyte One million bytes. More accurately 2 to 20th power or 1,048,576 in decimal notation.

Memo field Data field that holds a variable amount of text. The text may be stored in a companion file but it is treated as if it were part of the data record.

Memory Variable FoxPro allows you to store any data of your choice in the RAM (Random Access Memory) of the PC. In all, you can store up to 256 different data items. Almost anything, such as intermediate or final result of a calculation; current or the next bill number; a date; fixed number etc. can be stored in RAM. The data items stored in RAM are called memory variables. You need to assign a unique name called the memory variable name to each data item. This is required so that you can refer to a required variable by name and use it in calculations or for some other applications. For naming a memory variable, follow the same rules as used for naming a field. That is, a memory variable name can be letters, numerals or the underscore character (_). You can use spaces and punctuation marks in memory variable names. Although a memory variable name can begin with the underscore character, it is advisable to avoid it. In fact, FoxPro automatically crates a few variables that are called print system variables. The print system variables always begin with the underscore character. Memory variables play a very important role in FoxPro programming. (Programming is described later.) You can store the data entered by the user in memory variables, validate the data, process the data (e.g. calculate square root). Thus, you do not have to store the data directly in a database file. Finally, when the data has been validated and processed, you can store it in the database file.

Memory The computer's workspace physically a collection of RAM chips. It is an important resource, since it determines the size and number of programs that can be run at the same time, as well as the amount of data that can be processed instantly. The program's instructions are copied into memory from a disk or tape and are then extracted from memory for analysis, execution or processing (calculated, compared and copied). Then the results can be output from memory to a screen, printer, disk, tape or communications channel. As data is entered into memory, the previous contents of that memory space is lost.

Menu Bars A horizontal strip that appears at the top of the screen and contains menu pads.

Menu pads A word, phrase or icon on the menu bar that designates one menu. Positioning the cursor on a menu titile highlights the title and displays its options below it.

Microprocessor CPU on a single chip. In order to function as a computer, it requires a power supply, clock and memory. First-generation microprocessors were Intel's 8080, Zilog's Z80, Motorola's 6800 and

Rockwell's 6502. The first microprocessor was created by Intel.

Microsecond One millionth of a second.

Modify structure Database command that changes a file's structure. Field lengths and field names can be changed and fields can be added or deleted. It may convert the old data file into the new structure without data loss, unless fields have been truncated or deleted.

Mouse A small device that is electronically connected to a computer and is moved by hand on a flat surface in order to move the cursor on a video screen in the same directories. Button on the mouse allows users to issue commands and make responses or selections.

Multiprocessing Simultaneous processing with two or more processors in one computer or two or more computers processing together. When two or more computers are used, they are tied together with a high-speed channel and share the general workload between them. If one fails, the other takes over. It is also accomplished in special purpose computers, such as array processors which provide concurrent processing on sets of data. Although computers are built with various overlapping features, such as executing instructions while inputting and outputting data, multiprocessing refers specifically to concurrent instruction execution.

Multiprogramming Pertaining to the concurrent execution of two or more programs by a computer by interleaving their execution.

Network Arrangement of objects that are interconnected. In communications, the transmission channels and supporting hardware and software.

NOT Boolean logic operation that reverses the input. If a 0 is input, a 1 is output and vice versa.

Offline A device not directly connected to the CPU.

Online (1) Peripheral device (terminal, printer, etc). which is ready to operate. A printer can be attached and turned on, yet still not online, if the ONLINE button will usually turn it back online. (2) An online computer system refers to a system with terminals, but does not imply how the system is an online system that implies data entry and updating. A transaction processing system is an online system that updates the necessary files as the work comes in, such as in an order processing system. A realtime system is an online system that provides an immediate response to a question.

operating system Master control program that runs the computer. It is the first program loaded when the computer is turned on and its main part, called the kernel, reside in memory at all times. It is an important component of the computer system because its sets the standards for the application programs that runs in it. All programs must work through the operating system.

Optical Character Reader An input device which can read characters directly from an ordinary piece of paper by using a scanning mechanism. These characters are written in special type fonts.

Optimize To cause something to work as effectively as possible. For example, optimizing an application means to use code that causes the application to run as quickly as possible in a given environment.

OR A logical operation in which the bit patterns of two values are compared and in which all bits are turned on that are on in one or both of the two component values. Boolean logic operation that is true if any of the inputs is true. An exclusive OR is true if only one of the inputs is true, but not both.

Output Any computer-generated information displayed on screen, printed on paper or in machine readable form, such as disk and tape to transfer or transmit from the computer to a peripheral device or communications line.

Overflow The inability of computer (RAM) to handle a particular calculation, often caused by programming logic errors, for example, attempting to divide by zero.

Pack (1) To compress data in order to save space. Unpack refers to decompressing data. (2) Instruction that converts a decimal number into a packed decimal format. Unpack converts a packed decimal number into decimal. (3) In database programs, a command that removes records that have been marked for deletion.

Parameter list Communicates a list of constants, variables, and/or arrays between a calling program and a subprogram.

Pass by reference A mean of passing a variable to a function. The calling routine passes the address of the variable to the called routing which can then use that address to retrieve or modify the variable. When the function changes the value of the passed variable, the variable's original value in the calling program is also changed.

Peripheral Device In a computer system, any unit of equipment distinct from the central processing unit which may provide the system with outside communication. Peripheral devices are so called as they are attached to the periphery of the central processing unit or system box.

Point A measure of the size of a printer font, with one point being approximately 1/72.27 inches, 0.351 millimeters. Some software applications refer to point sizes, other to pitch sizes. The majority of the text in this book is sent in an 8 point font. To convert pitch to point, divide the pitch into 120, for example, 15 pitch = 120/8 point = 15. The greater the point size the greater the size of the font, inversely for pitch which is a measure of how many characters can be printed per linear inch.

Primary index The index that controls the current processing order of a file.

Procedure Manual procedures are human tasks. Machine procedures are lists of routines or programs to be executed, such as described by the job control language (JCL) in a mini or mainframe or the batch processing language in a personal computer in programming, another term for a subroutine or function.

Processing Manipulating data within the computer. The term is used to define a variety of computer functions and methods.

Processing symbol A rectangular figure used in flow charts to indicate a processing operation.

Processor May refer to software. A hardware device or software system capable of performing operations upon data.

Program A collection of instructions that tell the computer what to do. A program is also called software; hence, program, software and instructions are synonymous. A program is written in a programming language and is converted into the computer's machine language by software called assemblers, compilers and interpreters.

Project A project is a special file that keeps track of all programs, reports, labels, queries, format files and other type of files that are needed to create an application.

Pseudocode An algorithm expressed in English to conceptualize the algorithm before coding it in a programming language.

Random Access File Processing Same as Direct Access File Processing.

Random-access memory RAM – The computer's primary working memory in which program instructions and data are stored so that they can be accessed directly by the central processing unit (CPU) via the processor's high-speed external data bus. RAM often is called read/write memory to distinguish it from read/only memory (ROM), the other component of a personal computer's primary storage. In RAM, the CPU can write and read data. Most programs set aside a portion of RAM as a temporary work space for your data, so you can modify (rewrite) as needed until the data is ready for printing or storage on secondary storage media, such as a hard or floppy disk. RAM doesn't retain its contents when the power to the computer is switched off, so save your work frequently.

Real time systems Pertains to on line computer processing systems which receive and process data quickly enough to produce output to control, direct, or affect the outcome of an ongoing activity or process.

Recall Restore the records marked for deletion.

Record Group or related fields that store data about a subject (master record) or activity (transaction record). A collection of records make up a file. Master records contain permanent data, such as account number and variable data, such as balance due. Transaction records contain only permanent data, such as quantity and product code. A record is an entry in a database. For example, a payroll database may hold information on 300 employees and is therefore a 300 record database.

Record length A measure of the size of a record, usually specified in units such as characters.

Record pointer In a database management program, an onscreen status messages that states the number of the data record now visible (or in which the cursor is positioned).

Regular index Regular determines the order in which records are displayed but allows duplicate data to be entered into a field.

Relational database management system RDBMS – A relational database management program, especially one that comes with all the necessary support programs, programming tools and documentation needed to create, install and maintain custom database applications.

relational operator A symbol that specifies a compari-son between two values.

Relational	*Operator*	*Symbol*
EQ	Equal to	=
GT	Greater than	>
GE	Greater than or equal to	>=
NE	Not equal to	<> or # or!
LE	less than or equal to	<=
LT	less than	<

Relationship A connection between entities that has meaning for an appliction.

Remove button The Remove button moves the highlighted field from the selected fields list box to the available fields lsit box.

Remove All button Remove All button moves all the fields from the selected fields list box to the available field list box.

Replace In word processing programs, a feature that searches for a string and replaces it with another string. Always save your work before performing a replace operation. With most programs, you can improve the accuracy of the replacement operation by specifying capitalization and whole-word options. If you tell the program to match the capitalization pattern in the search string, such as Tree if you want the change only when tree begins a sentence, the program replaces only those strings that match the characters and capitalization pattern (Tree is replaced, but not TREE or tree).

Report Detail Band The area between the page header and the page footer, consisting of detail lines based on the records from the selected database(s).

Reserved word In a programming language or operating system a word – also called a keyword – that has a fixed function and can't be used for any other purpose. In BASIC, for example, the word REM is reserved to indicate the beginning of a remark. You can use a reserved work only for its intended purpose; you can't use the word for naming files, variables or other user-named objects.

Restore The Restore command reads the saved memory variables from disk back to your computer's memory.

Run-time error This is an error that occurs during program execution. A run-time error may occur during the program development stage or in real-life usage due to hardware failure. In the program development stage, run-time error may occur if a data file has not been previously closed and an attempt is made to open it. In real-life usage a run-time error will occur, for example, if the software application tries to access a printer that is out of paper, turned off or disconnected. Thorough and professional programming techniques ensure that the trauma of run-time errors is minimized. Preferably data should not be lost and the program should be recoverable at or close to the error point.

Run-time The period of time during which a computer program is a actually running.

Rushmore Technology A data access technique that permits sets of records to be accessed very efficiently, at speeds comparable to single record indexed access.

Scientific notation Display of numbers in floating point form. The number (mantissa) is always equal to or greater than one and less than 10 and the base is 10. For example, 2.345E6 is equivalent to 2,345,000. The number following E (exponent) represents the power to which the base should he raised (number of zeros following the decimal point).

Scope (1) CRT type of screen, such as used on an oscil-loscope or common display terminal. (2) In program-ming, the visibility of variables within a program. (3) In dBASE, a range of records, such as the "next 50" or "current record to end of file."

Security Protection of data against unauthorized access. Programs and data can be securred by issuing identifications numbers and passwords to authorized users of a computer individual, will ultimately have access to these codes. Data transmitted over communications networks can be secured by encryption to prevent eavesdropping.

Seek To move the access arm to the requested track on a disk. Assembly language instruction that activates a seek operation on disk. High-level programming language commmand used to select a record by key field.

Sequential access An information storage and retrieval technique in which the computer must move through a sequence of stored data items to reach the desired one. Sequential access media such as cassette tapes are much slower than random-access media, such as hard disk drives.

Sequential file A file that has been organized in ascending or descending record key sequence so that the records are written or retrieved one after another in sequence.

Serial access A storage device or medium where the access time is dependent upon the location of the data. Magnetic tape is a typical serial access device.

Sort To reorder data into a new sequence. Sorting capabilities are provided within the operating system and many application program, such as word processing and DBMSs.

Sorting Physical arrangement of records in a table. Sorting does not make any changes to the existing table rather it creates a new table that stores ordered data.

Source document A document that is the original formal record of a transaction, such as a purchase order or sales invoice.

Source program Program in its original form, as writ-ten by the programmer.

Special character Non-alpha or non-numeric character, such as @,#,$,%,&,* and +.

SQL Structured Query Language – pronounced "SQL" or "see qwill," a language used to interrogate and process data in a relational database. Originally developed by IBM for its mainframes, there have been many implementations created for mini and micro database applications. SQL commands can be used to interactively work with a database or can be embedded within a programming language to interface to a database.

Storage The retention of program instructions and data within the computer so that this information is available for processing purposes. See primary storage and secondary storage.

String (1) In programming, a contiguous set of alphanumeric characters that does not contain numbers used for calculations. Names, addresses, words and sentences are strings. (2) Any connected set of structures, such as a string of bits, fields or records.

String function String function are tools that let you control the way you can store or display strings. You can also use them to determine certain characteristics about them. There are string functions that let you convert numbers to characters, characters to numbers, decimal numbers to whole numbers (called integers), determine how many characters in a string, and so on.

String variable A unique variable such as NAME or DATE that you assign to a string value.

Structural Compound Index A structural compound index file is created when you include TAG<tag name> without including the optional OF <cd file> clause. Structural CDX files always have the same base name as the table. A structural compound *index file is automatically opened every time the table* is opened.

Structure chart A design and documentation technique to show the purpose and relationship of the various modules in a program.

Structure design A system design approach in which a difficult problem is broken into smaller problems that are small enough to manage but independent enough to sove separately.

Structured programming Variety of techniques that impose a logical structure on the writing of a program. Large routines are broken down into smaller, modular routines. The use of the GOTO statement in discouraged. For documentation, certain programming statements are indented, so that beginnings and endings of loops are easily identified. Structured languages, such as Pascal, Ada and dBASE, force the programmer to write a structured program.

Subroutine Group of instructions that perform a specific task. A large subroutine is usually called a module or procedure; a small one, a function or macro, but all terms are used interchangeably.

Syntax Rules that must be followed white coding program instructions, similar to grammatical rules for the English language.

Syntax error Error that occurs when a program cannot understand the command that has been entered.

System A group of integrated parts (people, methods, machines, and materials) that have the common purpose of achieving some objective(s).

System analysis Analyzing in detail the components and requirement of a system Analyzing in detail the information needs of an organization, the characteristics and components of presently utilized information systems and the requirements of proposed information system.

Systems analyst Persons responsible for the develop-ment of an information system. They design and modify systems by turning user requirements into a set of functional specifications which ate the blue-print of the system. They design the database or help design it if data administrators are available.

System flowchart A graphic diagramming tool used to show the flow of data media as they are processed by hardware devices and information processed procedures in an information system.

Table A dbf file created in a previous version of Visual FoxPro is a free table until it is added to a database.

Transaction Activity or request. Orders, purchases, changes, additions and deletions are examples of transactions that are recorded in a business informa-tion environment. Queries and other requests are also transactions to the computer, but are usually just acted upon and not recorded in the system. Transaction volume is a major factor in determining the size and speed of a computer system.

Transaction file Collection of records that record the activity of an organization. The data in transaction files is used to update the data in master files which contain the subjects of the organization. Transaction files also serve as audit trails and are usually transferred from active disk files to the data library after some period of time. As optical disks become more economical, transaction files will remain online in the computers so that an organization's history will be immediately available for adhoc queries.

Type Head Buffer A buffer that accepts and holds characters that are typed faster than the computer can process them.

Unique It selects and orders a subset of records based on the first occurrence of a value in the field you specify.

Updating The process of keeping master files accurate and up-to-date by processing them with the latest transactions contained in the transactionf file.

User Any individual who interacts with the computer at an application level. Programmers, operators and other technical personnel are not considered users when working in a professional capacity on the computer.

Validation In programming, providing that a program does its job. Many programmers prefer the term "validation" to "testing" or "debugging," since it has a more positive ring.

Variable In programming, a structure that holds data and is uniquely named by the programmer. It holds the data assigned to it until the program is finished. Variable are used to hold control values. In some languages, the type of data must be declared before it is assigned. A local variable is one that can be referenced only within the subprogram, function or procedure it was defined in. A global variable can be used by the entire program.

View Window The window lets you set up a special view of your data. You can open multiple tables and define relationship among them.

Window (1) The area that displays information on the screen. You can open or close a windows, move it around on the disktop, and sometimes change its size, scroll through it, and edit its contents. (2) The portion of a collection of information such as a document, picture, or worksheet that is visible in a viewing area on the display screen.

Wizard The wizard prompts you with simple questions as you go through a brief series of steps, in which you specify the table and fields that you want to use to create control on your report.

Zap Command that typically deletes the data within a file but leaves the file structure intact so that new data can be entered.

Zoom A feature of many graphics and some spreadsheet packages which allows the user to get a magnified view of a particular part of the graphics object (spreadsheet). This is a word borrowed from photography (zoom lens).

Index

I

F

G

H

I

J

K

L

M